BRIG GEN JAMES S WADSWORTH

A Full Blown Yankee
of the Iron Brigade

Service with
THE SIXTH WISCONSIN
VOLUNTEERS

by
Rufus R. Dawes

edited with an introduction by
Alan T. Nolan

UNIVERSITY OF NEBRASKA PRESS
LINCOLN AND LONDON

∞

First Bison Books printing: 1999

digit below:

3   2   1

...tion Data
...-1899.
...ers]
...service with the Sixth Wiscon-
...tion by Alan T. Nolan.
Originally published: Marietta, Ohio: E. R. Alderman, 1890.
Includes bibliographical references and index.
ISBN 0-8032-6618-9 (pbk.: alk. paper)
1. Dawes, Rufus R. (Rufus Robinson), 1836–1899—Diaries.
2. Dawes, Rufus R. (Rufus Robinson), 1836–1899—Correspondence.   3. United States. Army. Wisconsin Infantry Regiment, 6th
(1861–1865)   4. Wisconsin—History—Civil War, 1861–1865—
Regimental histories.   5. United States—History—Civil War, 1861–
1865—Regimental histories.   6. Wisconsin—History—Civil War, 1861–
1865—Personal narratives.
7. United States—History—Civil War, 1861–1865—Personal narratives.   8. Soldiers—Wisconsin—Diaries.   9. Soldiers—Wisconsin—
Correspondence.   I. Nolan, Alan T.
E537.5 6th.D3 1999
973.7'475—dc21
98-47486   CIP

Originally published in 1890 by E. R. Alderman & Sons, Marietta OH.
Reprinted from the 1962 edition by the State Historical Society of
Wisconsin, Madison. This Bison Books edition follows the original in
beginning chapter 1 on arabic page 5; no material has been omitted.

EDITOR'S FOREWORD

Service With The Sixth Wisconsin Volunteers was originally published in 1890 by E. R. Alderman & Sons of Marietta, Ohio.[1] Long classified as rare and prized as a collector's item, the book is a combination of the personal experiences of Rufus R. Dawes and a history of the regiment of which he was a member. In the vast literature of the American Civil War, it has long been recognized as exceptional. Its excellence is the product of three factors: the character and abilities of the author; the historical techniques and materials which he used; and the events in which he and his regiment participated. These factors—*author, technique* and *events*—combine to make the book a superb document of its kind. It is appropriate for an editor's foreword briefly to discuss each of these factors.

I

Although principally identified with Wisconsin Civil War history, Rufus R. Dawes was an Ohioan. One of the six children of Henry and Sarah Cutler Dawes, he was born at Malta in Morgan County, Ohio, in 1838. Appropriately enough, his birthday was on Independence Day, but his relationship to the American story was not only symbolic. His great-grandfather was William Dawes, Jr., Paul Revere's companion on the eve of Lexington and Concord, and his mother's family, too, was rooted in American history. She was the granddaughter of Dr. Manasseh Cutler, the great Massachusetts clergyman and patriot of the Revolutionary War and the early years of the republic.

[1] In 1937, a limited reprint of the book was issued, containing additional illustrations. The instant edition is a republication of the original 1890 edition.

Rufus Dawes spent his youth in Constitution, Ohio, near Marietta, and in Malta. But when the time came for college, he went to Wisconsin and entered the University of Wisconsin at Madison. After two years there, he returned to Ohio, to Marietta College, where he graduated in the Class of 1860.

In April, 1861, at the time of Sumter, Rufus and his father were on business in Juneau County, Wisconsin, but the onset of the war turned the youth at once to that more urgent matter. Allying himself with Wisconsin instead of Ohio, on April 25, he undertook to raise a company of volunteers in Juneau County. Less than a week later, one hundred men had enrolled. Taking the name of the "Lemonweir Minute Men," the men elected Dawes as their captain. A few weeks later, the company arrived at Madison and was assigned as Company K of the newly-organized Sixth Wisconsin Volunteers. Dispatched to Washington in July, the regiment was shortly thereafter assigned to the brigade which was later to be called the Iron Brigade. Appointed major of the Sixth Wisconsin on June 30, 1862, and to the lieutenant colonelcy of the regiment during the following year, Dawes ultimately became its colonel on July 5, 1864. Even before the colonelcy, he had frequently acted as the regimental commander of the Sixth and was its commander at Gettysburg. On August 10, 1864, his term of enlistment having expired, he was honorably discharged and returned to Marietta, Ohio. In 1866, he was brevetted a brigadier general of volunteers.

Dawes was seldom absent from the field during his term of service. On one occasion, he accompanied the regiment home on veteran furlough in January, 1864. While in Marietta, he married Mary Beman Gates of that community. It was a uniquely happy marriage and six children were born of the union. Continuing the family tradition of public service and renown, one of these children was Charles G. Dawes, Vice-President of the United States during the Coolidge Administration.

After the war, Dawes settled in Marietta and turned his attention to his family and to business pursuits. These were interrupted in 1880 when he was elected as a Republican to Congress, a seat which he lost in the election of 1882. Despite the onset of ill health, he remained a prominent figure in Ohio public affairs and was a strong contender for the Republican gubernatorial nomination in 1889. Following this episode, he was appointed by President McKinley as Minister to Persia, a post he declined because of physical incapacity. But he continued his interests in veterans' affairs, and in the temperance movement and education. In the latter respect, he served as a trustee of the Ohio Institute for the Deaf and Dumb and of Marietta College. Finally confined to a wheel chair, he died at Marietta in 1899.[2]

These are the basic biographical facts. They tell us something of Rufus R. Dawes, but his book tells us much more about him. At the outbreak of the war, he called himself an Abolitionist, still a relatively unpopular cause in 1861, especially in the Middle Western states. He wrote of "our destiny, the entire destruction of slavery," and "the eternal overthrow of a monied aristocracy based on slavery." Thus, in addition to a plain and unquestioning loyalty to the "old flag" and to the Union, Dawes also understood the implications of the war in relation to what he called "the great question of liberty." The book also testifies that its author was a secure and well adjusted man. It is wholly free of the pomposity and self-justification which characterize much autobiographical literature. And he was gentle, too, a characteristic which men do not enough admire but which so often marks the truly masculine spirit. Thus, on the eve of battle, he could write to his young fiancée, "You are mustered into service now and must endure your trials and hardships as a soldier, and I doubt not that they will be harder . . . than mine, for you see, you are a raw recruit. . . . If I do anything glorious I shall expect you to be proud of me." Between the lines, too, one finds the qualities of idealism and high-mindedness. There was nothing banal or sec-

---

[2] Biographical materials about Dawes and his family are from *A Memoir, Rufus R. Dawes* (New York, 1900), pp. 11–31; Alan T. Nolan, *The Iron Brigade* (New York, 1961), pp. 14, 376; *The National Cyclopedia of American Biography* (New York, 1910), Volume XIV, pp. 527–528. Dawes' commission dates appear in *Annual Report of the Adjutant General, State of Wisconsin* (Madison, 1865), p. 1339. The dates given are dates of the commissions, not issue dates or late muster dates.

ond-rate about Dawes and when one finishes the book he can accept the author's word about his own feeling for the men under his command: "I . . . esteem it an honor, worth a better life than mine, to be permitted to lead them in this glorious struggle."

In the light of his idealism about the war, it is fortunate that Dawes had another attribute, courage, a quiet and determined physical courage. This appears not in any self-conscious way. Indeed he wrote to his fiancée that "I do not want to fight" and noted an occasion behind a tree at Second Bull Run when "I must have shrunk to the dimensions of a wafer." But courage is nevertheless there in the swirling ordeal of the combat that he told about. A sense of humor was another of his gifts. In addition to the funny episodes which mark the pages, a humorous strain runs through much of his text. Complaining of the early period of the war and the elaborate equipment provided, Dawes remarked that "with us, ponderosity was military science." One of his musicians was described as a man who had "undertaken to crush the Rebellion with a trombone." And as lieutenant colonel commanding, he wrote of his headquarters in a residence in Virginia, with "three little astonished looking girls with their fingers in their mouths, hanging around the table watching me as I write." It should be especially marked that he was also able to look at *himself* humorously. Thus, when assembling his book in later years, he could characterize as "youthful vapor" some of his own high flown writings from the time of the war.

To all of Dawes' felicitous attributes of character may be added other qualifications of critical importance to a man writing a book. He was wonderfully observant and sensitive to everything around him. And he was a sophisticated and highly literate man, the product of a classical education which equipped him with narrative skills and permitted him to use the English language with uncommon skill and facility. With quiet irony, he mentioned Lee, "using his great power as a military leader, to destroy the Government he had sworn to defend." Turning to a less serious theme, the same satirical insight tells us of his metal scabbard "that tarnishes in half an hour." And he could sum up his feeling about an officer's expensive dress: "fancy uniforms are useless sleeping in the mud." Beyond the satire are the descriptions of the scenes that he saw. As he wrote about them, we, too, can see the "one hundred thousand miserable and discouraged men . . . wading through this terrible mud and rain" after the Federal disaster at Chancellorsville. And we can see the same men again, "tired, sore, sleepy, hungry, dusty and dirty as pigs" on the march to meet Lee at Gettysburg. With these descriptive skills, and with his other traits of character, Rufus Dawes was peculiarly qualified to write the book he chose to write. The fact that such a man was the author is the first element contributing to the value of the book.

II

The published memoirs of Civil War military personnel are frequently simply the *recollections* of aging men, written down long after the facts and sometimes marked by antagonisms and special pleadings. Most regimental histories are of similar ingredients. Published principally for the veterans themselves, they are usually composed largely of the reminiscences of the soldiers exchanged at regimental reunions and surely enlarged upon and improved by frequent repetition. Such materials have their flavor and interest, but they are of limited historical value. *Service With The Sixth Wisconsin Volunteers* stands apart from all such works of this kind.

Throughout the period of his service, Dawes kept a journal. He was also a prolific correspondent, writing long and articulate letters to his mother, his sister and to his fiancée, Miss Gates. After he and Miss Gates were married, she became the principal object of the letters, but their quantity increased and the quality did not diminish. To his wife, Dawes credited the keeping of these materials so that they were available to him when he began his book. They provided a contemporaneous chronicle of events, but he was not content to rely on them alone. He also turned to the *Official Records*, verifying and amplifying his own account by references to the reports of both Federal and Confederate participants.

Dawes' journal and his letters were marked by unusual richness of detail. His searching observation and his fluent pen worked to set down not only the obvious and dramatic, but also the ordinary and routine. Thus, his book provides a source of facts about the soldiers' attitudes and the *minutiae* of their daily lives, in and out of combat. The order of camp life was noted, beginning with reveille, proceeding through roll call, breakfast, police duty, guard mounting, inspection, drill, dress parade, retreat, tattoo, and taps. With both whimsy and truth, the soldiers' ordinary diet was recorded, "hard tack plain, hard tack fried, hard tack soaked, hard tack crumbled and stewed, or hard tack otherwise compounded." When his regiment withdrew at night from the front of a much larger enemy, the soldiers "muffled the rattling tin cups" to avoid discovery. In combat there was "the peculiarly mournful wail of the spent bullet," and when Dawes' commander was shot at his side, "I heard a distinct sound of the blow that struck him. He gave a convulsive start and clapped his hand on his leg, but he controlled his voice." After battle, we learn of the "troubled and dreamy sleep . . . that comes to the soldier on a battle field," and of the dolorous task of those assigned to find the dead and wounded: "Several dying men were pleading piteously for water, of which there was not a drop in the regiment, nor was there any liquor. Captain Kellogg and I searched in vain for a swallow for one noble fellow who was dying in great agony from a wound in his bowels. He recognized us and appreciated our efforts, but was unable to speak. The dread reality of war was before us in this frightful death, upon the cold, hard stones. The mortal suffering, the fruitless struggle to send a parting message to the far-off home, and the final release by death, all enacted in the darkness."

These, of course, are only samples of the recorded observations of the author. The fact that he had his own detailed and contemporaneous accounts before him, and his desire to write objective history as well as his own impressions, represent the second element in the excellence of his book.

III

Originally called "The Black Hat Brigade" because its men wore the regular army dress black hats instead of the more typical blue cap, the Iron Brigade was the only all-Western brigade which fought in the Eastern armies of the Union. It was perhaps the most distinguished infantry brigade in the Federal armies. Composed initially of the Second, Sixth, and Seventh Wisconsin Volunteers, and the Nineteenth Indiana Volunteers, the brigade also later included the Twenty-fourth Michigan Volunteers. Battery B of the Fourth U. S. Artillery, composed in large part of infantry men detached from the brigade, was not a part of the brigade but was closely associated with it.

Rufus King, a New Yorker who had moved to Milwaukee before the war, was the first commander of the brigade. He led the Western men until the spring of 1862, at which time the remarkable John Gibbon of North Carolina and West Point assumed command. To Gibbon is ordinarily assigned the credit for the peculiar élan and unique effectiveness of the brigade, characteristics which it maintained after Gibbon's promotion to division command and his replacement by General Solomon Meredith, promoted from the colonelcy of the Nineteenth Indiana.

In view of its ultimate casualty record, it is strange that the Iron Brigade waited so long to become a combat unit. It was organized on October 1, 1861, in camp at Arlington, Virginia. Assigned to the Army of the Potomac's First Corps, the brigade was not seriously engaged until almost a year following its organization. But at last on August 28, 1862, on the eve of the Federal defeat at Second Bull Run, its fighting career began at Brawner Farm. Led by General Gibbon, the Westerners showed their mettle in this vicious engagement, standing up to Stonewall Jackson's much larger Confederate force, in spite of the disadvantage of surprise and 33 per cent casualties. From that day until Gettysburg, the Iron Brigade was on hand for every significant Eastern battle, frequently at the vortex of the fighting and uniformly fighting with desperate and telling gallantry. On the first day of Gettysburg, numbered as the *First* Brigade of the *First* Division of the *First* Corps, the Western men outdid themselves against overwhelming numbers in the often neglected Federal holding action on McPherson's Ridge and Seminary Ridge, west of the town. At the close of that day, 1,212 of the brigade's 1,883 men were casualties, but not a backward step had been taken except on orders.

Shortly after Gettysburg, a series of Eastern regiments were incorporated into the brigade. In late 1864 and early 1865 three of the five Iron Brigade regiments either left the front or were merged with other regiments and lost their identity. The vaunted name "Iron Brigade" remained in use until the end of the war and some of its original members fought with Grant all the way to Appomattox. But by that time only Dawes' Sixth Wisconsin Volunteers and the Seventh Wisconsin Volunteers existed by name and, heavily infiltrated by late volunteers and drafted men, they were not the same regiments that had originally come from the West. But despite the relatively brief life of the organization, when the statistics were finally assembled, they accorded to the Iron Brigade a sad but proud distinction: a greater proportion of its men had been killed in combat than in any other Federal brigade. To this record, Rufus Dawes' Sixth Wisconsin Volunteers was no small contributor: Indeed, the records also showed that it stood tenth on the list of all Federal regiments in its number of men killed and died of wounds.[3]

This is the outline of the story which Rufus Dawes recorded at the time and later set down in his book. Although he wrote principally of the Sixth Wisconsin, its story could not be separated from those of the Iron Brigade and Battery B. Thus— and this is the third element contributing to the high quality of the book—Dawes chronicled *significant* military organizations engaged in *significant* events of the war. Although writing about combat is difficult, Dawes was at his best in telling of such activities. When Battery B was summoned at Brawner Farm to respond to the opening artillery fire from the enemy, he saw the battery come driving "down the turnpike on a gallop. Quickly

---

[3] Alan T. Nolan, *The Iron Brigade* (New York, 1961). Casualty statistics are those of William F. Fox, *Regimental Losses in the American Civil War* (Albany, 1889), pp. 116–17.

tearing away the fence, they wheeled into position in the open field, and the loud crack of their brass twelve pounders echoed the rebel cannon." Furious was the action at Antietam, in the bloody cornfield north of the famous Dunker Church. Dawes conveyed the ferocity of this most deadly action which befell the Sixth Wisconsin: "Men, I can not say fell; they were knocked out of the ranks by dozens. But we jumped over the fence, and pushed on, loading, firing, and shouting as we advanced. . . . The soldier who is shooting is furious in his energy. The soldier who is shot looks around for help with an imploring agony of death on his face." And there was also Gettysburg, the climax of the formal career of the Iron Brigade. Leading the Sixth in a celebrated charge on the railroad cut which concluded with the capture of an enemy regiment, perhaps the finest hour of the Sixth Wisconsin, Dawes wrote: "I ordered my men to climb over the turnpike fences and advance . . . (into) the heavy fire which they began at once to pour upon us from their cover in the cut . . . many were struck on the fences, but the line pushed on . . . 'Forward, charge!' was the order I gave. . . . With the colors at the advance point, the regiment firmly and hurriedly moved forward, while the whole field behind streamed with men who had been shot, and who were struggling to the rear or sinking in death upon the ground. The only commands I gave, as we advanced, were 'Align on the colors! Close up on the colors! Close up on the colors!' The regiment was being so broken up that this order alone could hold the body together. Meanwhile the colors fell upon the ground several times but were raised again by the heroes of the color guard. Four hundred and twenty men started in the regiment from the turnpike fence, of whom about two hundred and forty reached the railroad cut."

With equal skill, Dawes recorded the entire career of his regiment and its companions, until, physically exhausted and broken, he left it at Petersburg to be discharged. Moving in and out of the story are some of the major figures of the war as they were observed by Dawes, including Abraham Lincoln, and Generals Grant, McClellan, Hancock, and Doubleday. The scenes and descriptions of these men are valuable. Visiting the army after Antietam, the homely President "looked serious and careworn. He bowed low in response to the salute of our tattered flags." Referring to McClellan's 1861 order prohibiting the inauguration of army movements on Sunday, Dawes discerningly noted that since "he did not inaugurate them on any other day, it was not of much importance." And U. S. Grant appears at one of his first reviews as General-in-Chief, ignoring those regiments which cheered him, but doffing his hat to the Sixth Wisconsin because it did not. In addition to these materials about leading figures of the war, more detailed and intimate portraits appear of officers identified with the Iron Brigade. Surely Dawes correctly evaluated General John Gibbon: "Thoroughly educated in the military profession, he had also high personal qualifications to exercise command . . . and . . . splendid personal bravery." Iron Brigade commanders King and Meredith also frequently appear. And the book affords perhaps the only published eye-witness observations of a number of other figures of the war. Among these were Brigadier General Lucius Fairchild of the Second Wisconsin, a post-war Governor of Wisconsin; Brigadier General Lysander Cutler of the Sixth Wisconsin, the original colonel of that regiment; Brigadier General Edward S. Bragg, Dawes' immediate predecessor as colonel of the Sixth, a national political figure after the war; Colonel John A. Kellogg, Dawes' successor as colonel of the Sixth, commander of the regiment at Appomattox; and Colonel Frank A. Haskell, originally adjutant of the Sixth, author of a famous Harvard Classics' letter describing Gettysburg, who was killed at Cold Harbor as colonel of the Thirty-sixth Wissonsin.

* * *

Like Dawes himself, the brigade and regimental officers and enlisted men of whom he wrote were lesser figures of the war in any comparative sense. As distinguished as the Sixth Wisconsin and the Iron Brigade were, they were but little when considered as a part of the war as a whole. And the experiences of a single officer and his regiment and brigade, however interesting and colorful, are also of limited import in relation to the epic of the Civil War. But *Rufus R. Dawes* and his *regiment* and his *brigade* fought for the Union with signal honor, valor, and devotion. Because of Dawes and his regiment and his brigade, and the efforts of others like them, the Union lived. *Service With The Sixth Wisconsin Volunteers* improves our understanding of the central event of American history. Its availability in this new edition will be welcomed by those who seek such an understanding.

ALAN T. NOLAN

Indianapolis, Indiana
Spring, 1962

PREFACE.

With the hope that I may contribute something of value for the history of one of the most faithful and gallant regiments in the army of the Union, the Sixth Wisconsin Volunteers, and with the especial object of preserving for our children a record of personal experiences in the war, this book has been published.

A box of old letters and papers, collected during the war and carefully arranged and preserved by my wife, has been a chief source from which I have drawn the subject matter.

Contemporary statements and opinions have not been changed. In cases where subsequent knowledge disclosed an error, the fact is noted.

RUFUS R. DAWES.

MARIETTA, OHIO, November 10th, 1890.

CONTENTS.

————o————

CHAPTER I. PAGES 5-21.

CHAPTER II. PAGES 22-41.

CHAPTER III. PAGES 42-77.

III

Individual Records—The Cheering in the Wilderness Explained by a "Johnny"—The Story of William Jackson—Captain Marston Shot at Gettysburg—Seventeen Years Later—To my Living Comrades—Statistics From Colonel Fox and the Official Records.

PORTRAITS

ILLUSTRATIONS

COMPANY K.

"There's a cap in the closet
Old, faded and blue,
Of very slight value,
It may be, to you;
But a crown, jewel studded,
Could not buy it to-day
With its letters of honor,
'Brave Company K.'"

CHAPTER I.

The Call for Volunteers—The Lemonweir Minute Men—Anxious
Haste to "Crush the Rebellion"—Provoking Delays—Captain
Balfour's Opinion—Assigned to the Seventh Wisconsin—A
Poster—Ordered Into Quarters—Called to the Sixth Regiment
—Reception at Camp Randall—Company K Better Known
as Q—Officers of the Sixth—I Discover That I Have a Servant
—We are Uniformed in Gray—Mustered Into U. S. Service—Bull
Run—To the Front—The Glorious Passage East—Miss Ander-
son—The March Through Baltimore—Attacked by Plug Uglies
—Lieutenant Kellogg in the Battle of Patterson Park—On to
Washington—Kalorama Heights—Our Brass Band—First Sight
of General McClellan.

Fort Sumpter was fired upon, and recognizing the full import
of that event, on the fifteenth day of April 1861, President Abraham Lincoln issued his proclamation calling for seventy-five
thousand volunteers to suppress the rebellion by force of arms.
This first bugle call of war found the author of this book in the
sparsely settled County of Juneau in the State of Wisconsin.
I was then twenty-two years of age, and had come out of college
with the class of 1860. With the proclamation of the President
came the announcement that the quota of the State of Wisconsin would be only one small infantry regiment of seven hundred
and eighty men. It seemed quite evident that only by
prompt action I might secure what was then termed the "glorious
privilege" of aiding in crushing the Rebellion, which undertaking

it had been estimated by * one in high authority, could be accomplished in sixty days. It is pleasant to remember that at that day few questions were raised as to the rates of compensation for service, and so remote a contingency as realizing upon the promise of a pension was not considered. Nothing beyond the opportunity to go was asked. What seemed to most concern óur patriotic and ambitious young men was the fear that some one else would get ahead and crush the Rebellion before they got there. Drawing up the following pledge and signing it, I began the work of gathering Volunteers on the twenty-fifth day of April 1861.

"We, the undersigned, agree to organize an independent military company, and to hold ourselves in readiness to respond to any call to defend our country and sustain our government." It will be noted that the service offered was not limited to three months but was for "any call."

Forty-eight signers were secured as the result of my first day's work. Then John A. Kellogg, the Prosecuting Attorney of the county, would not be denied the privilege of signing my paper and joining with me in the work of raising a company of Volunteers. I argued with Kellogg, who was ten years my senior and a married man, that young men, without families, could crush the Rebellion, but he could not brook the thought of being deprived of sharing in the satisfaction and glory of that service, and feeling that this would be his only chance, he joined in the work of making up the company with the utmost zeal.

On the thirtieth day of April one hundred men, who had agreed to volunteer, met in Langworthy's Hall, in the village of Mauston, the county seat, to organize the company. There was no contest for the positions of Captain and First Lieutenant. But for the other offices there was active competition, and the meeting assumed something of the aspect of a political convention. After a discussion in which Badgers and other typical beasts and birds were considered for an appropriate name, we adopted the mellifluous title of "The Lemonweir Minute Men" from the peaceful and gently flowing river, in the beautiful

---

* Wm. H. Seward, Secretary of State, in President Lincoln's Cabinet.

valley of which most of our men resided. It would "remind us of home" said one, and this argument carried the day.

Extracts from a letter written to my sister in Ohio will serve to illustrate the spirit of these times and of this occasion. Their zeal might have been tempered had they known more of war, but a purer impulse of patriotism never burned in the souls of men, than that which inspired the unmercenary Volunteers of 1861.

MAUSTON, JUNEAU CO., WIS. MAY 4th, 1861.

I have been so wholly engrossed with my work for the last week or I should have responded sooner to your question: "Are you going?" If a kind Providence and President Lincoln will permit, I am. I am Captain of as good, and true a band of patriots as ever rallied under the star spangled banner. We hope to get into the third or fourth regiment, and if old Abe will but give a fair and merited share in the struggle to Wisconsin, we will see active service. The men expect and earnestly desire to go, and wait impatiently their turn. I shall esteem it an honor, worth a better life than mine, to be permitted to lead them in this glorious struggle. I am in hourly dread of hearing of some violence offered you on the border, and wish I might be permitted to bring to you, in your peril, some as strong hands and as true hearts as the Badger State can *boast.

STATE OF WISCONSIN, ADJUTANT GENERAL'S OFFICE.

MADISON, May 2nd, 1861.

CAPTAIN RUFUS R. DAWES,

MAUSTON, JUNEAU COUNTY,

Dear Sir : Enclosed please find commissions for your

---

*This is what I had heard from home. Letter from my mother dated Marietta, Ohio, April 28, 1861 :

"Governor Dennison has sent six cannon and two companies of the regular army to Marietta. Your Uncle (William P. Cutler) has not joined the Silver Greys for he will have to go to Congress in two months. He is one of the Committee of Safety. Business is prostrated, yet the people are hopeful and seem determined at all hazards to sustain the Government. Provisions here are abundant and cheap. The excitement is so great and so entirely engrossing that all other subjects are dismissed. People recognize the hand of God in these things and feel thankful that the North is right. To-day at church the soldiers marched in and took the front seats. What a sight for Marietta! The Ohio river perhaps will be the border. Before the end of the week there will be thousands of troops quartered in Marietta. I despair of giving you any idea of the excited state of things here."

company. You will be registered in your regular order, and called on when reached. Until further orders you will make no expenses on account of the State.

Very Respectfully Yours,

WM. L. UTLEY, Adjutant General.

Commissions enclosed :

Rufus R. Dawes,	. . .	Captain.
John A. Kellogg, .	. . .	First Lieutenant.
John Crane,	. . . .	Second Lieutenant.

The question of getting into active service now absorbed the minds of all, and great anxiety and impatience was displayed lest we should not be called, or other companies, later organized, should be preferred. On May 16th, I wrote to my brother, E. C. Dawes, then a student in college in Ohio, "I am working like a beaver to get my company into active service. We sent John Turner, (an influential citizen,) to Madison to see the Governor. I have a hundred men upon the muster roll. I have quite a number of raftsmen from the pineries. To endure the hardships of actual service none could be better fitted. Campaigning in the field would be a luxury in comparison to logging in the winter in the pineries. I don't believe there can be better soldiers."

During this period of doubt and anxiety, I found comfort in the judgment of one Captain Balfour, of Mauston. He differed from the general opinion as to the serious magnitude of the coming war. He was an old gentleman who had served as a Captain in the British army. He had been through campaigns in Spain and was present at the burial of Sir John Moore. He, and other young officers, he informed me, had taken turns in sitting on the throne of Spain which had been abandoned by Joseph Bonaparte, when Wellington's army had entered Madrid.

His wife, a hale and bright old lady, had been with him in these campaigns, serving as vivandiere of his regiment. Captain Balfour, then over eighty years of age, said "Don't fret, young man, your company will be needed. Those Southern people are determined upon war. It will take years to put them down. You'll see, you'll see! You have no Wellingtons or Napoleons in this country, and next to no experience in war. This is no job of sixty days." I constantly advised with this venerable soldier who gave me excellent counsel and suggestions of practical value, drawn from a long experience in field service.

Two weeks more passed away, much exciting news coming from Ohio,* and on the second of June, I find the following report of the condition of our affairs in a letter to my sister. "At present the prospect seems very good for our company remaining at home a month or two yet. We have been assigned to the seventh regiment. Six regiments are now under pay and the seventh will be called into camp when the fifth is mustered into the United States service. The first four regiments have already been mustered in. It is perhaps better to be so, though a severe trial to our patience. I went to Madison to see Governor Randall and the Adjutant General, but could get no higher on the list. Wisconsin has twelve regiments already, and we are well up to be in the seventh." On the 10th of June I write: "The first six regiments are now accepted by the General Government, and I expect to be ordered into quarters. I think we will be in ample time to go with the grand expedition down the Mississippi and hold a merry Christmas in New Orleans. This delay will make some hard work, recruiting to fill vacancies, but I can have a full company. George W. Bird and William F. Vilas are looking after my interests at Madison." These gentlemen had been old friends and college associates at the Wisconsin State University.

---

*Marietta had now become a Camp for the troops that made up the army for the campaign in West Virginia. From my mother:

MARIETTA, OHIO, May 27th, 1861.

"All of the first ladies in the city have given their names to nurse or furnish supplies for the sick. As yet we have no system, but hope to get organized in a day or two. The hospital is an old brick building near the Fair ground. There are thirty-nine sick men there to-day, and they are far from comfortable. But the Citizens are sending in things every day and we shall soon get fixed. Most of the men are sick with the measles. There is one case of typhoid fever. Another regiment (18th Ohio) came in to-day. Everybody is making bandages, lint, and Havelock caps. L—— has made five and a half dozens of plasters of mutton tallow, spread on linen rags, four inches square and done up neatly in oiled silk, very acceptable, the surgeons say." Such were the preparations for war in 1861.

EXECUTIVE OFFICE, MADISON, JUNE 14th, 1861.
CAPTAIN R. R. DAWES, LEMONWEIR MINUTE MEN,

MAUSTON, JUNEAU COUNTY.

Sir : The Governor desires to know whether your company is now full to at least eighty-three men for three years or the war. Quite a number of the companies on our Register fail to muster full at the appointed day. You will oblige by replying to this letter at the earliest day possible, and *stating a day on or after which you can stand ready to meet a mustering officer with a full company.* We expect to send off the first six regiments within four weeks, and two more will then be called into camp and equipped.

Yours Respectfully,

W. H. WATSON, Mil. Sec'y.

A Poster:

RALLY!
BOYS, RALLY!! RALLY!!!

ENLISTMENTS WANTED FOR THE LEMONWEIR MINUTE MEN!

HEADQUARTERS L. M. M., MAUSTON, JUNE 17th, 1861.

This company is ordered by the Commander in chief to hold itself in readiness to be mustered into the service on Monday, June 24th. Men are wanted to complete the full complement of one hundred and one. Come forward, boys, and place your names on the roll. R. R. DAWES, CAPTAIN.

To my sister on the 20th of June, I write: "I am at present tormented beyond measure by the delay in calling my company together. The men are scattered over nearly a whole Congressional district. Many influences operate now to deter and discourage the men, and I fear they will order us into camp without giving me time to collect my men or recruit for vacancies. But I have one glorious satisfaction. We have a place certain and nothing but the lack of a full company can stop us. I ride and travel night and day. It will take a load off my shoulders to have my men brought together." "Your excellent advice and the pin cushions will be very serviceable, and on behalf of the company I return their thanks. Please say to Mrs. E. B. Andrews that I appreciate highly my pin cushion made from Kossuth's vest." Some ladies of Marietta, Ohio, had sent to me, through my sister, one hundred pin cushions for my company.

On the 29th of June came the welcome telegram, which was received with the greatest enthusiasm, ordering us into quarters.

CAPTAIN R. R. DAWES: You can board your company at expense of the State at not more than two dollars and a half a week, until further orders. It is possible that you may be wanted for the sixth regiment.

W. H. WATSON, Military Secretary.

On the 6th day of July, in compliance with orders, the company, ninety-four men in all, took the cars for Madison to join the sixth regiment. We had been assigned to that regiment because of the failure of several other companies registered higher on the list in the Adjutant General's office. Our arrival, therefore, as it completed the organization of the regiment, was an event, increased in its interest and importance by the several previous disappointments. I received a telegram from the Colonel of the sixth regiment, while en route, asking the hour of our arrival. Had I suspected the reception that was being prepared for us, I think I should have entered protest. As we approached Camp Randall that afternoon, the fifth and sixth regiments, nearly two thousand men, were in line of battle to receive us with becoming state and ceremony. My company had had practically no drill. "By the right flank, right face" according to the Scott tactics, and "Forward march" was almost the sum total of my own knowledge of military movements. The men stumbled along in two ranks, kicking each other's heels as they gazed at the novel and imposing spectacle before them. A few wore broadcloth and silk hats, more the red shirts of raftsmen, several were in country homespun, one had on a calico coat, and another was looking through a hole in the drooping brim of a straw hat. I remember, also, that there were several of those ugly white caps with long capes, called "Havelocks." The men carried every variety of valise, and every species of bundle, down to one shirt tied up in a red handkerchief. My confusion may be imagined when I was met at the gate way of Camp Randall by Frank A. Haskell, the Adjutant of the sixth regiment, who was mounted on a spirited charger, and quite stunning in his bright uniform and soldierly bearing. With a military salute he transmitted an order from the Colonel "to form my company in column by platoon," and to march to Headquarters under escort of the Milwaukee Zouaves. Hibbard's Zouaves, (Co. B, 5thWisconsin,) was then considered the best drilled company in the state. Their appearance in bright Zouave uniform was fine. I answered Adjutant Haskell, "Good afternoon, Sir. I should be glad to comply with the wishes of the Colonel, but it is simply impossible." So we took our own gait in the direction of Headquarters. The maneuvres and the yelling of the Zouaves, who engaged in one of their peculiar drills, increased the distraction of my men, and they marched worse than before. However, we got into line in front of Headquarters and were briefly congratulated upon our arrival, in a few pertinent remarks by Colonel Lysander Cutler. The Colonel informed us in his speech that we would be designated as Company "K." But in recognition of our grand entree, the camp had already christened us Company "Q."

Fortunately, our first essay in military evolution at the evening dress parade, took place behind the backs of the regiment. Adjutant Frank A. Haskell came to my relief, and of his kindness on that occasion I have an appreciative memory. The fun he enjoyed in watching us, amply repaid his service. By our designation as Company "K" we were brought in camp, and in line, into close connection with Company "E," an alliance which proved congenial. The Captain of that Company appeared to be much gratified that a Captain had come in, who knew less than he did about military matters. Thus began an intimate association, which lasted through three hard years of trial, in which we were together. At this beginning of our acquaintance, I think a fellow feeling made us wondrous kind. In politics and law, Edward S. Bragg stood among the first men in his state, but in military matters he had yet, as the Indians would say, "a heap to know." The sixth regiment was an exceptionally fine body of officers and men, as their history may abundantly attest. There were many of the officers of the line, already well qualified by education and experience, for their duties. Company "A" was commanded by Captain Adam G. Malloy, who had been a soldier in the war with Mexico. His Company was being well instructed, and he was ambitious that they should justify their selection as first upon the list. Company "C," which had been made the color company, was commanded by Captain A. S. Hooe, whose father was a Major in the regular army. In that association he had grown to thorough knowledge of the drill. Company "F," of Germans from Milwaukee, had two of the most highly qualified officers with whom I met in all my service, Lieutenant Schumacher and Lieutenant Werner von Bachelle. Both had served in the armies of Europe, and as competent, exact and thorough drill masters, they were no where to be surpassed. It was to me an instructive pleasure to watch them drill their companies. The influence of this splendid company, and its Lieutenants, was marked in stimulating others to equal their performance. Both of these gallant men and model soldiers were killed in battle for their adopted country. The Captain of Company "H," which was also composed principally of Germans, was a character. He could, at that time, express himself only with much difficulty in English, He was a tall and stalwart soldier, rigid as a disciplinarian and exact as an instructor, as he had been educated in the military school at Thun, Switzerland. He had also served in European wars, and acted on the Staff of General Garibaldi. One saying of Captain Hauser in Camp Randall is memorable. Exasperated at his men who got into a huddle, he shouted, "Vell, now you looks shust like one dam herd of goose." Lieutenant John F. Marsh of Company "B," had served in the war with Mexico, and there were other officers of excellent qualification, among those upon the roster.*

---

*Colonel Lysander Cutler.
Lieutenant Colonel J. P. Atwood.
Major B. J. Sweet.

Surgeon, C. B. Chapman.	Adjutant, Frank A. Haskell.
First Ass't, A. W. Preston.	Quartermaster, Isaac N. Mason.
Second Ass't, O. F. Bartlett.	Chaplain, N. A. Staples.

CAPTAINS.	FIRST LIEUTENANTS.	SECOND LIEUTENANTS.
Co. A, A. G. Malloy.	D. K. Noyes.	F. C. Thomas.
Co. B, D. J. Dill.	J. F. Marsh.	H. Serrill.
Co. C, A. S. Hooe.	P. W. Plummer.	T. W. Plummer.
Co. D, John O'Rourke.	John Nichol.	P. H. McCauley.
Co. E, E. S. Bragg.	E. A. Brown.	J. H. Marston.
Co. F, W. H. Lindwurm.	F. Schumacher.	W. Von Bachelle.
Co. G, M. A. Northrup.	G. L. Montague.	W. W. Allen.
Co. H, J. F. Hauser.	J. D. Lewis.	J. T. Tester.
Co. I, Leonard Johnson.	F. A. Haskell.	A. J. Johnson.
Co. K, R. R. Dawes.	J. A. Kellogg.	Jno. Crane.

On July 9th, I reported progress in a letter to my sister as follows:

"After two months of incessant, aggravating and provoking labor, my company is in the sixth regiment. We came into camp on Saturday evening last and we are now under the severest kind of drill. We were at first quartered in barracks, and given old straw in which there was no scarcity of fleas, but last night we moved into our tents. My men are not more than half supplied with blankets, and, as we have cold drizzling weather, they have suffered. It is a new life to us all, but I hope we can get broken in without much sickness. I am studying up on tactics, drilling and attending to the business of the company, so that I have very little time to see my old friends in Madison." About this time we received from the State of Wisconsin payment for our services. To our surprise and gratification we were instructed to make up our pay roll from May 3rd., the date of our commissions. I remember that when I took my pay roll to that excellent gentleman, Simeon Mills, the Paymaster, he said, "I see, Captain, that you have omitted to put in your servant." I said, "I have no servant." Mr. Mills said, "I think you certainly have, as the Regulations require it." Seeing that he knew more about the subject than I did, I made no further objection to a servant's going on the pay roll. This was one of the farces of our military system. My treacherous memory forbids my recording here, whether my servant was described as having green eyes and red hair or red eyes and green hair; but I think the old pay roll will disclose a very remarkable descriptive list of this imaginary person. A Captain of infantry had sixty dollars per month as pay and sixty-eight dollars per month as "allowances." Thirteen dollars per month and thirty cents per day (one ration) was allowed for a servant, and one dollar and twenty cents (four rations) was allowed for subsistence. But the Captain was obliged to certify that he had a servant, and to describe him. Few Captains had servants, but all had one hundred and twenty-eight dollars per month.

Our regiment, strange to say, was uniformed by the State of Wisconsin in the color of the Confederacy, gray. These gray uniforms were of honest and excellent material, and we exchanged them with regret a few months later for the sleazy, shoddy blue, we received from the general government, at that early period in the war.

The question which absorbed the most attention next in Camp Randall, was the impending muster into the United States service. As the day approached, I found it was inevitable that I should lose four men, who could not or who would not be mustered in. One was too old, one was too young, one showed that he had no idea of going with us, and the last one had a presentiment that he would be killed. I labored with this last man, for he was a strong, hearty, good fellow, but he said that in a dream he had seen himself killed. This seemed absurd, but I had to let him go. Later in the war this man enlisted in a Wisconsin Cavalry regiment, and served his term without a scratch. Captain Bragg asked me if I did not want two of his men. I was anxious to muster in as many as possible, and did want badly two men. He said that one of his men wanted to serve his country as a fifer and the other as a drummer. The fifer could not fife, neither could the drummer drum. But none of my men in Company "K" could perform such service, and they were all desirous to serve as soldiers in the line. There seemed nothing in the way of this arrangement to swell my ranks by two, and so I took them in. Captain Bragg got nothing for his men, but he settled perplexing questions about the music in Company "E."

We were mustered into the service of the United States for the term of three years, unless sooner discharged, on the 16th day of July, 1861. The regiment mustered in ten hundred and forty-five men. In my company ninety-two men were mustered. In giving these figures, I follow the authority of my own contemporary letter.

Referring again to the old bundle of letters, carefully preserved by my sister, who herself, long years ago, passed away from us, I find that the movement of our army towards Bull Run, in Virginia, which was then in progress, aroused our expectation of moving Eastward. I find, also, that upon the occasion of the presentation by the State, of colors to the fifth and sixth regiments, there was a grand celebration and jollification at Camp Randall. There were about six thousand visitors present.

A fine supper, the gift of the ladies of Dane County, was served to both regiments in the dining hall. The camp was beautifully decorated, and no grounds were neater or more tastefully adorned than those of Company "K." To our First Sergeant, David L. Quaw, is chiefly due the credit.

My next letter is dated at Camp Cutler near Harrisburg, Pennsylvania, August 1st. "The disastrous affair at Bull Run caused us to be ordered this way. Our journey through from Madison to Harrisburg was like a triumphal march. Men, women and children, crowded in hundreds and thousands at every town and city, to hail us and to cheer us on our way to help rescue the down trodden flag. This shows how the people are aroused. At Milwaukee an abundant table was spread for us. At Racine, Kenosha, and Chicago the haversacks of our men were crammed with every delicacy. We came through by the way of the Pittsburg, Ft. Wayne and Chicago, and Pennsylvania Central Rail Roads. The trip was full of exciting and pleasing incidents. At Cresson, on the Allegheny Mountains, we met the family of Major Robert Anderson. You may be sure the Badger boys made the mountains ring with cheers for the daughters of the hero of Fort Sumpter. His oldest daughter is a very handsome young lady. The enclosed sprig please keep for me till the wars are over, as it was presented to me by Miss Anderson in acknowledgement of our compliment to her father. We expect to go from here to Harper's Ferry and will probably be attached to Gen. Banks' Division. The rebels are said to be advancing on Harper's Ferry. We therefore expect a fight in a few days. I wish my men were better drilled."

The question was raised, why Miss Anderson passed our old Colonel by and presented this little token to the youngest Captain in the line. It was wholly due to the superior lung power of Company "K."

We did move from Harrisburg, but it was not to Harper's Ferry nor to fight the enemy, for the next letter is from Baltimore. "We are encamped in Patterson Park, a beautiful grove overlooking the city, the bay, Fort McHenry and a broad extent of finely cultivated farms. We marched several miles through the streets of Baltimore last night, without arms. We were escorted by two hundred armed police. Our boys were well supplied with brick bats. The rebel Plug Uglies commenced an attack on Bragg's Company, "E," which marched just in front of my company, but it was promptly suppressed by the police. The streets were jammed with people, as we marched, and the excitement was very great. The sentiments expressed were spitefully hostile. There is a slumbering Volcano in Baltimore ready to break out at any success of the Rebellion. Your imagination cannot picture with what unction they would roll under their tongues such morsels as, "Bull Run you blue bellies!" "How do you like Bull Run?" "It was Yankees Run." We have come into a different atmosphere. I hope we may remain here awhile. We need drill badly* and our present

---

*Muster Roll of Company "K," 6th Wisconsin Volunteers, in August, 1861.

Captain, ... Rufus R. Dawes.
First Lieutenant . . . John A. Kellogg.
Second Lieutenant, . . John Crane.

SERGEANTS.

First Serg't, David L. Quaw. Second Serg't, Linnaeus Westcott.
Third Serg't, Eugene P. Rose. Fourth Serg't, H. H. Edwards.
Fifth Serg't, John Ticknor.

CORPORALS.

W. N. Remington, W. S. Campbell, Reuben Huntley,
Franklin Wilcox, Wm. H. Van Wie, John Holden,
Oliver Fletcher, Thomas Flynn.

MUSICIANS.

A. J. Atwell, E. G. Jackson.

PRIVATE SOLDIERS.

Charles A. Abbott,	Wm. Garland,	James W. Scoville,
Charles A. Alton,	Jacob Garthwait,	Edward Simons,
Daniel D. Alton,	S. Frank Gordon,	Erastus Smith,
Eugene Anderson,	Cassius Griggs,	Cyrus Spooner,
William Anderson,	Henry Gallup,	William Stevens,
Alonzo Andress.	William Hancock,	John St. Clair,
James L. Barney,	William Harrison,	James P. Sullivan,
Ira Butterfield,	Peter Helmer,	Hugh Talty,
Frederick Boynton,	Cyrus Hendrick,	Albert Tarbox,
Ralph Brown,	Edward Hendrick,	Silas Temple,
John Carsley,	Israel Hendrick,	Charles M. Taylor,
Geo. Chamberlain,	Thomas S. Hills,	A. R. Thompson,
Joseph A. Chase,	Llewellyn Hills,	John R. Towle,
Thomas Cleveland,	Volney Holmes,	Hoel Trumble,
Ephraim Cornish,	James W. Knapp,	Lyman B. Upham,
George W. Covey,	Bernard McEwen,	Richard Upham,
Chas. A. Crawford,	Daniel J. Miller,	William Valleau,
John A. Crawford,	E. Mitchell,	Stephen Whicher,

situation is all that could be desired. We are very closely confined in camp. No commissioned officer can leave without a pass from the Colonel. There is plenty of money in the regiment now, gold and silver. Our old Colonel Cutler is a very strict disciplinarian, and will tolerate no nonsense. He was Colonel of a regiment in Maine in the Aroostook war. Queer as it now sounds, the boast of our Colonel's military record was in serious earnest.

CAMP ATWOOD, PATTERSON PARK, August, 5th 1861.

"Our camp was attacked about midnight by the Plug Uglies of Baltimore. A fire was opened on our Guards, who promptly replied, and the bullets whistled occasionally through the camp. Several companies were turned out and quiet soon restored. Fortunately none of our men were struck." This little affair was our first contact with rebels who would shoot. In some respects it was a very laughable experience. When the firing began, which was after midnight, I formed my men in the company street and loaded up with brick bats. We had no guns. Companies "A" and "B" only had been armed as yet, and they were on guard duty contending with the foe. I sent Lieutenant Kellogg to the Colonel for instructions. This was super serviceable as the Colonel would have sent for us if he had needed our brick bats. Lieutenant Kellogg wandered around in the dark night and found the Colonel in the back part of the camp where the firing was the hottest. What instructions he received we never learned, as he fell into a dreadful hole in his reckless rush to bring them to us, and his condition of body and mind was such that he did nothing but swear a blue streak about his own mishap. With us the tragedy ended with a roaring farce. Lieut. Kellogg was of quick blood and it was not always safe to congratulate him as the only man wounded in the Battle of Patterson Park.

W. R. Davis,	Alex. Noble,	Charles West,
Willard Dutton,	Andrew J. Nott,	Chauncey Wilcox,
Thomas Ellsworth,	William Patterson,	Arlon F. Winsor,
A. G. Emmons,	Lorenzo Pratt,	Samuel O. Woods,
R. W. Emmons,	Waitstell Ranney,	Aaron Yates,
Abram Fletcher,	James Rodgers,	Volney DeJean, Wagoner.
Dennis Fuller,	Charles Reynolds,	

While we were at Patterson Park we were under the Command of General John A. Dix.

On the seventh day of August we moved on to Washington. The order came while the regiment was engaged in the evening Dress Parade, and it was received with enthusiasm. *Our orders were to move at once, and there was hurrying in hot haste. The regiment had been armed, while at Patterson Park, with Belgian muskets, a heavy, clumsy gun, of large caliber, and not to be compared with the Springfield rifled musket. We again marched through the streets of Baltimore at night. Our muskets were loaded and my letter says, "at half cock," and we received from all citizens the compliment of respectful silence. We started about midnight, in filthy cattle cars, and reached Washington City at daylight. We marched to the City Hall Park, and, late in the day to Meridian Hill, where we established our camp, a few rods from Columbia College, then being used as a hospital for the wounded from the Bull Run battle. This camp, called Kalorama, was, as indicated by its classic name, indeed beautiful for situation and for its magnificent view of the Capitol and the city. But the three weeks spent there were a great trial. There were in my company twenty-five men sick with the measles, and the other companies were in like manner severely scourged. The weather was intensely hot and the water was not good. Melons were freely sold in camp, and a general run of sickness was the result beyond our measles. On August fifteenth, we had in Company "K" thirty-five reported sick and unfit for duty. On August twenty-third, a more cheerful condition prevailed, as I write as follows to my sister:

"My men are getting through with their measles, and I hope to soon have out full ranks. We are drilling every day and improving rapidly. It is announced that we are soon to be reviewed by President Lincoln and Gen. George B. McClellan."

To my brother on August twenty-fourth, I wrote from Camp Kalorama:

"We are here at Washington yet, and I think likely to stay a

---

*General Dix says he had "telegraphic orders" to send General Rufus King and the two Wisconsin regiments (5th and 6th,) to Washington.

week or so. We were reviewed yesterday by the Brigadier, (Rufus King,) and our regiment never before appeared so meanly. It was enough to try the patience of a martyr, the performance of that contemptible brass band of ours. They played such slow time music that we passed the reviewing officer at about forty-seven paces a minute. We had to hold one leg in the air and balance on the other while we waited for the music. By the way, old Kanouse belongs to this band. He is sick, and I do not wonder at it. He goes along, pumping up and down on a big toot horn. He wants to get out of the band. I should think he would, for if a man in the regiment is caught in a rascally trick, the whole regiment yells, 'Put him in the brass band.'" Theodore D. Kanouse, who was an old college friend at the Wisconsin State University, often came to my quarters, and his witty comments upon the infelicity of his service in the band, were a source of amusement. He said he had undertaken to crush the Rebellion with a trombone and, willing to admit his own failure, he hoped the Government would not rely wholly upon its brass bands to accomplish that result. "As the regiment is at present organized, I am junior Captain in the fourth division, (Companies 'E' and 'K'). Captain Edward S. Bragg, of Company' E,' is rated as my senior. I really rank him though, by the date of my commission, and I propose to have this thing corrected.* Twice yesterday, on that ridiculous review, I gave orders when Bragg was at fault. Captain Bragg, though, is the brightest man in the regiment. He was a delegate to the Democratic National Conventions at Charleston and Baltimore. It is highly entertaining to hear him relate his experiences. Our Colonel (Lysander Cutler) is rigid in his discipline, and stern and unflinching in exacting the performance of all duties, and I believe will prove of determined courage. Frank A. Haskell is one of the best Adjutants in the army." Frank A. Haskell exercised at that time a marked influence upon the progress of the regiment in soldierly knowledge and quality. He was an educated gentleman, a graduate of Dartmouth College. He had belonged to the Governor's Guard, a military company at the Capitol of Wisconsin, and had been drawn by natural tastes

---

*Youthful vapor.

to some study of military tactics. Haskell had been born with every quality that goes to make a model soldier. He took great interest and pride in the instruction of the regiment, and so elevated his office, that some men then thought the Adjutant must at least be next to the Colonel in authority and rank. It was a good instruction in the school of a soldier to serve a tour of duty in the regimental guard. One especial and untiring effort of Adjutant Haskell was to exact cleanliness and neatness of personal appearance, an essential condition of true soldierly bearing. The cotton gloves, which he required the men to wear, were kept snow white, nor did he allow them to cover dirty hands. It was a dread ordeal for a man to step four paces in front and face the Adjutant before the assembled guard and in fear of this he went there clean at however great and unusual a sacrifice of customary habit. To see Haskell, "About face" and salute the Colonel before the regiment when we were on dress parade was an object lesson in military bearing.

On the twenty-sixth of August there was a general review of all the troops encamped on Meridian Hill. General George B. McClellan was the reviewing officer, and this was our first introduction. On that day I wrote to my sister:

"The General is a splendid looking man, just in the prime of life. The boys are all carried away with enthusiasm for him. Our Brigade is as well drilled as any I have seen, and is made up as follows: 2nd Wisconsin, 5th Wisconsin, 79th New York (Highlanders, uniformed in kilts), 32nd Pennsylvania, 2nd New York, (Fire Zouaves) and the 6th Wisconsin. General McClellan pronounced our regiment one of the best in material, appearance and bearing. We expect and hope to be in the first advance and this opinion expressed by the commander of the army is, I think, an earnest of things hoped for. The 5th Wisconsin—Colonel Amasa Cobb—is a fine regiment. The New York Fire Zouaves, the 79th Highlanders, and the 69th New York seem to be drunken rowdies. The 14th and 15th Massachusetts are the most neatly uniformed, the best equipped, the best provided for, and the best drilled regiments I have seen. Last night we had considerable excitement on account of an order to be ready to march at a moment's notice."

CHAPTER II.

BIVOUAC NEAR CHAIN BRIDGE, ON POTOMAC, ⎫
   SIX MILES ABOVE WASHINGTON,   ⎬
             SEPTEMBER 8th, 1861. ⎭

"It is very difficult now for me to write at all, so do not be alarmed at a little irregularity in my correspondence. We left the old camp on Kalorama Heights, a week ago to-morrow night (Sept. 2nd.) Since then we have been moving around from one place to another, wherever our presence has been deemed necessary. We left our tents, extra clothing, cooking utensils, everything but one woolen blanket and one oil cloth. We sleep on the ground with nothing above us but the canopy of heaven. To intensify our discomfort, the weather has been cold and rainy. This is rather a hard road to travel, but I keep healthy, hearty and happy, and feel better than when I first began to sleep in a tent. Our regiment has been doing picket duty along the Potomac river on the Maryland side from Chain Bridge to Falling Waters. My company has been deployed along about four miles. The rebel pickets and cavalry could be occasionally seen along the other side of the river. I have really enjoyed this week's work. The scenery on the Potomac here, is very romantic. The people generally sympathize with the rebels.

Our boys have fared sumptuously every day. They declared that even the pigs were secessionists and they burned them at the *steak* for their treason. Turkeys and chickens shared the same fate. It was impossible for me to restrain men who had been starved on salt-beef and hard tack, when they were scattered over four miles of territory and sneered at as Yankees by the people. The fact is I ate some pig myself. The present bivouac of the regiment is within a few rods of the ruins of Montgomery Hall, once, you know, General Washington's Headquarters. Across the river, opposite on a high hill, now the site of a powerful battery, is the spot where Clay and Randolph fought their duel."

CAMP NEAR CHAIN BRIDGE, SEPTEMBER 20th, 1861.

To my brother: "You are anxious to know whether we have any skirmishing. No. Our men are all at work constructing forts and digging trenches. You want to know what it has cost me to uniform. My sword, sash, and sword knot cost $35. My blue dress uniform, thirty-three dollars, undress uniform, seventeen dollars, and overcoat twenty-two dollars. Then I was fool enough to spend thirty dollars on gray, which is now of no use. Buff vest cost four dollars, army shoes, six dollars, and cap two dollars. My blue dress uniform turns red and is a confounded cheat. My sash is at least half cotton, and it is rapidly fading. My scabbard is metal that tarnishes in half an hour. The army is being terribly fleeced by the Washington sharps. Fancy uniforms are useless sleeping in the mud. Frank Haskell, our Adjutant, has been assigned to command of Company 'I' and P. W. Plummer of Company 'C' is acting as Adjutant. If you are going to be an Adjutant, set to work at once, learning how to 'About face' gracefully."

CAMP NEAR CHAIN BRIDGE, SEPTEMBER 23rd, 1861.

"The same 'masterly inactivity' is still the order of the day. Beauregard is strenuously preparing himself for an attack by McClellan. McClellan keeps thousands of men building fortifications to resist an attack by Beauregard. Yesterday from the dome of the Capitol of the United States, with the aid of a telescope, I distinctly saw the rebel flag waving on Munson's

Hill, six miles away. I could see a company of rebel soldiers also. This is a sorry spectacle."

The 5th Wisconsin regiment had been separated from us, and attached to a brigade, which was commanded by a young Brigadier who was yet unknown to fame, Gen. W. S. Hancock. Hancock's brigade was encamped at the opposite end of the Chain Bridge in Virginia. The General had a voice like a trumpet and we could hear him drilling his brigade. He would give some such order as, "On first division, third battalion, deploy column, quick, march!" and the regiments would proceed. Colonel Cobb of the 5th Wisconsin, a civilian appointee, would sometimes blunder, and we would hear in the same ringing, bell like tones, "Colonel Cobb, where the — — nation are you going with that battalion?" Amasa Cobb was a distinguished citizen at home and this was a source of extreme amusement to our men, some of whom would go down among the willows under the bank of the river, and shout across in fine imitation of General Hancock, "Colonel Cobb, where the — — nation are you going with that battalion?" The men called this performance, "Hancock whispering to his brigade."

CAMP LYON, NEAR CHAIN BRIDGE, SEPTEMBER 29th, 1861.

To my brother: "The army of the Potomac is in high spirits this morning. The Grand Army has moved forward and taken possession of Munson Hill and the whole line of rebel outposts without firing a gun. Our troops at the Chain Bridge did not move forward, but we were up nearly all night, to be ready to march at a moment's notice. But as General McClellan will not fight on Sunday, we do not now expect to move until to-morrow. (Reference is here made to a general order issued by McClellan in regard to inaugurating movements on Sunday. As he did not inaugurate them on any other day, it was not of much importance.) It is said that our brigade will go to the Arlington House, and probably pitch tents there, and perhaps advance in light marching order towards Fairfax Court House. It is said that some of our regiments in the movements last night, fired on each other, and that others, who were out of range but scared by the noise, threw away their guns and ran. Colonel Atwood has resigned, and Major B. J. Sweet has been promoted to Lieut.

Colonel and our little Captain Bragg of Co. 'E' has been promoted to Major. Companies 'E' and 'K' rejoice and are exceeding glad. but one or two of our Captains are mad at Bragg's promotion. He is the best man and I am glad of his advancement. They say the Colonel would have preferred to have Frank Haskell appointed Major, but Bragg captured the Governor.* Our old Colonel is as rugged as a wolf, and the regiment has great confidence in him, both as a man and an officer. We have not been roughing it lately, but have been living high. My Second Lieutenant has even struck up a flirtation with a young lady in Georgetown. Crane is making a fine young officer. He is one of the best instructors in the manual of arms in the regiment."

CAMP NEAR FORT CASS, ARLINGTON HEIGHTS, VA.,
OCTOBER 6th, 1861.

"We crossed the Potomac yesterday by the Aqueduct Bridge at Georgetown. We have joined the division commanded by Gen. Irvin McDowell. The 7th Wisconsin has been substituted for the 5th Wisconsin in our brigade. They have an old Dutch Colonel named Van Dor. The 19th Indiana regiment, commanded by Colonel Solomon Meredith, is now in our brigade.† We are encamped in the woods on the line of fortifications which extends from Chain Bridge to Alexandria in front of Washington, and near the Arlington House."

CAMP ARLINGTON, VA., OCTOBER 28th, 1861.

To my sister: "Ten officers‡ have left or been removed from

*This is camp chaff. Governor Alexander W. Randall, about that time, visited our camp at Arlington and this circumstance probably gave rise to such talk.

†Thus was originally made up the Iron Brigade of the Army of the Potomac. The camp at Chain Bridge may be considered as the beginning of the history of that body of troops, and this movement to Arlington its first march. The regiments comprising the brigade were now, 2nd Wisconsin, 6th Wisconsin, 7th Wisconsin and 19th Indiana, and these regiments remained brigaded together till the close of the war. It was fully a year from this time, however, before the brigade became known by its now historic title.

‡Officers who left the regiment about this time:

Capt. M. A. Northrup, Co. "G."	First Lieut. G. L. Montague, Co."G."
Capt. John O'Rourke, Co. "D."	First Lieut. J. D. Lewis, Co. "H."
Capt. Wm. H. Lindwurm, Co. "F."	2nd Lieut. P. H.'McCauley, Co. "D."
Capt. Leonard Johnson, Co. "I."	2nd Lieut. John Crane, Co. "K."
First Lieut. John Nichol, Co. "D."	2nd Lieut. A. J. Johnson, Co. "I."

our regiment for various reasons. My Second Lieutenant has resigned upon invitation of the Colonel. I feel indignant about it but am unable to prevent it. He was certainly a very promising young officer. First Sergeant, David L. Quaw, will be Second Lieutenant of my company in place of Crane. He will be a genial, companionable tent mate, but I doubt if he develops the fine soldierly qualities possessed by Crane."

Colonel Cutler applied a rigorous policy of weeding out line officers, who, for various reasons were not acceptable to him. Under the thin disguise of failure to pass examination before a certain commission of officers, of whom I believe, General James S. Wadsworth was President, several very promising officers were arbitrarily driven out of the regiment. The Irish Company "D" was entirely stripped of its officers, and too close a sympathy with them, by our young Irish Lieutenant, Crane, probably brought this attack upon him. Company "G" was also stripped of its officers. There was much bitter feeling in the regiment over these matters. Some, however, of the displaced officers had proved incompetent, and others might be termed incorrigible, so far as the discipline of the regiment was concerned. First Lieutenant, Philip W. Plummer, of Company "C," was appointed Captain of Company "G." He proved one of the most successful of our company commanders. Of patient temper and considerate judgment, he was yet a strict and exacting officer. The trim and soldierly First Sergeant of Company "E," William A. Reader, was made First Lieutenant of Company "G," and James L. Converse, the First Sergeant of Company "G," was promoted to Second Lieutenant. No more deserving officer was upon our rolls than James L. Converse, and he was faithful to the end, for he was killed in battle. Loyd G. Harris was advanced from First Sergeant to be Second Lieutenant of Company "C." Lieutenant John A. Kellogg was promoted to be Captain of Company "I" and Clayton E. Rogers, of Company "I," was promoted from the ranks to be Second Lieutenant. This brought upon the list an officer of great usefulness and remarkable courage and energy. David L. Quaw was made First Lieutenant and Sergeant John Ticknor, Second Lieutenant of my company, "K." The Irish Company, "D," which had been stripped of its Irish officers, was officered by the appointment of Lieutenant John F. Marsh of Company "B" as Captain, and Michael H. Fitch, the Sergeant Major, was appointed First Lieutenant, and Samuel Birdsall, Second Lieutenant. Thomas Kerr, who afterward reached the rank of Lieutenant Colonel, was with all others in the ranks of Company "D," overlooked. This appointment of strangers to command of the company, and disregard of their natural and reasonable preference as to nationality, made bad feeling among the men of that company. Marsh and Fitch were excellent officers and discreet men, and less difficulty resulted than was anticipated.

This changing around of officers, indiscriminately from company to company, was a new departure, and it gave to our regiment a violent wrench. Colonel Cutler had in all matters of command and discipline, the courage of his convictions, and his justification must be found in the fact that good results ultimately followed. Among the best results was bringing up from the ranks, a number of excellent young officers.

To my sister: (no date.) "A military life in camp is the most monotonous in the world. It is the same routine over and over every day. Occasionally we have a small excitement when on review. The other day an aristocratic old gentleman rode up in a splendid carriage, driven by a superb darkey in livery. It was William H. Seward. He is a particular friend of our Brigadier General, Rufus King. Caleb B. Smith, the Secretary of the Interior, has been in our camp several times. He visits Colonel Solomon Meredith. There was an inferior looking Frenchman at our review the other day, highly adorned with decorations, and gold lace, who is a mystery as yet. He is some sort of a foreign Prince. Our boys call him 'Slam Slam.' The finest looking military officer, McClellan not excepted, is our division commander, General Irvin McDowell. General King is a homely looking man, but he is a cultivated gentleman. General Blenker, who commands the division encamped upon our left, looks to me like a very common Dutchman.

If you have stockings and blankets for the soldiers, send them where they are needed, not here. If you could hear our men complain about being pack horses to carry the clothing forced upon them, you would not think they were suffering. Every man in my company has one cloth uniform coat, one overcoat, some men two,* three pairs of pants, three to five pairs of stockings, two woolen shirts, one undershirt, and most of them two pairs of shoes, and the regiment has been forced to send to Washington a large amount of good state clothing, (gray). Take the above mentioned articles in connection with two or three blankets, and pile them on to a man, in addition to his Belgian musket, cartridge box, and accoutrements, and you can appreciate the just cause for complaint of our knapsack drills. The plea is, that these drills make the men tough. Knapsack drills, reviews and inspections are the order of the day. General McDowell reviews us, then General McClellan, then General McClellan, and then McDowell. Every member of the Cabinet has been present on some of these occasions, but we have not yet had the President. How soon we will move, or what the plan of campaign will be, are subjects I have long ceased to bother my head about. We feel very sad over the battle of Balls Bluff. You may remember that the 15th Massachusetts was formerly brigaded with us. The officers were a fine set of men, and General Baker's brigade was for a long time encamped next to us at Chain Bridge. The most intelligent, best looking men I have seen in the service, belonged to the 15th Massachusetts."

The super abundant supply of clothing may be taken as a sample of the magnificent manner in which the grand army was being equipped. The resources of the government were freely lavished upon it. But "rooted inaction," as Horace Greely puts it, was upon us, in the hero of the hour, the commander of the army, whom in our imaginations we enthusiastically exalted to the skies as a great organizer, and a "Young Napoleon."

One of the reviews referred to in the foregoing letters was held at Bailey's Cross Roads. The troops were dismissed in the midst of the review, owing to some reported movement of the enemy, and McDowell's division marched back, taking the road toward

---

*One blue and one gray. When the men gave up the gray clothing, they were disposed to keep the overcoats, because of their superior quality.

Washington, to our camp on Arlington Heights. With our column rode a lady visitor; my authority is her own account. Our regiment marched at the head of the column, because we stood on the extreme right of the line. As we marched, the "evening dews and damps" gathered, and our leading singer, Sergeant John Ticknor, as he was wont to do on such occasions, led out with his strong, clear and beautiful tenor voice, "Hang Jeff. Davis on a sour apple tree." The whole regiment joined the grand chorus, "Glory, glory hallelujah, as we go marching on." We often sang this, the John Brown song. To our visitor appeared the "Glory of the coming of the Lord," in our "burnished rows of steel" and in the "hundred circling camps" on Arlington, which were before her.

Julia Ward Howe, our visitor, has said that the singing of the John Brown song by the soldiers on that march, and the scenes of that day and evening inspired her to the composition of the Battle Hymn of the Republic.* We at least helped to swell the chorus.

---

*BATTLE-HYMN OF THE REPUBLIC.

JULIA WARD HOWE.

Mine eyes have seen the glory of the coming of the Lord:
He is trampling out the vintage where the grapes of wrath are stored.
He hath loosed the fateful lightning of his terrible swift sword:
  His truth is marching on.

I have seen him in the watch-fires of a hundred circling camps;
They have builded him an altar in the evening dews and damps;
I can read his righteous sentence by the dim and flaring lamps,
  His day is marching on.

I have read a fiery gospel, writ in burnished rows of steel:
"As ye deal with my contemners, so with you my grace shall deal,
Let the Hero, born of woman, crush the serpent with his heel,
  Since God is marching on."

He hath sounded forth the trumpet that shall never call retreat;
He is sifting out the hearts of men before his judgment seat.
Oh! be swift my soul, to answer him! Be jubilant, my feet!
  Our God is marching on.

In the beauty of the lillies Christ was born across the sea,
With a glory in his bosom that transfigures you and me:
As he died to make men holy, let us die to make men free,
  While God is marching on.

CAMP ON ARLINGTON HEIGHTS, NOVEMBER 21st, 1861.

"Last Sunday I attended Dr. Gurley's church in Washington City. I went there to see President Lincoln. I think many others of the worshipers went there for the same purpose. Mr. Lincoln is very tall and very homely, but no one can look at him without being impressed with the serious earnestness of his face. On Tuesday we marched out to Bailey's Cross Roads to take part in the grand review. I must not write about what the papers are so full of. You know that it was the largest review of troops ever had in America, that sixty thousand infantry, nine thousand cavalry and one hundred and thirty pieces of artillery passed in review before McClellan, that the regiments marched by 'battalions en masse,' and that it took from 11 o'clock A. M. until 4 P. M. to pass the reviewing officer, and that the President, the members of the Cabinet, and all the celebrities, foreign and domestic, were present. But perhaps you have not seen that General McClellan was so overcome by the lofty pomposity of drum major William Whaley of this regiment, that he took off his hat when Whaley passed. But, sad to relate, Whaley was so overcome by this recognition, which took place while he was indulging in a top loftical gyration of his baton, that he dropped the baton. From the topmost height of glory he was plunged into the deepest gulf of despair. This drum major of ours we regard with pride and affection as the finest adornment of the regiment. He can hold his head higher, and whirl his baton faster than any other drum major in the Army of the Potomac. It is enough to make one sad, to see the stately Whaley leading that execrable brass band on dress parade, eternally playing the Village Quickstep, but when his own drum corps is behind him, 'Richard is himself again,' and he snuffs the air and spurns the ground like a war horse."

The marching of the regiment, which led the brigade and division at the grand review, had now become almost faultless. As the solid block of eight hundred stalwart western men, approached the Commanding General, marching in perfect time, and with free and easy stride, led by this truly splendid drum major, the great crowd at the reviewing stand continued cheering and clapping hands.

On the twenty-eighth of November, the regimental mess, composed of the field, staff and line officers, had a Thanksgiving dinner. We had built a large log dining hall, which was very comfortable, although home made. Our dinner was no small affair. Colonel Cutler also made each company in the regiment, the happy recipient of twenty mince pies, about a quarter of a pie to each man.

I here obtained a leave of absence for ten days, for a visit to Ohio.*

Letter received at Marietta, from Sergeant Upham:

HEADQUARTERS SIXTH REGIMENT, WIS. VOLS.

ARLINGTON HEIGHTS, VA., DEC. 31st, 1861.

"CAPTAIN DAWES,—*Dear Sir :*—I take this early opportunity of writing to you, knowing that you will be glad to hear from your company. I will tell you how we got along since you left. You remember that Lieutenant Quaw was on court martial, and that Lieutenant Reader was to take the company out on battalion drill, the afternoon you left. Well, Reader was unable to go. So this deponent formed the company, and when drill time came, there was no one to take it out. At the drum call I marched the company out and formed them in battalion, anxiously hoping that some commissioned officer would come to my relief, and wishing that Marietta were in a hot place so that you could have remained with us. Well, Captain Brown took charge of 'K,' and I felt as though a mountain had been lifted from my shoulders. We had a good drill. 'K' never did better. 'K' came into camp in good season and fell in immediately for dress parade, Lieut. Serrill taking command. Thus ended our first day without our Captain. Two men remained in off dress parade, Simons and 'Dick.'† They said you had excused them before you left,—a? in my mind. This morning all was bustle, preparing for monthly inspection. I made out the roll of the company, took the muster roll to the Adjutant, prepared my own accoutrements, and was

---

*The few days vouchsafed me sped swiftly. My brother had graduated from college, and he was now Adjutant of the 53rd Ohio Volunteers. His service was destined to be with the armies in the West, and he was soon to go to the front in the division commanded by General William T. Sherman. On the sixth day of January, 1862, I started to rejoin the regiment.

†Richard Upham, an Indian.

getting barbered when the drum beat. I left with my hair half combed and fell the company in. We were inspected by Captain Chandler. All the sons answered to their names, except Ralph Brown and A. G. Emmons. Even Hancock came up to be mustered. I am cross and ugly. I took two men to the officer of the guard to-day, for coming back to the company quarters when on guard duty. An imperative order to that effect was issued by the Colonel. Captain Brown says he wishes he had Company 'K.' They move so easily. Bully for Company 'K.' I will write again shortly, so as to keep you posted. I remain

Yours truly, LYMAN B. UPHAM."

I arrived in camp on the 9th day of January, 1862, the trip from Ohio to Washington consuming three days time.

We had many amusements in our winter camp on Arlington Heights. We played whist, chess, and other games on wintry days, and, despite restrictions on political discussion, in the articles of war, we discussed all questions of politics or religion, with the utmost freedom. Bragg was a Douglass or war Democrat, Brown and Kellogg, Republicans, and I was called an Abolitionist. But the baleful shadow cast by slavery over the border, and the fierce and brutal insolence of the slave catcher who was often seen on our free soil of Ohio, tended to make Abolitionists. Captain Edwin A. Brown was a singer. We were unconscious then, that his melodious voice predicted his own sad fate when he sang his favorite "Benny Havens, O." "In the land of sun and flowers, his head lies pillowed low."

The officers of the whole brigade would gather in our log dining hall and jokes would be ventilated, speeches made, and hilarious songs sung. The "Chinese song" as performed by Captain Hooe on those occasions, was so amusing that this reminder will recall it to all of our living comrades who heard it.

The men had one sport in this camp which was quite exciting. It was tossing men in a blanket. They became expert and would throw a man to an astonishing height and catch him in the blanket as he fell. I once took this whirling aerial flight, but only once, having no desire to repeat the experience. There was gambling in camp, that ever-present curse of camp life; but the strict orders of Colonel Cutler against this vice, and his vigorous discipline greatly restricted the evil in Camp Arlington. It was well that the regiment had so resolute a commander. He gave almost no passes to the city. Thieves, speculators, gamblers and vile characters of all kind had flocked to Washington to prey upon the army. This enemy in the rear was now more dangerous than the enemy in front. The great thoroughfare, Pennsylvania avenue, was constantly thronged with a surging crowd. The street was so muddy that it could not be crossed, and the western side only was used. In spite of the constant marching of the armed patrols, our soldiers were constantly made victims by the Harpies. Washington was a very sink hole of iniquity in other ways of evil. The unfinished dome of the United States Capitol, and the half built Washington Monument well typified the uncertainty of a continued national existence.

The grand old southern homestead of Arlington, with its quaint and curious pictures on the wall, its spacious apartments, broad halls and stately pillars in front, was an object of especial interest; but, abandoned by its owner, General Robert E. Lee, who was using his great power as a military leader, to destroy the Government he had sworn to defend, it was now a desolation. The military headquarters of McDowell's division was in the Arlington House, which was open to the public and hundreds tramped at will through its apartments.

Having ample time to plan campaigns, that indeed being the chief business of our lives at Arlington, and pursued by an increasing curiosity regarding a young lady then attending the seminary at Ipswich, Massachusetts, I threw out skirmishers in that direction. I sent sundry illustrated papers with pictures of our camps, and received from the enemy a return fire of catalogues and other Massachusetts publications. I was then a devout admirer of General McClellan and I received with disgust one of these missives directed to the "Army of the Potty Mac." But the seminary girls breathed the air of independent opinion in New England, and they were beyond the circle of McClellanism. This trifling skirmish resulted in no engagement.

ARLINGTON HEIGHTS, JANUARY 25th, 1862.

To my sister: "We are now having terribly muddy weather.

All drills are omitted. Unfortunately our turn for picket duty on the outposts came in the midst of this spell of bad weather. Your anxiety about 'the approaching battle' had better be postponed. Any movement of the army is impossible. As we marched up Munson's Hill, on our way to the outposts, the mud rolled down upon the men in a kind of avalanche. They waded up the hill through a moving stream of red clay mortar. Luckily I was ordered to act as Major, and had a horse to ride."

Six days from my Journal:

SATURDAY, FEBRUARY 1st, 1862.

"Went to the city (Washington) to-day. Had a pleasant visit with uncle William. (W. P. Cutler, member Congress.) In the evening we went to his rooms to call on Hon. Henry L. Dawes, of Massachusetts. Mr. Dawes treated me very politely. The Congressional Investigating Committee of which Mr. Van Wyck, of New York, is Chairman, was holding a session at his rooms. Mr. Holman* of Indiana, overhearing that I was an officer in the 6th Wisconsin, undertook to pump me on some charges somebody has been making against Colonel Cutler. It was all new to me, and I knew nothing at all about the matter. Mr. Dawes was evidently annoyed at this breach of his hospitality and Mr. R. C. Fenton called Mr. Holman sharply to order, and to a proper sense of the rudeness of his conduct. It was quite disagreeable.

SUNDAY, FEBRUARY 2nd, 1862.

Returned to camp in the morning. I found one of my men, private Ed. Hendrick, sick with the small pox. I had him removed to Washington. It is varioloid, and I hope may stop with this case.

MONDAY, FEBRUARY 3rd, 1862.

Was officer of the day. Rode over to Balls' Cross Roads to inspect guards. I never saw mud before, equal to that I encountered.

TUESDAY, FEBRUARY 4th, 1862.

Mud,—mud,—mud precludes drill, everything, to say nothing

---

*This does Mr. Holman an injustice. He fairly inferred that I was there to be examined as others had been. An evidence of the wonderful memory of details possessed by Mr. Holman is the fact that in 1882 he was able to recall this circumstance.

of an advance on Manassas. Was detailed to-day as a member of a General Court Martial.

WEDNESDAY, FEBRUARY 5th, 1862.

General Court Martial convened at headquarters McDowell's division, (Arlington House.) We tried one case and adjourned over until Friday. Colonel Cutler is President, and Capt. Hooe of our regiment, Judge Advocate.

THURSDAY, FEBRUARY 6th, 1862.*

A dull day in camp. Captain Brown and Captain Kellogg are jolly fellows to make time pass lightly. Kellogg sprained Brown's neck by an awkward blow with the boxing gloves."

During the continuance of bad weather, target shooting was about the only exercise required, and Colonel Cutler offered small prizes for excellence. Our Belgian muskets had been exchanged for Springfield rifles, a much lighter and better gun, and this gave great satisfaction. Washington's birthday was celebrated by Congress with appropriate ceremonies. Our brigade formed in a semi-circle in close column before the broad

---

*Page 718, Vol. 5, War Records, February 6th, 1862. McDowell's division was made up as follows:

KING'S BRIGADE.

6th Wisconsin,	960 men.
7th Wisconsin,	996 men.
2nd Wisconsin,	821 men.
19th Indiana,	892 men.
	3,669 men.

WADSWORTH'S BRIGADE.

21st New York,	735 men.
23rd New York,	878 men.
35th New York,	976 men.
20th New York,	915 men.
	3,504 men.

AUGUR'S BRIGADE.

30th New York,	800 men.
22nd New York,	837 men.
24th New York,	825 men.
14th N. Y. S. M., (Brooklyn,)	659 men.
	3,121 men.
2nd N. Y. Cavalry, (Ira Harris,)	982 men.
Batteries of artillery,	663 men.
Total division strength,	11,939 men.

portico of the Arlington House, and listened to the reading of Washington's farewell address, and to an excellent oration from our Brigadier General, Rufus King. The columns were then deployed and battalion volleys of blank cartridges were fired in honor of the day. The inspiration of the occasion was felt more deeply because we stood upon ground once owned by Washington.

On Sunday, the 9th day of March, my uncle, Mr. Cutler, accompanied by Edward Ball, Sergeant at Arms of the House of Representatives, came over to Arlington to visit me in camp. I turned out my company "K" for their inspection. They addressed the men briefly, and assured them that they would soon be called to more active duties, and on that evening we received our marching orders. At 4 o'clock on Monday morning, March 10th, 1862, the old camp on Arlington Heights was broken up. The whole army of the Potomac advanced in full marching order in the direction of Centreville. We expected battle, and our men were in that verdant and idiotic frame of mind, which was then termed "spoiling for a fight." After a hard day's march we encamped two miles west of Fairfax Court House, and on Tuesday morning, March 11th, we were informed that the rebels had evacuated Centreville and Manassas. I quote the comments of my journal, as to the manner in which the announcement of this fact was received. "The men were greatly disappointed. They had made their wills, and written their farewell letters, and wanted to fight a battle. The fortifications at Centreville are by no means so formidable as they have been represented. I saw two saw-logs in the embrasures representing cannons. So much for wooden guns." We remained in camp near Centreville until Saturday, March 15th. At noon on this day the brigade marched back toward Alexandria, and the rain poured down in dismal torrents all the afternoon. We passed an exceedingly disagreeable night in bivouac near Alexandria, and on Sunday morning returned to the old camp on Arlington Heights. General Irvin McDowell had been assigned to the command ot an army corps, composed of three divisions. (*Franklin, McCall, King.) General Rufus King succeeded to the

---

*Page 755, Volume 5, Official War Records.

command of McDowell's division, which was now designated as "King's division," Colonel Cutler succeeded General King in command of the brigade, and Lieutenant Colonel Sweet, succeeded to command of the regiment.

We now understood that we were to accompany the Army of the Potomac, under General McClellan, which was then embarking at Alexandria, for Fortress Monroe. We received orders on March 18th, to go to Alexandria, and we fully expected to embark. We were instead ordered into camp near Alexandria and while our tents were being pitched, we were directed to march back again to Fairfax Seminary. The order was obeyed with much grumbling and scolding, and without our supper. The rainy, cold, dismal weather, together with the pungent and blinding smoke of the camp fires of green wood, rendered camp life at Fairfax Seminary, extremely unpleasant. The little shelter tents, usually called "dog tents," occupied by the men, proved like most army material at that period of the war, to be of the poorest quality, and leaked badly. On March 25th, the sun had broken through the clouds, and there was, as might be expected, a grand review conducted by General Irvin McDowell. The divisions of Generals Franklin, King, and McCall were out in full force, perhaps 25,000 men. Two days later there was another review, upon which occasion Lord Lyons, the English Minister, was present with General McClellan.

One white day from my journal.

SATURDAY, MARCH 29th, 1862.

The regiment was paid this morning. I got a pass to Washington. The men of my company sent by me $610 to be remitted in drafts to their friends. Got drafts of Rittenhouse & Company.

Tiresome and monotonous camp life ensued until April 4th,* when the regiment marched—not to embark at Alexandria, but towards Fairfax Court House. We pushed on until April 6th, when we encamped near Bristoe Station. During this march an

---

*ADJUTANT-GENERAL'S OFFICE, APRIL 4th, 1862.

GENERAL McCLELLAN: By direction of the President, Gen. McDowell's army corps has been detached from the force, under your immediate command, and the General is ordered to report to the Secretary of War. Letter by mail.　　　　　　L. THOMAS, Adjutant-General.

amusing excitement was created by the 14th Brooklyn regiment. The men of that regiment were from the city, clerks, book-keepers and business men. They were full of shrewd devices to avoid unnecessary hardships. They were then uniformed in short Zouave jackets, made in the cutaway style, often seen on youngsters of about six years of age, and profusely adorned with buttons. Their pantaloons were red. When we were somewhere near Centreville, they captured in a field, a quiet and peaceable looking young bull. After much ingenious labor, they succeeded in harnessing him to a cart, using an old horse harness for this purpose. Then, loading up the cart with a pyramid of their heavy knapsacks, they endeavored to persuade the bull with their bayonets to march along with the troops. The terrified animal would at first only go backwards, but finally goaded beyond endurance by the bayonets, he made a sudden bolt. Our troops, all unconscious of impending danger, were marching quietly along the turnpike, when there arose a shout, "Clear the track ! Clear the track !" Men on foot, and mounted officers needed no second warning, but crowded against the fences to give the bull the road. Down the turnpike came the rushing bull, the air about him filled with flying knapsacks. He completely routed our brigade. He soon upset the cart and kicked himself loose. When we saw him last he was still at full speed., and the "Red Legs" were hunting knapsacks.

The following from my Journal :

TUESDAY, APRIL 8th, 1862.

"There is rain and snow to-day. Company officers are supplied only with shelter tents. Our camp is very muddy. It is difficult for officers to get anything to eat, as our wagon is loaded with hard tack, and very poor ham only. I paid Jake* ten dollars to-day."

WEDNESDAY, APRIL 9th, 1862.

"Rain and snow to-day. I was not able to get my wet boots on, this morning, and was obliged to lie in my 'dog tent' until afternoon. As I could not stay in the tent without continually lying on the bunk, it was tedious. The rain and snow storm has

---

*Jake was my colored servant, and while in a comfortable camp, he was a very good one.

continued all day, confining all the men to their shelter tents. We have no mail, no papers, no literature of any kind. The men beguiled the weary hours, by croaking like frogs, quacking like ducks, and barking like dogs. I gave Jake a gold dollar and sent him in quest of something to eat. The base wretch has deserted me, and 'done gone' to Baltimore. That is what he wanted his $10 for. I got supper at a house at Bristoe Station. Breakfast and dinner I had none."

One performance of our men in these dismal rain storms, was quite comical. It was called, "The bull frog of Bull Run." A leader would shout: "When our army marched down to Bull Run, what did the big bull frog say?" Hundreds of men would respond in deep bass, bull frog croaks: "Big thing! Big thing!!" Then the leader would ask, "When our army came back from Bull Run, what did the little frogs say?" "Run Yank! Run Yank!!" would be screeched in response, in excellent imitation of a swamp full of frogs. "What does the bully Sixth say?" Again the bull frog bass would respond, "Hit 'em again! Hit 'em again!!" Brave boys! how they contended against adverse circumstances, with their cheerful and courageous spirit.

While near Bristoe, we received news of the great battle of Pittsburgh Landing. Our army was said to have gained a victory, after suffering a terrible loss. General King kindly gave me the use of the Government telegraph, but I was unable to learn anything of my brother, who, I knew, must have been in the engagement. On Sunday, the 13th, we marched from camp near Bristoe to Catletts Station. Here we enjoyed the good fortune of a "high, dry, and excellent camp ground."

(Letter.)   St. Stephen's Chapel, Va.,

April 14th, 1862.

"Our troops are engaged in repairing railroads, and building bridges. We are advancing through a beautiful country, but, deserted by its people, and desolated by the armies, it seems likely to become a wilderness. At present, my company, and company 'E,' are doing outpost duty under command of Major Bragg. My own headquarters are at St. Stephen's Chapel, a handsome little Episcopal church, with pulpit and pews uninjured. It is the most comfortable quarters I have had for a long time."

(Journal.) TUESDAY, APRIL 17th, 1862.

"We were relieved from picket duty by the 21st New York. We were sorry to go back to camp. Our tour of duty at St. Stephen's Chapel was a picnic."

General Augur's brigade, of King's division, marched forward to opposite Fredericksburgh, after some skirmishing near Falmouth, and on Monday, the 21st of April, our brigade marched from Catletts Station towards Fredericksburgh. In accordance with our customary fate, a severe rain storm prevailed all day. The creeks were overflowing, and we were so delayed at the crossings, that we made only six miles. The brigade bivouacked for the night in a muddy field. The men were wet, wood scarce and wet, mud deep, air chilly, and everything in a forlorn condition. As a remedy, a heavy whiskey ration was issued. It was the first experiment of the kind in the history of our regiment, and it proved a miserable failure. There were many who would not drink their liquor at all, and others, as a result, obtained a double or triple portion. My journal says: "A thousand drunken men in the brigade, made a pandemonium of the camp all night."

We reached Falmouth opposite Fredericksburgh at four o'clock on Wednesday, April 23rd. Our hearts were made glad by finding our mail waiting for us. I heard fully from my brother that he was engaged in the bloody battles of April 6th and 7th, at Shiloh, and in the skirmish of the morning of the 8th, at Fallen Timber. He had escaped without injury, though fighting with a courage and valor honorable to himself, and gratifying to his friends, as he was placed under very trying circumstances.

(Letter.) CAMP OPPOSITE FREDERICKSBURGH,
APRIL 26th, 1862.

"We are now encamped on the heights north of the Rappahannock river, opposite Fredericksburgh, which is an old fashioned, compactly built, little city, situated in a beautiful valley. Our troops do not occupy the town, but, as the hills north of the river are high, our batteries command it. Above the town, the river is full of rapids, but vessels come up to the town, and a U. S. gun boat was here yesterday. We hope to push on toward Richmond and join McClellan's army. Our camps are now flooded with negroes, with packs on their backs, and bound for freedom. No system of abolition could have swept the system away more effectually than does the advance of our army. Behind us the slaves, if they choose, are free. All civil authority is gone." Our military authorities refused to have anything to do with the negroes. But with the sympathy and active assistance of the soldiers, the poor slaves were breaking their fetters in spite of their masters. Some men in one of our New York regiments, so roughly handled a slave owner, who was trying to recapture his slave in camp, that the provost guard interfered to protect him, but not to catch the slave. Meanwhile the slave made good his title to liberty, by taking refuge with the soldiers. I wrote from this camp: "So far the slave holders have vainly called upon our military authorities, for assistance in returning fugitives. Thus the great question of liberty is working its own solution. The right must, and surely will, triumph in the end. Let us thank God, and take courage."

CHAPTER III.

Saturday, April 26th, 1862.

"Some men in our brigade bought to-day of citizens, large amounts of tobacco and other goods, with fac-simile confederate currency. The people refused United States treasury notes when offered, but sought this bogus confederate money with avidity. Indeed, I think myself, it looks a little better than the original rebel money. An order was issued to-day, forbidding this kind of swindling."

On Sunday, we marched out four miles, on the line of the Acquia Creek Railroad. Here we were engaged in building a great pole trestle bridge over Potomac creek.

The work was under direction of Herman Haupt, a volunteer engineer officer on the staff of General McDowell, and the bridge was considered a triumph of military engineering. I quote from General Andrew Hickenlooper, a description of this bridge. He says: "It was five hundred feet in length, and eighty feet in height, composed of unhewn trees and saplings, cut in the adjoining woods and placed in position by the troops of General McDowell's command. So rapidly was the work executed that the whole was completed within a period of nine days, which, allowing twelve working hours a day, required the placing in position of five hundred pieces of timber every hour. And so well was the work done that for several years it carried in safety from ten to fifteen heavy trains per day and resisted the destructive influence of several devastating floods." Lieutenant D. L. Quaw was in command of a large force getting out this bridge timber. Lieutenant Clayton E. Rogers was also doing work with his accustomed vim, having a large band of choppers. After this service, we again encamped opposite Fredericksburgh. No event worthy of mention transpired until Thursday, May 8th, when Brigadier General John Gibbon took command of our brigade and Colonel Cutler returned to the command of the regiment. General Gibbon graduated from West Point in 1847. In 1854 he was at West Point as Assistant Instructor of Artillery, which shows that he was considered, even then, master of his profession. The "Artillerists Manual," published in New York in 1859, was from his pen and was considered an extremely useful work. He was Captain of Battery "B" 4th U. S. Artillery in the regular service. He soon manifested superior qualities as a brigade commander. Thoroughly educated in the military profession, he had also high personal qualifications to exercise command. He was anxious that his brigade should excel in every way, and while he was an exacting disciplinarian he had the good sense to recognize merit where it existed. His administration of the command left a lasting impression for good upon the character and military tone of the brigade, and his splendid personal bravery upon the field of battle was an inspiration. The brigade was now known as "Gibbon's brigade."

We were ordered to procure an entire outfit of new hats and a supply of clothing. There was complaint on the part of the men at being obliged to draw overcoats at the beginning of summer in a hot climate.

On the evening of the 10th of May, there was an alarm over the river beyond Fredericksburgh. The men received the announcement that they would probably be needed for a fight with a tremendous shout. They said "a year's fight was bottled up in them and it was spoiling to come out." It transpired, however, that there were not enough rebels in the vicinity to accommodate our men with the desired fight.

We now had a large force of men engaged upon the timber work of the railroad bridge across the Rappahannock river. This bridge was of the same character as that of the Potomac Creek, and it was six hundred feet in length by sixty-five in height.

Meanwhile General McClellan's army was pressing on toward Richmond. A strong feeling possessed us that we were to be a mere side show while others performed the real acts of war. We had now been nearly a year in active service and could boast only of the inglorious battle at Patterson Park. This circumstance is the more notable, since statistics show that, when the war was ended, our brigade had lost more men killed in battle than any other brigade in the whole army of the Union.

About this time I visited in the cemetery at Fredericksburgh, the tomb of Mary, the mother of Washington. The rebel soldiers, who had been encamped in this vicinity, had set targets against this sacred monument and it was shamefully defaced by bullets fired against it.

On Saturday, May 17th, the regiment was fully supplied with white leggings, black felt hats adorned with feathers, and white cotton gloves. These decorations were received with the greatest merriment, but we all felt proud of the fine appearance of the battalion. My journal says: "General Gibbon attended our dress parade to-day, and the regiment was in 'fine feather.'" The next day, a gay looking young rebel Captain came in with a flag of truce. The men, delighted to see a live rebel, flocked around him by hundreds. On the 19th of May, the great railroad bridge across the Rappahannock was completed, and a locomotive passed over into Fredericksburgh.

It is worthy of record, that on our pay-day, the men of my company, "K," sent home in various small sums to their families and friends, over $800, nearly one half of the entire pay received. General Shield's division joined us on the 23rd of May, and on this day President Abraham Lincoln and the Secretary of War, Edwin M. Stanton, were present at a review of our brigade. On Saturday, May 24th, the journal says: "The soldiers of Shield's division have christened us the 'bandbox brigade.' Our boys retort that they would rather wear leggings than be lousy. Shield's division are the dirtiest ragamuffins we have yet seen in the service." At this time General McDowell, himself a precise and exacting soldier, said of our brigade: "Many times I have shown them to foreign officers of distinction, as specimens of American Volunteer soldiers, and asked them if they had ever anywhere seen even among the picked soldiers of royal and imperial guards, a more splendid body of men, and I have never had an affirmative answer." The brigade was not excelled in the precision and accuracy of their movement by any other body of troops I have ever seen, not excepting the cadets at West Point. Beyond a doubt, it was this year of preparation that brought the "Iron Brigade" to its high standard of efficiency for battle service.

The next day we had marching orders, and to the great joy of the men, we moved toward Richmond. The men said: "As soon as old Abe saw our brigade, he knew it could take Richmond, and he has sent us to do it." But we marched only eight miles south of Fredericksburgh, and encamped for several days in the woods. We here received news of the disastrous retreat of General Banks in the Shenandoah valley, before the swift advance of Stonewall Jackson.

The next two weeks journal, is the record of experiences on a wild goose chase by McDowell's corps, after Stonewall Jackson, who was in the Shenandoah valley.

THURSDAY, MAY 29th, 1862.

"We marched at ten A. M., northward, and camped for the night, six miles north of Fredericksburgh, on the road to Catletts Station. It was a hard tramp. Sixty pounds is an awful load for a man to carry on a hot summer day."

Friday, May 30th, 1862.*

"We marched at 8:30 A. M. The weather was hot and sultry. One hundred and fifty men fell out of the ranks exhausted, on the march to-day. It rained in the afternoon. We camped six miles from Catletts Station. It was one of the hardest marches the regiment ever had. Twenty miles was the distance marched."

A few weeks later (Fredericks Hall raid) upon an equally sultry day, our regiment marched thirty-five miles without knapsacks. The men were here absurdly over burdened. They had been required to carry each an overcoat, an extra pair of shoes, and an extra pair of pants. These superfluous articles, added to the necessary hundred rounds of ball cartridges, shelter tent, gum and woolen blankets, haversack full of rations, canteen full of water, musket and accoutrements, were a load beyond the strength of ordinary men. Our young boys were broken down by the needless overtaxing of their strength. I can not say who was responsible for such management. I know, however, that General McDowell, whether justly or unjustly, was thoroughly cursed for it. Vast numbers of new overcoats, and many knapsacks were flung away by the exhausted men on this march. The men said they were "issuing overcoats to the rebel cavalry," and it is very likely that they were. I know well the weight of those monstrous knapsacks from personal experience. Many a mile I carried a knapsack on my shoulders to aid the tired and weak of my company. I well remember seeing strong men carrying two knapsacks, and sometimes stout Abe Fletcher loaded up with three, to help the "little fellows"† along. At Gettysburg, this kind hearted man fell dead at the front of battle. But the smallest man in the company was a

---

*See pages 309—310, Volume 12, Part III, War Records, for strength and composition of McDowell's corps on May 31st. 1862. Present for duty in the corps, officers, 2,023, men, 42,422. In King's division, officers, 466, men, 8,560.

†The "little fellows" of Company "K" were Silas W. Temple, John R. Towle, Charles M. Taylor, George E. Chamberlain, Cassius Griggs and Aaron Yates. They were young, slight, round cheeked boys, who endured their hardships with a cheerful patience that won us all. The leather straps cut their shoulders, and the weight was too heavy under the hot sun, and pressed upon their lungs. They were not fitted to become beasts of burden, nor were they thus rendering the cause a useful service.

marvel. He was a diminutive Irishman, named Hugh Talty. In recognition of his shortness he was called "Tall T." He would often carry an extra knapsack for the "little fellows." In the distribution of new clothing, there was a difficulty in properly "sizing up" the company. "Tall T" was under the smallest size contemplated in the Regulations, and he could never be fitted. Poor "Tall T" sometimes had pantaloons that would almost button around his neck. I gave this matter particular attention. "Who's your tailor, 'Tall T?'" once shouted a man as we marched. "The captain, be gob," came back like a flash from "Tall T."

There was another little Irishman in the company whom we called "Mickey," (James P. Sullivan.) For genuine sallies of humor at unexpected times, I have never seen his equal. He was a heroic soldier, and he was shot and severely wounded, three different times in battle. "Micky" and "Tall T" were both shot, and laid in the same hospital together at Gettysburg. They softened the sufferings of many by their unconquerable good humor and genuine wit. Such men are of priceless value in an army.

The most caustic comment I can make on this campaign, is to quote the remarks of a deserter from Stonewall Jackson's army, who came to us at some time during the marching. He said, "You uns is pack mules, we uns is race horses." "All old Jackson gave us, was a musket, a hundred rounds and a gum blanket, and he 'druv us so like hell,' that I could not stand it on parched corn." Another saying of some Johnny from Jackson's corps was quoted then. He said: "We uns durst leave our mammy. You uns is tied to granny Lincoln's apron string."

Our men called their knapsacks, "Saratoga trunks." The weary details of the hot and dusty tramp need not be repeated. We marched from Fredericksburgh to Warrenton, and then from Warrenton to Fredericksburgh, opposite which city we were again encamped on June 10th, 1862. With Jackson, celerity was success. With us, ponderosity was military science.

The most pleasant incident of the expedition, was our camp, in a beautiful grove near the village of Warrenton, which is delightfully situated, overlooking an extensive mountain landscape. Here we enjoyed a luxury, not common in that region, good, pure water. Some of the first families of Virginia, made their homes here, but we found the first people particularly bitter in their hostility.

It was my custom to attend church with my company, while we were in camp near Fredericksburgh. On Sunday, June 15th, I attended the Episcopal church with fifty men. The men enjoyed attending church, as it seemed homelike. We were kindly received, and made welcome by the minister, but so much can not be said for the people.

In the camp near Fredericksburgh, our enlisted men had their brasses scoured, guns wiped, white gloves washed, and shoes blacked by the contrabands who swarmed about them. How these people lived being a mystery to me, I one day cornered a very black, but quick witted little imp, called "Mink." "Mink," said I, "where did you come from?" "Bides hole, sah!" (Boyd's Hole, below Fredericksburgh.) "What do you eat?" "I picks up a bone, sah!" "Where do you sleep?" "I sleeps under a leaf, sah!" "What do you do?" "I teaches school, sah!" Sure enough, investigation proved that this little black "Mink" was teaching a class of other contrabands their letters, which he had already quickly learned himself. As "Mink" explained matters to me, our colored barber, who came with us from Wisconsin, "done bossed the school," but the colored barber himself could not read. He was only useful in keeping order.

(Journal.)   SATURDAY, JUNE 14th, 1862.

"Served to-day on a board of survey with Lieutenant Colonel Lucius Fairchild, 2nd Wisconsin, and Captain Linsley, 19th Indiana. We condemned a large amount of wormy hard-tack. There seems to be some chance of our going to Richmond yet."

SUNDAY, JUNE 15th, 1862.

"I marched eighty men of my company to church in Fredericksburgh. We went to the Episcopal church. We were made to feel at home. Requested Colonel Cutler to settle definitely the question of seniority among captains."

There were four of the original captains remaining on the rolls who had been mustered into the United States service on the same day, July 16th, 1861. There still remained an unsettled question as to their relative rank.

(Journal.) MONDAY, JUNE 16th, 1862.

"Colonel Cutler ordered the seniority question settled by lot. Captains Dill, Hooe, Hauser and I repaired to the Colonel's headquarters. The Colonel put four scraps of paper into his hat, marked severally 1, 2, 3, and 4. The drawing resulted: Dawes, 1; Hooe, 2; Hauser, 3; Dill, 4. Much favored by fortune. Lieutenant Colonel Sweet sent in his resignation to-day. Now comes a tug of war. Colonel Cutler wants Haskell appointed Major."

TUESDAY, JUNE 17th, 1862.

"Colonel Cutler has asked an expression of the officers for Major. A caucus called for to-night. —— deserts me and works for Haskell. O, treachery! Was appointed officer of the brigade guard, and did not attend the caucus. Final vote: Haskell, thirteen, Dawes, fourteen."

WEDNESDAY, JUNE 18th, 1862.

"A very exciting day in the regiment. No report made of the caucus. It did not come out right. Captain Brown battles for me like a hero. Haskell told me he should get the appointment if he could. I told him, I should do the same, as it was my right in order of rank, and we shook hands over it. Sent my papers to Bill Vilas. He will give them a hustle if he gets the papers in time. Major Bragg works hard for me. He says, 'this attempt to dragoon the officers into over-riding the rights of captains, will not win.'"

FRIDAY, JUNE 20th, 1862.

"Colonel Cutler, General Gibbon, General King, and, I suppose, all Madison, Wisconsin, recommend Haskell. Lieutenant Colonel Sweet, Major Bragg, seven Captains, fourteen Lieutenants, and three regimental staff officers recommend my appointment. —— signed a private recommendation for me.*

---

*—— was trying to carry water on both shoulders, and as usual in such cases, it tipped over and spilled upon him. Colonel Cutler was an able commander, but not a good politician. It was a blunder to ask for an expression of preference by the officers, especially when he was already supported by the solid line of Brigadier Generals.

SUNDAY, JUNE 22nd, 1862.

"I attended the Episcopal church with my company. Private Hoel Trumbull ran away from us, but was caught and locked up in the guard house. He spent a season in meditation. He thinks, on the whole, the church would have been the lesser evil. Colonel Sweet has received notice of the acceptance of his resignation."

(Letter.)   CAMP OPPOSITE FREDERICKSBURGH,
JULY 1st, 1862.

"For a week I have been fighting a bilious fever, but now have the mastery and am rapidly recovering. I have also won another victory which will please you. I have received a commission as major and am no more a captain. I sent my papers for presentation to the Governor of Wisconsin (Edward Salomon) to my friend, William F. Vilas, at Madison. Vilas writes that he called at the Governor's office and sent in word that he wished to see him in connection with the majorship of the Sixth regiment."

"The Governor came to the door and said: 'Mr. Vilas, I do not wish to hear anything more upon that subject. The friends of Mr. Haskell have already harassed me beyond my patience. I shall make no appointment until I hear more fully from the regiment.'

'Oh! but,' says I, 'I happen to be on the other side of that question.' 'Walk right in Mr. Vilas,' says he, 'I am glad to see you'. I went in and presented your case the best I could, and have since learned with great pleasure that your commission has been issued. Accept of my dexter in token of heartiest congratulation."

"This promotion comes very fortunately just before active operations against the enemy, which I doubt not will soon take place, since Gen. Pope has been sent to command our army."

When Colonel Cutler assumed command of the brigade, Haskell went upon his staff. It was an unfortunate step, as it put entirely out of the line of promotion one of the finest officers Wisconsin sent to the war. General Gibbon, who was intimately associated with him, has said that Haskell "was better qualified to command an army corps than many who enjoyed that honor." He continued to serve on staff duty until 1864 when he was appointed Colonel of the 36th Wisconsin. He was killed at the battle of Cold Harbor, while exposing his own life to encourage his regiment to attack the enemy's works.

"We hail the coming of General Pope with much satisfaction. There is a strong feeling among the soldiers against McDowell. He is considered incompetent, if not disloyal." This harsh opinion of General McDowell is only suffered to appear as a moderate expression of the prejudice existing at that time among our officers and men against him. This whole question was considered in the McDowell Court of inquiry, and I make no effort to explain the cause.

July 4th was celebrated with festivities and merry-making. Gibbon's brigade gathered upon a large plain, where there was horse racing, foot racing, and other amusements and athletic exercises. There was a great mule race, a sack race, and a greased pig. Wagon master, William Sears, of our regiment, won the mule race. The prize in this case was for the mule that got through last. Each rider accordingly whipped another's mule, holding back his own. Sears rode a balky mule which would go backward whenever whipped. Captain Hollon Richardson, of the seventh Wisconsin, won the foot race.

NEAR FREDERICKSBURGH, JULY 10th, 1862.

"I am not near Richmond, nor likely to be. General Pope is charged with the same old duty of guarding Washington. So unless the rebels move on Washington, our future presents a peaceful aspect."

CAMP OPPOSITE FREDERICKSBURGH, JULY 18th, 1862.

"General Pope's bombastic proclamation has not tended to increase confidence, indeed the effect is exactly the contrary. (Pope's celebrated order, concerning Lines of Retreat, and Bases of Supply, is here referred to.) For the present, I do not anticipate that we will move from Fredericksburgh. Should Stonewall Jackson make another raid, we will likely take the same tramp in pursuit of him. King's division with some detachments under General Doubleday, are now the only troops here. I think General Pope does not reinforce us here, for fear of General Jackson in the valley. Of course we feel eager to be something more than ornamental file-closers. Our regiment has been more than a year in the service; and in soldierly bearing, perfection in drill, and discipline, we do not yield the palm to the regulars in any service."

CAMP OPPOSITE FREDERICKSBURGH, JULY 28th, 1862.

"We have just got back after a dash toward Orange Court House. This is one of the fruits of the policy of our new commander, General Pope. Our boys are growing enthusiastic in the prospect of a general who has a little life. We left camp by order of General Pope, on July 25th, and marched fifteen miles on the Gordonsville plank road, to a point where the road forks. We remained in this position, while other troops made a raid within five miles of Gordonsville. The rebels are concentrating in some force at that point, and I think General Pope will offer battle. If the forces are nearly matched, we will defeat them. I judge of the Southern army by the character of the prisoners we have taken, and our division is superior to such troops. When we were at the front, an old negro slave came in the middle of the night to our picket line. He said that "Massa Bullock," a Lieutenant in the rebel army, was in a house, a mile away. I took forty men, surrounded the house, and captured him. He was a fine young scion of a first family of Virginia. He was not in uniform, and he denied my right to take him as a soldier. When the darky identified him, he asked me if I would 'take the word of a nigger.'? But when I proposed that he take the oath of allegiance,* he said that I might take a horse to water, but I could not make him drink. So I brought the gentleman in as a prisoner of war. General Pope's orders are carried out in good faith, and, so far as I know, no abuse has been perpetrated."†

The colored man who came to our picket line was very old. I felt suspicious of a trap, and questioned him closely as to his motives in making such disclosures. He said "Fore God, Massa, we knows you uns is our friends. Its the Lord's will, that the colored folks help you uns." I told him that if he led us into an ambush, he would certainly be the first one killed; but he led the way, audibly praying God to sustain him.

---

*See Volume XII, Part 1, Page 271, War Records, as to oaths of allegiance.

†Reference to orders concerning foraging.

MAJ: GEN. IRVIN McDOWELL.

T. J. Jackson

"STONEWALL" JACKSON.

From the consolidated morning report of Major General Pope, July 31st, 1862, the number of men present for duty, in the ranks of Gibbon's brigade was 40 companies, 2,664 men. To this must be added at least 150 for commissioned officers, making a total of about 2,800 for duty in the brigade. This was just before engaging in the hard and bloody campaign of forty-five days, covering the battles of Gainesville and Bull Run Second, under General Pope, and the battles of South Mountain and Antietam, in the Maryland campaign. In these operations, Gibbon's brigade suffered a loss of 1,592 men killed or wounded, and by its heroic conduct, acquired the historic title of the "Iron Brigade;" by whom first applied, I do not know.

THE FREDERICKS HALL RAID.

The regiment left camp opposite Fredericksburgh, at 2 o'clock, on the morning of August 5th, 1862, as a part of an expedition intended to cut the Virginia Central Railroad. General Gibbon was in command of the force sent forward for this purpose. He divided his force, placing Colonel Cutler in command of about one thousand men.* The troops were without knapsacks, and stripped for a race. Colonel Cutler marched by the Orange plank road for several miles, and then turned south, passing by a narrow road through Spottsylvania Court House. Cutler's flying column marched thirty-five miles on this day, one of the very hottest of the summer. General Gibbon's force (about 3,000 men) marched on the Telegraph road, running south from Fredericksburgh. They accomplished fifteen miles. He discovered that the rebel General, J. E. B. Stuart. was advancing by the Bowling Green road on his left, with a strong force. All possibility of General Gibbon's force surprising the enemy was gone, and he moved his troops over to the Spottsylvania road, to cover the retreat of Colonel Cutler's detachment. Unconscious of the happenings narrated, our column had reached a place called Mount Pleasant, fifteen or twenty miles from the railroad. Here, at eleven o'clock at night, a courier from General Gibbon, caught us sound asleep in bivouac, except the

---

*Six companies of the Ira Harris cavalry, two guns of Gerrish's (N. H.) battery, under Lieutenant Edgell, and 650 of our best men of the Sixth were present in the ranks.

proper guards. General Gibbon sent by his courier to Colonel Cutler, the facts of the situation, and directed him to act according to his judgment. Colonel Cutler called a midnight council of the field officers. Besides the Commander, there were present, Colonel J. Mansfield Davies, Lieutenant Colonel Judson Kilpatrick, Major H. W. Davies of the cavalry, Lieutenant Edgell of the artillery, and Lieutenant Colonel E. S. Bragg and Major R. R. Dawes of the infantry. Colonel Cutler explained that we were many miles in advance of our supporting column, and that General Stuart, with a force estimated at five thousand men, was behind us. Before us was the North Anna river, an unfordable stream, with wooden bridges that could be easily burned. Seven miles beyond the river was the railroad. The main force under General Gibbon had abandoned the effort to reach the railroad. The question was, should we go on and attempt to destroy the railroad as originally proposed, taking our chances of peril in front and rear, or should we fall back upon Gibbon's force which was waiting for us. Lieutenant Colonels Kilpatrick and Bragg, argued strongly in favor of going on.* They urged that this was the safest, as well as the most honorable course and such was the decision of the council. At the earliest dawn, the column started for the railroad. The men were given an intimation of the situation, and told that everything depended upon their speed. About one hundred and fifty of the foot-sore and weary men were left at Carl's bridge, over the North Anna, under Captain P. W. Plummer, to hold it for our retreat. When we approached Fredericks Hall station, Kilpatrick charged in with the cavalry, and cut the telegraph wires, and picketed the roads. Lieutenant Edgell put his guns in position to cover the retreat, and our men were kept hard at work for some time, destroying the railroad track, and the torch was applied to all Confederate Government and railroad property.† We then hurried back to

---

*Lieutenant Edward P. Brooks, Acting Adjutant, was present at this council, and he has written of it, "Bragg, Dawes, and Kilpatrick insisted on going on."

†Brooks says: "Burned Government warehouse, several thousand bushels of corn, fifty hogsheads of tobacco. Found ten barrels of peach brandy, and the men took a supply in their canteens, which refreshed them."

get across our wooden bridge. We made a great march upon that day Private William L. Riley, of Company "I," made the following note in his journal: "Part of the regiment left at a bridge. The rest goes on to Fredericks Hall station, and returns to Waller's tavern; about forty miles accomplished in one day. Big marching for infantry" We tore up about two miles of railroad track, so says Colonel Cutler.*

On the afternoon of August 9th, 1862, an order was received by telegraph directing that King's division should join General Pope at Cedar Mountain which was forty-five miles distant. On this day was fought the bloody battle of Cedar Mountain between Stonewall Jackson's corps and our troops under command of General N. P. Banks. On the early morning of August 10th we left the old camp opposite Fredericksburgh, never to return. The regiment marched twenty-one miles that day and on the evening of the 11th arrived near the scene of Cedar Mountain battle. General Jackson's army had retreated beyond the Rapidan. On this evening my contraband, whom I had employed in place of Jake, also deserted me. He smelled the battle from afar and "done got out." Sergeant Howard F. Pruyn of company "A" had in his employ a bright little yellow boy who had attracted my notice. The Sergeant could not keep a servant while on the march. I asked him if he thought this boy could do my work. He said he was a good and willing boy, but that he did not know anything and could not do my work. I was not in a position to be exacting, so I took him on trial. His name, William Jackson, will appear often in the after pages. A more excellent servant or a more faithful friend than he proved throughout the remainder of my service in the war could scarcely have been found.

---

*General Gibbon says in his official report of this affair: "I can not refer in too high terms, to the conduct of Colonel Cutler. To his energy and good judgment, seconded as he was by his fine regiment, the success of the expedition is entirely due." In Colonel Cutler's official report, occur these words: "I wish especially to notice Lieutenant Colonel Kilpatrick, and Major Davies of the cavalry, and Major Dawes of the infantry, for the prompt and efficient manner, in which they caused all my orders to be executed, also for the very valuable suggestions I received from them." See report Brigadier General Rufus King, Page 121, Volume XII, Series 1, Official Records of the War. Brigadier General John Gibbon, Page 122, Volume XII, Series 1, Official Records of the War. Colonel Lysander Cutler, Page 123, Volume XII, Series 1, Official Records of the War.

We were now encamped directly upon the battle ground of Cedar Mountain, where we remained for a week. We were obliged to bury many of the rebel dead whose corpses, left half buried upon the field, were intolerable. This was our first contact with one of the real horrors of war. Private Riley's journal mentions the fact that while we were in this camp, there was a roll-call every two hours, which, he says was a "new wrinkle." The object was of course to keep the men at hand for action, as we were in the presence of a largely superior force of the enemy. On the 19th day of August, we began our retreat before the advancing army of General Lee. We marched back fifteen miles toward the Rappahannock and camped that night five miles from the river. On the early morning of August 20th, we resumed our northward march. Riley says that his company "I," under Captain Kellogg, was sent to build a bridge across the river above the railroad station and that they worked all night, completing their bridge at daylight.

On the 20th day of August, our regiment crossed the Rappahannock, at the crossing of the Orange and Alexandria Railroad. We encamped a mile from the bridge. On the afternoon of that day, cavalry of the enemy appeared on the opposite bank of the river. By the clouds of dust rising on all the roads, we could trace the advance of the rebel army. On the morning of the 21st of August, the enemy opened fire on our troops from a battery of artillery, about a mile above the bridge, the first artillery we had ever heard in actual battle. One of our batteries wheeled into position on a gallop, cheered by the excited shouts of our men, and was admirably served in reply. Private William Riley says of this artillery duel, which was witnessed with great interest by our novices: "Our battery got the better of them in a few shots, showing a better practice, and more accurate shooting. Our shells burst close to their guns, while the enemy fired wide of their mark." Gibbon's brigade was ordered to the right of King's division, and we marched along in the rear of the batteries, now all placed in order of battle to fire upon the enemy. As we came into range of the enemy's battery, they turned their fire full upon the sixth Wisconsin. This was our initiation. The shell whizzed and burst over us and around us. The men marched steadily, keeping their places, and holding their heads high. They soon learned that a discreet and respectful obeisance to a cannon ball is no indication of cowardice.

When our brigade had taken position, six companies of our regiment were ordered forward to cover the brigade front, and to advance as skirmishers to the river. Lieutenant Colonel Bragg was in command of these companies, I was second. General Patrick's brigade skirmish line, next on our left, was ordered to join us, and be governed by our movement. But Patrick's line did not wait, and Colonel Bragg, seeing Patrick's skirmishers advancing, ordered the right of his own line forward, before our deployment on the left was completed. By this accident, company "E," under Captain Edwin A. Brown, was switched off, and lost from the line, and no connection was made with General Patrick's skirmishers. Our line also swung away from the proper front, and in place of advancing toward the river, we gradually changed to moving up parallel with the river, opening at every step, the gap between us and General Patrick's skirmishers. The thick woods concealed all from our view. After passing through the woods, we came upon a body of cavalry with blue overcoats. I galloped up to the officer in command and asked him if he had seen any rebels. He said, "Yes, Sir, plenty of them,—just in that point of woods, not five minutes ago." So we pushed on pell mell across an open field toward "that point of woods." Sharp musketry skirmishing broke out directly behind us. It was Captain Brown with our lost company "E," and Lieutenant Charles P. Hyatt, with a platoon of company "B," gallantly driving this rebel cavalry, for such it was, across the river. But we had been sent on a fool's errand by a rebel company, who were dressed in Union blue overcoats. Brown's and Hyatt's men killed and wounded several of the enemy, and captured a Lieutenant and two private soldiers. These officers and their men won the first glory for the sixth Wisconsin on the field of actual battle. The interpretation of our movements by Private William L. Riley is amusing. He says, "Went up the river to reconnoitre fords."

Toward night our regiment was ordered to advance nearer the

river. The rebels saw the movement, and opened fire upon us with a battery of artillery. Colonel Cutler halted, established guides, and aligned forward into the position assigned before he would allow the men to lie down. He said "you must get used to it." Fortunately the rebels were poor artillerists and did not hit us, so nobody was hurt. We learned to "lie down" in battle, later in our experience, without waiting to establish guides. In this new position, we were under a heavy artillery fire. During an interval, Colonel Cutler brought up his colored servant, an excellent cook, to make a pot of hot coffee, which he invited me to share with him, but, just as we sat down to enjoy our feast, the coffee-pot was knocked from the fire at least twenty feet in the air by a rebel shell. The darky, not stopping for his coffee-pot, left the field at the speed of a race horse. Our experiences the first day under fire, as we lost no men, were really valuable in showing the men, that artillery fire was not so dangerous as they had anticipated. During the next two days we were subjected by the rebels to, what I call in my journal, "several good shellings."

On August 23rd, we marched to the village of Warrenton. The rebel troops, judging from the clouds of dust which we could see beyond the river, were moving also. We marched to the Rappahannock at Warrenton Sulphur Springs, where we supported a battery, and were under fire of artillery nearly all day of August 26th.* At the Sulphur Springs, on August 27th, we were ordered to march with the utmost haste back to Centreville. The enemy was in great force between us and Washington, (Stonewall Jackson's corps.†) As we marched

---

*On this day, Lieutenant Edward P. Brooks, our Acting Adjutant, was ordered to report to General Pope, to act as guide to the columns of troops from the Army of the Potomac. He guided General Philip Kearney's division, and rendered other service so excellent in character, that General Pope gave him letters of the highest commendation.

†Lieutenant Arthur C. Ellis, of Company "B," himself disabled from marching, was with the wagon train of our brigade at Manassas Junction, when the cavalry of General J. E. B. Stuart reached there. Our brigade park of twenty-one wagons, was a short distance from the headquarters wagon train of General Pope. General Pope's wagons, and all others in the vicinity, excepting those of our brigade, were captured and destroyed by Stuart's cavalry. But Lieutenant Ellis rallied the crippled and sick men from our brigade, and directing them to lie on the

through Warrenton, wagon-loads of hard tack and pork were being destroyed, but the emergency seemed to be considered so great that the troops were not allowed to halt and fill their nearly empty haversacks, and some of our men were marching hungry. Time would have been gained by stopping a few moments to eat. We passed through New Baltimore and camped for the night near Buckland's Mills. Before daylight on August 28th, we were again on the march. About the middle of the forenoon, we halted for some time in the road near Gainesville. Quite a large body of rebel prisoners passed us here. Artillery fire was heard toward the Bull Run battle field. We pushed on for two miles, when we turned off from the turnpike into a piece of timber on the right hand side of the road. Here we remained until four o'clock in the afternoon. Beef was killed, and a ration issued. About this hour, General McDowell, according to his own testimony, became convinced that the troops who had been firing on our men, "were a small reconnoitering party, not worthy of mention to the Commanding General," and he ordered King's division to march on the turnpike to Centreville. General McDowell himself then left his corps, and having, he says, "important business with General Pope," he went to find that General and in the search became "lost in the woods." He remained lost in the woods during the entire night.

General Stonewall Jackson, at that very hour, was forming a column of eighteen thousand men along the Warrenton turnpike to attack General McDowell, and this force was scarcely two miles away. After watching our extraordinary movements for a season, Jackson says: "By this time it was sunset. * * * I determined to attack at once, which was vigorously done by the divisions of Taliaferro and Ewell" (six brigades). This attack, it will be seen, struck the second Wisconsin and nineteenth Indiana regiments.

Our division moved, as ordered, back to the turnpike and then along the turnpike toward Centreville, first, Hatch's brigade; second, Gibbon's; third, Doubleday's; fourth, Patrick's.

---

ground under the wagons, successfully defended, and saved from capture our train. The attack upon them was made at midnight. It was a very gallant deed, and of especial value to us, as all of our papers and much property were with the wagons.

The Battle of Gainesville.

General Hatch, in advance, sent the 14th Brooklyn regiment as advance guard and flankers. I remember seeing the line of their red legs on the green slope of the same hill from which the enemy fired upon us, but they discovered no enemy. Our brigade moved along the turnpike on that quiet summer evening as unsuspectingly as if changing camp. Suddenly the stillness was broken by six cannon shots fired in rapid succession by a rebel battery, point blank at our regiment. The shell passed over the heads of our men, and burst in the woods beyond. Surprise is no sufficient word for our astonishment, but the reverberation had not died away when gallant old Colonel Cutler's familiar voice rang out sharp and loud, "Battalion, halt! Front! Load at will! Load!" The men fairly jumped in their eagerness; and the iron ramrods were jingling, when—"Bang! Bang!" went the rebel cannon again. Again they overshot our men, but a poor horse was knocked over and over against the turnpike fence. "Lie down!" shouted Colonel Cutler. Fortunately a little bank along the roadside gave us good cover. Battery "B," 4th U. S. artillery, now came down the turnpike on a gallop. Quickly tearing away the fence, they wheeled into position in the open field, and the loud crack of their brass twelve pounders echoed the rebel cannon. Thus opened our first real battle. General Gibbon ordered the 2nd Wisconsin and 19th Indiana regiments to move forward upon the enemy. This attack of General Gibbon was made upon the theory that a comparatively small force of the enemy was present. (See reports of Gibbon and Doubleday.) No sooner had the 2nd Wisconsin shown its line in the open field, than there burst upon them a flame of musketry, while Confederate batteries distributed along about a mile of front opened with shell and and round shot. Under this terrible fire the second was obliged to change front before they could return a shot. We could not see them nor the 19th Indiana, owing to the intervening woods, but we heard the awful crash of musketry, and we knew there was serious work ahead. Captain J. D. Wood, of Gibbon's staff, came galloping down the turnpike with an order for the sixth to move forward into action. "Forward, guide centre," ordered the

Colonel. The word here ran down the line from a remark of Captain Wood's, that the second was being slaughtered, and when Colonel Cutler shouted "March," every man scrambled up the bank and over the fence, in the face of shot and shell, with something the feeling that one would hurry to save a friend from peril. My horse partook of the fierce excitement, and ran up the bank and leaped a fence like a squirrel. I could now see the men of the second Wisconsin. They were under the concentrated fire of at least six times their own number of the enemy. Our regiment, five hundred and four men in ranks, pushed forward rapidly in perfect line of battle, field officers and Adjutant E. P. Brooks mounted and in their places, and colors advanced and flying in the breeze. Colonel Cutler was on a large dark bay, well known to all the men as "Old Prince." Colonel Bragg rode a pure white horse of high mettle, which was skittish and unmanageable. My own sturdy old mare was always steady under fire.

The regiment advanced without firing a shot, making a half wheel to the left in line of battle as accurately as if on the drill ground. Through the battle smoke into which we were advancing, I could see a blood red sun, sinking behind the hills. I can not account for our immunity from the fire of the enemy while on this advance. When at a short range, Colonel Cutler ordered the regiment to halt and fire. The seventh Wisconsin now came forward and passed into the ranks of the second Wisconsin. Our united fire did great execution. It seemed to throw the rebels into complete confusion, and they fell back into the woods behind them. We now gave a loud and jubilant cheer throughout the whole line of our brigade. Our regiment was on low ground which, in the gathering darkness, gave us great advantage over the enemy, as they overshot our line. The other three regiments of the brigade were on higher ground than the enemy. There was space enough vacant between our regiment and the others for a thousand men. Colonel Cutler sat upon his horse near the colors at the center of the regiment. Lieut. Colonel Bragg was on the right and, being myself upon the left, I was in good position to observe the progress of the battle. It was quite dark when the enemy's yelling columns again came forward, and they came with a rush. Our men on the left loaded and fired with the energy of madmen, and the sixth worked with an equal desperation, This stopped the rush of the enemy, and they halted and fired upon us their deadly musketry. During a few awful moments, I could see by the lurid light of the powder flashes, the whole of both lines. I saw a rebel mounted officer shot from his horse at the very front of their battle line. It was evident that we were being overpowered and that our men were giving ground. The two crowds, they could hardly be called lines, were within, it seemed to me, fifty yards of each other, and they were pouring musketry into each other as rapidly as men could load and shoot. Two of General Doubleday's regiments (56th Pennsylvania and 76th New York,) now came suddenly into the gap on the left of our regiment, and they fired a crashing volley. Hurrah! They have come at the very nick of time. The low ground saved our regiment, as the enemy overshot us in the darkness. Men were falling in the sixth, but our loss was small compared to that suffered by the regiments on the left. I rode along our line and when near Colonel Cutler, he said, "Our men are giving ground on the left, Major." "Yes, Sir," said I. I heard a distinct sound of the blow that struck him. He gave a convulsive start and clapped his hand on his leg, but he controlled his voice. He said, "Tell Colonel Bragg to take command, I am shot." Almost at the same time "Old Prince" was shot; but he carried his master safely from the field. I rode quickly to Lieut. Colonel Bragg and he at once took command of the regiment. There was cheering along our line and it was again standing firmly. General Doubleday's two regiments by their opportune arrival and gallant work, aided much in turning the battle in our favor. The "Little Colonel" (Bragg,) always eager to push forward in a fight, advanced the regiment several rods. But soon the enemy came on again just as before, and our men on the left could be seen on the hill, in the infernal light of the powder flashes, struggling as furiously as ever. I could distinctly see Lieut. Colonel Fairchild, of the second Wisconsin and Lieut. Colonel Hamilton of the seventh Wisconsin, and other officers whom I recognized, working among and cheering up their men. Men who had been shot were streaming back from along the whole line. Our regiment was suffering more severely than it had been; but, favored by the low ground, we kept up a steady, rapid, and well aimed fire. As I galloped backward and forward along the line, my horse encountered ditches. Excited by the firing, cheering, and whizzing of the rebel shells, she would squat and jump a long distance in crossing them. How long our men withstood this last attack, I can not estimate, but, in the history of war, it is doubtful whether there was ever more stubborn courage than was displayed by the second and seventh Wisconsin and nineteenth Indiana regiments, on this field of battle. The only reason why I speak less of the 19th Indiana regiment is because I could not see them so distinctly. Our line on the left gradually fell back. It did not break but slowly gave ground, firing as savagely as ever. The rebels did not advance. Colonel Bragg directed our regiment to move by a backward step, keeping up our fire and keeping on a line with our brigade. But one of the companies of the right wing ("C") became broken by the men marching backward into a ditch. Colonel Bragg halted the regiment to enable them to reform their line, and upon this ground we stood until the enemy ceased firing. The other regiments of the brigade fell back to the turnpike. After an interval of quiet, Colonel Bragg called upon the regiment to give three cheers. No response of any kind was given by the enemy. It was now about nine o'clock, and the night was very dark. Feeling assured the battle was over, measures then were taken to secure the burial of our eight dead men, and to hunt up our sixty-one wounded. Three men were missing.* The regiment moved back by the left of companies and formed in the edge of the piece of woods. By direction of the Colonel, I rode toward the left to ascertain the location of our other troops. I came suddenly in the darkness upon a marching column. Fortunately, I kept still and soon discovered myself to be by the side of a rebel regiment. I rode quietly along for a short distance with them and turned off into the darkness unheeded. General Gibbon directed us to remain

---

*One of our best officers, Lieutenant Jerome B. Johnson, of Company "E," was found severely wounded. Surgeon A. J. Ward, of the second Wisconsin, remained with our wounded men.

where we were. The enemy, a short distance away, was caring for their wounded and burying their dead. We could hear their conversation, but ordered our picket line not to fire or in any way to disclose our proximity.

About half past twelve o'clock at night we marched back through the woods to the turnpike. Painful to relate, to this woods many of our wounded had gone when shot in the battle. They were now scattered about under its dark shadows, suffering and groaning and some were dying. In the pitchy darkness we stumbled upon them. This was the battle for which we had so long been yearning. On the turnpike we found hasty preparations for retreat and at about one o'clock A. M. we silently filed away in the darkness, muffling the rattling tin cups, and turning our course toward Manassas Junction. As major I rode at the rear of our regiment. Presently there sifted out from the marching column numbers of wounded men, who were struggling to keep with their comrades and to avoid falling into the hands of the enemy.* I saw Captain John F. Marsh, who had been shot in the knee, drop to the rear, and dismounting from my horse, I lifted him to the saddle, marching through on foot myself. My steady old mare did the service of a good Samaritan. Each stirrup strap and even her tail were an aid to help along the weak and weary. The cry at such times is for water, water. There was none left in the canteens. But we deemed ourselves very fortunate. We had lost 72 from our 504 men in battle. But the second Wisconsin! 298 men of the splendid second Wisconsin had been killed or wounded in the fight and they had taken not more than 500 men into action. The 7th Wisconsin and the 19th Indiana had suffered in almost the same terrible proportion. Of twelve field officers in the brigade, but four remained for duty, and two of them were of our regiment. The second Wisconsin regiment had been almost mortally wounded. Never afterward could be filled the places of such soldiers as went down at Gainesville. For free and easy movement, combined with exact

---

*A second Wisconsin man, E. S. Williams, whose leg was later amputated, in some manner crawled over that nine miles, and another man of that regiment, Hugh Lewis, went over the road on that fearful night, to have his arm amputated in the morning.

precision and perfect time, that battalion had a little surpassed us all on the brigade drill ground. The *elan* of the old second Wisconsin could not be excelled. It has passed into the history of our country, as the regiment which had the largest number of men killed in battle, in proportion to its numbers, of any regiment engaged in the war for the Union. Gainesville contributed much to this unequalled list of dead upon the field of glory. But the weary and dreadful lists of battle casualties can not be repeated here, they must be looked for upon the official records of the war. About daylight we reached our bivouac near Manassas and flung ourselves exhausted upon the ground for rest.

Leaving the tired brigade in its heavy slumber, we may consider briefly the Battle of Gainesville.

The cold figures speak for the battle power shown by our glorious brigade, more eloquently than language can express. Stonewall Jackson sent into action six brigades of infantry and three batteries of artillery. The brigades were: Trimble's, Lawton's and Early's of Ewell's division, and Starke's, Baylor's, and Taliaferro's, of the Stonewall division, thirty regiments of infantry, at least eight thousand men. The batteries in action were, Wooding's, Pogue's, and Carpenter's. Our force engaged could not have exceeded three thousand men. The officially reported loss of Ewell's division was seven hundred and fifty-nine.* The loss of the Stonewall division was not less. Gibbon's brigade lost seven hundred and fifty-four and General Rufus King has testified that the entire loss of our six regiments and one battery† engaged, was one thousand men. It is now made quite certain by the Confederate Official Records that our troops inflicted upon them a loss of fifteen hundred men. This is reasonably explained by the fact that the Confederate force twice advanced in columns of attack. Our men stuck desperately and persistently to one deployed line, from which they delivered a steady and well aimed fire. At the time of the hottest firing, the troops were stationed approximately as shown in the diagram given. The Confederate brigades are arranged

---

*See Page 813, Volume 12, Part II, War Records.
†"B," 4th U. S. artillery.

in the order that seems to be indicated by their own official reports. I have not attempted to locate their artillery.

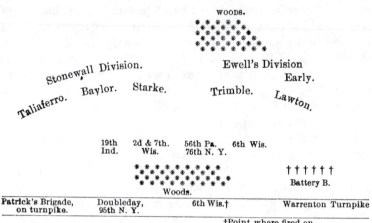

WOODS.

Stonewall Division.   Ewell's Division

Taliaferro.   Baylor.   Starke.   Trimble.   Early.   Lawton.

| 19th Ind. | 2d & 7th. Wis. | 56th Pa. 76th N. Y. | 6th Wis. |

Woods.

Battery B.

| Patrick's Brigade, on turnpike. | Doubleday, 95th N. Y. | 6th Wis.† | Warrenton Turnpike |

†Point where fired on.

I do not feel that our army commander, General Pope, has in his official statements of this battle, done justice to our troops engaged. I much prefer the more worthy tributes from the Generals who were opposed to us upon that bloody field. The Confederate General, T. J. Jackson, says in his official report in regard to this battle: "The conflict was fierce and sanguinary. The federals did not attempt to advance, but maintained their ground with obstinate determination. Both lines stood exposed to the discharge of musketry and artillery until about nine o'clock, when the enemy slowly retired, yielding the field to our troops. The loss on both sides was heavy and among our wounded were Major General Ewell and Brigadier General Taliaferro."

The Confederate General, William B. Taliaferro, who commanded Jackson's old division, three brigades in the battle, says in his official report: "Here one of the most terrific contests that can be conceived occurred. The enemy never once attempted to advance upon our position, but withstood with great determination the terrible fire which our lines poured upon them. For two hours and a half, without an instant's cessation of the most deadly discharges of musketry, round shot and shell, both lines stood unmoved, neither advancing and neither broken nor yielding, until at last, about nine o'clock at night, the enemy slowly and sullenly fell back and yielded to our victorious troops."*

General John F. Reynolds says, "After the firing ceased I saw General King, who *determined to maintain his position.*† I left about 9 o'clock P. M., to return to my division, promising to bring it up early in the morning to his support."‡ General Reynolds commanded the Pennsylvania Reserve division, twenty-five hundred of the best possible quality of veteran soldiers. But a Council of War was afterward held by the Generals of King's division. The old adage was again verified that "A Council of War never fights." General King has written as follows: "Then came the question, what next to be done. The enemy in greatly superior force barred the way in which the division was marching. The only alternative was to deflect to the right to join the bulk of Pope's army in the vicinity of Manassas." It seems however that the bulk of Pope's army was not then at Manassas. This movement was an abandonment of the ground we held between Lee's army and Jackson's isolated corps. Brigadier General Gibbon, who so gallantly attacked the enemy with his single brigade, says in his own official report: "I sent repeated and earnest requests to Division headquarters (General King) for assistance." "I sent repeatedly and urgently to Generals King, Doubleday and Patrick for assistance, but the two regiments of Doubleday's brigade was the only assistance furnished me." General Doubleday sent his two regiments however, to assist Gibbon, without orders to do so from General King. He says in his report: "Receiving no orders, and unable

---

*In Volume XII, Series 1, Part II, War Records, may be found official reports of the battle of Gainesville.

Brigadier General John Gibbon,...............................Pages 377 and 379.
Letter of General Gibbon,...Page 380.
Report Lieutenant Colonel E. S. Bragg,......................... " 382.
   "   General A. Doubleday,.. " 369.
   "   "   J. P. Hatch,.. " 367.
   "   Casualities, ... " 380.

†Golden words for General King.

‡Page 393, Volume XII, Series I, Part II, War Records.

to obtain them, I almost immediately sent two regiments of my brigade, the 56th Pennsylvania, under Colonel S. A. Meredith, and the 76th New York under Colonel W. P. Wainwright, to aid Gibbon. Knowing he would be overpowered if not succored, I immediately complied with his earnest request and sent him the two regiments referred to, leaving myself but one regiment (95th New York) in reserve." General Gibbon says: "Patrick's brigade remained immovable and did not . fire a shot," and he says also, "No superior general officer was in the vicinity with the requisite knowledge and authority to order up troops to our support."

I have searched the official records in vain for further explanation of the management of this battle. Our Corps Commander, General McDowell, had no part in the affair, for he was "lost in the woods."

What a painful contrast is presented in the records of the Generals of the enemy. The rebel Corps Commander, Stonewall Jackson, conducted the battle in person. Two rebel Generals of Division were shot in the fight, (Ewell and Taliaferro). Jackson had exact knowledge of the field, a clear purpose, concentrated action by his troops, and his Generals led their men to battle. On the afternoon of this day, August 28th, 1862, was lost the only opportunity that occurred in that campaign to attack Jackson with superior forces while separated from Lee. The verdict of history is likely to be, that the opportunity was "lost in the woods."*

The best blood of Wisconsin and Indiana was poured out like water, and it was spilled for naught. Against a dark background of blunders, imbecilities, jealousies and disasters in the Pope campaign, stands in bright relief the gallant conduct of our heroic leader, John Gibbon. Whatever history may do for others, his fame is as safe as that of the faithful and gallant heroes of the brigade he commanded.

But let us now return to our sleeping brigade at Manassas. A

---

*See Pages 328 to 331, Volume XII, Part 1, War Records. The McDowell Court of Inquiry. "The court finds that he, (McDowell) separated himself from his command at a critical time, without any orders from his superior officer and without any imperative necessity."

fresh beef ration has been issued and hot coffee has been made, and at nine o'clock all are listening to the sounds of battle that come from the old Bull Run field. There is a heavy sound of cannon and an occasional ripple of musketry. We were near the railroad track, which branches off at Manassas Junction. I was myself aroused from a sleep by the heavy tramp of hurrying feet. I arose to see the corps of General Fitz John Porter passing by us toward the battle field. At the time they were passing, the cannon were roaring so loudly that the men fully believed they were marching directly to battle. They appeared fresh and in good spirits and the corps was a remarkably fine body of troops. The men marched rapidly, appeared to be well fed, and there was a great contrast between them and our own exhausted troops. As things are in a battle campaign they were in excellent condition. They showed quite a contempt for us as of "Pope's army." They said: "We are going up to show you 'straw feet' how to fight." The lesson did not prove to be impressive. All through the ranks of Porter's Corps was a running fire of disparagement of us as "Pope's" soldiers, something quite inferior to the Army of the Potomac. Of course our men retorted. There was one regiment of Zouaves with baggy trousers (Duryea's I think). I remember one of our men said: "Wait till you get where we have been. You'll get the slack taken out of your pantaloons and the swell out of your heads."

We remained until some time in the afternoon when we marched back toward the field of battle where a heavy engagement seemed to be in progress. We moved along the Manassas Gap Railroad and turned on to the road to Sudley Springs. As we marched up to the battle field that afternoon, we could see heavy clouds of dust stretching away toward Thoroughfare Gap. This of course was caused by the advancing army of General Lee, but it was interpreted to us at the time as indicating that Jackson was retreating to join Lee. Private Riley states in his journal: "Upon our arrival at the Warrenton turnpike, General McDowell, who sat upon his horse by the road side, said, 'We have been driving the enemy all day.'" Riley also says in his journal that General McDowell used this language: "Give him a good poke, boys. He is getting sick," meaning the enemy. General

McDowell wore a peculiarly shaped cap at this time which was commented upon by the men.

King's division was formed in two lines of battle in a large open field, but Gibbon's brigade was detached and ordered away, and we marched toward the right, nearly a mile and a half. We went into position in support of batteries of artillery, relieving troops who marched toward the front. It was about sunset. King's division, excepting ourselves, had become involved in a very sharp battle with the enemy. Listening to this musketry, we deemed ourselves exceedingly fortunate to have escaped a fight. Our one night's experience at Gainesville had eradicated our yearning for a fight. In our future history we will always be found ready but never again anxious.

A few artillery shots from the enemy whistled over us, but we soon fell into a profound and much needed slumber.

BATTLE OF BULL RUN SECOND.

The sun rose clear on the morning of August 30th, 1862, and during the forenoon the troops of our army were moving quietly into position. From our hill we had an excellent view of the field. The whole of our army was spread before us, but intervening timber hid the enemy from our sight. The drift of talk was that the rebels were falling back. About three o'clock in the afternoon, we were ordered forward to "pursue the enemy." We marched on the Warrenton turnpike, perhaps half a mile, when our brigade was formed into two lines of battle in an open field on the right hand side. General Patrick's brigade was in front of us, formed also in two lines of battle. We had thus at our point of attack four lines of battle. Before us was woods, beyond which a railroad embankment. Behind this embankment quietly awaiting the attack were our antagonists at Gainesville, the veteran army corps of Stonewall Jackson. Just before we entered the edge of the woods, our brigade was changed to one line of battle with the sixth Wisconsin on the right. As the troops entered the woods a very heavy artillery fire broke out upon our left, (Longstreet's). Musketry opened in our front. Bullets, canister, shell, and the men said, " scraps of railroad iron," tore through the limbs and brush over us and around us. We pushed on, advancing as the lines in front of us advanced and lying down on the ground when they stopped. There was no order to charge upon the enemy, and we wondered why such orders were not given. Thus we slowly advanced. Suddenly, the lines in our front broke and the men ran back in great disorder. The rebels raised a tremendous shout, and poured in a heavy fire of musketry. The sharp artillery fire of the enemy which enfiladed our line, added to the panic and confusion. Colonel Bragg shouted, "Sixth Wisconsin, kneel down! Captains, keep your men down! Let nobody tramp on them!" General Gibbon himself came running up on foot with his revolver drawn, shouting, "Stop those stragglers!—Make them fall in!—Shoot them if they don't!" It was a new experience, but we were not swept away. Our men were down with bayonets set, when the fugitives began to swarm upon them. All the officers were struggling to stop stragglers and force them to join our ranks. Many were held with us, but no Union troops were left in front of us. General Gibbon directed Colonel Bragg to throw forward a company as skirmishers. This was a fearful duty. Colonel Bragg called for my old company "K."

> "Who faltered or shivered?
> Who shunned battle stroke?
> Whose fire was uncertain?
> Whose battle line broke?
> Go ask it of history,
> Years from to-day,
> And the record shall tell you,
> Not 'company K.'"

The boys immediately sprang up under command of Captain David L. Quaw, and deployed forward upon a run. We could see them firing and dodging from tree to tree. They met a rebel skirmish line coming forward through the woods, and they drove it back upon the rebel line of battle. The spirit and conduct of company "K" was beyond praise. The panic and retreat of our own troops and the exultant shouts of thousands of rebel soldiers did not daunt these men. Captain Quaw says that "after the rebel skirmishers retreated, there arose up from behind a railroad bank, a mass of rebel soldiers several ranks deep. I shouted to my men to 'tree.' I jumped behind a small tree myself, where I must have shrunk to the dimensions of a wafer.

A dozen bullets hit that tree. I did not wait for the rebels to fire again, but ordered the men back to the regiment."

All the troops that had been in the woods, except the sixth Wisconsin, had now retreated and gone to the rear. Brigadier General John Gibbon, be it ever remembered to his honor, remained with our regiment. He said he had received no orders to retreat and he should stay until he got them. The regiment was now lying on the ground, subjected to a fire from rebel sharp-shooters and quite a number of our men were killed or wounded by them. A bullet would strike a man who would writhe, groan and die or spring up, throw away his impediments and start for the rear. Our men peered through the leaves, shooting at the puffs of powder smoke from the muskets of the rebels. As I walked along the line, some men of company "I" said: "Major, don't go near that tree." I was not aware what tree, but had wit enough to jump away. Spat, went a bullet against a tree, cutting a corner from my haversack. They had noticed that the tree had been several times struck by the bullets of a sharp shooter. A soldier of a New York regiment lay wounded in front of our line. He begged piteously for water and for help. First Sergeant, Charles Lampe, of company "F" went to give him a swallow from his canteen and was himself shot dead by the merciless bullet of the sharp-shooter. Private William Bickel-haupt, of company "F," had been shot through the body, and I heard the poor little boy, for such he was, in plaintive broken English telling his comrades what to write to his "Mutter."

It now being evident that no staff officer could bring us orders of any kind, General Gibbon directed Colonel Bragg to form a line of skirmishers to cover the retreat of the regiment, and to move to the rear. The skirmishers were quickly deployed and Colonel Bragg ordered the regiment to face about and march back. But the rebels redoubled their fire, killing and wounding quite a number of our men. Bragg immediately ordered the regiment to face to the front. Our skirmishers were hotly engaged with the enemy. By a slow backward step, we moved out of the woods. Upon reaching the open ground, Colonel Bragg faced the regiment by the rear rank and took a steady double quick. It was full three quarters of a mile over the open fields to the place where our new lines were forming. The sixth Wisconsin regiment alone upon the plain, in full sight of both armies, marched this distance. General Rufus King in describing this scene says: "The sixth Wisconsin, the very last to retire, marched slowly and steadily to the rear, with column formed and colors flying, faced the front as they reached their new position, and saluted the approaching enemy with three cheers and a rattling volley." General King is in error as to the volley. We should have killed our following skirmish line by such firing. The regiment was ordered into position in support of battery "B," 4th U. S. artillery. We were on a high point, commanding the Warrenton turnpike and the open fields over which we had retreated. Just as the line was being formed, a solid shot cut off the tail of a fine bay horse ridden by Lieutenant James Stewart, of battery "B." *The shot gave the horse a deep cut across the rump, the scar of which lasted his life-time. The horse's tail flew into the faces of men of our regiment, switching them severely.

It was now late in the afternoon. The rebels (Longstreet's corps) directed a heavy fire of artillery on us, and began a general advance of their infantry toward our left. We could see regiment after regiment of the enemy moving in column by division, and forming into line of battle as they advanced upon our men. From the point where we lay upon the ground, the view of the battle was extensive. Our batteries were all actively firing upon the advancing columns of the enemy. Their artillery was also in action. The solid shot and shell struck around us and whizzed over us. Occasionally a horse would be killed by them, and one man's head was carried away entirely. Such sights very severely test one's nerves. A solid shot will plow into the ground, spitefully scattering the dirt, and bound a hundred feet into the air, looking as it flies swiftly away like an India rubber playing ball. We could see every movement of the left wing of our own army, and of the right wing of the rebel army. Our lines were in open fields in front of a strip of woods. The rebel musketry fire was pouring from the woods upon our men who were closing together and rallying under the attack.

---

*This horse was called "Tartar."

Regiments would sweep splendidly forward into the front line,
fire a crashing volley into the woods and then work with great
energy. But they quickly withered away until there would
appear to be a mere company crowding around the colors. The
open fields were covered with wounded and stragglers, going to
the rear. The rebels charged up a ravine endeavoring to
capture an Ohio battery upon our immediate left. The second
and seventh Wisconsin had been consolidated and were under
command of Lieutenant Colonel Lucius Fairchild. Colonel
Fairchild had his men change front and attack the enemy, who
were quickly driven back and the battery saved. We could now
see that our troops upon the left were being driven back in
confusion over the open fields. This outflanked our position,
and it was evident that we must soon draw back our line.
General Joseph Hooker, who was mounted on a white horse,
rode up among the guns of our artillery and carefully noted the
situation of affairs. He ordered batteries and infantry to retire.
Regiments moved steadily by the right of companies to the rear,
the batteries moved also in retreat. A rebel line in our front
rose up from the ground and advanced slowly after us. It was a
strange sight, our blue line slowly retreating, and the long gray
line slowly and quietly following. When we halted and formed
again, the rebels halted and lay down on the ground. It was
growing dark. There was still a heavy roll of musketry to
our left and some sharp firing on our right. By nine o'clock, all had
died away.* About ten o'clock, General Philip Kearny came up

---

*CASUALTIES IN THE BATTLES OF GAINESVILLE AND BULL RUN.

	Killed		Wounded.		Missing.		Aggregate.
	Officers.	Men.	Officers.	Men.	Officers.	Men.	
Sixth Wisconsin Volunteers		17	4	87		11	119
Second Wisconsin Volunteers	2	51	8	205	1	31	298
Seventh Wisconsin Volunteers	1	30	8	145		33	217
Nineteenth Indiana Volunteers	1	46	7	161		44	259
Total	4	144	27	598	1	119	893

in rear of our regiment, which now lay across the Warrenton turnpike near the stone bridge over Bull Run. He informed us that our brigade was to be the rear guard of the army which was in full retreat. We had not before suspected the real extent of the disaster. General Kearny remained with us anxiously watching the front, and Colonel Bragg and I had much conversation with him. It was after midnight when we started for the rear. Mock camp fires had been built to deceive the enemy. We lay down to rest at a point three miles from the battle field and on the early morning of August 31st, we drew back across Cub Run, forming a line of battle on the eastern bank. About noon of that day we marched from Cub Run to Centreville. We bivouacked near Centreville. Late at night, I was sent out to establish a line of pickets. Our men, after the privations, labor, and intense excitement of three successive days in battle, were unfitted for such duty. One man placed on picket post in the woods, in the bewilderment of his senses, got himself faced toward our camp instead of toward the enemy. When he was approached by his comrades to relieve him, he mistook them for the enemy and fired upon them and killed Rudolph Fine of Company "I."

On September 1st, 1862, we marched six miles toward Fairfax Court House. On the afternoon of this day occurred the battle of Chantilly, in which fell General Philip Kearny. We were in line of battle, but at some distance to the right of the troops engaged. A heavy storm was prevailing during this battle. The noise of the artillery and musketry intermingling with the roll of very sharp thunder produced a striking effect. The darkness incident to a sky overcast with heavy, rolling clouds, lighted up alternately by flashes of lightning and the flames of artillery, made a scene long to be remembered. Several wagon trains became jammed together on the turnpike and a great panic ensued. Wagons were two or three abreast, and the mules going at a full gallop. There came a sudden crash and a jam, and wild cursing and shouting by the drivers.

September 2nd, we marched twelve miles to Upton's Hill, within six miles of Washington and went into position. As the column approached Upton's Hill, the announcement was made that General George B. McClellan had been placed in command of all the troops. There was genuine enthusiasm at this news. General John P. Hatch who was commanding our division, swung his sword and called for cheers, which were given with an uproarious good will and repeated. Open sneering at General Pope was heard upon all sides. It began with the advent of the troops from the Army of the Potomac, and it spread through our whole body. General Pope made a grave blunder when he assailed the ingrained hero worship of General McClellan, which possessed our troops. The force of this feeling can be little understood now, because conditions akin to those which affected us have passed away. Such a feeling, as that for General McClellan, was never aroused for another leader in the war. An intense party spirit attended these conditions. The Army of the Potomac was smarting under criticism, and was disappointed at its own failure to meet the unduly elevated hopes and expectations of the people. Richmond had not been taken. Pope was now defeated, and there were those even in high position, who seemed to glory in the fact. Those were dark days for the administration of President Lincoln. He pursued the only course left to him, and he acted wisely in placing General McClellan again in command. The animadversions against the President himself, for what was called "interference" with the plans of his Generals, were common and severe throughout the army.

(Letter.)   UPTON'S HILL, SEPTEMBER 5th, 1862.

My dear mother:—"I have tried in several ways to send you word of my safety. We have had a terrible ordeal. We were in battle or skirmish almost every day from August 21st to 31st. Our brigade has lost eight hundred men; our regiment, one hundred and twenty-five. The country knows how nobly our men have borne themselves. I have been at my post in every battle."

On Upton's Hill, we received our delayed mail. Colonel Bragg found several letters urging him to stand as a War candidate for congress. From Bragg's reply to such solicitation, I give an extract: "Say to Judge Flint that I shall not decline a nomination on the platform, the Government must be sustained, but my services can not be taken from the field. I command the regiment, and can not leave in times like these." Brave words from our gallant "little Colonel."

Colonel Cutler had a curious experience in Washington, which well illustrates conditions in that city after the Pope campaign, and how they affected the temper of the great War Minister, Edwin M. Stanton. Colonel Cutler had bought a new uniform, and as soon as he could walk, he went with great difficulty, leaning on two canes, to pay his respects to the Honorable Secretary of War. The office of the Secretary was, as usual, crowded, and the Colonel patiently waited for his turn to be received. As the Colonel approached, the Secretary, with a glance at the new coat and bright brass buttons, blustered out as only Mr. Stanton could, "What in h—l and — — nation are you doing in Washington? Why don't you go to your regiment, where you are needed?" Colonel Cutler answered: "If I had not been shot and a fool, I would never have come here. Good day, Mr. Secretary."

CHAPTER IV.

In the reorganization of the army which took place at Upton's
Hill, our brigade was designated as *4th brigade, 1st division, 1st
army corps, Army of the Potomac. The Army of Virginia,
which was the title of General Pope's command, was now
obliterated. General John P. Hatch was in command of our
division, and that magnificent soldier, General Joseph Hooker,
commanded our first army corps. Army corps from this time
were known rather by their numbers, than by the names of their
commanders. McDowell's 3rd corps was changed to be the 1st
corps. We marched from Upton's Hill via Washington City, and
Rockville, Maryland; and on September 12th, 1862, I wrote to
my mother from Lisbon, Maryland:

"Our army is moving up again to the battle field. Probably
before this reaches you the conflict will be over. If so, you will
know that I was there. My health is good and I am ready to
take my chances. Do not feel that our task is easy or sure of
successful accomplishment. The battle will be desperate and
bloody, and upon very equal terms. Give my love to all."

Our camp on the quiet Sabbath morning of September 14th,
1862, was in the valley of the Monocacy, near Frederick,
Maryland. There are few fairer landscapes in our country
than this valley affords from its eastern range of hills. The

---

*Page 170, Volume 19, Part I, War Records, Organization of the
Army of the Potomac. In our brigade, Lieutenant Colonel Bragg commanded the sixth Wisconsin, Lieutenant Colonel Lucius Fairchild, the
second Wisconsin, Captain John B. Callis, the seventh Wisconsin, and
Colonel Solomon Meredith the nineteenth Indiana.

morning was bright, warm, and clear. The bells of the city of Frederick were all ringing. It was a rejoicing at the advent of the host for her deliverance, the Army of the Potomac. The spires of the city were glistening in the morning sunlight. To the south-west could be distinctly heard the muttering of cannon. This was General Stonewall Jackson attacking the garrison at Harper's Ferry. From right to left along the valley below us, were stretched the swarming camps of the blue coats, and every soldier felt his courage rise at the sight. Through a wooded and uneven country, by different and devious routes, the columns of the grand army had marched forward. We had known something of their progress, but had not so felt their power as we did now when they were concentrating before us. The deep feeling of almost affectionate admiration among the soldiers for the commander of our army, General McClellan, was often thus expressed: "We have got a General now, and we will show the country what we can do."

At eight o'clock A. M., our brigade marched forward on the National turnpike, the sixth Wisconsin in advance. Our entry into the city was triumphal. The stars and stripes floated from every building and hung from every window. The joyful people thronged the streets to greet and cheer the veterans of the Army of the Potomac. Little children stood at nearly every door, freely offering cool water, cakes, pies and dainties. The jibes and insults of the women of Virginia, to which our men had become accustomed, had here a striking contrast in a generous and enthusiastic welcome by the ladies of Frederick City. At eleven A. M. we reached the summit of the Katoctin mountain. Fences and trees showed marks of a skirmish of the evening before. From the summit of this mountain a splendid view was spread before us, in the valley of Middleton. Over beyond the valley, eight miles away, from along the slopes of the South Mountain, we could see arising the smoke of battle. We hurried along down the road toward the scene of action, every gun of which we could see and hear. Our march through the little village of Middleton was almost a counterpart of our reception at Frederick City. The people were more excited as the cannon boomed loud and near, and bloodstained soldiers were coming in from the field of battle. Hearing that a colonel of an Ohio regiment had been brought in to Middleton, wounded, I made a special inquiry and found that it was Lieutenant Colonel Hayes of the 23rd Ohio. (Rutherford B. Hayes.) We marched on beyond Middleton about a mile and a half and then turned into a field to make our coffee. The fires were not kindled, when an order came to fall in and move forward. It was announced that General Hooker had said "that the crest of that mountain must be carried to-night." General Hatch's division turned from the National road toward the right, but an order was received assigning Gibbon's brigade to a special duty. The brigade countermarched and advanced again on the National road for half a mile. We then turned to the left into a field and formed in two lines of battle. The seventh Wisconsin and nineteenth Indiana were in the front line; the second and sixth Wisconsin in the second line. We had in the ranks of our regiment four hundred men. Simmon's Ohio battery, planted in this field, was firing shell at the rebels on the summit of South Mountain. Before us was a valley, beyond which by a steep and stony slope, rose the South Mountain range. From our position to the summit of South Mountain was perhaps two miles. Two miles away on our right, long lines and heavy columns of dark blue infantry could be seen pressing up the green slopes of the mountain, their bayonets flashing like silver in the rays of the setting sun, and their banners waving in beautiful relief against the background of green.

Battle of South Mountain.

Turner's gap through which the National turnpike passes over the mountain, was directly in our front. To attack this pass was the special duty for which we had been selected. To our left along the wooded slopes, there was a crash of musketry, and the roll of cannon, and a white cloud of battle smoke rose above the trees. From Turner's gap in our front, and along the right on the summit of the mountain, the artillery of the enemy was firing, and we could see the shells bursting over and among our advancing troops. For nearly an hour we laid upon the grassy knoll, passive spectators of the scene. The sun was sinking behind the mountain, when our order came to move forward.

The two regiments in front (7th Wisconsin and 19th Indiana) moved in line of battle. Our regiment and the 2nd Wisconsin followed at supporting distance, formed in double columns. Thus we went down into the valley and began to climb the slope of the mountain, which was smooth at first and covered with orchards and cornfields. The regiment was halted in an orchard and two companies ("B," Captain Rollin P. Converse and "K," Lieutenant John Ticknor) were sent forward as skirmishers. Our skirmishers immediately encountered skirmishers of the enemy and drove them slowly up the mountain, fighting for every inch of the ground. Nothing could be finer than the conduct of these two companies, or more gallant than the bearing of their young leaders. The officer commanding the skirmishers of the second Wisconsin, Captain Wilson Colwell, was killed.

For half a mile of advance, our skirmishers played a deadly game of "Bo-peep," hiding behind logs, fences, rocks and bushes. Two pieces of artillery of battery "B" moved up on the turnpike under Lieutenant James Stewart, and when the skirmishers were checked, they would wheel into action and fire shell at the houses, barns or thickets, where the rebels found a cover. The enemy now turned upon us the fire of their batteries, planted in the pass near the mountain top, but their shot flew over.

General Gibbon mounted upon his horse and riding upon high ground where he could see his whole line, shouted orders in a voice loud and clear as a bell and distinctly heard throughout the brigade. It was always " Forward ! Forward ! " Just at dusk we came to a rough, stony field, skirted on its upper edge by timber. Our skirmishers had encountered the enemy in force and were behind a fence. The seventh Wisconsin in front of us, climbed the fence and moved steadily forward across the field and we followed them, our regiment being formed in double column. Suddenly the seventh Wisconsin halted and opened fire, and we could see a rapid spitting of musketry flashes from the woods above and in front of us, and wounded men from the seventh began to hobble by us. The sharpest fire came from a stone wall, running along in a ravine toward the left of the seventh. Captain John B. Callis was in command of that regiment. He ordered a change of front, throwing his right forward to face the wall; but there burst from the woods, skirting the right of the field, a flame of musketry which sent a shower of bullets into the backs of the men of the right wing of the seventh Wisconsin. Many men were shot by the enfilading fire to which they could make no reply. Captain Hollon Richardson came running toward us shouting: "Come forward, sixth!" Sharp and clear rang out on the night, the voice of Bragg: "Deploy column! By the right and left flanks, double quick, march!" The living machine responded to this impulsive force with instant action, and the column was deployed into line of battle. The right wing of our regiment came into open field, but the left wing was behind the seventh. "Major!" ordered Bragg, "take command of the right wing and fire on the woods!" I instantly ordered: "Attention, right wing, ready, right oblique, aim, fire, load at will, load!" The roll of this wing volley had hardly ceased to reverberate, when Bragg said: "Have your men lie down on the ground, I am going over you." "Right wing, lie down! Look out, the left wing is going over you!" was the command. Bragg had brought the left wing behind the right wing and he ordered them forward over the men of the right wing as they laid upon the ground. The left wing fired a volley into the woods, and the right wing advanced in the same manner over them and fired a volley into the woods. Once more Bragg gave a volley by the left wing. There were four volleys by wing given, at the word of command. In a long experience in musketry fighting, this was the single instance I saw of other than a fire by file in battle. The characteristic of Colonel Bragg in battle, was a remarkably quick conception and instant action. The conduct of the men was worthy of their commander. In the deployment of the column under fire, they hurried over the rough and stony field with the utmost zeal, and while many men were struck by the bullets of the enemy, there was neither hesitation nor confusion. After the four volleys by wing and a welcome cheer by the seventh Wisconsin, there was positive enthusiasm. Our whole line was slowly advanced up the mountain, the men shouting and firing. The rebels behind the stone wall and in the timber would shout: "O, you d——d Yanks, we gave you h—ll again at Bull Run!" Our men would shout back: "Never mind Johnny, its no McDowell after you now. 'Little Mac' and 'Johnny Gibbon' are after you now." The rebels fell back from the woods, but stuck to the stone wall. The hostile lines had approached each other closely and the fire was deadly. It was dark and our only aim was by the flashes of the enemy's guns. Many of our men were falling, and we could not long endure it. Colonel Bragg took the left wing, directing me to keep up the fire with the right wing, and crept up into the woods on our right, advancing a considerable distance up the mountain. He gained higher ground than that of the enemy in our front, and from this position opened fire.

Colonel Bragg directed me to join him with the right wing. Owing to the thick brush and the darkness of the night, it was a difficult matter to scramble up the stony side of the mountain. To add to our difficulties, the rebels opened fire upon us; but our gallant left wing fired hotly in return and the junction was completed. Our cartridges were getting short and our guns were dirty with bad powder. Gradually by direction of Colonel Bragg we ceased firing and lay still on the ground. A man in company "A" exclaimed: "Captain Noyes, I am out of cartridges!" It is likely that the enemy in the woods above us heard him, for they immediately opened upon us a heavy fire. We returned the fire, and for a short time the contest was very sharp. This was the last of the battle. When all was again still, Colonel Bragg felt sure that he could hear the enemy withdrawing. He ordered, "Three cheers for the Badger State." They were given and brought no reply. A few volunteer skirmishers crept forward into the woods in front of us. Further pursuit was impossible. We were nearly out of ammunition and our guns so dirty that we could hardly use them. We lay among thick bushes on the steep rough slope of a mountain in almost total darkness.

We did not dare to let the men sleep. Colonel Bragg sent to General Gibbon for ammunition. General Gibbon replied that it was impossible for him to furnish it, but that he hoped that we would soon be relieved by other troops. He said that we must hold the position we had gained so long as there was "an inch of our bayonets left." The night was chilly, and in the woods intensely dark. Our wounded were scattered over a great distance up and down the mountain, and were suffering untold agonies. Owing to the difficulties of the ground and the night, no stretcher bearers had come upon the field. Several dying men were pleading piteously for water, of which there was not a drop in the regiment, nor was there any liquor. Captain Kellogg and I searched in vain for a swallow for one noble fellow* who was dying in great agony from a wound in his bowels. He recognized us and appreciated our efforts, but was unable to speak. The dread reality of war was before us in this frightful death, upon the cold, hard stones. The mortal suffering, the fruitless struggle to send a parting message to the far-off home, and the final release by death, all enacted in the darkness, were felt even more deeply than if the scene had been relieved by the light of day. After a long interval of this horror, our stretcher bearers came, and the poor suffering heroes were carried back to houses and barns. At last word came that General Sumner's troops were marching up the mountain to relieve us. How glad we were to hear it, they only can know who have experienced the feeling of prostration produced by such scenes and surroundings, after the excitement of a bloody battle. It was after midnight, and it seemed to us bitterly cold. The other regiments of our brigade had marched down the mountain, but our relief—where was it? We sent Adjutant Brooks to General Gibbon, who said that our relief had been ordered, and would certainly come. But it did not come. Colonel Bragg finally sent Adjutant Brooks to Brigadier General Willis A. Gorman, the brigade commander, who had orders to relieve us. The Adjutant reported that he offered to lead the way to prevent the possibility of confusion or mistake, but that General Gorman's reply was: "I can't send men into that woods to-night. All men are cowards in the dark." He forgot that the men whom he condemned to shivering and misery for the rest of the night had fought and won a bloody battle in the dark. We were not relieved until eight o'clock in the morning of September 15th, when the 2nd

---

*William Lawrence of company "I."

New York regiment of Gorman's brigade came up. As soon as it became daylight, we examined the field of battle, and found many dead and wounded rebels. The troops opposed to us were five regiments of a brigade commanded by Colonel A. H. Colquitt, the 6th, 23rd, 26th and 28th Georgia, and 13th Alabama regiments. One rebel soldier from Georgia, wounded in the head, his face a gore of blood, fled from us as we approached. We could hardly persuade him that it was not our purpose to kill him.*

General George B. McClellan was stationed in the same field where Simmon's Ohio battery was planted and he had watched our brigade in the engagement. He wrote the following to the Governor of Wisconsin: "I beg to add my great admiration of the conduct of the three Wisconsin regiments in General Gibbon's brigade. I have seen them under fire acting in a manner that reflects the greatest possible credit and honor upon themselves and their state. They are equal to the best troops in any army in the world."

After being relieved by the second New York we marched down the mountain to the National turnpike and the men began to build fires to make coffee and cook their breakfast, but we were ordered to march immediately to the Mountain House on the top of South Mountain. It was hard, but the men fell in promptly and marched along munching dry hard tack. It was now 24 hours since they had had their coffee. Our brigade was put by General Hooker in the advance in the pursuit of the enemy and our regiment marched at the head of the column. We pushed along the turnpike down the western slope of the mountain. Presently old gray haired men, citizens of Maryland, came rushing up to meet us. They seemed almost frantic with joy. They swung their hats and laughed and cried without regard for appearances. One respectable old gentleman who trot-

---

*Official reports of action at South Mountain, may be found in Volume 19, Part I, War Records.

ted along beside my horse said; "We have watched for you, Sir, and we have prayed for you and now thank God you have come."

Here his feelings got the better of him and he mounted a bank and began to shout. The last I saw of him, he was shouting and thanking God and the 19th Indiana was responding with lusty cheers. As we approached the village of Boonesboro, it seemed deserted, but when our column entered the streets, doors and windows flew open and the people thronged out to greet us. Flags that had been hidden in the darkest corner were now unfurled. These people informed us that the rebel infantry had passed through the town in haste and in much disorder. Colonels were in some cases, they said, carrying regimental banners. They said that General Lee was present when the retreat commenced. We turned to the left in Boonesboro toward Antietam creek. Our cavalry in front were picking up hundreds of prisoners, stragglers and wounded men from the retreating army. We pushed on five or six miles, passing through the village of Keedysville. When we were on the hill west of that place, the rebels opened fire on us from batteries planted in front of the village of Sharpsburg. We turned off the turnpike into a field and marched into a ravine, where we had protection. Still fragments of bursting shell fell thick in the fields around us. Our batteries came galloping along the turnpike and wheeling rapidly into position along a ridge they returned the fire of the rebel artillery. Unmindful of this clatter, our men rallied for the fences and building fires made their much needed coffee with little regard for the fragments of shell flying around.

After drinking coffee I went up to the ridge where our batteries were firing upon the enemy. I could see on the hills beyond the creek (Antietam) a rebel line of battle stretching over the fields. General Joseph Hooker was there at this time with his field-glass and I heard him say that from appearances the force of the enemy was at least forty thousand. It was now three o'clock in the afternoon. We marched up the Antietam more out of range of the rebel batteries and bivouacked for the night. Our greatly exhausted men were soon sound asleep. At several times during the 16th of September the cannonading was heavy and from our position, we had a good view of the combat.

About four o'clock in the afternoon, General Hooker's army corps began to cross Antietam Creek. The division of Pennsylvania Reserves crossed on the bridge above Keedysville, while General Doubleday's* division, to which we belonged, forded the creek at a shallow place below. The troops advanced slowly toward the Sharpsburg and Hagerstown Turnpike. We passed over open fields and through orchards and gardens, and the men filled their pockets and empty haversacks with apples. About dusk, sharp musketry and cannonading began in our front. It was nine o'clock at night when our brigade reached the position assigned it. The men laid down upon the ground, formed in close column, muskets loaded and lines parallel with the turnpike. Once or twice during the night, heavy volleys of musketry crashed in the dark woods on our left. There was a drizzling rain, and with the certain prospect of deadly conflict on the morrow, the night was dismal. Nothing can be more solemn than a period of silent waiting for the summons to battle, known to be impending.

About daylight, General Doubleday came galloping along the line, and he ordered that our brigade be moved at once out of its position. He said we were in open range of the rebel batteries. The men were in a heavy slumber. After much shaking and kicking and hurrying, they were aroused, and stood up in their places in the lines. Too much noise was probably made, which appears to have aroused the enemy. The column hurriedly changed direction, according to orders, and commenced moving away from the perilous slope which faced the hostile batteries.

We had marched ten rods, when whiz-z-z! bang! burst a shell over our heads; then another; then a percussion shell struck and exploded in the very center of the moving mass of men. It killed two men and wounded eleven. It tore off Captain David K. Noyes's foot, and cut off both arms of a man in his company. This dreadful scene occurred within a few feet of where I was riding, and before my eyes. The column pushed on without a halt, and in another moment had the shelter of a barn.† Thus

---

*General Doubleday succeeded General J. P. Hatch, wounded at South Mountain.

†Poffenberger's barn.

opened the first firing of the great battle of Antietam, in the early morning of September 17th, 1862. The regiment continued moving forward into a strip of woods, where the column was deployed into line of battle. The artillery fire had now increased to the roar of an hundred cannon. Solid shot and shell whistled through the trees above us, cutting off limbs which fell about us. In front of the woods was an open field; beyond this was a house, surrounded by peach and apple trees, a garden, and out-houses.† The rebel skirmishers were in this cover, and they directed upon us a vigorous fire. But company "I" deployed as skirmishers, under command of Captain John A. Kellogg, dashed across the field at a full run and drove them out, and the line of the regiment pushed on over the green open field, the air above our heads filled with the screaming missiles of the contending batteries. The right of the regiment was now on the Sharps-burg and Hagerstown Turnpike. The left wing was obstructed in its advance by the picket fence around the garden before mentioned. As the right wing passed on, I ordered the men of the left wing to take hold all together and pull down the fence. They were unable to do so. I had, therefore, to pass the left wing by the flank through a gate with the utmost haste, and form again in the garden. Here Captain Edwin A. Brown, of company "E," was instantly killed. There is in my mind as I write, the spectacle of a young officer, with uplifted sword, shouting in a loud imperative voice the order I had given him, "Company 'E,' on the right by file into line!" A bullet passes into his open mouth, and the voice is forever silent. I urged the left wing forward with all possible speed. The men scrambled over briars and flower-beds in the garden. Beyond the garden, we entered a peach orchard. I hurried forward to a rail fence skirting the front edge of the orchard, where we overtook the right wing. Before us was a strip of open-field, beyond which on the left-hand side of the turnpike, was rising ground, covered by a large cornfield, the stalks standing thick and high. The rebel skirmishers ran into the corn as we appeared at the fence. Owing to our headlong advance, we were far ahead of the

---

† David R. Miller's house.

general lines of battle. They were in open fields, and we had the cover of the houses and orchard. Colonel Bragg, however, with his usual battle ardor, ordered the regiment forward. We climbed the fence, moved across the open space, and pushed on into the corn-field. The three right companies of the regiment were crowded into an open field on the right-hand side of the turnpike. Thus we pushed up the hill to the middle of the corn-field.

At this juncture, the companies of the right wing received a deadly fire from the woods on their right. To save them, Colonel Bragg, with a quickness and coolness equal to the emergency, caused them to change front and form behind the turnpike fence, from whence they returned the fire of the enemy. Meanwhile, I halted the left wing, and ordered them to lie down on the ground. The bullets began to clip through the corn, and spin through the soft furrows—thick, almost, as hail. Shells burst around us, the fragments tearing up the ground, and canister whistled through the corn above us. Lieutenant Bode of company "F," was instantly killed, and Lieutenant John Ticknor was badly wounded. Sergeant Major Howard J. Huntington now came running to me through the corn. He said: "Major, Colonel Bragg wants to see you, quick, at the turnpike." I ran to the fence in time to hear Bragg say: "Major, I am shot," before he fell upon the ground. I saw a tear in the side of his overcoat which he had on. I feared that he was shot through the body. I called two men from the ranks, who bundled him quickly into a shelter tent, and hurried away with him. Colonel Bragg was shot in the first fire from the woods and his nerve, in standing up under the shock until he had effected the maneuver so necessary for the safety of his men, was wonderful. I felt a great sense of responsibility, when thrown thus suddenly in command of the regiment in the face of a terrible battle. I stood near the fence in the corn-field, overlooking the companies on the turnpike which were firing on the enemy in the woods, and where I could see the left wing also. I noticed a group of mounted rebel officers, whom I took to be a general and staff. I took a rest over the turnpike fence, and fired six shots at the group, the men handing me loaded muskets. They suddenly scattered.

Our lines on the left now came sweeping forward through the corn and the open fields beyond. I ordered my men up to join in the advance, and commanded: "Forward—guide left—march!" We swung away from the turnpike, and I sent the sergeant-major (Howard J. Huntington) to Captain Kellogg, commanding the companies on the turnpike, with this order: "If it is practicable, move forward the right companies, aligning with the left wing." Captain Kellogg said: "Please give Major Dawes my compliments, and say it is impracticable; the fire is murderous."

As we were getting separated, I directed Sergeant Huntington to tell Captain Kellogg that he could get cover in the corn, and to join us, if possible. Huntington was struck by a bullet, but delivered the order. Kellogg ordered his men up, but so many were shot that he ordered them down again at once. While this took place on the turnpike, our companies were marching forward through the thick corn, on the right of a long line of battle. Closely following was a second line. At the front edge of the corn-field was a low Virginia rail fence. Before the corn were open fields, beyond which was a strip of woods surrounding a little church, the Dunkard church. As we appeared at the edge of the corn, a long line of men in butternut and gray rose up from the ground.. Simultaneously, the hostile battle lines opened a tremendous fire upon each other. Men, I can not say fell; they were knocked out of the ranks by dozens. But we jumped over the fence, and pushed on, loading, firing, and shouting as we advanced. There was, on the part of the men, great hysterical excitement, eagerness to go forward, and a reckless disregard of life, of every thing but victory. Captain Kellogg brought his companies up abreast of us on the turnpike.

The Fourteenth Brooklyn Regiment, red legged Zouaves, came into our line, closing the awful gaps. Now is the pinch. Men and officers of New York and Wisconsin are fused into a common mass, in the frantic struggle to shoot fast. Every body tears cartridges, loads, passes guns, or shoots. Men are falling in their places or running back into the corn. The soldier who is shooting is furious in his energy. The soldier who is shot looks around for help with an imploring agony of death on his face.

After a few rods of advance, the line stopped and, by common impulse, fell back to the edge of the corn and lay down on the ground behind the low rail fence. Another line of our men came up through the corn. We all joined together, jumped over the fence, and again pushed out into the open field. There is a rattling fusilade and loud cheers. "Forward" is the word. The men are loading and firing with demoniacal fury and shouting and laughing hysterically, and the whole field before us is covered with rebels fleeing for life, into the woods. Great numbers of them are shot while climbing over the high post and rail fences along the turnpike. We push on over the open fields half way to the little church. The powder is bad, and the guns have become very dirty. It takes hard pounding to get the bullets down, and our firing is becoming slow. A long and steady line of rebel gray, unbroken by the fugitives who fly before us, comes sweeping down through the woods around the church. *They raise the yell and fire. It is like a scythe running through our line. "Now, save, who can." It is a race for life that each man runs for the cornfield. A sharp cut, as of a switch, stings the calf of my leg as I run. Back to the corn, and back through the corn, the headlong flight continues. At the bottom of the hill, I took the blue color of the state of Wisconsin, and waving it, called a rally of Wisconsin men. Two hundred men gathered around the flag of the Badger state. Across the turnpike just in front of the haystacks, two guns of Battery "B," 4th U. S. artillery were in action. The pursuing rebels were upon them. General John Gibbon, our brigade commander, who in regular service was captain of this battery, grimed and black with powder smoke in himself sighting these guns of his old battery, comes running to me, "Here, major, move your men over, we must save these guns." I commanded "Right face, forward march," and started ahead with the colors in my hand into the open field, the men following. As I entered the field, a report as of a thunderclap in my ear fairly stunned me. This was Gibbon's last shot at the advancing rebels. The cannon was double charged with canister. The rails of the fence flew high in the air. A line of union blue charged swiftly forward from

*Hood's old Texas brigade, and Law's brigade.

our right across the field in front of the battery, and into the corn-field. They drove back the rebels who were firing upon us. It was our own gallant 19th Indiana, and here fell dead their leader, Lieutenant Colonel A. F. Bachman; but the youngest captain in their line, William W. Dudley, stepped forward and led on the charge. I gathered my men on the turnpike, reorganized them, and reported to General Doubleday, who was himself there. He ordered me to move back to the next woods in the rear, to remain and await instruction. Bullets, shot, and shell, fired by the enemy in the corn-field, were still flying thickly around us, striking the trees in this woods, and cutting off the limbs. I placed my men under the best shelter I could find, and here we figured up, as nearly as we could, our dreadful losses in the battle. Three hundred and fourteen officers and men had marched with us into battle. There had been killed and wounded, one hundred and fifty-two. Company "C" under Captain Hooe, thirty-five men, was not in the fight in front of the corn-field. That company was on skirmish duty farther to our right. In this service they lost two men. Of two hundred and eighty men who were at the corn-field and turnpike, one hundred and fifty were killed or wounded. This was the most dreadful slaughter to which our regiment was subjected in the war. We were joined in the woods by Captain Ely, who reported to me, as the senior officer present, with the colors and eighteen men of the second Wisconsin. They represented what remained for duty of that gallant regiment.

The roar of musketry to the front about the corn-field and the Dunkard church had again become heavy. Stragglers and wounded streamed in troops toward the rear. This tide growing momentarily stronger, General Gibbon directed me to form a line of the whole brigade, perhaps five hundred men present, to drive back, at the point of the bayonet, all men who were fit for duty at the front. But, soon, the troops engaged about the Dunkard church fell back, and the whole line was formed in rear of batteries, planted on the ridge near Poffenberger's house. We were on the ground from which, at the early dawn, our regiment had moved forward to begin the battle.

At the very farthest point of advance on the turnpike, Captain

Werner Von Bachelle, commanding Company F, was shot dead. Captain Bachelle was an ex-officer of the French army. Brought up as a soldier in the Napoleonic school, he was imbued with the doctrine of fatalism. His soldierly qualities commanded the respect of all, and his loss was deeply felt in the regiment. Bachelle had a fine Newfoundland dog, which had been trained to perform military salutes and many other remarkable things. In camp, on the march, and in the line of battle, this dog was his constant companion. The dog was by his side when he fell. Our line of men left the body when they retreated, but the dog stayed with his dead master, and was found on the morning of the 19th of September lying dead upon his body. We buried him with his master. So far as we knew, no family or friends mourned for poor Bachelle, and it is probable that he was joined in death by his most devoted friend on earth.

It was about noon when we got to our position in rear of the batteries, and we were greatly astonished and rejoiced to meet here our gallant Lieut. Colonel, Edward S. Bragg, who had come back to join us on the field of battle. He was severely wounded and unfit for duty, but he was there, and we had believed him to be dead.

Captain John A. Kellogg showed great ability as a commander of men in battle. He rallied several hundred stragglers of every regiment engaged and organized them as a regiment; posting his line behind a stone wall on the right hand side of the turnpike near the Poffenberger house. He did this while I was deploying the brigade to stop stragglers, as ordered by General Gibbon. General Doubleday, our division commander, seeing his line and not knowing how to account for it, galloped up shouting, "What regiment is this?" "A regiment of stragglers, Sir," said Kellogg. "Have you any orders?" "Stick to the stone wall." Captains P. W. Plummer and Rollin P. Converse, Lieutenants Charles P. Hyatt, Lyman B. Upham and Howard V. Pruyn were always in the lead. But the same is true of all of our line officers who were there. Whoever stood in front of the corn field at Antietam needs no praise. Captain Converse was shot through both thighs, as we were about to advance in pursuit of the running rebels. He convulsively threw his sword into the soft ground and said, "Hyatt; I can't run after them, I am shot, take command," and he hobbled off, refusing help.

The excitement of the men at the point of the battle when the rebels began to run before us, is illustrated by curious incidents. Private Thomas Barcus of company "I," like Captain Converse, was shot in such a manner as to disable the flexor tendons of his legs. Finding he could not run, he shouted, "Here is where you get your stiff legs!" Corporal Sherman of company "D," after shooting several times at a rebel color, saw it fall. At that moment a bullet went through his arm. He was boasting in a loud voice that he had "fetched it," and seemed greatly surprised to find his own arm paralyzed.

During the remainder of the day we were in position in support of the heavy line of batteries. About 4 P. M., while the musketry of General Burnside's battle upon the left was crashing, the enemy suddenly opened upon us a heavy fire of artillery. Our cannon, I believe about forty in number, replied with great vigor, and for half an hour a Titanic combat raged. We lay as closely as possible to the ground. I was upon the same oil-cloth with Captain John A. Kellogg, when a large fragment of shell passed into the ground between us, cutting a great hole in the oil-cloth, and covering us with dirt. It was a mystery how this could be and neither of us be struck.

Right here on the front line two enterprising reporters were gathering lists of killed and wounded and items of the battle, when this cannonading suddenly opened. One, whose name I have forgotten, reporting for the "New York Herald," got down and hugged the ground like an old soldier. As he lay near me, he was showered with dirt plowed up by the fragment of shell, but he "stood fire." The other, Mr. L. L. Crounse, of the "New York Times," frantically straddled his horse, and buried his spurs in the animal's flanks. Bowed flat, his hat gone, and in headlong flight over the fields toward the rear, he presented a spectacle amusing to the soldiers. Amid the thunder of cannon and screaming of shell, a great shout was set up to cheer Crounse upon his ride. But Crounse doubtless got his report in first.

The piles of dead on the Sharpsburg and Hagerstown Turnpike were frightful. The "angle of death" at Spottsylvania, and the Cold Harbor "slaughter pen," and the Fredericksburgh Stone

Wall, where Sumner charged, were all mentally compared by me, when I saw them, with this turnpike at Antietam. My feeling was that the Antietam Turnpike surpassed all in manifest evidence of slaughter. When we marched along the turnpike on the morning of September 19th the scene was indescribably horrible. Great numbers of dead, swollen and black under the hot sun, lay upon the field. My horse, as I rode through the narrow lane made by piling the bodies along beside the turnpike fences, trembled in every limb with fright and was wet with perspiration. Friend and foe were indiscriminately mingled.

In climbing the two post and rail fences that lined the turnpike, great numbers of men were killed. They climbed these fences as the shortest cut to the woods, through fear of retreating before the fire over the open fields. In climbing, they made themselves an easy mark. Our own troops climbed these fences under the same circumstances on their several retreats from the woods around the Dunkard Church.

In front of the haystacks where Battery B, 4th U. S. Artillery, had been planted was seen a horse, apparently in the act of rising from the ground. Its head was held proudly aloft, and its fore legs set firmly forward. Nothing could be more vigorous or life-like than the pose of this animal. But like all surrounding it on that horrid aceldama, the horse was dead.

The student of this battle will be well repaid by a careful study of the Confederate reports. The troops we first encountered in the early morning and drove into the woods around the Dunkard Church were the same we met at Gainesville, the Stonewall division of Jackson's Corps. The troops who in turn drove us back were Hood's Texas brigade, who originated the rebel yell, and from them we heard it on this occasion in all its terror. Colonel W. T. Woffard commanded the Texas brigade. In Law's brigade in line with the Texans was the second Mississippi regiment afterward encountered by us at Gettysburg. It will be seen that we get even with this regiment in that battle. It will be of interest to observe how closely my own account of our movements given above, which was written for my mother while I was in winter quarters at Belle Plaine, Virginia, in January, 1863, accords with the official reports of the enemy.

IN LINE OF BATTLE, NEAR SHARPSBURG, MARYLAND, }
(Letter.) SEPTEMBER 18, 1862. }

"MY DEAR MOTHER :—I have come safely through two more terrible engagements with the enemy, that at South Mountain and the great battle of yesterday. Our splendid regiment is almost destroyed. We have had nearly four hundred men killed and wounded in the battles. Seven of our officers were shot and three killed in yesterday's battle and nearly one hundred and fifty men killed and wounded. All from less than three hundred engaged. The men have stood like iron. We are now under General Joseph Hooker. Lieut. Colonel Bragg was wounded yesterday and I commanded the regiment during most of the battle. The battle may be renewed at any time."

It will be noticed in this letter that for the first time in my contemporary writing, I speak of the men as having stood "like iron." It is probable that the title of "Iron Brigade" was applied before the date of this letter.

It is evident that I was not aware when this letter was written that General Joseph Hooker, our corps commander, had been shot in the battle of the day before.

*This battle closed the campaign of forty-five days, which may properly be called the first battle epoch in the history of the brigade. During this time, the brigade was on eleven different days subjected to the battle fire of the enemy.

---

*See Official Records of the War, Volume 19, Part 1.

Report Lieutenant Colonel E. S. Bragg,	Page 254.
Report Captain John B. Callis,	" 257.
Report General A. Doubleday,	" 223.
Report General John Gibbon	" 248.
Report General Joseph Hooker,	" 235.
Report Captain W. W. Dudley,	" 257.

CONFEDERATE REPORTS.

Colonel W. T. Woffard, Texas brigade,	Page 927,	Vol. 19, War Records.
General J. B. Hood,	Page 922,	Vol. 19, War Records.
Lieut. Col. M. W. Gary,	Page 930,	Vol. 19, War Records.
Lieut. Col. P. A. Work,	Page 931,	Vol. 19, War Records.
Colonel E. M. Law,	Page 934,	Vol. 19, War Records.
Lieut. Col. B. F. Carter,	Page 934,	Vol. 19, War Records.
Captain Ike N. M. Turner,	Page 937,	Vol. 19, War Records.
General J. R. Jones,	Page 1006,	Vol, 19, War Records.
Major H. J. Williams,	Pages 1010—1012,	Vol. 19, War Records.
Colonel Edmund Pendleton,	Page 1015,	Vol. 19, War Records.

CASUALTIES IN THE BATTLE OF SOUTH MOUNTAIN.

	Killed		Wounded.		Missing.		
	Officers.	Men.	Officers.	Men.	Officers.	Men.	Aggregate.
Sixth Wisconsin Volunteers......................		11	1	78		2	92
Second Wisconsin Volunteers	1	5	1	20			27
Seventh Wisconsin Volunteers..............		11		115		21	147
Nineteenth Indiana Volunteers..............		9	2	35		7	53
Total......	1	36	4	248		30	319

CASUALTIES IN THE BATTLE OF ANTIETAM.

	Killed		Wounded.		Missing.		
	Officers.	Men.	Officers.	Men.	Officers.	Men.	Aggregate.
Sixth Wisconsin Volunteers..................	3	20	5	110		9	147
Second Wisconsin Volunteers......		18	6	57		9	90
Seventh Wisconsin Volunteers.........................		9		26		5	40
Nineteenth Indiana Volunteers........	1	5	1	71		25	103
Total........	4	52	12	264		48	380

In Vol. 19, Part I, Page 189, War Records, will be found a corrected statement of casualties of 6th Wisconsin at Antietam, aggregating 152.

CHAPTER V.

The regiment was now in a condition of exhaustion from the severity of its service and from its losses in battle. Colonel Cutler and Lieutenant Colonel Bragg were wounded, disabled, and absent, and I remained for some time in command. Captains Brown and Bachelle were dead. Captains Noyes, Marsh and Converse were wounded and disabled. Lieutenant Bode had been killed and Lieutenants Jerome B. Johnson and John Ticknor had been wounded, and two hundred and sixty enlisted men had been killed or wounded in the campaign. I have included the men reported "missing" as among the killed or wounded. Such was almost invariably the fact. The wounded man, when shot, went to the rear and availed himself of the first assistance found. Often he fell into the hands of stretcher bearers or ambulance drivers of another corps. He would be taken first to their field hospital and finally to Washington, or perhaps, to Baltimore to the general hospital. We would hear from him in an urgent appeal for his "descriptive list" to be sent "at once" to the hospital where he was located. This important paper he needed to draw his pay. Meanwhile our return of killed, wounded and missing had been made, and it remains upon the

Official Records of the War. ·The companies were disorganized by the loss of officers, and a period for rest and reorganization was a necessity.

(Letter.)   CAMP NEAR SHARPSBURG, SEPTEMBER 23rd.

"I have for a day or two been suffering from a severe attack of bilious sick-headache, a result of the late terrible excitement and trying times. We are encamped amid a dreadful stench of the half-buried thousands of men and horses on the battle field.

Captain Edwin A. Brown, of company "E," my best friend in the regiment, was shot dead at Sharpsburg. That gallant soldier, Captain Von Bachelle, was shot dead and his Newfoundland dog lay dead upon his body."

One of our sergeants made the blunder of sending to Mrs. Bragg a message that her husband had been killed, instead of sending it to Mrs. Brown. The results were sensational and very sad.*

The Republican Union Congressional convention for the fourth district of Wisconsin, which met at Fond du Lac, September, 24th, 1862, adopted resolutions seconding the nomination of Colonel Bragg, as an independent War candidate for congress, on his own platform. The following is one of the resolutions adopted: "Resolved, that we recognize in Edward S. Bragg, a

---

Extracts from a newspaper published at Fond du Lac, Wisconsin:
"The entire people of Fond du Lac have been, during the last few days the subjects of the most painful emotions, and two families and their connections prostrated with grief, when but one was really afflicted. Last Friday morning, a pang of intensest pain ran from heart to heart, on reception of a telegram that Lieutenant Colonel E. S. Bragg was killed in the battle of the 17th inst. The dispatch was sent from Hagerstown, Md., by a sergeant of company "I," directed to Mrs. Bragg, stating that her husband was killed, and that his body would be forwarded by express to this city. The news was considered reliable almost beyond a doubt. The city council convened, made arrangements to take charge of the funeral in a city capacity, and appointed a committee to proceed to Chicago to escort the body home. His family, plunged in grief, had made every arrangement for the funeral and burial, when, lo! light came back to that home, and a dark cloud threw its shadow across another threshold. The committee sent after Colonel Bragg's body, found when they reached Chicago, that it was Captain Edwin A. Brown, instead of Colonel Bragg, who was killed, and telegraphed to that effect, Sunday last. The news created a new and painful excitement. What was gained in one direction, was lost in another. The city council determined they would take the same course in regard to conducting the funeral, that had been marked out when it was supposed that Colonel Bragg had fallen."

true patriot, pledged to the support of the government and in every way qualified to represent the people of this district in the next congress of the United States, and we cheerfully recommend him to the people for their suffrages, notwithstanding upon questions of civil administration, he sustains a creed different from ours. He is true to the country, and in this trying hour we will know no subdivision of the National friends."

CAMP NEAR SHARPSBURG, MARYLAND,
OCTOBER 2nd, 1862.

(Letter.)

"We are now encamped at a beautiful spot on the banks of the Potomac river, enjoying the rest that we so greatly needed. All has been quiet since the battle until yesterday, when there was cannonading at a distance, all day. Our camp is about one mile from the village of Sharpsburg."

On the third day of October, the Army of the Potomac was reviewed by President Abraham Lincoln. The line was formed in almost the position occupied by the army of General Lee at the opening of the battle. We had about two hundred and fifty men in our ranks at this review. Our battle flags were tattered, our clothing worn, and our appearance that of men who had been through the most trying service. Mr. Lincoln has said that he staked the question of publishing his Proclamation of Emancipation upon the result of this battle. Recognizing Antietam as a victory, he had issued his preliminary paper of September 22nd, 1862, and he now visited the bloody field, where under the gracious favor of God, to whom he had appealed, we had defeated the invasion of the North, and made it possible for him to proclaim the purpose of our government to emancipate all slaves in the territory that was in rebellion. Mr. Lincoln was manifestly touched at the worn appearance of our men, and he, himself, looked serious and careworn. He bowed low in reponse to the salute of our tattered flags. As I sat upon my horse in front of the regiment, I caught a glimpse of Mr. Lincoln's face, which has remained photographed upon my memory. Compared with the small figure of General McClellan, who, with jaunty air and somewhat gaudy appearance, cantered along beside him, Mr. Lincoln seemed to tower as a giant.

CAMP NEAR SHARPSBURG, MARYLAND, ⎱
(Letter.)   OCTOBER 5th, 1862. ⎰

"General Abner Doubleday now commands our division, and General John F. Reynolds commands our corps."

Major General John F. Reynolds continued to command the first army corps until July 1st, 1863, when he was killed in front of the attacking column of our brigade, in the battle of Gettysburg.

(Letter.)   CAMP NEAR SHARPSBURG, OCTOBER 9th, 1862.

"A fine new regiment has been added to our brigade. They are a splendid looking body of men, entirely new to the service. It is the twenty-fourth Michigan, commanded by Colonel Henry A. Morrow. Their ranks are full now, and they are, as we were, crazy to fight."

CAMP NEAR BAKERSVILLE, MARYLAND, ⎱
(Letter.)   OCTOBER 21st, 1862. ⎰

"We have changed our camp and are not so pleasantly situated as when on the bank of the Potomac river. There, we had a fine view of the river which sweeps around in a beautiful bend, and of a broad extent of pleasant farming land, and romantic mountain scenery in Virginia. The regiment is gaining strength by men returning every day. Colonel Cutler is still feeble from the effect of his wound at Gainesville. The box of fruit you sent me is still missing. I have great hopes of getting it to-night. As I sent a man to Washington on some business, he will bring it with him if it is there. You ask me how I live— Dr. O. F. Bartlett and I mess together, and we have a good wall tent with a fly as a sunshade. We have a portable stove which keeps us comfortable. While in camp, our table is well supplied and our servants are good cooks. We have good bread, butter, and potatoes. Our mess chest is filled at the beginning of a march and put in the regimental headquarters wagon. When separated from our wagon train, we have hard times. I have often been glad to share the rations of the men, who will not let me suffer so long as they have a hard tack."

Later in the war, the admirable pack mule system of transportation of officers' provisions relieved them of the difficulty here complained of, and added greatly to their comfort when in the field. Before the introduction of pack mules, it was quite common for the officers' supplies to become exhausted by separation from the wagon trains.

Dr. O. F. Bartlett had already been promoted to be Surgeon of the third Wisconsin regiment. He was a gentleman of dignity of manner, and a surgeon of great skill. It will be observed that in my mess arrangements I was partial to the doctors.

(Letter.)   CAMP NEAR BAKERSVILLE, OCTOBER 26th, 1862.

Since assuming command of the regiment, I have been kept busy. There is a great deal of work with the regiment, and a good deal of outside labor has been imposed upon me. Sending descriptive lists to our wounded men in the hospitals is no small job. I was ordered to assist Captain McClellan of the staff of General George B. McClellan, in the inspection of the regiments of Doubleday's division. Two regiments were assigned to me yesterday, the 14th Brooklyn and the 24th New York. It was a wearisome task to inspect them, and disagreeable, as all deficiencies and faults must be reported directly to headquarters of the army."

In a memorandum book of 1862, I find notes in pencil of the inspection of three regiments. I regret that the notes of the other regiments inspected by myself were not preserved. These notes give some insight into the condition of the troops after the battle of Antietam, a subject upon which there was a controversy.* It can safely be said that two at least of the regiments here noted, were in very bad condition for active service. I give notes of inspection of the 24th New York.

"Regiment consolidated into a battalion of four companies.

Field officers present, none. Captain Miller, commanding.

Actual muster, 120 enlisted men for duty. Total enlisted men present in camp, 153, absence of 16 men from muster not satisfactorily accounted for. Condition of arms, ordinary. Cartridge boxes minus tin magazines, 12. Clothing and shoes, bad."

In the 14th Brooklyn regiment there were no field officers present and the regiment had been consolidated into a battalion

---

*Volume 19, Part I, Pages 10 to 75, War Records.

of four companies. In one company there were 74 men present, of whom for various reasons, 43 were non-effective. The principal reason was that they were without arms. The men of this regiment were all satisfactorily accounted for and the arms inspected were in good condition.

The result of Captain McClellan's inspection of the sixth regiment of Wisconsin volunteers was noted as follows:

"Field officers present, one.

Line officers present, ten.

Company		present effectives,		non-effectives,		total,	
"	"A,"	present effectives,	46;	non-effectives,	5;	total,	51.
"	"B,"	"	32;	"	1;	"	33.
"	"C,"	"	44;	"	3;	"	47.
"	"D,"	"	33;	"	3;	"	36.
"	"E,"	"	26;	"	0;	"	26.
"	"F,"	"	21;	"	1;	"	22.
"	"G,"	"	22;	"	0;	"	22.
"	"H,"	"	14;	"	1;	"	15.
"	"I,"	"	40;	"	5;	"	45.
"	"K,"	"	35;	"	4;	"	39.

Effectives, 313; non-effectives, 23; total, 336.

There were 81 defective cartridge boxes in the regiment. There were no men without arms. The condition of arms was "very good." The absent were all accounted for. The condition of clothing was generally *bad, and shoes very bad." The tin magazines in the cartridge boxes were to keep the powder dry. In battle the men would often throw them away in order to more quickly and easily get at their cartridges; but the cartridge box was thus ruined for further service. It would no longer keep the cartridges dry. Instruction had been given to particularly examine all cartridge boxes. The inspection was very thorough and rigid, and it disclosed that the army was in a destitute and almost disorganized condition.

(Letter.)   CAMP NEAR BAKERSVILLE, MARYLAND,   }
                                  October 27th, 1862.   }

"Colonel Bragg writes that he regards his election to Congress

---

*See Vol. 19, Part I, Pages 10 to 75, War Records.

as probable, but since the Ohio election, I have little faith. Colonel Cutler writes that he hopes to be back soon. He has become subject to sciatica and his painful wound is not half healed.

It is true that the army is in a suffering condition for clothing and shoes. Our regiment was never before nearly so destitute. I have used every exertion to obtain a supply of clothing, and only this morning succeeded in getting some underclothing for the men. Pants or coats I cannot get."

To these contemporary statements of the condition of the troops should be added the explanation, that we had passed through the battles and labors of the Pope campaign as well as those of the Maryland campaign, since we had received supplies of clothing and shoes. Our brigade had entered the Pope campaign overloaded with clothing and abundantly supplied with everything needed, but the feathers in our hats were drooping and the white leggings, which, as a protection to the feet and ankles, were now more useful than ornamental, had become badly soiled.

(Letter.)   CAMP IN VIRGINIA, October 31st, 1862.

"At last the Army of the Potomac is moving and we are once more upon the sacred soil. A big fight or a foot race will come off shortly. I mustered the regiment for pay to-day. I hope the money will come when we can do something with it. The continued absence of the Paymaster is becoming a serious annoyance."

            BEFORE SNICKER'S GAP, VIRGINIA, ⎱
(*Letter.)   NOVEMBER 2nd, 1862.   ⎰

"The campaign has opened again and we are pushing after the enemy once more. They threw a few shells from Snicker's Gap yesterday, indicating their presence there. If we encounter them, I shall have the honor of leading the regiment."

At this time, our newly appointed Assistant Surgeon, Dr. John C. Hall, reported to the regiment for duty. He proved to be a gentleman of great intelligence and fine literary taste. We became congenial friends and were intimately associated in the most pleasant and friendly relations for all of the remaining time of my service.

---

*Volume 19, Part I, Page 990, War Records.

Eng⁴ by Geo E Perine NY

HON. JOHN B. CALLIS

CAMP NEAR WARRENTON, VIRGINIA,
(Letter.)   NOVEMBER 7th, 1862.

"After hard marching, we are stopped by a snow storm. This is to us a familiar spot. It is cold, and exceedingly disagreeable campaigning now. Colonel Cutler has returned and he is in command of the brigade. He is really unfit for duty. I still command the regiment. General Gibbon has been promoted to command Rickett's division. We are sorry to lose him, for a brave and true man, tested as he has been, is a jewel here."

On November 1st, 1862, my brother, with the army in the west, was promoted to be major of his regiment. He was an adjutant. He had been jumped over all the captains in the line. The principle I so firmly stood for in our regiment, was trampled under foot in his regiment, and—I was glad of it.

(Letter.)   WARRENTON, VIRGINIA, NOVEMBER 9th, 1862.

"We are still here waiting for provisions. To-day the regiment is without a cracker to eat, but our men bear it without a murmur. No regiment in the army endures privations more patiently. The new regiment, (24th Michigan) do not take it so easily. They have been shouting: 'Bread! Bread!' at the top of their voices all day."

While we were in this camp, on November 7th, 1862, General George B. McClellan was relieved from the command of the Army of the Potomac, by President Lincoln, and General Ambrose E. Burnside appointed to that ill-starred responsibility. There was considerable expression of feeling. No acts of insubordination occurred. There was talk of resignations by officers, but in our brigade, the sturdy faithfulness of Colonel Lysander Cutler, then commanding, and his known determination of character, had an excellent restraining influence. He declared that he would recommend for dismissal, for tendering a resignation while in the presence of the enemy, any officer who offered to resign for such a reason. There were no resignations sent to his headquarters.

CAMP NEAR WARRENTON, VIRGINIA,
(Letter.)   NOVEMBER 10th, 1862.

"I am afraid that Colonel Bragg was defeated for congress. It is manifest that the cowardly sneaks who stay at home intend to sell out the country. Think of Horatio Seymour, an infamous peace Democrat, carrying the state of New York over General James S. Wadsworth.

We have just learned that General Gibbon has been promoted to Major General. His honors were fairly won. He is one of the bravest of men. He was with us on every battle field."

BIVOUAC IN THE BRUSH TEN MILES FROM ANYWHERE, IN }
(Letter.)   STAFFORD CO., VA., NOVEMBER 20th, 1862. }

"After a weary march of a week, we are encamped at the head waters of Acquia creek. We have been marching through a cold and driving rain storm, and to-day we are drying off. We are in the grand division commanded by *General William B. Franklin, and, the orders say, 'on the left of the army'. The men say they are willing to be left when more bloody fighting is to be done. The roads are in a desperately muddy condition, and we were all day yesterday moving the division two miles. Lieutenant Colonel Bragg has returned to the regiment. He was badly defeated in his race for congress, and all because he is a war man. They are for peace at any price, in his district."

The officers were desperately straitened for provisions on this march. Our headquarters wagon with officers' rations, was stuck in the mud miles away. Colonel Bragg detailed Private Adams, of company "C," who was a genius in that line, to forage for us. He gave him money to buy provisions. Adams could buy nothing of the spiteful rebel women, and he could find but little in that barren. At last he found a pig, killed and dressed, and hanging to the limb of a tree by a kitchen window, but there was a "safe guard" from corps headquarters, standing with loaded musket over that pig. Adams went into ambush until after dark, when he came safely into camp with a leg of fine young pork. I am safe in saying it was the sweetest and best I ever ate.

(Letter.)   CAMP OPPOSITE FREDERICKSBURGH, VIRGINIA, }
                                   NOVEMBER 25th, 1862. }

"I do not expect to be able to visit home this winter. The authorities are excessively strict and it would be scarcely possible for me, although I have not slept in a house for eight months, to

---

*Volume XXI, Page 48, War Records.

get permission to go even to Washington. Colonel Solomon Meredith is now a Brigadier General and he is to take command of our brigade."

(Letter.) CAMP NEAR BROOKS STATION, Nov. 30th, 1862.

"HON. W. P. CUTLER:—If possible, I will procure a pass and come up to the city, but it is doubtful whether I can. I have not been off duty nor slept out of camp for eight months and have been in every skirmish and battle ; but owing to the practices of that worse than contemptible class of officers who shirk duty and hang around Washington, we who do our duty can get no privileges."

(Letter.) CAMP AT BROOKS STATION, DEC. 1st, 1862.

"Our great army has once more come to a halt. There is an aspect of winter quarters for the army, but no one expects that our Commanding General will publish orders to that effect. O, no, 'Richmond must fall,' 'Lee's army must be bagged.' There must be another bloody battle. Nothing less will appease our valiant 'stay-at-home rangers.' You are not prepared to believe that our army at Antietam was checked at every point. You think McClellan a traitor. I did not make a fool of myself at the time of McClellan's removal as some officers did. I do not yet know whether the army has suffered from the change Wait and see how much better Burnside does, before 'rejoicing' over the removal of McClellan.

We have fixed up very comfortably in this camp. I am now tenting with Dr. A. D. Andrews, who is a pattern of neatness.

A law of congress invests a field officer in each regiment with the powers and functions of a regimental court martial. I am the court in this regiment. A full record of proceedings and evidence in each case tried has to be made *pro forma*, which involves much labor. My standard of fines for misdemeanors ranges from three dollars to thirteen dollars, the maximum allowed by law. As for example, "for killing a rabbit," ("rabbits" are covered with wool in this country)—about four dollars; "for a knock down," eight dollars, and for getting drunk and kicking up a row generally, thirteen dollars.

(Letter.) CAMP AT BROOKS STATION, VIRGINIA, }
DECEMBER 5th, 1862. }

"General Wm. B. Franklin's grand division is on the move.

We had ourselves comfortably fixed for the winter. General Solomon Meredith is in command of the brigade."

The next letter shows the temper prevailing in the army in regard to an attack upon the entrenched position of the enemy at Fredericksburgh. It was written to my sister, December 10th, 1862: "The country is clamoring for General Burnside to drive his army to butchery at Fredericksburgh. What we think of the probability of Burnside's attacking Fredericksburgh is best shown in the fact that we are building winter quarters. Not by order, oh, no! No general would dare give such an order, as the country would demand his head immediately. But if General Burnside allows himself to be pushed into a battle here, against the enemy's works, the country will mourn thousands slain, and the Rappahannock will run red with blood expended in fruitless slaughter."

Doctor John C. Hall approached Colonel Bragg the night before Fredericksburgh with the inquiry: "Going to have a battle, Colonel?" "Yes." "We can whip them, can't we?" "Not by a d—d sight over there. After they have killed a few thousand, and ruined as many more, we'll come creeping back, and be lucky if we get back at all." The sequel is this, says Bragg: "When we crept back three days afterward, Dr. Hall said: 'Colonel, I owe you an apology.' For what? said I. 'Well, I must confess I thought from your talk before the battle, that one of our best regiments had got into the hands of a man, whose heart was not in the war. That's what I want to apologize for. I find you knew more about this matter than I did. I watched you when the shells flew. I saw you under fire at your post, and then I went over the bank myself, fully satisfied to leave the cause in your keeping.'"

(Letter.) OPPOSITE FREDERICKSBURGH, DEC. 17th, 1862.

"Another great battle has been fought. Terrible as it was to some, to us it was really almost nothing compared with Antietam. We feel very grateful to have escaped our perils with so wonderfully small a loss. No man in the regiment was killed, and only four were wounded, all of whom we believe will live."

*The Battle of Fredericksburgh.

"On the early morning of December 12th, 1862, in the midst of a dense fog, a heavy bombardment of artillery was opened on the town of Fredericksburgh. A crossing of the Rappahannock in pontoon boats was forced later in the day. Our brigade lay quietly on the heights opposite Fredericksburgh until about four o'clock in the afternoon of this day, when we moved toward a pontoon bridge about a mile below the town. From the Stafford Heights we had a fine view of the broad open plain on the south side of the river, upon which long lines of battle were being formed by our troops. General Franklin's grand division was assigned to duty on the left flank of the army. After crossing the bridge, our march was directed down the south bank of the river for nearly two miles. Our column was in plain view of the rebel artillerists, posted on the hills at about the distance of one mile. Battery after battery opened fire upon us, as we moved along. Owing to the distance and their bad practice, no damage was inflicted. The shell whistled over us, and a panic took place among our colored servants, who were following the regiment. They were loaded down with coffee pots, frying pans and officers' rations, and they fled hastily over the river bank, tumbling from top to bottom, and scattering our officers' provisions. The brigade reached a stone house, known as Bernard's, at dark. We bivouacked that night in a fine grove of trees around the house. The night was very cold. I worked industriously with my darky boy, William, who had returned from under the bank, scraping together a great heap of leaves under a large tree for a bed. Colonel Lysander Cutler came limping along on his wounded leg, and looking wistfully at my comfortable arrangement for the night, requested the favor of sleeping with me. He said I was young and would keep him warm. The privilege was gladly granted. Colonel Cutler was a heroic man to be there at

---

*Report General A. Doubleday,............Page 465, Volume 21, War Records.
   "   "   Solomon Meredith,..... " 475, "   "   "   "
   "   Colonel L. Cutler,................ " 479, "   "   "   "
   "   Colonel L. Fairchild,............ " 478, "   "   "   "
Organization Burnside's Army,........... " 148, "   "   "   "
   "   Lee's Army,................ .... " 1070, "   "   "   "
Casualties "Iron Brigade,".................. " 139, "   "   "   "

all, as he was fifty-five years old, a great sufferer from the effects of his wound, and much subject to sciatic rheumatism. On this night a private soldier whom I will call only by his his nick-name, "Banta," let an old sow out of her pen at the Bernard house, and the animal ran with a "wush" over a young doctor on General Wm. B. Franklin's staff, who was sleeping on the ground near by. "Banta" was seized and tied to a tree, and released only upon the urgent intercession of Colonel Bragg.

"Old Mat," a colored servant to the officers of company "C," had been bred a slave on the Bernard plantation, and when two of our stalwart axe-men commenced cutting down some of the fine old trees in front, striking alternate blows from opposite sides, the darky could not contain himself,—his old love for his home and its surroundings was evidenced in this way: "Boys, what you doin' dar! You brake dat old man's heart if you cut down dat tree! His grandfather planted dat tree!"

About daylight of the 13th, the troops were formed for the advance upon the enemy. The battle field was covered by an exceedingly dense fog and nothing could be seen. The brigade was formed in grand column by regiments, our regiment being second line from the front. Thus we moved through the fog in four lines of battle. The artillery of the enemy was firing vigorously at us and the shot and shell whistled and shrieked around us, but, owing to the fog, none struck in our columns. The divisions of Generals Meade and Gibbon, belonging to Franklin's grand division, soon became heavily engaged. We heard the crash of their musketry, and braced ourselves for the conflict, we believed to be before us. But, after moving a considerable distance and no enemy having been encountered, the fog cleared away and we found ourselves on a great open plain, facing toward the Massaponax river on the extreme left flank of the army. We were without shelter of any kind and during the entire day were exposed to a fire of the rebel artillery, posted on a hill near Hamilton's crossing. The rebel cavalry under General J. E. B. Stuart, formed to charge the left flank of our army. Diagonal squares were formed by the regiments of our brigade to receive a charge of cavalry, while a heavy fire of artillery was directed upon us. Our squares were as formidable as those of Napoleon at the Pyramids. The rebel cavalry wisely refrained from charging upon these squares, and I have always felt that the "Iron Brigade" was in the right place at Fredericksburgh. It was the manifest purpose of General Lee to attack the left flank of our army with this heavy column of cavalry. Late in the afternoon, the enemy opened upon us the concentrated fire of all his artillery on Hamilton's Heights, forty or fifty guns. Our men lay flat upon the ground and took it with wonderful courage and patience. I have never known a more severe trial of nerve upon the battle field, than this hour under that infernal fire. With nothing to do but crouch close to the ground, our eyes were riveted upon the cannon on the hill firing point blank at us. They seemed endowed with life in their tremendous and spiteful energy. There would be a swift outburst of snow white smoke, out of which flashed a tongue of fire, and the cannon would leap backward in its recoil; then followed the thundering report, in the midst of which the missile fired at us would plow deep into the ground, scattering a spray of dirt and bound high over us or burst in the air, sending fragments with a heavy thud into the ground around us. Like fiends who stirred infernal fires, the rebel artillerymen could be seen working around their guns. Several times I saw the awful plowing of the earth in the very midst of our battle lines of men lying upon the ground. There was instant death in the track of it. We were relieved from this fire only by the darkness of the night, and our regiment was moved forward to the Bowling Green road. Hearing this movement, the enemy began firing upon us with canister. We could hear the sharp rattle of shot upon the ground. As the night was very dark, the firing was necessarily at random, and the danger not great, but the sound of the shot striking the ground was frightful.

This night was intensely cold. We formed long lines of officers and men together, who would lie down on their oil cloths, spoon fashion to keep each other warm. We would soon get so cold on the side next to the ground, that we would have to turn over. The command, "About face," would be given, and the whole line of men would roll over together to lie a few moments on the other side. At short intervals the rebel battery would blaze away with its horrible shot rattling on the frozen ground. The shot seemed to fly about one foot above us, so that, while one was freezing as he lay down, he was tortured with the fear of being torn to pieces if he ventured to stand up or walk around. While the regiment was lying here on the Bowling Green road, General Meredith was relieved from the command of the brigade and Colonel Cutler again assigned to that duty.*

Colonel Cutler moved the regiment back to its old position on the left, which we occupied without change until the general retreat of the army. The line of the brigade extended diagonally from the Bowling Green road to the Rappahannock and it constituted the extreme left flank of the army. During both day and night, December 14th and 15th, a sharp fire was kept up between our skirmishers and those of the enemy, and at intervals a brisk cannonade took place. At one time the enemy planted a Whitworth rifled cannon beyond the Massaponax in position to enfilade our lines of battle lying on the plain. They fired solid bolts down about two miles of our line. The whistle of this shot was shrill and peculiar. When it bounded into the air after striking the ground, it looked like a corn cob whirling over and over. One shot struck a knapsack and flung a pack of playing cards many feet into the air, scattering them in all directions. †Capt. R. A. Hardaway of the Confederate army, had charge of this gun.

The twenty-fourth Michigan made a good appearance in this their first engagement. They were exceedingly anxious to go always to the front, and, resting upon our hard earned laurels, we were generously willing that they should do so. But there was little choice of place on that open plain. No soldiers ever faced fire more bravely, and they showed themselves of a fibre worthy to be woven into the woof of the "Iron Brigade." Col. Morrow was equal to all requirements, enterprising, brave, and ambitious, he stepped at once into a circle of the best and most experienced regimental commanders in the Army of the Potomac.

Lieutenant Clayton E. Rogers, of company "I," was serving on the staff of General Doubleday, who commanded our division.

---

*See report of General Abner Doubleday, Page 465, Vol. 21, War Records.
†Vol. xxi. Pages 642 to 644, War Records.

I give from another writer an account of Lieutenant Rogers' ride to save the pickets on the stormy night of our retreat:

"Splendidly mounted, Lieutenant Rogers rushed down to the extreme left with no regard to roads but straight as a bee flies. The left once gained, he moderates his pace and whispers into the ear of each astonished officer, 'Order every man in your command to fall back steadily and silently, gradually close up your ranks and move swiftly to the bridges. Whisper these orders into their ears man by man.' So, quietly but rapidly he speeds down the picket line while the propitious storm howls with unabated fury. One by one our drenched boys are falling back and drawing in together. Silently as shadows the whole picket line steals across the plain. And now as the ranks closed up for rapid marching, 'double double quick' is about the pace.

The wild sweep of the storm sounds ever and anon terribly like the murmur of excited pursuit but no rebel thunder bolt comes darting out of the darkness. No rebel bullet strikes down a single man. Half an hour after the order was whispered into the ear of the soldiers the whole picket line is moving swiftly down the bank and reaches the bridge; only one bridge remains, for the other had been already removed, and at it's head stand the engineers all ready to cast off the pontoons and float them across the river. Another moment and the floating causeway trembles beneath the quiet tread of the rejoicing column and Lieutenant Rogers, grimly smiling, as the last files reach the bridge, moves over also."

General Doubleday says in his official report: "Before daylight Lieutenant Rogers of the sixth Wisconsin Volunteers, acting aide-de-camp, drew them (the pickets) all in successfully to the last man. They owe their safety, in my opinion, to the judgment and coolness of this young officer." Lieut. Colonel Williams of the 19th Indiana is, also, highly commended in the official reports. (See Reports of Doubleday and Cutler.)

The brothers, Clayton E. and Earl M. Rogers were at this time Lieutenants in company "I," under Captain John A. Kellogg. These were three strong men, and their company had become an exceedingly fine body of soldiers. Many of the men of this company were pioneers who had gone west to subdue the wilderness known in the early history of Wisconsin as "Bad Ax" county. Clayton Rogers was squarely built and of a powerful frame. He possessed great energy and he was an indefatigable worker. He seemed to be absolutely fearless in battle. Earl Rogers was tall and slight but firmly knit. He was an especial favorite in the regiment, being familiarly called "Bony" from a fancied resemblance to Napolean Bonaparte. He had an epi-grammatic manner of expression that gave his sayings pertinence and force. "Bony" Rogers was of the finest type of a gallant and dashing soldier, and he was a remarkably keen and quick witted man.

After crossing the pontoon on the night of the 15th, our brigade bivouacked in the woods about two miles from the river. While we were here, the enemy fired upon us with their Whitworth rifled cannon which must have been planted three miles away. Colonel Bragg, Dr. John C. Hall and I were sitting at breakfast in a wall tent, when crash went one of these Whitworth bolts through the limbs of a tree directly over us. This startled us somewhat but we put on the appearance of paying no regard to it. Oh, no, we did not mind it. Another bolt came with its unearthly scream on the line, barely missing the ridge pole of the tent. We had no further appetite for breakfast in that locality, and we scattered without delay.

On December 16th, 1862, Mr. Cutler in Congress at Washing-ton noted in his memorandum book some of the results of the defeat: "This is a day of darkness and peril to the country.—The great trouble is the loss of confidence in the management of the army. Under McClellan nothing was accomplished. Now Burnside fails on the first trial. McClellan's friends chuckle and secretly rejoice over the result.—The Democrats cry peace and compromise, clamor for McClellan, denounce the radicals, do everything to embarrass the government. Judge (W. D.) Kelly of Pennsylvania, made a capital speech in the House to-day, in favor of the Proclamation, which is now being attacked by the Democrats, in hopes the President will not enforce it."

The proclamation was to be in force from and after January 1st, 1863.

(Letter.)   CAMP NEAR BELLE PLAINE, VIRGINIA, }
DECEMBER 25th, 1862. }

"We are now in camp near the Potomac river, at a place called Belle Plaine. We have a fine view of the broad river and are pleasantly located. We are building substantial winter quarters, and hope to be permitted to remain here all winter. I have just returned from Washington city where I enjoyed a pleasant visit with Uncle William (Wm. P. Cutler) and other friends there. I brought out to-day the canned peaches you sent me. They were pronounced magnificent by all of our mess at our Christmas dinner. (The mess referred to consisted of Dr. A. W. Preston, Dr. John C. Hall, Dr. A. D. Andrews, and Major R. R. Dawes. Upon this occasion Lieutenant Colonel E. S. Bragg was an honored guest.)

This army seems to be overburdened with second rate men in high positions, from General Burnside down. Common place and whisky are too much in power for the most hopeful future. This winter is, indeed, the Valley Forge of the war. The Doctors and I have built a very substantial log-house with two rooms and a good floor. Dr. Andrews is ingenious in fixing up little conveniences and Dr. Preston likes to have things nice. Dr. Hall and I get the benefit of their skill. All is quiet on the Rappahannock since the battle.

General James S. Wadsworth is now in command of our division, in place of Gen. Doubleday who is a gallant officer. I saw him at Antietam, where he commanded our division. He was remarkably cool and at the very front of battle, near battery B—at the haystacks. He was with Major Anderson at Fort Sumter. He urged Anderson to open fire upon the rebels to prevent their constructing works. But Anderson was reluctant to open fire at all. Doubleday sighted and fired the first gun of the war at Fort Sumpter."

(Letter.)   CAMP NEAR BELLE PLAINE, JANUARY 10th, 1863.

"I was agreeably astonished by an arrival. An orderly came to my quarters yesterday and said, 'Major, there is a box for you at brigade headquarters.' I found nobody at headquarters who knew whence or how it came and of course nobody had any charges to prefer. There was a mixture of jelly and dried apples but I managed to save everything but a little jelly and a glass bottle of catsup that had been broken. The labels were smeared with a peculiar plaster of jelly and catsup, so that it was impossible for me to make out to whom I am indebted for all of the luxuries. I deciphered enough to learn that several of my friends contributed. If they could know how good such things taste after a dreary routine of hard tack and ham they might appreciate the depth of my gratitude. We had another high old dinner at the Doctors quarters, as our cabin is called."

The regiment was very comfortably quartered in this camp at Belle Plaine. The men had all built substantial log houses and provided themselves with rude but comfortable beds. By long association officers and men of the First Army Corps had become familiarly acquainted with each other. This greatly enlarged our social circle. A large room was constructed, the walls being of logs, near the camp of our regiment for public gatherings and merry making. Here the young officers had periodical meetings, and there were hilarious songs, speeches and other amusing public performances.

*"BURNSIDE'S STICK IN THE MUD."

Tuesday forenoon, January 20th, 1863, the regiment left its comfortable quarters near Belle Plaine and marched toward the Rappahannock river. Nothing worthy of note occurred until about four o'clock in the afternoon, when it began to rain. It was a cold and driving storm which aided by the gale penetrated the clothing and cut the faces of the men as they staggered along. It was with the greatest difficulty that the artillery and wagon trains were dragged through the deep mud. As General Burnside floundered through the mire, a teamster whose mules were hopelessly stuck in the mud, respectfully raising his cap said: "General, the auspicious moment has arrived." (He quoted the expression from the General's well-known order of march.) We bivouacked for that night near Stoneman's switch on the Acquia Creek R. R. The storm raged and howled, and the rain poured in torrents during the night. "Early in the morning," to quote another, "the troops began to wade on to glory." The

---

*Volume XXI, Page 752, War Records.

rain still poured down upon us. The column floundered on until about three o'clock in the afternoon, advancing at the rate of one mile an hour. We bivouacked in lines of battle facing the Rappahannock, having made about five miles during the day. We were in the woods and not far from the river. We remained here during the night and all of Thursday, January, 22nd. Friday morning, the effort to cross the river having been abandoned, we started back for our old camp near Belle Plaine. The mud, the cold winter rain, the wild wind and smoke of camp fires of wet wood, had inflicted discomforts, even miseries, upon our men not easily described, and the ignoble "mud campaign" will ever hold its place in the memories of all the soldiers of the Army of the Potomac as firmly as the hardest fought battles.

When we started to return, numbers of the men reported themselves to the Surgeons as sick and unfit to march. There was but a single ambulance at command, which was soon overloaded. It was a hard decision for our surgeons as to who should ride and who march. As the column was about to move, a man came out of the ranks with his knapsack and accoutrements on and declared himself too sick to march. The Surgeon put his knapsack, gun, and all his load into the ambulance, but could not displace sick men who were already in the overloaded vehicle. The poor fellow succeeded in marching about half the distance to our camp, when he laid down in the mud in a fence corner and died. He had not before been even reported on the sick-list. It was only another form of the casualties which in a thousand ways destroyed human life in the war.

When in the evening we reached our old camp at Belle Plaine, we found our comfortable and elaborately constructed loghouses occupied by the fifty-fifth Ohio regiment. Our men were angry and high words were likely to culminate in a row, when the matter was happily adjusted by an invitation from Colonel John C. Lee, commanding the Ohio regiment, to come in and share the quarters with them. He said the fault was not with them, but with the General who had ordered them to go into our quarters. The greatest hilarity and good feeling prevailed between the two regiments after this and the men of the fifty-fifth, pitying our forlorn condition, gave up the best they had for supper. The next day the fifty-fifth was ordered away. We now remained settled in our winter camp at Belle Plaine. The Surgeons and myself resumed possession of our house. We spent many cheerful hours during the long winter evenings in social chat or deep discussion, and the days were passed in the monotonous routine of camp duty.

On January 26th, W. P. Cutler noted as follows in his journal: "To-day it is said that Burnside has been relieved at his own request, and Hooker put in his place. Our Potomuc army is so far a failure, and seems to be demoralized by the political influences that have been brought to bear upon it. All is confusion and doubt. The President is tripped up by his generals, who seem to have no heart in their work. God alone can guide us through this terrible time of doubt, uncertainty, treachery, imbecility and infidelity. Thaddeus Stevens jokingly remarked that he thought there was a God when he was as young as Kellogg of Michigan, (who said we must remember him) but he had given it up lately."

The complete failure of General Burnside, in the mud campaign, added to his disaster at Fredericksburgh, ended his career as commander of our army and *General Joseph Hooker now succeeded him. General Hooker was much admired in the army. He was grand in his personal appearance and military bearing but his assignment to the command did not restore confidence to the country. At this dark period of the war, grave apprehension existed among members of congress as to the condition for service of the Army of the Potomac. It was alleged that it was demoralized, defective in it's discipline, and that the body of the soldiers was particularly hostile to the policy of Emancipation. It was said that the army was incensed at the Administration because of the removal of General McClellan, and that this feeling was intensified by the flat and dismal failure of Burnside, the weakest army leader the war had yet developed. The papers of the Hon. Wm. P. Cutler, now deceased, show that in secret caucus of members of the 37th Congress this supposed condition of affairs was anxiously discussed by the

*Pages 3 to 5. Vol. xxv. Part II, War Records.

members of the Republican, or war party. With a view of getting my unbiased testimony, Mr. Cutler wrote me several letters, now lost, in which he made inquiry concerning these matters. He concealed appearance of concern on his own part.

(Letter)   CAMP NEAR BELLE PLAINE,
FEBRUARY 15th, 1863.

To HON. WM. P. CUTLER:—"I can speak certainly only of the old brigade. You can depend upon it that it is not demoralized. I am now and have been nearly all winter serving as a member of a general court martial. I see no difference between this winter and last winter in the character or number of offenders brought to trial. There is as high a tone of discipline throughout the army as there ever was when it was under command of General McClellan.

I would get a leave of absence for a few days and go home, but under General Hooker's orders, so long as either of the other field officers are away, I cannot get one. Since Col. Cutler has been wounded, there is little likelihood of our having three officers here or of my getting away."

(Letter)   CAMP NEAR BELLE PLAINE,
FEBRUARY 10th, 1863.

"It is easier for you to say 'get a furlough' than it is for me to get 'a leave of absence.' I think however, as you say, that I have earned that privilege, if any one has. I spent nine months of last year without a single night out of camp. I am not yet a Lieutenant Colonel. The Senate has not confirmed the nomination of Colonel Cutler, which is necessary to make him a Brigadier General. From all I can learn they will do so and I expect soon to be promoted.

There is talk of organizing the old regiments into battalions of four hundred men each. In that event, I would have command of one. I enclose to you to keep carefully a fragment of our Wisconsin State color. This flag has become much tattered and some of the old rags that were trimmed off I have saved. It was this flag that I carried to the battery at the battle of Antietam."

The Northumberland County Raid.*

An expedition under command of Col. Lucius Fairchild and consisting of 236 men of the 2nd and 250 men of the 6th Wisconsin regiments left Belle Plaine, February 12th, 1863, and embarked upon the steamer Alice Price. The steamer proceeded down the Potomac river. The day was fine and a sail upon the broad and beautiful river was much enjoyed by our men, to whom it was a novelty. The troops were in light marching order and carried six days rations. Howard J. Huntington, in a letter published in the Baraboo, Wisconsin, Republic says: "Just at dusk, we were halted by a U. S. gunboat, guarding the Potomac, from whom friend or foe must obtain permission ere they can pass." On Friday morning we turned into Cone river, a small inlet in Northumberland county, Virginia. Here the officers of the steamer caused the lead to be cast for sounding. It was evidently the first time many of our men had ever witnessed this performance and they appear to have been much impressed by it. When the steamer landed, Colonel Fairchild marched to Heathville, several miles in the interior, collecting mules, horses, bacon and forage of all descriptions.

He left me with about two hundred men in command at the steamboat. A foraging party under command of Major John Mansfield of the second Wisconsin, discovered a large amount of bacon stored upon the premises of one Dr. Smith. I rode to the plantation and found a fine establishment, and convincing evidence from the extraordinary amount of stores accumulated that there was smuggling from Maryland. Major Mansfield had very properly seized Dr. Smith† as a prisoner of war. He was diligently transferring the bacon to the steamer. As I rode by a row of negro quarters, an old negro slave with his hat under his arm, his voice tremulous with fear and excitement, said: "Massa, is you the big ossifer?" I asked him what he wanted. He said: "We heard you'uns would make us colored people free. The people want to go with you. Some says we can go and some

---

*Report Col. L. Fairchild,.............Vol. xxv, Part I, Page 16, War Records.
Letter Gen. Joseph Hooker,......... "   "   " II, " 88, "   "

†My notes say Jacob Smith. Colonel Fairchild's report has it James Smith.

says we can't go." I told him that they could go if they chose, and rode off, while the old man profoundly blessed the "good God" who had sent us there. When I got back to the steamer, I found the prisoner, Dr. Smith, an intelligent and gentlemanly man and I had a pleasant conversation with him. Hearing a commotion we went to the outer guard of the boat where a strange scene met our eyes. There were men, women and children, about seventy slaves, gathered upon the beach. They were of every age and size from the old patriarch who had interviewed the "big ossifer," to babes at the breast. They had their worldly all with them. I gave Dr. Smith to understand that his slaves were free under our flag, and could go on the boat if they chose, and that he should not interfere with their decision.

In the evening the troops returned from Heathville and, Colonel Fairchild out-ranking me, all questions were taken out of my hands. Forty-three horses and mules had been captured by Colonel Fairchild. A part of the horses and mules (28) were mounted by men and sent over-land under command of Lieutenant D. B. Daily of the second Wisconsin. In regard to the seventy slaves, I quote from Howard J. Huntington's contemporary account of what took place on Saturday morning: "At this stage of the proceedings, something unusually interesting took place. Dr. Smith had been allowed to go to his house for some purpose, previous to his departure for Washington, and we were a little surprised to see the guard returning with him accompanied by a young lady." This lady* was a remarkably handsome and manifestly superior woman. Her husband was said to be a colonel in the army of General Lee. Huntington continues: "It was the Doctor's sister. She had come to make a plea for her own and her brother's property. They made straightway for the cabin where they found Colonel Fairchild, and immediately the court opened. The appeal was strong and skillful, but the Colonel was equal to the emergency and kept in view the fact that he was acting for the government that sent him. She seemed to understand that we were going to take her slaves, whether they wished to go or not, but the Colonel assured her that he did not ask

---

*I made no contemporary record of this lady's name. In 1870, my recollection was "Mrs. Brockenbrough."

them to leave and that if she could induce them to remain, she might do so." The lady went among the slaves with tears in her eyes and implored them by every recollection and attachment of a life-time, and by the sacred memories of their dead, not to go away, and she painted in high colors the miseries that would be inflicted upon them when they became "free niggers" up north.

The slaves regarded her with affection and the highest respect, and they were deeply moved. But there were friends of freedom and fair play among the men who carried muskets. They warned the negroes that before our steamer was out of sight the chains would be on them, and they would be driven south. They told them that their liberty was here, to take it. I remember the squeaking tenor voice of private Edwin C. Jones, of company "E," asking, "Shall these babes be slaves? Almighty God forbid it!" The negroes all went on the boat. The lady's maid hung weeping upon her, but she went with her people to be free. To quote Huntington again: "The young lady was escorted home safely by the guard, and after burning some boats which had been used for smuggling, we started for home, where we arrived Sunday evening." As the steamer passed up the Potomac, the officers gathered in the cabin and there was a sharp discussion of the policy of emancipation. Some officers expressed themselves opposed to it, while Dr. John C. Hall, in his strong and eloquent support of the proclamation, was quite able to cope with them in the discussion. An interested listener to this debate was our prisoner, Dr. Smith. The impression it made upon him was surprising to Dr. Hall and myself. A few books had been taken from his premises which were gathered up and returned to him. Calling Dr. Hall and myself to the outer guard of the steamer, he presented each of us with a book. My own present was a small copy of Shakespeare. He said it was a token of respect for the "manly position" we had taken in the argument. He condemned in strong terms the views of the officers opposed to us in the discussion and said if they really believed what they argued, he looked upon them as "murderers without cause of his people, and robbers of his property."

Sunday night, in a pouring rain, the regiment disembarked and marched back to our camp. The mud was very deep, and in the pitchy darkness, the men plunged and staggered through it with great difficulty and serious loss of temper. Suddenly some wag sung out with the peculiar intonation of the lead heaver: "Four fathom." Instantly from some other part of the column came out in drawling intonation, "Four and a half." Then another shouted: "Quarter less twain," but when the squeaking voice of orator Jones sang out "No bottom," the regiment raised a universal shout, and waded into camp without further complaint.

(Letter.)   CAMP NEAR BELLE PLAINE, FEB'Y 24th, 1863.

To W. P. Cutler:—"The conscription law passed by the Senate gives great satisfaction to all patriots in the army. It is a move in the right direction to fill up the old regiments. The prime fault of our military system has been to continue to send new organizations into the field, raw and green, while the old regiments, trained and tried, and their officers made fit by experience to lead, are allowed to dwindle down to nothing. I think the country has no cause to distrust the Army of the Potomac. I have conversed with many officers, and all express themselves hopefully and respectfully of our Commander. For myself, I see much that is encouraging in the long continuance of the war. The more I come in contact with Southern ideas and institutions, the more firmly I become convinced that there can be no understanding between us so long as a vestige of their accursed institution of slavery remains. I expect no peace until its destruction is accomplished. Two years of bloody and unsuccessful war have brought our people to a point that they could have reached in no other way. They are willing to give us the men and the money, the power, and I say, do not let us stop short of our destiny, the entire destruction of slavery."

CHAPTER VI.

A Visit to Ohio—A Public Address—Promoted—General James S. Wadsworth—Preparations for the Campaign—General Lysander Cutler—Col. Bragg's Letter with our old Flag—Reviewed by the President—General Joseph Hooker—How to get Ready for a Battle Campaign—Twenty-fourth Michigan Makes a Raid —Campaign Opens—I Entrust Dr. A. W. Preston with Letters to be Mailed Only if I am Killed—Fitz Hugh's Crossing—Experiences at Chancellorsville—Dismal Retreat—Dr. Preston Mails my Letters—Resulting Troubles and Excitements—My Mother Refuses to Take my own Word that I am Killed.

On March 10th, 1863, I started for a visit to Ohio. I had a leave of absence for fifteen days. It was a needed and delightful relaxation from the exacting duties of the military service, and it was my fate to transact business of great importance, as will soon appear. While at Marietta, I received an invitation from prominent citizens to deliver a public address.*

I quote from the published report of this address, such extracts as give the contemporary opinions and observations of a soldier in the Army of the Potomac, upon subjects of importance in its history.

MARIETTA, OHIO, March 16th, 1863.

MAJOR RUFUS R. DAWES. Dear Sir:—"The undersigned, believing it would be gratifying to many of our citizens to hear from you in regard to the war, and the state of the country, would respectfully invite you to address the public of Marietta, at the Court House at such time as you may designate.

> R. E. Harte,
> Thos. W. Ewart,
> E. W. Evans,
> F. A. Wheeler,
> Chas. R. Rhodes,
> Wm. S. Ward,
> Thos. Wickes,
> S. P. Hildreth and others."

Editorial from the Marietta, Ohio, Register.

"Lieutenant Colonel Dawes was on a visit to his home in this city. He accepted an invitation by many citizens, and addressed the people on the evening of March 19th, at the Court House, which was crowded with an audience of ladies and gentlemen The address gave the highest satisfaction and was listened to with almost breathless interest. It was delivered in a forcible and eloquent manner. At the close, the audience voted heartily to request a copy for publication."

" 'Is the Army of the Potomac demoralized?'

I have belonged to the Army of the Potomac during almost
the whole of its existence, and I have no hesitation in saying,
that in point of discipline and general efficiency, the standard is
higher this winter than ever before. I think the men are in
better spirits. There are several reasons for this opinion. They
are now old soldiers, inured to the toils, hardships and dangers
of the service, and skillful in making the best and most of the
comforts with which they are provided. The paymasters have
been around this winter and arrearages have been paid up.
Nothing is more disheartening and demoralizing to the soldier
than to feel that his family is suffering at home for want of his
small and richly earned wages. The men are better provided
this winter with good and healthful rations, than at any time
before in the history of our army. Fresh bread, onions, potatoes,
and fresh beef are regularly furnished in addition to the old
stipend of hard tack and side meat. An encouraging system of
furloughs, as a reward of soldierly conduct, has been instituted.
You can hardly realize with what satisfaction the soldiers hailed
general order number three,* on the subject of furloughs. In
short, the soldiers feel that their personal comfort and happiness,
so far as attainable in the army, is being looked after and they
feel encouraged. Breaches of discipline and soldierly conduct
have been more surely punished this winter than usual. Orders
have been enforced against political discussions, and disrespect-
ful and treasonable language towards the government or superior
officers. Copperhead newspapers no longer monopolize the
circulation among the soldiers, and, by the prompt dismissal of
disaffected and disloyal officers, the army is being purged of the
damnable heresy, that a man can be a friend to the government,
and yet throw every clog in the way of the administration and
the prosecution of the war. No, the Army of the Potomac is
not demoralized nor has it ever been.

'How does the army like General Hooker?'

The army likes General Hooker. They like him because he
is 'fighting Joe Hooker.' They like him because of the onions

---

*Page 11, Volume XXV, Part II, War Records.

and potatoes he has furnished them, and they like him because he is the commander of the Army of the Potomac, and they expect him to lead them to victory. Victory is what we want no matter whether Hooker, Burnside or McClellan leads us. The bones of our comrades and dear friends are bleaching all over the battle grounds of the east. We have marched and we have countermarched, toiled and suffered, without realizing the hopes and expectations of the country. Now we want, and we expect, under 'fighting Joe,' such a triumph as will place us right upon the records of history, and the glory and blessings of which will repay us for the disasters and sufferings of the past. The fighting of an army depends more upon the courage and good faith of subordinate commanders than seems to be understood throughout the country. From such, or many other causes, General Hooker may fail, but, we feel that his heart is in the work, that he is a fighting man and we have great hope.

'How does the army like the Emancipation Proclamation?'

If there remains any one in the army, who does not like the Proclamation, he is careful to keep quiet about it. We are hailed everywhere by the negroes as their deliverers. They all know that 'Massa Linkum' has set them free, and I never saw one not disposed to take advantage of the fact. The negroes will run away if they get a chance, whenever they are assured of their freedom, and that the Proclamation places it beyond the power of any military commander, however disposed, to prevent. Slavery is the chief source of wealth in the South, and the basis of their aristocracy, and my observation is that a blow at slavery hurts more than battalion volleys. It strikes at the vitals. It is foolish to talk about embittering the rebels any more than they are already embittered. We like the Proclamation because it hurts the rebels. We like the Proclamation because it lets the world know what the real issue is. We like the Proclamation because it gives a test of loyalty. As Governor Andrew Johnson, of Tennessee, says: 'If you want to find a traitor North, shake the Emancipation Proclamation or the writ of habeas corpus at him and he will dodge.' We like the Emancipation Proclamation because it is right, and because it is the edict of our Commander in Chief, the President of the United States.

'How does the army like the conscription law?'

They like the conscription law or any other law that promises to fill the shattered ranks of their battalions. As soldiers anxious for military glory, we want our army strengthened, so that we may achieve military success. As patriots, we desire such a force put in the field this summer as may conquer a peace. The old regiments, reduced by battle and disease to mere skeletons, are looking anxiously for recruits. Each has its own record, its own battles inscribed upon its banners, and each wishes to retain its own identity, which it can only do by being filled up.

We hail the act with joy, because it indicates a determination on the part of the Government to meet the crisis. We feel encouraged and feel hopeful. Our soldiers need encouragement as well as reinforcement. They want to feel that they are sustained and sympathized with by their friends at home. Nothing, in my opinion, has been more demoralizing to the Army of the Potomac, than letters from home to soldiers, advising them 'to get out of it, if they can,—that they have done their share,—and that the war is to be hopelessly protracted.' If you wish success, write encouraging letters to your soldiers. Tell them that they are engaged in a good and glorious cause, cheer them on as enthusiastically as you did when they entered the service as volunteers. Tell them that victory will be sure to crown their faithful efforts. Do not fill the ears of your soldiers with tales of troubles and privations at home, caused by their absence. Worse troubles would come to you should rebel arms prevail. Many a poor fellow is brought before the severe tribunal of a court martial, whose greatest crime is listening to and obeying the suggestions of father or mother at home. We like the conscription law because it brings matters to a focus. If it can be enforced, we shall bring an army into the field that must sweep all before it. If it can not be enforced, the future is very hopeless.

'What does the army think of the Copperheads?'

They think that any citizen of the North, who by word, deed, or influence, throws a clog in the way of an earnest and vigorous prosecution of the war, so long as there is a rebel in arms, gives aid and comfort to the enemies of his country and deserves their fate. The army is unanimous in this opinion. The chief hope of traitors South, now is in the co-operation of traitors, North. The war is now being prosecuted on correct principles, and for a great purpose, the re-establishment of republican government throughout the land on the basis of free institutions, and the eternal overthrow of a monied aristocracy based on slavery. The consummation of so grand an enterprise will be a step forward in the history of the world. The world is moving forward, and carrying us with it. We can not resist the progress of events. However prejudices of Copperheads may be galled at the policy of the government or the conduct of the war, all of them of sound judgment are realizing that they have but one salvation, to stand by the government in its peril. Our enemy is too strong, too earnest, too much determined to rule or ruin, to admit of any compromise or half way ground.

The traitors at home who clog the government in its righteous struggle, will go down to history with infamy. If the voice from the army helps to open their eyes to this fact, I beg to add my voice again. We want to fight this war until we conquer a peace on terms that will be honorable, and a peace that can be lasting. The traitor who aids and comforts the enemy by standing in the way of this, has our heartiest contempt as a coward, who dares not maintain his true principles by an honorable appeal to arms.

Do not expect overwhelming victories of us. The rebel army in our front is too skillful in maneuvering, too expert in retiring, too strong in bayonets, to be 'gobbled up or bagged.'

Your Army of the Potomac will go out this spring, purged of disloyalty, the men stronger in health, and better in spirits than ever before. Remember that the same men are there who charged again and again the deadly rifle pits at Fredericksburgh, who swept over the crest at South Mountain, and who struggled on the bloody fields of Antietam. The army is more anxious for victory than you can be, and rest assured that when it is again called to battle it will do its duty."

(Letter.) WASHINGTON, D. C., MARCH 21st, 1863.

"I got through safely to this point in twenty-four hours. I have just met Frank Haskell who comes directly from Madison,

Wisconsin. He says my commission as Lieutenant Colonel has been issued."

(Letter.)   CAMP NEAR BELLE PLAINE, MARCH 25th, 1863.

"I am safe and sound in camp. There are great preparations everywhere in the army for hard campaigning, and doubtless it will be attended by hard fighting. We are to use two pack mules to a regiment, and we are to carry ten days rations. Field officers are required to furnish their own transportation. General Hooker is putting his army in a thorough state of preparation. General Lysander Cutler has been assigned to the command of the second brigade, first division, first army corps. He will be a near neighbor. Captain John A. Kellogg will act as Adjutant General on his staff. The Governor has commissioned Bragg, Colonel; myself, Lieutenant Colonel, and Captain John F. Hauser, Major. The regiment is in fine trim this spring. Indeed, all I said in my speech about the army is strictly true. My visit home was pleasant indeed and I shall go into the new campaign with courage and hope, renewed by the sympathy and encouragement I received at Marietta. I am glad to be on record in that speech. I don't want stock in anything better than that kind of doctrine just now. I have just got back from a visit of compliment to General James S. Wadsworth, our division commander, by the officers of our regiment. Our officers went in a body with the brigade brass band."

General Wadsworth was a strong character, and his command of our division left a deep impression upon its history. The amount of army supplies handled at the Belle Plaine Landing was enormous, and the roads to that point became terrible. In vain were they corduroyed with pine logs, the sharp-hoofed mules would go down in the mud and mire. General Wadsworth got oxen and he kept them "stall fed" near his own headquarters. It was a rare treat to our men to see the old General take a gad and "whisper to the calves." He took great interest in the oxen and was often seen at the landing giving instructions in driving them. He was an intensely practical commander, indefatigable as a worker, and looking closely after details. No commander could do more for the personal comfort of his men.

"All leaves of absence are now cut off. Dr. Andrews is in

great trouble. He was too late to get his leave of absence and has to go into the campaign without the privilege of the long-hoped for visit to his little family. He feels it very deeply. War is in many respects brutalizing, but the fortitude and moral courage to bear up cheerfully and manfully under its discipline is ennobling. Some men, it makes, and more, it ruins.

There is some prospect that I may command the regiment in the coming battles. General Wadsworth talks of calling on Colonel Bragg to assist him on his staff. He has great confidence in Bragg's coolness, courage, and experience in battle."

(Letter.)   CAMP NEAR BELLE PLAINE, APRIL 4th, 1863.

"The indications here of immediate movement are not so strong as they were a few days ago. We can only tell by the straws which way the wind is blowing. Leaves of absence and furloughs are again being granted to a limited extent, and officers' wives are again permitted in camp, from which they had been banished.

General Cutler is doing finely with his new command. Our regiment turns out four hundred men in ranks for duty, and they look fat, healthy, and contented. Everything with us is amicable and friendly. No back-biting nor underplotting. Our two-year old regiment has never yet had an officer court martialed."

A correspondent in the army at this time wrote the following pleasant and very correct description of General Lysander Cutler :

"Commanding the second brigade of this division is General Lysander Cutler, a native of Massachusetts, formerly Colonel of the sixth Wisconsin volunteers, since promoted for skill and bravery in the field. Last evening, in company with my friend, Colonel Livingston, I rode over to take tea with the General. He is an elderly gentleman, spare of frame, with silvery hair, a beard nearly white, and beneath heavy eyebrows of an iron-gray color, are keen, penetrating dark eyes. His step is somewhat uneven, owing to a severe wound received at Gainesville. From behind a somewhat grave and severe aspect, shines out a kindly, even genial manner that wins you at once."

The old blue color of the State of Wisconsin was now returned to the Governor to be exchanged for a new flag which had been provided. That Colonel Bragg was as skillful with the pen as with the sword, may be evidenced by his beautiful and appropriate letter which accompanied our old flag:

HEADQUARTERS SIXTH REGIMENT WISCONSIN VOLUNTEERS, NEAR BELLE PLAINE, VIRGINIA, APRIL 4th, 1863.

His Excellency the Governor of Wisconsin:

SIR—On behalf of the regiment I have the honor to command, I return to the State of Wisconsin the regimental color presented this regiment in the summer of 1861.

We part with it reluctantly, but its condition renders it unserviceable for field service. When we received it, its folds, like our ranks, were ample and full; still emblematical of our condition, we return it, tattered and torn in the shock of battle. Many who have defended it, "sleep the sleep that knows no waking;" they have met a soldier's death; may they live in their country's memory.

The regiment, boasting not of deeds done, or to be done, sends this voiceless witness to be deposited in the archives of our State.

History will tell how Wisconsin honor has been vindicated by her soldiery, and what lessons in Northern courage they have given Southern chivalry.

If the past gives any earnest of the future, the "Iron Brigade" will not be forgotten when Wisconsin makes up her jewels.

I have the honor to be, very respectfully, your obedient servant,

EDWARD S. BRAGG,

Colonel commanding sixth regiment Wisconsin Volunteers.

(Letter.)   CAMP NEAR BELLE PLAINE, APRIL 8th, 1863.

*"Our corps is to be reviewed to-morrow by the President and his wife. I was invited by General Meredith on the day of the cavalry review to go with him to call on the President and Mrs.

---

*Present at this review, by President Lincoln, was a correspondent of the Cincinnati Gazette, who wrote to his paper as follows:

"When the fourth brigade of the first division of the corps, the 'Iron Brigade' as it is sometimes called, marched up, there was a universal manifestation of admiration and applause.

The proud, elastic, but firm military tread, the exact and uniform movement, as if every company and every regiment were moved by one impulse and inspirited by one soul, demonstrated that these men had the spirit of the true soldier. 'This,' remarked General Hooker to the President, 'is the famous fourth brigade.' 'Yes,' rejoined the President, 'it is

Lincoln, but I did not go. Colonel Bragg and Dr. Hall went, and their caustic comments are highly amusing. General Joseph Hooker is actually the finest looking man in the Army of the Potomac.

In our Spring election, the regiment gave one hundred and eighty-four Republican majority and the three Wisconsin regiments something over six hundred."

The Apollo like presence of General Hooker, his self-confident, even vain glorious manner, his haughty criticism of others and his sublime courage at the battle front have combined to make impressions upon the public judgment that obscure his most valuable traits of character and his best qualities as a commander. Poetry has placed his glory above the clouds of Lookout Mountain. But history is more likely to dwell upon the fact that he received the Army of the Potomac, rent by internal jealousies, discontented, discouraged and humiliated under the stigma of defeat. With indefatigable zeal he addressed himself to the task of its re-organization and, if I may so expresss it, re-inspiration. It was for Hooker to arouse the drooping spirits of the grand army and he accomplished the task. He had the true Napoleonic idea of the power of an "Esprit de Corps." It was he who first devised the beautiful, and to the soldiers inspiring system of corps badges. Forever the trefoil of the second corps, the crosses of the fifth and sixth corps, the arrow, the cartridge box with forty rounds, and the other corps badges of the war, will be the almost worshipped symbols of a glorious service.

(Letter—To a new correspondent.) Camp near Belle Plaine, April 13th, 1863.

"We are busy getting ready for the grand movement, which must begin soon. We may start to-morrow or next day. Let

---

commanded by the only Quaker General I have in the army.' (General Meredith being by birth and early education, a Quaker.")

Captain James Stewart of battery "B," has written of this review:

"After I had passed in review, riding 'Tartar,' I was sent for, to allow the President to look at the horse's wound. As soon as Mr. Lincoln saw it, he said to the general officers about him: 'This reminds me of a tale!' which he proceeded to relate to their great amusement. But his little son, 'Tad,' mounted on a pony, followed me and insisted on trading horses. I told him I could not do that, but he persisted in telling me that his papa was the President, and would give me any horse I wanted in trade for 'Tartar.' I had a hard time in getting away from the little fellow."

J. Hooker
Maj Genl

S Meredith

BREVET MAJ GEN S MEREDITH

me tell you how we get ready for a campaign. First ten days rations must be provided for our regimental headquarters mess. So the darkies are posted off to the commissary's to buy two hams, twenty-five pounds of hard tack, one dollar's worth of coffee, and fifty cents' worth of tea; to the sutlers for a can of prepared milk and five pounds of soda crackers, and rations are provided, except, that we load down the darkies when we start, with soft bread. This truck is loaded upon our 'transportation,' which is a mule with an irresistible tendency to lie down when he gets tired of marching. Next we procure a wedge tent and four or five blankets, then an oil cloth and an extra pair of boots for each, then two skillfully packed bundles of woolen shirts, and finally a bag of corn. All of this, when we march, adorns the back of our transportation mule. The valises are neatly packed up to be left in the wagon. Papers are arranged, wills made, pistols cleaned, tourniquets* carefully stored away in a safe pocket, debts paid up, and the mess is ready to march. If in addition to this, you have to get the regiment ready, your work is not done. First your ten days rations for the men must be looked after. (General Hooker's marching orders required ten days rations to be carried on the persons of the men.) Next, your supply of ammunition, and the condition of the arms, next is your supply of food and clothing, and finally, your weak squad must be weeded out and sent off. Your officers must be reminded of their duties, and the existing orders regulating a march refreshed in their minds. Your knapsacks must be thoroughly inspected and all superfluous articles, such as bibles and playing cards, must be thrown away.

Our regiment goes out in fine condition this spring, as does the whole army. We are not so strong in bayonets, but our four hundred men know how to fight. Orders have been issued from the War Department for the consolidation of regiments. We are yet too large to come within the order. But, by its terms, the Colonel would be mustered out and I would be left in command. To command the old sixth with her glorious record; would fully satisfy the full measure of my own military ambition.

---

*An instrument to stop the flow of blood.

Those 'great triumphs' to which you refer, were too closely contested to be inspiring, considering the infamous doctrines of the opposition. God grant that our army may strike a great blow for the cause, for this is the darkest hour of our struggle."

*On April 20th to 23rd, the twenty-fourth Michigan under Colonel Henry A. Morrow, made a raid upon the right flank of General Lee's army at Port Royal. They crossed the Rappahannock river in boats. This affair won for Colonel Morrow much commendation, and established his reputation as an efficient and enterprising commander.

On the evening of April 28th, the day we marched, believing myself on the eve of personal risk in battle, I placed some letters I had received, in an envelope which I carefully sealed and addressed to the lady who sent them. I then entrusted the package to Dr. A. W. Preston, charging him to return it to me unless I was killed in the impending battle, in which event he must put it in the mail. He faithfully promised to do this.

(Journal.)   TUESDAY, APRIL 28th, 1863.

Ordered to march at twelve o'clock, noon. Rumor says the eleventh and twelfth corps moved yesterday, and the booming

---

*Volume XXV, Part I, Page 1113, War Records.
    "   "   " II,   "   507,   "   "
    "   " · "   "   "   511,   "   "

A rebel will was found by a soldier of the twenty-fourth Michigan infantry, in the little village of Port Royal.

"In the name of God, Amen, I, John Cooper, of the County of Carolina, and State of Virginia, being of sound mind and health, and of disposing memory, do make this my last will and testament, hereby revoking all others heretofore made. *Imprimis*: It is my will that after my funeral expenses and just debts have been paid, all my estate, both real and personal, be vested forever in my beloved daughter, Nancy, begotten of my beloved wife, Charlotte, and such other children as may be born during our coverture, to be equally divided between my said daughter Nancy and my other children as aforesaid, reserving, however, a support to my wife Charlotte, out of my estate during her widowhood.

Secondly, I do hereby *emancipate and set free* my beloved wife Charlotte and my daughter Nancy, and such other children as may be begotten on the body of my wife Charlotte.

In testimony whereof, I have hereunto set my hand and affixed my seal, this 26th day of March, in the year of our Lord, one thousand eight hundred and fifty-four.

                                                JOHN COOPER.
Signed, sealed, acknowledged, published and delivered in our joint presence.   STAFFORD H. PARKER.
                                                WILLIAM CATLUT."

of cannon proclaims that somebody is stirring. I finish my journal to-night, uncomfortably located in the oak brush, some-where near the Rappahannock river. About noon to-day, Lieut. Clayton Rogers, who is acting on General Wadsworth's staff, came galloping down with an order for the sixth and seventh Wisconsin to move out to quell a mutiny. The mutiny was a small affair of a few two years men of the 24th New York, who claimed that their time had expired. A few pointed remarks by General Wadsworth, rendered pungent by the presence of our regiment with loaded muskets, brought them to their senses and they quietly fell in.

It is said that our regiment and the twenty-fourth Michigan have been selected by General Wadsworth to cross the river in pontoon boats to protect the laying of the pontoons."

(Letter.)   In Line of Battle below Fredericksburgh,
                        May 1st, 1863.

"We left our old camp near Belle Plaine at noon of the 28th and bivouacked that night near the river four miles below Fred-ericksburgh. About midnight we marched again, hoping to surprise the enemy by rushing two regiments over in pontoon boats, capturing the rifle pits along the opposite bank and thus clearing the way for a pontoon bridge. For this perilous duty, our regiment and the twenty-fourth Michigan were selected. The troops moved slowly in the fog, rain and darkness, and so much noise was made by the mules in the pontoon train, that little hope remained of surprising the enemy. About daylight when the engineer corps had launched only half of their boats into the river, they were opened upon by the musketry of the enemy posted in rifle pits beyond the river. A panic ensued in the pontoon train. There was a grand skedaddle of mules with lumbering pontoon boats, negroes and extra-duty men. We cleared the track and let them go by us in their frantic and ludicrous flight. We had completely failed to surprise the enemy. A fog hung over the river and as soon as it cleared away, an order came from General Wadsworth to Colonel Bragg to move the regiment to the bank of the river and fire across at the enemy. We double quicked forward in line, threw ourselves flat upon the ground and commenced firing but we could gain nothing. The rebels were on higher ground and in rifle pits and their fire was more destructive to us than ours could be to them. The twenty-fourth Michigan and fourteenth Brooklyn were also sent to the river bank. But the three regiments were soon moved back into a ravine. It now seemed that the Rappahannock must be reddened with our blood if the crossing was to be forced. The river was about two hundred yards wide and very deep and the banks were high and steep. Pontoon boats enough to carry about four hundred men were lying in the water at a landing place called Fitz Hugh's crossing or Pollock's Mill, with one end caught upon the shore and oars to row the boats were lying in the bottom of them. Of course, they were directly under the enemy's fire. About nine o'clock, the sixth Wisconsin and twenty-fourth Michigan regiments were ordered to cross the river in these boats and attack the rifle pits. I confess that a shrinking from the proffered glory came over us. To be shot like sheep in a huddle and drowned in the Rappahannock appeared to be the certain fate of all if we failed and of some if we succeeded. The regiment was ordered into line at once to prepare for the rush. Knapsacks were unslung and piled upon the ground. We selected men from each company who were to row the boats and instructed them in their duty. Colonel Bragg briefly and plainly stated to the regiment what was expected of them and the plan for the execution of the movement. The plan was simple and fully comprehended by the men. A line of troops was to be moved forward to the edge of the river bank who would fire over our heads at the enemy while we crossed the river in the boats. Batteries of artillery were planted on the hills back of the plain, which would also fire upon the enemy.* These dispositions were soon made and we moved out upon the plain. We had to pass over an open field and down a sloping bank to reach the boats,

---

*Official Reports of Fitz Hugh's Crossing may be found in Vol. XXV, Part I, War Records:
Major General John F. Reynolds, Pages..................................253 and 256.
Brigadier General J. S. Wadsworth, Page..262.
Colonel E. S. Bragg, Page..271.
Colonel W. W. Robinson, Page ....273.
Brigadier General Solomon Meredith...267.
  Losses in the sixth Wisconsin regiment at Fitz Hugh's Crossing were 3 killed, 13 wounded; 90 prisoners were captured.

and during this time, we received the fire of the enemy. When our battle line appeared, the rebels turned their fire upon us. 'Now for it, boys. By the right of companies to the front. Run, march,' came in sharp, jerky emphasis from Colonel Bragg. The evolution was performed like clock-work, and the companies moved for the boats at the top of their speed.

The men plunged into the boats and threw themselves upon the bottom of them as they had been instructed. Here was our only mistake; the men were on the oars. "Whiz" came the bullets. To halt or flinch in the deadly storm was disgrace if not death. Nervous and quick orders were given something like this: "Heave off your boats! Up with the oars!" Here fifteen of our men were shot. Once clear of the shore, the oars-men worked like heroes and our regiments along the river bank and the batteries opened fire upon the rebels. When we got across the river, we jumped into the mud and water, waist deep, waded ashore, crawled and scrambled up the bank, laying hold of the bushes. Very few shots were fired before the rebels were throwing down their arms or running over the plain. Our men were greatly excited, but we gathered them together and moved in line of battle to a brick house."

(Journal.)   SATURDAY, MAY 2nd, 1863.

"The enemy shelled us for two hours this morning. Nobody hurt in our regiment. The division was safely withdrawn from the south side of the river. The rebels did not interfere with the movement. We marched rapidly up the river. The sun was intensely hot. We camped in the woods at ten P. M."

About five P. M. of this memorable day, General Stonewall Jackson swept down upon and stampeded the eleventh corps of our army. Dr. A. W. Preston of our regiment was on hospital duty in that part of the field. At some time during the panic, he says, he gave the letter I had entrusted to him to a mail carrier. Two days afterward, he discovered his mistake, and greatly chagrined, having forgotten if he ever knew, to whom the letter was addressed, he wrote to my sister, Miss Lucy Dawes, assuring her that I was alive and well.

(Journal.)   SUNDAY, MAY 3rd, 1863.

"Marched to the battle field of Chancellorsville at two o'clock in the morning. Crossed the river at Banks Ford and took position on the battle field in the second line. The musketry fire in the woods near our left, was for an hour to-day, as heavy and incessant as I ever heard. Impossible to know how things are going. It seems certain that the battle is indecisive. Many rumors are flying around, the gravest one that Hooker is wounded and Couch in command of the army. Our corps is in the second line, supporting the fifth corps, which is in rifle pits. Not a single shot or shell has come dangerously near us to-day."

(Journal.)   MONDAY, MAY 4th, 1863.

"Hot firing on the picket line in the night. An attack by the enemy expected, and men forbidden to take off their blankets."

This seems to have been a cruel and unnecessary order. The blankets were in a roll over the shoulder and it is difficult to imagine what harm could come from the use of them. Colonel Bragg and I did not use our own blankets because of this order, feeling that we ought to share the hardships with the men. No fires were allowed. Colonel Bragg and I lay down together on the same oil cloth. I remember distinctly that Bragg wore his spurs, and that he kicked in his sleep.

(Journal.) "Ordered under arms at ten o'clock this forenoon. Twenty-fourth Michigan has just moved to the right, and our regiment is to support them in case of a fight. At half past eleven nothing has come of it. Just got permission to get dinner. Boys are all cooking coffee. Drizzling rain at intervals this afternoon. At five P. M. there was a very sharp fight at the same place on our left. At this writing, six P. M., there is a heavy cannonading in the direction of Fredericksburgh. (General Sedgwick's battle at Salem Church.) Ten P. M., heavy volleys of musketry on our left and quite a sharp fusilade on our right. Constant alarms until midnight. The last report is that the rebels were the attacking party last evening at five o'clock and that they were driven back with a loss of six hundred men. Slept a troubled, dreamy sleep."

(Journal.)   TUESDAY, MAY 5th, 1863.

"Foggy this morning. At this writing, eight A. M., scattering musketry fire, a mile away to our left. This developed into a heavy fight of about twenty minutes duration. The sun will be very hot to-day. Heavy whisky rations being dealt out to the men. Reports say, the rebels charging our works come out to a certain point unmolested, and then set up a fiendish yell and rush forward upon our rifle pits, as yet, only to be driven back by the musketry of our men, and the canister of the batteries. The slaughter must be terrible. Rumor says this morning, that General Sedgwick has been driven from the heights of Fredericksburgh. There was heavy fighting somewhere down there all night. Whisky enough was sent here to make the whole regiment dead drunk.

Eleven o'clock A. M.—Orders are: 'Be ready to move at once to the right.' It is said that we are to lead in an attack. It is always so. Guess our time has come. False alarm. Some mistake by one of the nine-months Colonels on the right. Lie down again and try to kill time. Very hot. Orders to be under arms at sunset. Very heavy thunder storm at five P. M. Miserable situation,—Colonel Bragg and I and *Huntington, all crouched under one oil cloth in the driving rain. At dark, rumor has come of a general retreat. Mules are packed and sent to the rear. The rain continues pouring down, and our condition that of unmitigated discomfort. Picket firing the entire night."

(Journal.)   WEDNESDAY, MAY 6th, 1863.

"About three o'clock this morning the infantry began to move for the rear. Our brigade† moved the last of our corps at 3:30 A. M. Mud very deep and a drizzling rain. At five A. M., we reached the pontoon bridge at United States Ford. Forty thousand men are not yet over. Our division formed in line of battle to protect the passage of the troops. Crossed at eight A. M., unmolested. Soaking rain and chilly. One hundred thousand miserable and discouraged men are wading through this terrible mud and rain. We cannot understand it in any other way than as a great disaster. Feel sick and dispirited myself. We trudged along slowly through mud and rain until two P. M. Camped in a pine jungle. Pitched wedge tent. Found our blankets wet and I am sick."

---

*Lieutenant Howard J. Huntington was Acting Adjutant.

†The "Iron Brigade" was often selected as the rear guard, upon the retreats of our army.

(Journal.)   THURSDAY, MAY 7th, 1863.

"Marched to-day. Camped near White Oak Church. Sick all day. Threatened with fever."

(Journal.)   FRIDAY, MAY 8th, 1863.

"In camp to-day. Too sick to write a journal."

Here it will be necessary, for a proper appreciation of our real experience in the war, to follow the letters mailed by Dr. Preston. They went directly to their destination.

Miss Mary B. Gates, Marietta, Ohio, was the address upon them. This lady had completed her education at Ipswich Seminary, in Massachusetts, and I had met her at her home in Marietta. Differences of opinion upon the merits of General McClellan and indeed upon all other subjects had been happily reconciled. She was twenty years of age, and of her charming qualities of mind and person it is not for my partial pen to write. She had received two letters from myself since the campaign had opened and she was anxious for further information from the front. On the early morning of May sixth, she hastened to the Post Office. She found a letter. No suspicion of harm to me was aroused, however, as the letter was plainly directed in my own hand. The first sentences she read can be given here:

"We are advancing upon the enemy. I doubt not that we must have a bloody battle. I leave this package where I have perfect confidence it will be sent to you in case I am killed, and only in that event."

The scenes that ensued are not the business of the public, and will not be described. My mother, who with her two sons had been much under fire, said she would "take Rufus' word for anything but the fact that he was killed." This was consoling, but still not until four days afterward was there a relief from painful apprehension, when my sister received the following epistle from the army:

> HEADQUARTERS FOURTH BRIGADE, }
> FIRST DIVISION, FIRST ARMY CORPS, }
> MAY 4th, 1863. }

MISS LUCY DAWES, MARIETTA, OHIO.

My dear Madam:—Your brother, Lieutenant Colonel Dawes of the sixth Wisconsin Volunteers, is *alive* and *well*.

Why I send you this letter is, the Colonel left with me a letter addressed to you, to be sent you in case he should fall in the then coming engagement,—and although he came out safe, and is now in good health, yet I have either lost the letter with some other papers or sent it to you by accident when mailing other letters for the North. In great haste. I am very respectfully your obedient servant,

A. W. PRESTON, Surgeon-in-Chief, Fourth Brigade.

Chapter VII.

(Letter to M. B. G.) CAMP NEAR WHITE OAK CHURCH,
MAY 18th, 1863.

"The two years and nine months troops are by reason of the expiration of their enlistment, leaving us every day. Our army is being materially weakened, and so far as I know, is getting small reinforcement. We have had several alarms of an advance by the enemy, but I apprehend nothing of the kind. He is too discreet. I shall not be surprised if matters on the Rappahannock remain for a time '*in statu quo.*'

The reason General Hooker recrossed the river was because he was outgeneraled and defeated,—a humiliating confession, I own, but I believe true.

I have taken up my work again. I have tried twenty-three cases and made a finding and record in each this forenoon. Is not that summary justice? This is business which accumulated while I was sick. I fined one incorrigible little scamp for paddling across the Rappahannock on a slab and trading coffee to the rebel pickets for whisky, with which he made half of our men on picket drunk.

The weather is fine and we are beautifully located in a grove near the White Oak Church. The church is mythical, but it is a pleasant name to mark a pleasant locality. Drilling, parading, reviewing and court martialing go on again as usual before the battle."

(Letter to M. B. G.) Camp near White Oak Church, ⎱
                                    May 21st, 1863. ⎰

"We are under orders to march at daylight with three days' rations and without knapsacks. It is now three o'clock A. M. *Colonel Henry A. Morrow, of the twenty-fourth Michigan, commands the expedition. The equipment of the troops indicates a reconnoitering affair of some kind."

This expedition was composed of one thousand two hundred men, (19th Indiana, 2nd and 6th Wisconsin) and it was ordered to march down the Northern Neck to the relief of our cavalry, and for a general reconnoisance. The weather was hot, and as I had not fully recovered from my sickness, I was scarcely able to endure the march. Colonel Morrow stationed me in command of one hundred and sixty men at a cross roads near King George Court House, while the main body marched on down the Neck. The object in stationing this force was to guard the line of retreat. I constructed an earth work at the cross roads and remained in position until the return of the troops, five days afterward.

My situation in the enemy's country made it necessary to keep my small force constantly in hand. The chicken-hungry boys were in a land replete with pigs and poultry. I established a guard around my post, and still the men slipped out. Captain Hart, of the nineteenth Indiana, had borrowed my horse and ridden off, probably to buy a chicken. Finally, exasperated at the depletion of my force, I sent out a patrol with strict orders to arrest every man or officer found. Soon I heard a shout: "The patrol has caught the Colonel!" And, there was my well known old mare coming in, with Captain Hart mounted on her, under the bayonets of the patrol-guard. Of course, the Captain had a pass, but my brash order to the patrol was considered to have countermanded it.

Captain Charles H. Ford, recently promoted to the command of company "H," is highly commended by Colonel Morrow, for quickly putting up a bridge on this expedition. Charley Ford was over six feet tall, and his soldierly bearing was very fine. He was acting aide on the staff of General Wadsworth. General

---

*See Volume XXV, Part I, Page 1112, War Records, for complete and interesting report of Colonel Henry A. Morrow.

Wadsworth would have none but efficient men around him. It is patent that he considered the sixth Wisconsin a good place to find such men. Two of our officers (Captain Ford and Lieutenant C. E. Rogers) were on his staff.

A serious loss befell our regimental headquarters mess on this expedition. Colonel Bragg's fiery and untamed white war-horse which he rode at Gainesville, had become afflicted with a hoof disease which was prevalent in the army. The horse had been reduced to the menial service of a pack mule. On his back was our complete and elaborate equipment of cooking utensils, tableware and provisions. When crossing a bridge, whether from fright, or a desire to commit suicide by drowning, or to get rid of the degrading burdens on his back, the horse deliberately jumped into the deep water beneath and sank at once below the surface. After an astonishingly long interval he reappeared, blowing water like a whale, but every vestige of our property was at the bottom of the stream.

(Letter to M. B. G.)   CAMP NEAR WHITE OAK CHURCH, }
MAY 27th, 1863. }

"Our corps received marching orders to-day, but we are not off yet, and as it is evening, I presume we shall not go. It is probable that the occasion of these orders was apprehension of an attack by the enemy. Our army is being daily weakened by troops going home.

Under such circumstances, I do not look for offensive operations by this army unless the enemy withdraws heavily to the assistance of Vicksburg. Indeed, an attack by the enemy upon this army is not wholly improbable. Our news from Vicksburg is cheering to-night, but our people are so sanguine and the habit of counting chickens before they are hatched is so firmly established, that we can not tell how much of it to believe. The paymaster has come to-day, making our boys happy. If we are going to march under our orders, I do not want my pay. Last December, during the battle of Fredericksburgh, I had to leave a large sum of money with one of our surgeons.

Our Major, John F. Hauser, is a character. He is a German, a soldier by profession, forty-five years of age and with a commanding figure. He has a voice like a trumpet. Over twenty years ago he was at Thun, in Switzerland, at a military school. Louis Napoleon was there, and the Major says he knew him well. To use the Major's own language : 'I spree mit him many time.' He says he served as lieutenant on the staff of General Garibaldi. He seems to have entertained a high respect, almost reverence for Garibaldi."

(Letter to M. B. G.)   CAMP NEAR WHITE OAK CHURCH, }
                                            MAY 30th, 1863.   }

"I am going this morning for two days duty as field officer of the day, in command of our division picket. All here now think that General Lee is going to attack this army. If the rebels are to lose Vicksburg, I do not see why it is not possible that he should make a desperate push here to neutralize the great disaster west. Well, this most unfortunate Army of the Potomac is yet a power, and when thrown upon its defense can not be defeated by the whole force of the rebellion. I am not sure that an offensive campaign by the enemy, is not to be hoped for by the country. Perhaps the 'Johnnies' will come to my picket line. I have eight hundred men, and can begin a pretty good battle. I will try to bother them some before they get their pontoons down.

We had a review of the first army corps yesterday. It is running down in numbers. We have great rumors about our destiny this summer. Some say we are going to Baltimore to relieve the eighth army corps, so long on duty in that vicinity. That would be grand. But my opinion is, that the veterans of the old first army corps, renowned on so many bloody fields for unflinching valor, like the old guard of Napoleon, will be considered as 'too good lookers on' to be spared from the battle front."

(Letter to M. B. G.)   MAY 31st, 1863.

"I have been on picket for two days and for a wonder had good weather throughout my tour. This is a laborious duty. An officer is held oppressively responsible for the vigilance and good conduct of his pickets. He is required to visit his line four times a day and once at night to inspect it. This involves thirty-two miles ride. I found one poor fellow asleep on duty. What do you think his punishment would be if brought to trial by his Colonel?—'Shot to death with musketry.' I voted that sentence four times last winter when serving on general court martial, but thanks to our kind-hearted 'Father Abraham,' none were executed, for which I feel very thankful.

Our picket line runs along the edge of the bank of the Rappahannock river. The rebels on the opposite bank are about two hundred yards away. There is no hostility and the men sit dozing and staring at each other, and when there are no officers about, they exchange papers and communicate with each other in as friendly a manner as if there was no cause for enmity. Riding along this bank with the red sash over my shoulder, the insignia of the officer of the day, the rebel pickets would sometimes aim their guns at me just to see how nicely they could pop me over. Not enjoying this harmless sport, it generally occurred to me, when I saw a fellow aiming at me, that I had urgent business somewhere else, and I would immediately gallop away to attend to it.

Colonel Bragg is very sick. The Major's ugly little horse kicked him a few days ago on the foot, which is also now a serious affair. He is trying to stay here in his tent, but he will probably be obliged to go to the hospital.

Our brigade is now designated as the first brigade, first division, first army corps; and the sixth Wisconsin is the first battalion. This makes us by designation, the first regiment in the volunteer army of the United States. As a brigade, we are one of the oldest in the army, and deserve the title. There is great dearth of news. All is very quiet on the Rappahannock. I shall be in command of the regiment until the Colonel gets well, which may not be very soon."

(Letter to M. B. G.)　　　Camp near White Oak Church,
　　　　　　　　　　　　　　June 4th, 1863.

"The whole corps has orders to march at daylight. This is something unexpected. The only guess I can give is that the enemy is trying to cross the river to move on our right flank. I have plenty of work to get my family ready to move. Reveille is sounding all through the corps.

The artillery bugles sound beautifully in the morning air. May be in a day or two we will hear the familiar roar of the big guns. Of course I will write again upon the very first opportunity. But remember I am a poor soldier campaigning, and make due allowance for short and unsatisfactory letters."

(Letter to M. B. G.)   JUNE 5th, 1863.

"We were sold again. After turning out at midnight and packing our traps, and preparing for a battle which somebody seemed to think impending, our orders were countermanded. So we have rebuilt our canvas cities and settled down again. The fact is, somebody is very much exercised lest the terrible Lee may do something dangerous. Three times now of late this army has been turned out of house and home to lie sweltering in the sun, only to have its marching orders countermanded. The boys have long ago learned to take such things philosophically. They tear down and build up cheerfully with the shrewd observation, that 'it is only Johnny Reb fooling the balloon again.' If we are to be all summer at the mercy of the balloon, I fear you will get no other letters than those written on the eve of an active campaign. Colonel Bragg is still quite ill. The command of the regiment devolves upon me. He cannot participate in our next campaign. He is wholly unfit for duty in the field.

Later—Our army is most of it on the march. The rebel army moved last night which explains it."

The whole of the rebel army had not moved. The corps commanded by General A. P. Hill still remained at Fredericksburgh.

(Letter.)   FRIDAY EVENING, 10 P. M.

"We march at daylight and it is the general belief that we will cross the Rappahannock and attack the enemy here. I shall command the regiment."

(Letter to M. B. G.)   JUNE 6th, 1863.

"Both armies are moving. Something important is impending. The Sixth corps has crossed the river and occupied the plain below Fredericksburgh, and every few moments comes the boom of their cannon. This, however, may be a feint to hold the enemy here. All of the enemy's tents over the river have disappeared. We are now lying in line of battle supporting the sixth corps, which is on the other side of the river. I think it likely, however, that we may yet take the double quick in the direction of Bull Run. There is considerable cannonading over the river but no serious engagement."

This excessive readiness inflicted great discomfort upon the troops. The men would lie hour after hour on the ground in the hot sun with everything packed for marching. As we lay thus, Sam, an extraordinarily homely looking darky of broad African type, who worked for Colonel Bragg, fell sound asleep in the dust of the road under the hot sun. Ed. Brooks, our Adjutant, who loved practical jokes, took his canteen and poured water into the large cavity of Sam's ear. Sam was aroused indeed. He rose up, shook his head like an angry lion, and seized a soldier's musket from the gun stacks. Only Brooks' agility saved him from being thrust through by a bayonet. It was with difficulty and a dollar that Sam was appeased. No water was afterward poured in his ear.

Extracts from a daily journal kept by Dr. John C. Hall:

THURSDAY, JUNE 4th, 1863, 8 A. M.

"We are sitting like Marius among the ruins, not of a splendid city but of our encampments, and we have been since daylight. Our tents are taken down and packed, our blankets are rolled, our valises filled, breakfast eaten, mules and darkies loaded, and we are 'ready to march.' But we lack orders to 'fall in' and march. The sun looks red and hot. * * * 12 M., were ordered to 're-pitch our tents'"

FRIDAY, JUNE 5TH, 1863.

"* * * We were ordered to be packed up ready to march at 5½ in the morning."

SATURDAY, JUNE 6th, 1863, 10½ A. M.

"Played the same game we did two days ago. Nearly all night spent in getting ready to march at daylight, but here we still remain in that disagreeable state of uncertainty that a soldier so often experiences. Orders have just come to pitch tents 'if desirable' but we may expect to move at any time. * * In the army we don't know anything but what we see. We rely on guessing. I will make a guess: Johnny Reb has fooled 'fighting Joe.' Has Johnny hid? Has he evacuated? Where is he? Joe can't say and the balloon is nonplused and in disgrace."

General Hooker's reconnoitering balloon could be constantly seen in the air, and it was a subject of much humorous speculation.

149

(Letter to M. B. G.)   Camp near White Oak Church, }
Sunday Evening, June 7th, 1863. }

"We are again in camp to-night after roasting in line of battle for two days in the hot sun. Our movements are mysterious. There are three brigades of the sixth corps on the plateau below Fredericksburgh and they have been there for two days skirmishing with the enemy. But they do not advance an inch beyond the old line of demarkation, the Bowling Green Road. The rebel army is manifestly preparing for some movement. General Hooker, not feeling strong enough to attack them seems to be trying to keep them here by shaking his fist at them. If he becomes satisfied that they have withdrawn heavily to reinforce their armies elsewhere, he may attack them, but the inevitable apron string will draw us back to old Bull Run if the enemy appears on our right flank. Let them go to Maryland. A small force can hold the entrenchments in front of Washington while the Army of the Potomac, threatening their communications, would bring them to battle or cause them to retreat with the same certainty that gravitation brings down a building with the underpinning knocked out. Let the rebel army go into Maryland, the farther the better, and if we can not defeat them with that advantage, we can never crush the rebellion. They cannot in my judgment go too far into Pennsylvania with the army of the Potomac between them and their base. The rich Pennsylvania Dutchmen can well be allowed to suffer for one year a loss of their cattle, hogs and crops to get the rebel army of Virginia, the right arm of the rebellion, in such a trap. When I had finished that sentence, my candle fell down and rolled over this sheet of paper which accounts for its wretchedly bad appearance and for my failure to complete the crushing of the rebellion. Colonel Bragg has gone to Washington. His foot is very sore and bad. He may go to Wisconsin before returning, and I am likely to be in command of the regiment for some time."

(Letter to M. B. G.)   Camp near White Oak Church, }
June 10th, 1863. }

"It is a continued series of alarms, orders and counter-orders here. Both armies are maneuvering and threatening. Our troops on the south side of the river are securely entrenched and can not be driven back without a bloody struggle. The rebels, however, show no serious disposition to attack them. Meanwhile we are in camp, parading and drilling again as usual. I think we have the cleanest and healthiest regiment in the first army corps. There are only two men sick, and they are marked for light duty.

I have just had to leave my writing to attend to an unpleasant duty. This was the order I received: 'You will detail from your regiment two lieutenants and twenty wholly reliable men, to report at once to the Provost Marshal of the first division, to execute the sentence of death, etc.' The victim's name is John P. Woods of the nineteenth Indiana regiment. His crime was, 'desertion and misbehavior in presence of the enemy.' He will be shot next Friday. The men, I assure you, dislike to be called upon for such duty. The miserable man is seated upon his coffin a few rods in front of a platoon of men. All fire at the dropping of a white handkerchief, each, in mercy, aiming at a vital part and each hoping that his is the blank cartridge with which one musket is charged. Lieutenant Clayton E. Rogers, who is the Provost Marshal of General Wadsworth's division, feels very badly that he is obliged to perform this duty.

I must brag a little about our regiment. We have the healthiest regiment in the corps. We have a harmonious, quiet and satisfied set of officers. There is no intriguing, courtmartialing or backbiting, which is common in the army. The arms, accoutrements and clothing are kept in excellent condition. Let me tell you the routine of camp-life. Reveille is the first thing in the morning for the soldier. When it is sounded, the companies are formed in their streets and the roll is called, one commissioned officer to be in attendance. In one hour, comes the breakfast call. Next, the police call, when it is required that the whole camp shall be swept as clean as a floor. Next comes guard mounting at 8:30 A. M. A critical inspection is made by the adjutant of the men of the guard details, and slovenliness and carelessness is punished. Then comes a company inspection by the captains, and especial attention is paid to the personal cleanliness of the men, which accounts for the exceptional good health of our regiment. Next, I conduct a battalion drill which is over at ten A. M. I enjoy this drill, as our regiment is not to be surpassed, and I feel very proud of their splendid movements. We rest then during the heat of the day until four P. M., when Major Hauser conducts a theoretical drill of the officers of the line. At half-past five, I hold dress parade, and at half-past six, the captains conduct a company drill. At seven o'clock, the Retreat is sounded and guard dismissed. At nine P. M., Tattoo is sounded and the evening roll-call is made, and at ten P. M., Taps are beaten, all lights are put out and the day is done. The most orderly, quiet, systematic community in the world is a well ordered regiment in camp. The rebels fired briskly quite a while last night on our troops who are over the river, but shot very wild. One or two of their shells exploded in our camp."

The next letter, written at one o'clock on the morning of June 12th, 1863, inaugurates our march which culminated in the battle of Gettysburg.

(Letter to M. B. G.) "We are to march this morning positively. I think the whole army is going, for the order is from General Hooker. If so, it will be your second time 'under fire, searching those dreadful lists.' You are mustered into the service now and must endure your trials and hardships as a soldier, and I doubt not they will be harder to bear than mine, for you see, you are a raw recruit. Whether we march in advance or retreat, against the rifle pits beyond the river or toward the plains of Manassas, I will write at every opportunity. The regiment will go out strong in health and cheerful in spirit, and determined always to sustain its glorious history. It has been my ardent ambition to lead it through one campaign, and now the indications are that my opportunity has come. If I do anything glorious I shall expect you to be proud of me."

(Letter to M. B. G.)   Bivouac near Centreville, Va., }
                                June 15th, 1863. }

"Here we are again on our annual visit to Bull Run. I think, however, we shall miss our annual drubbing. We broke camp at daylight Friday morning, (the twelfth.) We marched that day about twenty miles under a scorching sun and through suffocating clouds of dust. You can hardly imagine what our poor loaded soldiers suffer on such marches. We camped Friday night at Deep Run. We marched at daylight Saturday and camped for the night near Bealton station. We marched Sunday morning and all day Sunday and all night, and until the middle of the afternoon to-day, when we reached this point, tired, sore, sleepy, hungry, dusty and dirty as pigs. I have had no wink of sleep for two nights. Our army is in a great hurry for something. I hope we can be allowed to stay here to-morrow, to recruit our energies. The indications now are that we will. Indeed our poor worn out fellows must have some rest. We have had no mail and no papers since leaving camp. I must go to sleep. My darky boy, William, has got my oil cloth fixed for a shade, and I am going to wrap up in my blanket and lie down on the ground with my haversack for a pillow, and I will have a sounder, sweeter, more refreshing sleep, than if I was in the softest bed. When you pity my deplorable condition, remember my noble boys who have had ten times the toil and have come through without a murmur."

On this hot march our pack mule laid himself down, in spite of William's efforts to the contrary, in the water of Deep Run, seriously damaging the rations of our regimental headquarters mess.*

(Letter to M. B. G.)   BIVOUAC NEAR LEESBURG, VA.,
                                        JUNE 18th, 1863.

"†We are still toiling along on our weary way with only such

---

*This story, from the humorous pen of Loyd G. Harris, evidently refers to the circumstance. The mess, however, consisted of Major Hauser, Adjutant Brooks, Lieutenant Colonel Dawes, and the three surgeons.

"'Willyum' was a quiet colored boy who waited on our Colonel and Lieutenant Colonel.

Once on a long march we had halted for the night. The camp fires were blazing in full glory, and the air was thick with appetizing smells from the coffee-pots and frying-pans. 'Willyum' and the pack mule that carried the baggage and mess utensils for the field officers were both missing. Our gallant Colonel and the quiet Lieutenant Colonel, were getting decidedly hungry, when 'Willyum' came in.

'Where is the pack mule?' the Colonel asked.

'Why, sah, just as we war coming by de big pond, 'bout a half a mile back, I thought I'd gib him a drink, an' de ole fool just laid down wid de whole pack in de water, an' I reckon I will want 'bout ten men to git him out.'

The mule and pack were rescued in a damaged condition, but the field officers had a late meal that night."

Lieutenant Harris commanded company "C" during the Gettysburg campaign, Captain Thomas W. Plummer having been wounded at Fitz Hugh's Crossing.

†Volume XXVII, Part I, Page 140, War Records.

halts or rests as are absolutely essential to renew the strength of man and beast. We are hurrying to the rescue of Pennsylvania and Maryland as I never knew the Army of the Potomac to hurry before. And yet I suspect that we are anathematized for our slow motions. 'Where is the Army of the Potomac?' is, I presume, the indignant exclamation of many good people in the land to-day. Our march yesterday was terribly severe. The sun was like a furnace, and the dust thick and suffocating. Many a poor fellow marched his last day yesterday. Several men fell dead on the road. Our boys have all come through so far, accepting the hardships as a matter of course, and remaining cheerful and obedient. I assure you I feel proud of them"

Upon this march General James S. Wadsworth showed great solicitude for the suffering men. There was an ambulance loaded with the valises of the officers serving on his staff. These valises the old General ordered thrown out, and the ambulance filled with the knapsacks and muskets of the exhausted soldiers. But the papers of the division headquarters were in these valises and all were diligently sought and gathered up during the night. It was said that the General threw out his own valise.

"One of my greatest hardships is to get no mail. Sometimes a little package of headquarters letters are brought through. Suppose you put First Brigade, First Division, First Army Corps on your letters. I got a letter from my sister which was directed in that way. We got the newspapers to-day. Our brigade newsboy got them through in some way. The head-lines say: *'Rebels in Pennsylvania'*—*'Another battle at Antietam on the tapis.'* I hope not. I never want to fight there again. The flower of our regiment were slaughtered in that terrible corn-field. I dread the thought of the place. If there is a battle, watch the papers to see if General John F. Reynolds and General James S. Wadsworth figure in it. By them you can trace me. (As it proved, the first flash of the telegraph from Gettysburg was, that General John F. Reynolds had been killed while leading a charge of the "Iron Brigade," and that Wadsworth's division had opened the great battle, suffering severely in the fight.) Colonel Wm. W. Robinson of the seventh Wisconsin, has temporary command of the brigade. It is said that General Meredith will be Military

Governor of Indiana. I write under continual marching orders, and a perpetual pressure of business. An ordnance report, clothing report, picket detail and other duties, stop my writing."

(Letter to M. B. G.)   BIVOUAC ON BROAD RUN, TEN MILES ⎱
FROM LEESBURG, VA., JUNE 19th, 1863. ⎰

"I have pitched my tent to-night in a splendid grove of grand old oaks on the banks of Broad Run. Nothing could be more pleasant or romantic than our situation to-night, but the boom of hostile cannon toward *Aldie Gap takes away something from the romance. Our march to-day was short and well conducted, and our men are washing themselves in the pure waters of Broad Run and so are feeling fresh and more cheerful. It is eight days to-night since we have had a regular mail, and we do not expect any soon. It rains through my tent on the paper which causes the spots. It is very dark, too, to-night, and we came near having to march, as orders came to that effect, and ambulances were sent for the sick. The impression was, when we camped this evening, that we would remain here a day or two and I had my camp systematically arranged with reference to regularity and cleanliness."

(Letter to M. B. G.)   BIVOUAC NEAR BROAD RUN, ⎱
LOUDON CO., VA., JUNE 21st, 1863. ⎰

"Our long watched for mail, caught us last night. The cannon are sounding in the direction of Leesburg and there is quite a battle† being fought there this Sabbath morning. Our men seem to have driven the rebels, and the firing seems to have receded. Have had a very busy forenoon. Ordnance to inspect, camp to be put in condition, candidates for the invalid corps to be examined, and I got twelve letters in the mail. You see that we are in camp again. I suppose we are waiting for the 'favorable opportunity to fall upon Lee and destroy him.' Lee, meanwhile, ravages Pennsylvania at his leisure, but there is one thing,—'Washington is safe.' "

I have a letter from Eph, (my brother). He says: 'Of course I have heard all about your troubles, or rather the tribulation of

---

*Volume XXVII, Part I, Page 53, War Records.
†Volume XXVII, Part I, Page 53, War Records.

the folks at home through Doctor What's-his-name's mistake. Being relieved by a telegraphic dispatch from any apprehension for your safety, I could not help looking at the ludicrous side of the question and it was decidedly funny. To tell you the truth, I had an idea that you had something of a liking for the young lady, and thought the matter would some day come to a crisis. Our regiment numbers in the aggregate 595, of whom 535 are 'present for duty.' The absentees are mostly detached. We have no sick men and have had but one man die of disease with the regiment in six months, though we have marched several hundred miles.' The week's marching in the dust and heat has been hard on the men. One of our men in company 'I' has become a lunatic from the effect of the heat. The newspapers say there were a thousand cases of sunstroke in our army. I stand the sun very well, but it has made me brown as sole leather. We are no holiday soldiers. I sent my boy, Billy, all over the country to-day to find something to eat. Nothing was forthcoming but a little wet flour and our biscuits were very soggy, but it was a relief from hard tack. Did you ever eat a hard tack? Get one and eat it if you can for my sake. There are reports of a chicken of rebel proclivities, and Billy has laid a campaign to capture it. So I hope for better things to-morrow. My boy, Billy, is a good provider, but this desert is too much for him. Hard tack, ham, fresh beef and coffee without milk is the ceaseless round of our bill of fare."

(Letter to M. B. G.)   CAMP ON BROAD RUN, }
                                JUNE 24th, 1863. }

"General Hooker shows no disposition to press the enemy so long as he confines his attention to the Pennsylvania Dutchmen and leaves Washington alone. The prospect is very dark with us just now. But if we open the Mississippi, and I think we will, and can thwart General Lee in this effort to carry the war, as the rebels say, 'into Africa,' we will have accomplished for this summer, perhaps, all we have any right to expect. Our cause is just and we will get success as soon as we deserve it. As an Ohio man, I shall feel deeply humiliated if Vallandigham is elected the next Governor.

I had a chance to do a good thing this morning and it gave me pleasure. One of our men of company 'C,' a fat cheeked, sleepy boy, was sent to me under guard by the field officer of the day of Wadsworth's division, to be dealt with for sleeping on his picket post, for which the penalty is death when in the presence of the enemy. The poor fellow, who, like Joe in Pickwick, slept because of a big supper on rebel chicken, was sadly frightened. That demon, official duty, required that I should prefer charges and send him to a general court martial for trial. But with a sharp lecture and warning, I released him from arrest and sent him to his company. His demonstration of gratitude was quite affecting. He will remember the Lieutenant Colonel commanding the Sixth, as long as he lives. (His life, poor fellow, was short. He fell dead eight days afterward in the charge on the railroad cutting at Gettysburg.)

Our living has improved much within a day or two. We now get butter, eggs, milk, mutton, and indeed almost everything but fruit. I do not expect to taste a strawberry this year. When in camp we generally live comfortably enough. It is on the march that we have to suffer. Our provisions and a wedge-tent, we carry on a pack mule. Everything else I carry on my horse. I have a good horse. She knows the orders on battalion drill almost as well as the men do. She will follow the column on a night march no matter how dark. This is important, as to lose the road in the night is fatal to a Colonel. He leads astray all troops behind him."

(Letter to M. B. G.)   Bivouac near Middleton, Md., }
       June 27th, 1863. }

"We are once more at the old South Mountain battle ground. We left our camp near Guilford station on Broad Run, early on the morning of the twenty-fifth. We marched all night and crossed the Potomac at Edwards Ferry. We proceeded via Poolsville and encamped for the night near Barnesville. We marched next morning at daylight, and through deep mud and a drizzling rain all day, and encamped near Jefferson, in the valley of Middleton. This morning we started early and reached this point at two o'clock P. M. Our marches, except to-day, have been long and toilsome. What do you think of trudging along all day in a soaking rain, getting as wet as a drowned rat, taking supper on hard tack and salt pork, and then wrapping up in a wet woolen blanket and lying down for a sleep, but waked up during the night three or four times to receive and attend to orders and finally turning out at three o'clock in the morning to get the regiment ready to march? Well—that is soldiering, and it is a great deal more comfortable soldiering, than to march through suffocating clouds of dust under a hot sun. In the dust, men are dogged and silent. In the rain they are often even hilarious and jolly.

The campaign has now been fairly inaugurated on Northern soil. General Meredith and I rode together this evening over our battle ground on South Mountain. The grass has grown green over the graves of our brave boys, who lie buried there. The inscriptions on the head boards are already scarcely legible and with their destruction seems to go the last poor chance that the sacrifice these men have made for their country shall be recognized and commemorated."

We did not then suspect that all would be gathered up by our Government and buried in beautiful National cemeteries, to be forever cared for, and their memories held in perpetual honor.

"General Meredith pointed out to me the grave of a private soldier of the nineteenth Indiana regiment, who had been a professor in a western college, and a man of marked scholarship and refinement. What could be more unselfish and noble than the sacrifice this man has made for his country."

(Letter to M. B. G.)   BIVOUAC IN PENNSYLVANIA }
ON MARSH CREEK, NEAR GETTYSBURG, JUNE 30th, 1863. }

"We left South Mountain in great haste on the 28th, and marched to Frederick city through a drizzling rain as usual. Next day we moved from Frederick to Emmitsburg, Md., and to-day we came here, where we are having a muster for pay. I don't think I ever before saw at this time of the year such a long continued, misty, drizzling storm as we have been marching through since we crossed the Potomac. *General Meade as commander of the army was a surprise."

Meade lacked the martial bearing and presence of Hooker. Few of our men knew him by sight. He was sometimes seen riding by the marching columns of troops at a fast trot, his hat

---

*Volume XXVII, Part I, Page 61, War Records.

brim turned down and a poncho over his shoulders. The only sign of rank was a gold cord on his hat. At the muster for pay, I read to the regiment, General Meade's address to the troops.

"We have marched through some beautiful country. It is refreshing to get out of the barren desert of Virginia into this land of thrift and plenty. Our reception in Maryland was hardly so enthusiastic as last summer, but in Pennsylvania, everybody, great and small, is overjoyed at the coming of our banners."

Our regiment had the advance and first crossed the Pennsylvania line.

"The rebel stealing parties are running away ahead of us and I presume the whole rebel army is concentrating to give us battle."

As we marched through Emmitsburg, the advance of the army, some students in the Catholic college welcomed us with great enthusiasm and several of them marched along with us beyond the town, giving the above information. They were much interested in watching the movements of our advance guard and flankers, the feelers of the army. They wanted to see us "flush the enemy."

"I am kept full of business on such hurried marches, scarcely from morning to night getting a moment I can call my own."

The unfinished letter was here placed in my pocket to await a convenient opportunity to complete it, and the next entry upon the sheet is as follows: "July 1st A. M. Orders have just come, 'pack up, be ready to march immediately.' I will finish this letter the first chance I get."

I put the unfinished letter again in my pocket and rode on at the head of my regiment to Gettysburg. The letter is finished in a nervous scrawl written with a pencil.

"LINE OF BATTLE ON A HILL NEAR GETTYSBURG, {
JULY 2nd, 1863, 8 A. M. {

God has preserved me unharmed through another desperate bloody battle. Regiment lost *one hundred and sixty men killed and wounded. I ordered a charge and we captured a regiment. †Major Stone, commanding the second Mississippi,

---

*Actual loss one hundred and sixty eight.

†This, as will be seen was an error. It was Major John A. Blair. J. M. Stone was the Colonel, but he had been shot and disabled.

surrendered his sword and regiment to me. There are no communications now with the North, but sometime I hope you will get this."

(Letter.)   IN LINE OF BATTLE BEFORE GETTYSBURG, }
                                    JULY 4th, 1863, 12 M.   }

"I am entirely safe through the first three of these terrible days of this bloody struggle. The fighting has been the most desperate I ever saw. On July 1st, our corps was thrown in front, unsupported and almost annihilated. My regiment was detached from the brigade and we charged upon and captured the second Mississippi rebel regiment. Their battle flag is now at General Meade's headquarters, inscribed as follows: 'Captured by the sixth Wisconsin, together with the entire regiment, kept by Sergeant Evans for two 'days, while a prisoner in the hands of the enemy.' "

This battle flag with its inscription is in the Ordnance Museum of the War Department at Washington, D. C. Its official number is forty-eight.

"The Sixth has lost so far one hundred and sixty men. Since the first day we have lost only six. O, Mary, it is sad to look now at our shattered band of devoted men. Only four field officers* in the brigade have escaped and I am one of them. I have no opportunity to say more now or to write to any one else. Tell mother I am safe. There is no chance to telegraph. God has been kind to me and I think he will yet spare me."

                    IN LINE OF BATTLE BEFORE GETTYSBURG, }
                                    JULY 4th, 6 P. M.   }

†"What a solemn birthday. My little band, now only two hundred men, have all been out burying the bloody corpses of friend and foe. No fighting to-day. Both armies need rest from the ex-

---

*The field officers of the brigade fared thus in the battle: Second Wisconsin, Colonel L. Fairchild, lost an arm; Lieutenant Colonel G. H. Stevens, killed; Major John Mansfield, severely wounded. Seventh Wisconsin, Lieutenant Colonel John B. Callis, shot through the body; Major Mark Finnicum, wounded. Nineteenth Indiana, Lieutenant Colonel W. W. Dudley, lost a leg while acting as color bearer; Major Lindley wounded. Twenty-fourth Michigan, Colonel H. A. Morrow, wounded; Lieutenant Colonel Flannagin, lost a leg; Major Wright, wounded. The four who escaped injury were Colonel W. W. Robinson, seventh Wisconsin Col. S. Williams, Nineteenth Indiana, and Major Hauser and myself.

†I was twenty-five years old on this day.

haustion of the desperate struggle. My boys until just now have had nothing to eat since yesterday morning. No regiment in this army or in any other army in the world ever did better service than ours. We were detached from the brigade early on the first day and we operated as an independent command. I saved my men all I could and we suffered terribly to be sure, but less than any other regiment in the brigade. We captured a regiment. I don't know as we will get our just credit before the country, but we have it with our Generals."

I went in person taking the captured battle flag to General Meade, at headquarters of the Army of the Potomac. The object of this visit was to obtain, if possible, permission to send the battle flag to the Governor of Wisconsin to be retained at the capitol of Wisconsin as a trophy. In this effort I was unsuccessful, and I brought the flag back. As I passed along from General Meade's headquarters to Culps' Hill, carrying the rebel battle flag loosely folded over my arm, I took my course over the ground where General Pickett made his charge. Many wounded Confederate soldiers were still lying on this ground. A badly wounded Confederate sergeant who had lain upon the ground during the night, called to me in a faint voice: "You have got our flag!" It was a sergeant of the second Mississippi regiment. The men of this regiment who had escaped from the railroad cut and other casualties on July first, had taken part in this attack. This man informed me that the commander of his regiment at the time of its surrender was Major John A. Blair, and he gave me many particulars in regard to the history of the regiment. No introductions took place at the railroad cut. I do not know whether this sergeant survived his wound. I did all in my power to secure for him aid and attention.

HEADQUARTERS SIXTH WISCONSIN VOLUNTEERS,
LINE OF BATTLE BEFORE GETTYSBURG,
JULY 4th, 1863.

"*Sir:*—I have the honor to report that the accompanying battle flag of the second regiment of Mississippi Confederate Volunteers was captured by the regiment under my command under the following circumstances: Shortly after the opening of the action on the morning of July first, my regiment was by command of General Doubleday, detached from the brigade and ordered to the support of the right of the division (Wadsworth's) which was being forced back and outflanked by the enemy. I moved as rapidly as possible upon the advancing line of the enemy, joining with the fourteenth Brooklyn and ninety-fifth New York on my left. A brisk fire was opened throughout our line which soon checked the enemy, and forced him to take refuge in a railroad cut. I ordered a charge upon the cut. The men moved forward, well closed and on a run. When our line reached the edge of the cut, the rebels ceased firing and threw down their arms. Major Blair commanding the regiment in my front, the second Mississippi, surrendered his sword and regiment. The battle flag was taken before the surrender by Corporal F. Asbury Waller of company 'I' and sent to the rear in charge of Sergeant Wm. Evans of company 'H' who was badly wounded. The Sergeant was taken prisoner by the enemy and held for two days in Gettysburg. With the assistance of some ladies, whose names I have not learned, he successfully concealed the color and finally when the enemy retired, brought it safely to the regiment. I have the honor to be, very respectfully,

R. R. Dawes,

Lieutenant Colonel commanding sixth Wisconsin Volunteers."

This report was directed to General Wadsworth's adjutant general.

(Letter to M. B. G.)   On the march, July 6th, 2 P. M.

"We have stopped for a few moments near Emmitsburg. I am entirely well. I telegraphed to mother day before yesterday. This has been a terrible ordeal. Our loss is 30 killed outright, 116 wounded, several of whom have died since, and 25 missing, all from 340 men taken into battle. My horse was shot under me early in the fight, which perhaps saved my life. The experience of the past few days seem more like a horrible dream than the reality. May God save me and my men from any more such trials. Our bravest and best are cold in the ground or suffering on beds of anguish. I could tell a thousand stories of their heroism: One young man, Corporal James Kelly of company "B," shot through the breast, came staggering up to me before he fell and opening his shirt to show the wound, said 'Colonel, won't you write to my folks that I died a soldier.' Every man of our color guard was shot and several volunteer color bearers. There was not a man of them but would die before the honor of the old Sixth should be tarnished. I do not know what is in store for us but you know that with my earliest chance, I will write you fully of what has happened."

This history would be incomplete with no glimpse of how the new recruit stood fire at home. As the thunders of Gettysburg rolled over the land, there was intense excitement on the part of all the people. Telegraphic bulletins were posted every few hours. This is from M. B. G. to R. R. Dawes:

HOME, JULY 4th, 1863.

"Your birthday, and I have been all the time anticipating so much pleasure in writing to you to-day but it is only to-night that I have felt that I could write at all. It has seemed utterly impossible for me to write to you, not knowing you were where my letters could ever reach you or my prayers ever avail you. I feel that I can now—not that I think you are out of danger by any means—but I believe you will be spared. I shall not undertake to tell you how slowly and sorrowfully the last three days have dragged along. The first news we heard of the battle was that the first army corps was engaged and General Reynolds killed. About noon to-day I began to feel more hopeful that you had got through safely, but this afternoon we hear that the first corps is engaged again. When will they ever let you rest? From the papers, to-night, I conclude you came safely through Wednesday (July 1st) but your corps commander killed and your brigade commander wounded. I shall watch, oh, so anxiously, for tidings this week, praying that God in His mercy may spare you."

MARIETTA, OHIO, JULY 7th, 1863.

"I am beginning to feel as if I could write to you again, not quite sure you are safe yet but taking heart from the fact that we have had no bad news and we have the list of killed and wounded in the sixth Wisconsin up to Thursday evening. We hope you were not in that division of the first corps which was engaged Friday (July 3rd). If you are only safe how we shall rejoice! Of all times to think that you should have commanded the regiment in this great victory! Don't you suppose I was proud of you and the sixth Wisconsin, last night, when I read of your regiment, the fourteenth Brooklyn and the ninety-fifth New York capturing a whole brigade? There has been greater rejoicing over your victory in Pennsylvania than I have ever known, and within the last half hour dispatches have come saying that Vicksburg is ours. 'Great Babylon is fallen, is fallen.' I do not know how as a Nation we are going to bear our success, but I know as an individual I can't bear much more of any thing."

CHAPTER VIII.

THE SIXTH WISCONSIN AT GETTYSBURG.

*When General James S. Wadsworth's division of the first army corps marched toward Gettysburg on the morning of July first, 1863, the sixth Wisconsin was the last regiment in the order of march for the day. The brigade guard, two officers and one hundred men, marched immediately behind us, which accounts for their assignment to the regiment for duty when we became involved in battle. The column moved on the Emmitsburg Road. Three hundred and forty officers and enlisted men marched in the ranks of the regiment. All were in the highest spirits. To make a show in the streets of Gettysburg, I brought our drum corps to the front and had the colors unfurled. The drum major, R. N. Smith, had begun to play "The Campbells are Coming," and the regiment had closed its ranks and swung into the step, when we first heard the cannon of the enemy, firing on the cavalry of General Buford. The troops ahead turned across the fields to the left of Gettysburg, toward the Seminary Ridge. We stopped our music, which had at least done something to arouse the martial spirit of old John Burns, and turned to engage in the sterner duties involved in war. When the head of the regimental column reached the crest of Seminary Ridge, an aide of General Meredith, Lieutenant Gilbert M. Woodward, came on a gallop with the order, "Colonel, form your line, and prepare for action." I turned my horse and gave the necessary orders. The evolution of the line was performed on the double quick, the men loading their muskets as they ran. Hastening forward on a run to get to our position on the left flank of the "Iron Brigade," which, regiment after regiment, *en echelon*, was dashing into the McPherson woods, another aide, Lieutenant Marten, came gal-

---

*For organization Army of the Potomac, see Page 155, Volume XXVII, Part I, War Records.

loping up and said, "Colonel, *General Doubleday is now in command of the first corps, and he directs that you halt your regiment." General John F. Reynolds had been killed, but the fact was not disclosed to us by Lieutenant Marten. I halted the men and directed them to lie down on the ground. The brigade guard now reported to me for duty in the impending battle, and I divided them into two companies of fifty men each, and placed them upon the right and left flanks of the regiment.

The brigade guard comprised twenty men from each of the five regiments of the "Iron Brigade." The two officers, Lieutenant Lloyd G. Harris, sixth Wisconsin, and Lieutenant Levi Showalter, second Wisconsin, were capable men and excellent leaders. Eighty-one men of the other regiments of the brigade were thus, by the emergency of sudden and unexpected battle, brought into the ranks of our regiment.

The situation on the field of battle of all the troops now engaged, will be made clear by a diagram. Two brigades of each army confronted each other. Archer's brigade opposed the "Iron Brigade," and Joseph R. Davis's brigade opposed Cutler's brigade of Wadsworth's division. Hall's battery was with Cutler's brigade.

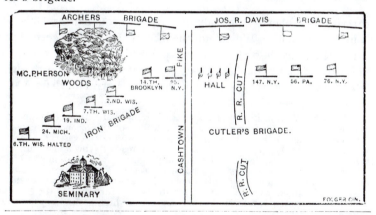

*I deemed the extremity of the woods, which extended to the summit of the ridge, to be the key of the position, and urged that portion of Meredith's brigade, the Western men assigned to its defense, to hold it to the last extremity. Full of the memory of their past achievements, they replied cheerfully and proudly, "If we can't hold it, where will you find men who can?"—Doubleday's Report.

Excepting the sixth Wisconsin, the whole of Wadsworth's
division was hotly engaged in battle with the enemy. Lieutenant
Meredith Jones came with orders from General Doubleday. He
said, "*General Doubleday directs that you move your regiment
at once to the right." I immediately gave the order to move in
that direction at a double quick. Captain J. D. Wood came and
rode beside me, repeating the order from General Meredith and
saying the rebels were "driving Cutler's men." The guns of
Hall's battery could be seen driving to the rear, and Cutler's men
were manifestly in full retreat.

The following diagram illustrates the change of front made to
throw the regiment on the flank of the victoriously advancing
enemy. Across our track as we hurried on, passed some officers

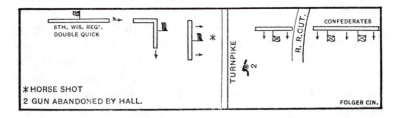

carrying in a blanket the body of our corps commander, General
John F. Reynolds. We did not then know that he had been shot.

Suddenly my horse reared and plunged. It did not occur to
me that she had been shot. I drew a tight rein and spurred her
when she fell heavily on her haunches. I scrambled from the

"*The sixth Wisconsin, together with the brigade guard, under Lieutenants
Harris, of the sixth Wisconsin, and Showalter, of the second Wisconsin,
had been detached by my order, to remain with me as a reserve. There
was no time to be lost, as the enemy was already in the woods, and advancing at double quick to seize this important central position and hold
the ridge. The "Iron Brigade," led by the second Wisconsin in line, and
followed by the other regiments, deployed *en echelon* without a moment's
hesitation, charged with the utmost steadiness and fury, hurled the enemy
back into the run, and reformed their lines on the high ground beyond the
ravine.

The second Wisconsin, in this contest, under the gallant Colonel Fairchild, was particularly distinguished. It accomplished the difficult task of
driving superior numbers of rebel infantry from the shelter of the woods,
and to it also belongs the honor of capturing General Archer himself. He
was brought in by Private Patrick Maloney, of company "G." It is to be
lamented that this brave Irishman was subsequently killed in the action."

MAJ GEN GEO G. MEADE

A. Doubleday.

ground, where I had been thrown sprawling, in front of the regiment, and the men gave a hearty cheer. The gallant old mare also struggled to her feet and hobbled toward the rear on three legs. She had been struck in the breast by a minnie ball, which penetrated seventeen inches. For years she carried the bullet, which could be felt under the skin behind the left shoulder blade—but woe to the man who felt it, as her temper had been spoiled. For the rest of the battle I was on foot. The regiment halted at the fence along the Cashtown Turnpike, and I gave the order to fire. In the field, beyond the turnpike, a long line of yelling Confederates could be seen running forward and firing, and our troops of Cutler's brigade were running back in disorder. The fire of our carefully aimed muskets, resting on the fence rails, striking their flank, soon checked the rebels in their headlong pursuit. The rebel line swayed and bent, and suddenly stopped firing and the men ran into the railroad cut, parallel to the Cashtown Turnpike. I ordered my men to climb over the turnpike fences and advance I was not aware of the existence of the railroad cut, and at first mistook the manuever of the enemy for retreat, but was undeceived by the heavy fire which they began at once to pour upon us from their cover in the cut. Captain John Ticknor, always a dashing leader, fell dead while climbing the second fence, and many were struck on the fences, but the line pushed on. When over the fences and in the field, and subjected to an infernal fire, I first saw the ninety-fifth New York regiment coming gallantly into line upon our left. I did not then know or care where they came from, but was rejoiced to see them. Farther to the left was the *fourteenth Brooklyn regiment, but I was then ignorant of the fact. Major Edward Pye appeared to be in command of the ninety-fifth New York. Running to the major, I said, "We must charge." The

---

*Colonel E. B. Fowler fourteenth Brooklyn, in his official report, has given the impression that he ordered the sixth Wisconsin regiment to make this charge. He gave us no orders whatever. I did not know he was on the field until the charge was over. I called Colonel Fowler's attention to the matter and he stated as an explanation that he sent an officer to give me such an order. Colonel Fowler was retreating his regiment when we arrived at the turnpike fence. He then changed front and joined our advance. The fourteenth Brooklyn and ninety-fifth New York jointly had not more men in action than the sixth Wisconsin.

gallant major replied, "Charge it is." "Forward, charge!" was the order I gave, and Major Pye gave the same command. We were receiving a fearfully destructive fire from the hidden enemy. Men who had been shot were leaving the ranks in crowds. With the colors at the advance point, the regiment firmly and hurriedly moved forward, while the whole field behind streamed with men who had been shot, and who were struggling to the rear or sinking in death upon the ground. The only commands I gave, as we advanced, were, "Align on the colors! Close up on the colors! Close up on the colors!" The regiment was being so broken up that this order alone could hold the body together. Meanwhile the colors fell upon the ground several times but were raised again by the heroes of the color guard. Four hundred and twenty men started in the regiment from the turnpike fence, of whom about two hundred and forty reached the railroad cut. Years afterward I found the distance passed over to be one hundred and seventy-five paces. Every officer proved brave, true, and heroic in encouraging the men to breast the deadly storm, but the real impetus was the eager and determined valor of our men who carried muskets in the ranks. I noticed the motions of our "Tall Sycamore," Captain J. H. Marston, who commanded company "E." His long arms were stretched out as if to gather his men together and push them forward. At a crisis he rose to his full height, and he was the tallest man in the regiment, excepting Levi Steadman of company "I," who was killed on this charge. How the rebels happened to miss Captain Marston I cannot comprehend. Second Lieutenant O. B. Chapman, commanding company "C," fell dead while on the charge. The commission of Lieutenant Thomas Kerr as captain of company "D," bears the proud date of July first, 1863—in recognition of his conduct. The rebel color was seen waving defiantly above the edge of the railroad cut. A heroic ambition to capture it took possession of several of our men. Corporal Eggleston, of company "H," sprang forward to seize it, and was shot and mortally wounded. Private Anderson. of his company, furious at the killing of his brave young comrade, recked little for the rebel color, but he swung aloft his musket and with a terrific blow split the skull of the rebel who had shot young Eggleston. This soldier was well known in the regiment as "Rocky Mountain Anderson." Lieutenant William N. Remington was shot and severely wounded in the shoulder, while rushing for the color. Into this deadly melee came Corporal Francis A. Waller, who seized and held the rebel battle flag. His name will forever remain upon the historic record, as he received from Congress a *medal for this deed.

My notice that we were upon the enemy, was a general cry from our men of: "Throw down your muskets! Down with your muskets!" Running forward through our line of men, I found myself face to face with hundreds of rebels, whom I looked down upon in the railroad cut, which was, where I stood, four feet deep. Adjutant Brooks, equal to the emergency, quickly placed about twenty men across the cut in position to fire through it. I have always congratulated myself upon getting the first word. I shouted: "Where is the colonel of this regiment?" An officer in gray, with stars on his collar, who stood among the men in the cut, said: "Who are you?" I said: "I command this regiment. Surrender, or I will fire." The officer replied not a word, but promptly handed me his sword, and his men, who still held them, threw down their muskets. The coolness, self-possession, and discipline which held back our men from pouring in a general volley saved a hundred lives of the enemy, and as my mind goes back to the fearful excitement of the moment, I marvel at it. The fighting around the rebel colors had not ceased when this surrender took place. I took the sword. It would have been the handsome thing to say, "Keep your sword, sir," but I was new to such occasions, and when six other officers came up and handed me their swords, I took them also. I held this awkward bundle in my arms until relieved by Adjutant Brooks. I directed the officer in command, †Major John A. Blair, of the second Mississippi regiment, to have his men fall in without arms. He gave the command, and his men, (seven officers and two hundred and twenty-five enlisted men) obeyed. To Major John F. Hauser I assigned the duty of marching this body to the provost-guard.

---

*See Page 282, Volume XXVII, Part II, War Records.

†Colonel J. M. Stone, since Governor of Mississippi, was in command at the opening of the battle, but he had been wounded and disabled.

Lieutenant William Goltermann of Company "F," volunteered to command a line of volunteer skirmishers, which I called for as soon as Major Hauser moved his prisoners away. This line of men took possession of the ridge toward the enemy and guarded against a surprise by a return of the enemy to attack. One gun of Hall's second Maine battery stood upon the field before the railroad cut and between the hostile lines. After the surrender, Captain Rollin P. Converse took men enough for the purpose and pulled this gun to the turnpike, where Captain Hall took it again in charge.

Corporal Frank Asbury Waller brought me the captured battle flag. It was the flag of the second Mississippi Volunteers, one of the oldest and most distinguished regiments in the Confederate army. It belonged to the brigade commanded by Joseph R. Davis, the nephew of Jefferson Davis. It is a rule in battle not to allow sound men to leave the ranks. Sergeant William Evans of company "H," a brave and true man, had been severely wounded in the thighs. He was obliged to use two muskets as crutches. To him I intrusted the battle-flag, and I took it from the staff and wrapped it around his body.

Adjutant E. P. Brooks buckled on one of the captured swords, and he still retains it, but the other six were given to a wounded man and delivered to our chief surgeon, A. W. Preston. The enemy, when they took the town, captured the hospital and the swords. No discredit to the doctor is implied, as his hands were full of work with wounded men.

*After this capture of prisoners in the railroad cut there was a

---

*The line officers present at the battle of Gettysburg were as follows; the first named is the company commander when the fight opened : Lieutenant Howard F. Pruyn, company "A," wounded; Lieut. H. J. Huntington, company "A ;" Captain R. P. Converse, company "B;" Lieutenant Charles P. Hyatt, company "B;" Lieutenant Loyd G. Harris, company "C," wounded ; Lieutenant O. D. Chapman, company "C," killed ; Lieutenant Thomas Kerr, company "D ;" Captain J. H. Marston, company "E ;" Lieutenant Michael Mangan, company "E," wounded ; Lieutenant Oscar Graetz, company "F ;" Lieutenant William Goltermann, company "F ;" Lieutenant James L. Converse, company "G ;" Lieutenant John Timmons, company "G ;" Lieutenant John Beeley, company "H," wounded ; Lieutenant H. B. Merchant, company "H," wounded ; Lieutenant Earl M. Rogers, company "I ;" Captain John Ticknor, company "K," killed ; Lieutenant William N. Remington, company "K," wounded ; Lieutenant Wm. S. Campbell, company "K." Captain Charles H. Ford and Lieutenant C.

lull in the battle. Our comrades of the "Iron Brigade," who had charged so brilliantly into the McPherson woods, had been completely victorious. They had routed Archer's brigade, capturing its commander and many of its men, and then they had changed front to move to the relief of Cutler's brigade, but our charge upon the railroad cut, and its success, obviated that necessity. By this charge Joseph R. Davis' brigade was scattered or captured.* We had fairly defeated, upon an open field, a superior force of the veterans of the army of General Lee. It was a short, sharp, and desperate fight, but the honors were easily with the boys in blue.

While the regiment is being reorganized, let us follow Sergeant William Evans. Weak and faint from loss of blood, he painfully hobbled to Gettysburg, and became exhausted in the street. Brave and faithful friends came to his relief. Two young women assisted this wounded soldier into their home, and placed him upon a bed. The Union troops soon began to retreat in confusion through the town, and the cheers of the victorious enemy could be plainly heard. Evans begged of his friends to hide the rebel flag. They cut a hole in the bed-tick beneath him, thrust in the flag, and sewed up the rent. The flag was thus safely concealed until the enemy retreated from Gettysburg, and on the morning of July 4th Evans brought his precious trophy to Culp's Hill and gave it to me there.†

E. Rogers were acting on the staff of General Wadsworth. Captain John A. Kellogg was the very efficient Chief of the Staff of General Lysander Cutler. His service was distinguished by his accustomed activity and bravery in battle. Lieutenant Levi Showalter, the second Wisconsin officer commanding the improvised company of the brigade guard on the right of the regiment, was shot and severely wounded. He was a gallant officer and led his men with a spirit equal to any commander in the line.

*Volume XXVII, Part II, Page 638, War Records. General Henry Heth says in his report: "Davis' brigade was kept on the left of the road that it might collect its stragglers, and from its shattered condition it was not deemed advisable to bring it again into action on that day."

The strength of General J. R. Davis' brigade May 31st, 1863, for duty, officers and men, was 2,577 in its four regiments There were three regiments in this battle, or approximately 1,933 men, three fourths of 2,577. War Records, Volume XVIII, Page 1086.

†A letter just recieved from Captain Loyd G. Harris makes the following important statement regarding the rebel battle flag, and gives the name of the brave women who saved it for us: "After I was wounded, Lieut. W. N. Remington, Lieutenant John Beely and myself, were in a temporary hos-

BATTLE FLAG OF THE SECOND MISSISSIPPI REGIMENT, CAPTURED AT
GETTYSBURG.

In his official report General Doubleday says that when Cutler's regiments were overpowered and driven back, "the moment
was a critical one, involving the defeat, perhaps the utter rout of

---

pital in Gettysburg. Acting on the advice of the surgeon, we found pleasant
quarters with the family of Mr. Hollenger, and while there were joined by
one of our sergeants (William Evans I think) who had the rebel flag. This
was about noon. Just after our dinner, firing began in the front. I went
up stairs and from an upper porch could plainly see the movement of the
eleventh corps but not the first corps. They (the eleventh corps) were
over-lapped by the enemy and soon in full retreat. I went below and told
Remington and Beely to hurry out and get to the rear as fast as they could.
Mrs. Hollenger partly fainted, and assisted by her husband I helped to carry
her to the cellar. There were two young lady daughters, (Miss Julia was
the name of one of these young ladies). I bade them all good bye, and
when I went out, had a narrow escape from being shot down or captured, but
by going through houses, after I passed two cross streets, found my companions in an ambulance. Once with them we lead the retreat."

There was brought to me on Culp's Hill, July 4th, when our wounded
men returned, a bouquet of flowers with the compliments of Miss Sallie
Paxton. This lady had seen our charge upon the railroad cut.

our forces."* Later in the day we marched through the railroad cut, and about one thousand muskets lay in the bottom of it. Only one regiment surrendered as an organization, and that was the second Mississippi Volunteers. The ninety-fifth New York took prisoners, as did also the fourteenth Brooklyn. All the troops in the railroad cut threw down their muskets, and the men either surrendered themselves, or ran away out of the other end of the cut.

THE ADVANCE ON THE RAILROAD CUT.

Seminary Ridge is in the foreground. Later in the battle, battery "B" was planted here and in the timber showing on the right. The regiment when supporting this battery was in the timber, and it was there that we reorganized after our charge upon the railroad cut.

We next advanced, by order of General Wadsworth, to the ridge† west of the Seminary Ridge. Here we encountered a

---

*The moment was a critical one, involving the defeat, perhaps the utter rout of our forces. I immediately sent for one of Meredith's regiments, the Sixth Wisconsin, a gallant body of men, who I knew could be relied upon. Forming them rapidly perpendicular to the line of battle on the enemy's flank, I directed them to attack immediately. Lieutenant-Colonel Dawes, their commander, ordered a charge, which was gallantly executed. The enemy made a hurried attempt to change front to meet the attack, and flung his troops into the railroad cut for safety. The Ninety-fifth New York volunteers, Colonel Biddle, and the Fourteenth Brooklyn, under Colonel Fowler, joined in the charge; the cut was carried at the point of the bayonet.   *   *   *   *   *

†Occupied by the enemy in the picture.

heavy line of rebel skirmishers, upon whom we opened fire, and drove them into Willoughby Run. But the enemy turned upon us the fire of six pieces of artillery in position just south of the Cashtown Turnpike beyond Willoughby Run, and beyond the houses in the picture. The shell flew over us and burst around us so thickly that I was obliged to order the men to lie upon the ground under the brow of the ridge. The "Iron Brigade" was in the McPherson Woods, half a mile to our left. The space between us and that brigade was occupied by Colonel Roy Stone's Pennsylvania Bucktails. General Lysander Cutler's brigade was now upon our right. This was our position when the general attack was made by the rebel army corps of Hill and Ewell combined, at half past one o'clock in the afternoon. The first brunt of it struck the gallant brigade of Bucktails. They were fighting on Pennsylvania soil. Their conduct was more than heroic, it was glorious. I can not describe the charges and counter-charges which took place, but we all saw the banner of the one hundred and forty-ninth Pennsylvania planted in the ground and waving between the hostile lines of battle, while the desperate fight went on. This color was taken by the enemy.

Under pressure of the battle, the whole line of Union troops fell back to the Seminary Ridge. I could plainly see the entire movement. I saw Captain Hollon Richardson who acted as an aide to Colonel W. W. Robinson, now in command of the "Iron Brigade," carrying on his horse and waving aloft, the colors of the seventh Wisconsin, as the proud brigade slowly drew back from the McPherson Woods to the Seminary Ridge. We received no orders. Being a detached regiment it is likely that we were overlooked. The enemy (Ewell's corps) advanced so that the low ground between us and the Seminary Ridge in our rear was swept by their fire. It would cost many lives to march in line of battle through this fire. I adopted the tactics of the rebels earlier in the day, and ordered my men to run into the railroad cut. Then instructing the men to follow in single file, I led the way, as fast as I could run, from this cut to the cut in the Seminary Ridge. About a cart load of dirt was ploughed over us by the rebel shell, but otherwise not a man was struck. The ranks were promptly reformed, and we marched into the woods on the Seminary Ridge to the same position from which we had advanced. The whole first army corps was now in line of battle on the Seminary Ridge, and here that grand body of veteran soldiers made a heroic effort to stay the overwhelming tide that swept against them.*

Battery "B," fourth U. S. artillery, under command of Lieutenant James Stewart, came up, and General Wadsworth directed me to support it with my regiment. James Stewart was as brave and efficient a man as ever fought upon a battle field. His battery was manned by men detailed from the volunteers, many of them from our brigade. And now came the grand advance of the enemy. During this time the attack was progressing, I stood among the guns of battery "B." Along the Seminary Ridge, flat upon their bellies, lay mixed up together in one line of battle, the "Iron Brigade" and Roy Stone's "Bucktails." For a mile up and down the open fields in front, the splendid lines of the veterans of the army of Northern Virginia swept down upon us. Their bearing was magnificent. They maintained their alignments with great precision. In many cases the colors of regiments were advanced several paces in front of the line. †Stewart fired shell until they appeared on the ridge east of Willoughby Run; when on this ridge they came forward with a rush. The musketry burst from the Seminary Ridge, every shot fired with care, and Stewart's men, with the regularity of a machine, worked their guns upon the enemy. The rebels came half way down the opposite slope, wavered, began to fire, then to scatter and then to run, and how our men did yell, "Come on, Johnny! come on!" Falling back over the ridge they came on again more cautiously, and pouring upon us from the start a steady fire of deadly musketry. This killed Stewart's men and horses in great numbers, but did not seem to check his fire.

---

*The first corps only consisted of about 8,200 men when it entered the battle. It was reduced at the close of the engagement to about 2,450.— Doubleday's Report.

†See Report of confederate Colonel Abner Perrin, Volume XXVII, Page 661, Part II, War Records, and General A. M. Scales, Page 670, and Colonel W. J. Lowrance, Page 671. These reports show the terrible effect of Stewart's fire upon the enemy. In 1882 I visited the ground with General A. M. Scales and he stated that the fire of battery "B" was the most destructive he had known in the war.

RETREAT.

Lieutenant Clayton E. Rogers, aide on General Wadsworth's staff, came riding rapidly to me. Leaning over from his horse, he said very quietly: "The orders, colonel, are to retreat beyond the town. Hold your men together." I was astonished. The cheers of defiance along the line of the first corps, on Seminary Ridge, had scarcely died away. But a glance over the field to our right and rear was sufficient. There the troops of the *eleventh corps appeared in full retreat, and long lines of Confederates, with fluttering banners and shining steel, were sweeping forward in pursuit of them without let or hindrance. It was a close race which could reach Gettysburg first, ourselves, or the rebel troops of Ewell's corps, who pursued our eleventh corps. Facing the regiment to the rear, I marched in line of battle over the open fields toward the town. We were north of the railroad, and our direction separated us from other regiments of our corps. If we had desired to attack Ewell's twenty thousand men with our two hundred, we could not have moved more directly toward them. We knew nothing about a Cemetery Hill. We could see only that the on-coming lines of the enemy were encircling us in a horseshoe. But with the flag of the Union and of Wisconsin held aloft, the little regiment marched firmly and steadily. As we approached the town, the buildings of the Pennsylvania College screened us from the view of the enemy. We could now see that our troops were retreating in a direction at right angles to our line of march. We reached a street extending through Gettysburg from the college to Cemetery Hill, and crossed it. We were now faced by the enemy, and I turned the course toward the Cemetery Hill, although then unconscious of the fact. The first cross street was swept by the musketry fire of the enemy. There was a close board fence,

---

*Doctor John C. Hall was on duty in a building used for a hospital near the railroad station in Gettysburg. From the north window he had, he says, a "perfect view" of the retreat of the eleventh corps. In his journal of July second, 1863, he wrote of it: "Away went guns and knapsacks, and they fled for dear life, forming a funnel shaped tail, extending to the town. The rebels coolly and deliberately shot them down like sheep. I did not see an officer attempt to rally or check them in their headlong retreat. On came the rebs and occupied the town, winning at that point a cheap victory."

FLAG OF SIXTH WISCONSIN AS CARRIED AT GETTYSBURG, THE LAST
BATTLE OF THIS OLD COLOR.

inclosing a barn-yard, on the opposite side of the street. A board
or two off from the fence made what the men called a "hog-hole."
Instructing the regiment to follow in single file on the run, I
took a color, ran across the street, and jumped through this
opening in the fence. Officers and men followed rapidly. Taking
position at the fence, when any man obstructed the passage-way
through it, I jerked him away without ceremony or apology, the
object being to keep the track clear for those yet to come. Two
men were shot in this street crossing. The regiment was reformed in the barn-yard, and I marched back again to the street
leading from the Pennsylvania College to the Cemetery Hill. To
understand· why the street was crossed in the manner described,
it should be remembered that men running at full speed, scattered
in single file, were safer from the fire of the enemy than if
marching in a compact body. By going into the inclosure, the
regiment came together, to be at once formed into compact order.

It was in compliance with the order, to keep my men together. The weather was sultry. The sweat streamed from the faces of the men. There was not a drop of water in the canteens, and there had been none for hours. The streets were jammed with crowds of retreating soldiers, and with ambulances, artillery, and wagons. The cellars were crowded with men, sound in body, but craven in spirit, who had gone there to surrender. I saw no men wearing badges of the first army corps in this disgraceful company. In one case, these miscreants, mistaking us for the rebels, cried out from the cellar, "Don't fire, Johnny, we'll surrender." These surroundings were depressing to my hot and thirsty men. Finding the street blocked, I formed my men in two lines across it. The rebels began to fire on us from houses and cross-lots. Here came to us a friend in need. It was an old citizen with two buckets of fresh water. The inestimable value of this cup of cold water to those true, unyielding soldiers, I would that our old friend could know.

After this drink, in response to my call, the men gave* three cheers for the good and glorious cause for which we stood in battle. The enemy fired on us sharply, and the men returned their fire, shooting wherever the enemy appeared. This firing had a good effect. It cleared the street of stragglers in short order. The way being open I marched again toward the Cemetery Hill. The enemy did not pursue ; they had found it dangerous business. We hurried along, not knowing certainly that we might not be marching into the clutches of the enemy. But the colors of the Union, floating over a well ordered line of men in blue, who were arrayed along the slope of Cemetery Hill, became visible. This was the seventy-third Ohio, of Steinwehr's division of the

---

*The whole retreat from the commencement was most creditable to the troops engaged. There was no hurry and no confusion, but the regiments fell back calmly, turning from time to time to check the enemy's advance by volleys of musketry, and again retreating. From the admixture of so many different regiments at the seminary, it became impossible to reorganize them in good order without a delay which would have exposed the men to certain destruction. I saw, however, no running or undue haste. All the troops passed tranquilly on, although the enemy was firing into them from the side streets, and all reformed promptly on their arrival at Cemetery Hill, and in a very short time were again ready for service. The sixth Wisconsin marched through the streets in a body, stopping from time to time to return the fire of the enemy, and giving hearty cheers for the good old cause and the sixth Wisconsin Volunteers.—Doubleday's Report.

eleventh army corps. With swifter steps we now pressed on up the hill, and, passing in through the ranks open to receive us, officers and men threw themselves in a state of almost perfect exhaustion on the green grass and the graves of the cemetery. The condition of affairs on Cemetery Hill at this time has been a subject of discussion. If fresh troops had attacked us then, we unquestionably would have fared badly. The troops were scattered over the hill in much disorder, while a stream of stragglers and wounded men pushed along the Baltimore Turnpike toward the rear. But this perilous condition of affairs was of short duration. There was no appearance of panic on the Cemetery Hill. After a short breathing spell my men again promptly responded to the order to "fall in." Lieutenant Rogers brought us orders from General Wadsworth, to join our own brigade, which had been sent to occupy Culp's Hill.* As we marched toward the hill our regimental wagon joined us. In the wagon were a dozen spades and shovels. Taking our place on the right of the line of the brigade, I ordered the regiment to intrench. The men worked with great energy. A man would dig with all his strength till out of breath, when another would seize the spade and push on the work. There were no orders to construct these breastworks, but the situation plainly dictated their necessity. The men now lay down to rest after the arduous labors of this great and terrible day. Sad and solemn reflections possessed, at least, the writer of these papers. Our dead lay unburied and beyond our sight or reach. Our wounded were in the hands of the enemy. Our bravest and best were numbered with them. Of eighteen hundred 'men who marched with the splendid brigade in the morning, but seven hundred were here. More than one thousand men had been shot. There was to us a terrible reality in the figures which represent our loss. We had been driven, also, by the enemy, and the shadow of defeat seemed to be hanging over us. But that afternoon, under the burning sun and through the stifling clouds of dust, the Army of the Potomac had marched to the sound of our cannon. We had lost

---

*Colonel W. W, Robinson, of the seventh Wisconsin regiment, was in command of the brigade, having succeeded General Meredith, who had been wounded.

the ground on which we had fought, we had lost our commander and our comrades, but our fight had held the Cemetery Hill and forced the decision for history that the crowning battle of the war should be at Gettysburg.*

It is a troubled and dreamy sleep at best that comes to the soldier on a battle field. About one o'clock at night we had a great alarm. A man in the seventh Indiana regiment, next on right, cried so loudly in his sleep that he aroused all the troops in the vicinity. Springing up, half bewildered, I ordered my regiment to "fall in," and a heavy fire of musketry broke out from along the whole line of men. At three o'clock in the morning, according to orders, the men were aroused. The morning of the second day found us lying quietly in our breast-works near the summit of Culp's Hill. We were in the shade of some fine oak trees, and enjoyed an excellent view of nearly the whole battle field. Our situation would have been delightful, and our rest in the cool shade would have been refreshing, if it had not been for the crack, crack, of the deadly sharpshooters on the rebel skirmish line. Owing, probably, to the crooked line of our army, the shots came from all directions, and the peculiarly mournful wail of the spent bullet was constantly heard.

LONGSTREET'S ATTACK ON SICKLES.

Our line faced toward the town of Gettysburg. For hours I watched the rebel troops with a field-glass, as their heavy columns of infantry marched toward our right. We could see them forming in the fields beyond Rock Creek, and knew that they were preparing to attack Culp's Hill. Until four o'clock P. M., but little sound was heard except the monotonous noise of the sharpshooter.

---

*In the sixth Wisconsin, Adjutant Edward P. Brooks is mentioned for greatly aiding the successful capture of the two regiments in the railroad cut, by throwing a body of men into the cut so as to enfilade the rebel line. Corporal F. Asbury Waller, of company I, captured the colors of the second Mississippi previous to the surrender of that regiment. Major Hauser was particularly brave and efficient. Captain John Ticknor and Lieutenant Orrin D. Chapman, who were killed in the charge, were a great loss to the service. Captain Rollin P. Converse and Lieutenant Charles P. Hyatt, of company B, and Lieutenant Goltermann, of company F, were also among the highly distinguished. The commander of the regiment, Lieutenant-Colonel R. R. Dawes, proved himself to be one of the ablest officers on the field.—Doubleday's Report.

At this hour, from the Cemetery Hill and from a long distance in that direction, the storm of battle suddenly broke out. Artillery and musketry thundered and crashed together. Amid the tumult we could plainly hear the rebel charging yell. We momentarily expected that the rebels in the valley of Rock Creek would advance upon us. But they did not come, and gradually our attention became absorbed by the awful combat on our left. We could plainly see that our troops were giving ground. Thousands were streaming to the rear. Our suspense and anxiety were intense. We gathered in knots all over the hill, watching the battle. It seemed to us a long time that this savage, but to all appearances unfavorable, struggle went on. The rebel line certainly was advancing. The rebel yell certainly was predominant. Brigade after brigade moved in, but the tide was against us. As the sun was low down a fine sight was seen. It was two long blue lines of battle, with twenty or thirty regimental banners, charging forward into the smoke and din of battle. To all appearances they saved the field. But a sound came now from the woods to our right, that made us jump for our breastworks. It was the rebel yell, sounded by thousands of voices. It was almost dusk, and beginning to be quite dark in the woods. I ran to my post, and ordered: "Down, men, watch sharp, keep your eyes peeled! Shoot low, shoot low, the hill is steep; quiet, now; steady!" After these orders and cautions, the men peered sharply into the woods to "let them have it" as they came up the hill against us. But there is no attack upon us. The crash of Union muskets breaks out on our right, and we know that the attack is on the twelfth corps. Soon a staff officer came along, calling: "Where is Colonel Dawes?" I answered: "Here." He said: "Take your regiment, sir, and report to General Greene." I said: "Where is he?" "He is over in the woods where they are attacking." I commanded: "Attention, battalion, right face, forward by file right—march!" and we started for General Greene. Who he was I did not know, but the musketry showed where to go. The first mounted officer I saw proved to be General C. S. Greene, of the twelfth army corps. Taking from his pocket a card, he wrote in the darkness his name and command, which he handed to me. He then directed me to form my regiment, and go into the breastworks; to go as quickly as possible, and to hold the works after I got there. I did not then understand, nor did he, that the rebels already had possession of these works. Facing the regiment to the front, I ordered: "Forward—run; march!" We received no fire until we neared the breastworks, when the enemy who had possession of them, lying on the lower side, and who were completely surprised at our sudden arrival, rose up and fired a volley at us, and immediately retreated down the hill. This remarkable encounter did not last a minute. We lost two men, killed—both burned with the powder of the guns fired at them. The darkness and the suddenness of our arrival caused the enemy to fire wildly. We recaptured the breastworks on our front, and the fourteenth Brooklyn, which came in on our right, also got possession of the works. We remained here until midnight, when we were relieved by troops of the twelfth corps, who had left these works to support General Sickles' corps against Longstreet's attack and now returned. We then marched back to our own breastworks on Culp's Hill.

During the whole day of July 3rd, we occupied our intrenchments on Culp's Hill. They seemed a *coign* of vantage. We had the zip of the sharpshooter's bullet, the "where is you" of cannon shot, the ringing whistle of the ragged fragments of bursting shell, all around us. At some hours of the day, especially during the great cannonade preceding Pickett's charge, the air seemed full of missiles fired by the enemy. But no man was touched, and we were devoutly thankful that such immunity was granted us.*

This letter from Colonel J. M. Stone, then, and at the present time, Governor of the State of Mississippi, was in reply to my letter asking for some recollections of our meeting at Gettysburg.

STATE OF MISSISSIPPI, EXECUTIVE DEPARTMENT, }
JACKSON, JUNE 4th, 1876. }

COLONEL R. R. DAWES, MARIETTA, OHIO.

"*My Dear Sir:*—I have the honor to acknowledge the receipt of your esteemed letter of the 1st inst. and I thank you for the

---

*For casualties Army of Potomac see Page 112, Volume XXVII, Part I, War Records.

complimentary mention of the officers and men composing the second regiment of Mississippi Volunteers, which regiment I had the honor to command during the late war. I have a distinct, but sad recollection of the events of July 1st, 1863, in the vicinity of Gettysburg. In consequence of a wound received a few minutes prior to the final issue, I did not have the pleasure of meeting you and your gallant men in the railroad cut. The loss of my regiment in that terrible conflict (if my memory serves me correctly) was one hundred and eighty-two killed and wounded. I have frequently heard Major Blair (afterward Lieutenant Colonel) and other officers and soldiers of my regiment, speak in the highest terms of yourself and the officers and men of the sixth Wisconsin. I remember well the fight in the cornfield in front of the church at Antietam, (Sharpsburg.) I was in command, was twice wounded, but not disabled, and remained and commanded until the battle ended.

You can communicate with Colonel John A. Blair, at Tupelo, Lee County, Mississippi. He will doubtless be much pleased to hear from you. With assurances of my highest regard, and sincere desire for mutual and perpetual good feeling and friendly relations, I am very respectfully yours, J. M. STONE.

Official reports describing the action of the sixth Wisconsin in the battle of Gettysburg may be found as follows, in Volume XXVII, Part I, War Records:

General Abner Doubleday, Pages..243 to 257
General James S. Wadsworth, Page...266
Lieutenant Colonel Rufus R. Dawes, Pages.......................................275 to 278

References to the sixth Wisconsin will be found in Reports of
General Lysander Cutler, Page..283
Colonel Edward B. Fowler, Page..286
Major Edward Pye, Page 287
General John W. Geary, Page...827
General George S. Greene, Page..856
Captain Lewis R. Stegman, Page...865

Confederate Reports, Volume XXVII, Part II, War Records:
General Joseph R. Davis, Page...648
Major General Henry Heth, page...637
Lieutenant General A. P. Hill, Page...606

Reports of the commanders of the other regiments of the "Iron Brigade" may be found in same volume:
Colonel Henry A. Morrow, Page...267
Major John Mansfield, Page..273
Colonel W. W. Robinson, Page...278

CASUALTIES IN THE BATTLE OF GETTYSBURG.

	Killed		Wounded.		Missing.		Aggregate.
	Officers.	Men.	Officers.	Men.	Officers.	Men.	
Brig. Com. Staff..			2				2
Sixth Wisconsin Volunteers............................	2	28	7	109		23	169
Second Wisconsin Volunteers.........................	2	25	10	144	5	47	233
Seventh Wisconsin Volunteers........................		27	11	98	1	42	179
Nineteenth Indiana Volunteers.......................	1	25	23	111	4	57	221
Twenty-fourth Michigan Volunteers................	8	46	14	206	3	84	361
Total..	13	151	67	668	13	253	1165

CHAPTER IX.

(Letter to M. B. G.)   BIVOUAC NEAR BOONESBORO, MD.,
JULY 9th, 1863.

"Until we get our wagon train I am reduced to the extremity of writing with a pencil. Our pursuit of the retreating enemy has been rapid. We have marched night and day and we have beaten the rebel army. At last the Army of the Potomac has done what, well-handled, it might have done long ago, out-marched, out-maneuvered and defeated the great rebel army of General Lee. Our men have toiled and suffered as never before. Almost half of our men have marched barefooted for a week. Such energy as is now exhibited would have crushed the rebellion long ago. Colonel Bragg came back to us last night. I do not think he can endure the hot sun, as he is still sick. This battle service has always made me sick, but I think I will get through this time. You can hardly know the strain of such days as those three at Gettysburg. We have had severe rains since the battle. I have not slept in a dry blanket or had on dry clothing since crossing the Potomac before the battle. If we can end this war right here, I will cheerfully abide the terrible risk of another battle, and certainly personal discomforts are small comparatively. I feel very hopeful now, and prouder than I can tell you that the old army has vindicated itself. I hope the Quartermaster will be up to-night with my valise, so I will not be obliged to write with a pencil."

Owing to the great necessity for medical attendance upon the wounded at Gettysburg, our three surgeons, who were all experienced and skillful operators, were kept at Gettysburg. A young civilian doctor, whose name I have lost, was sent to attend our regiment upon this march. He was provided with no horse or equipment, and I was obliged to share mine with him.

(Letter to M. B. G.)   NEAR SOUTH MOUNTAIN, }
                 JULY 9th, 1863. }

"I wrote you an illegible letter this morning with a pencil, and sent it in a rebel envelope. We are again near the rebel army, and unless they 'escape' over the river, we may expect a battle. Last night a shell burst within half a mile of us. Our army is worn out with toil and suffering, and looks hopefully for a season of rest after the enemy is driven from our soil. General Meade has shown himself equal to the emergency. We have had as yet no opportunity to make reports of the battle, or to do anything but march, and I presume we will not until Lee's army is destroyed or beyond the Potomac. The only paper I have seen since the battle is a Baltimore Clipper. The second Wisconsin regiment can not muster fifty muskets. Still this little representative remnant has been with the advance since the battle, and will probably open the next fight as it did the last. One thing will appear, that the Army of the Potomac saved Pennsylvania and the North. Not one shot was fired at Gettysburg by the Pennsylvania militia."

WILLIAMSPORT.

(Letter to M. B. G.) LINE OF BATTLE NEAR FUNKSTOWN, MD., }
                    JULY 11th, 1863. }

"To-day we have expected a battle, but the sun is now twenty degrees above the highest summit of South Mountain, and not so much as a musket shot has broken the stillness. Perhaps the rebels have crossed over the river but that is not likely."

(Letter to M. B. G.)   LINE OF BATTLE NEAR HAGERSTOWN, }
                  JULY 12th, 1863. }

"We are again confronting the rebel army which is strongly entrenched in position near the Potomac river and another deadly struggle·seems certain. I can not write more than that. I am to-night, alive and well, and have received all of your letters up to July fourth. This battle must end our campaign for the present."

(Letter to M. B. G.)   NEAR HAGERSTOWN, JULY 14th, 1863.

"*I wrote the last note in full expectation of having soon to charge on the enemy's entrenchments. No pleasant prospect to one who saw the awfully murderous repulse of the rebel charging columns at Gettysburg. All day yesterday, we lay quietly roasting in the hot sun and this morning the rebel army has retreated across the river. We may now reasonably hope for rest. The incessant and toilsome marching from Fredericksburgh to Gettysburg, the terrible battle, and the hurried pursuit of the enemy to this point has been the most trying campaign of this army. Our men have become ragged and shoeless, thousands have marched for days barefooted over the flinty turnpikes. The army has shown a willingness and alacrity under its toils, sufferings and privations, that entitle it to the gratitude of the Nation and I think for once it will receive it."

There has been discussion upon the question whether General Meade should have attacked the rebel army in its position near Williamsport, Maryland, on the thirteenth of July. It is my belief that our army would have been repulsed if they had attacked the enemy in this entrenched position. Our later experiences at Spottsylvania and at Cold Harbor, and in many other unsuccessful assaults is a sufficient indication of the fact.

(Letter to M. B. G.)   CAMP NEAR KNOXVILLE, MARYLAND, ⎱
JULY 16th, 1863. ⎰

"We have one day of rest. I have had to use all kinds of schemes to get my letters to the mail, sometimes leaving them with citizens or dropping them in village post offices or sending them by newspaper boys. The State of Wisconsin has at last furnished us with a beautiful stand of colors upon which our battles are inscribed : '*Rappahannock, Gainesville, Bull Run, South Mountain, Antietam, Fredericksburgh, Fitz Hugh's Crossing, Chancellorsville, Gettysburg,*' and who can tell what more is in store for this shattered little fragment of veteran heroes before next

---

*July 13th to 15th 1863, occurred the terrible draft riots in New York City.

July, when our term of service will expire. Five hundred and seventy-five men have been killed or wounded in these battles and I have been through them all with scarcely a scratch. We are stopping here a few days to get new clothing and shoes and to refit the troops for another campaign in Virginia. The prospects are brightening. The opening of the Mississippi river is the grand success of the war.

We have never been so pressed for time. Accounts, returns, muster-rolls, correspondence, everything was given up to driving the enemy from Pennsylvania. I have just signed our muster-rolls for the muster of July 1st. (This refers to the muster for pay made on June 30th at Marsh Creek just before engaging in the battle of Gettysburg). By our losses at Gettysburg and in other battles, our regiment is reduced below the minimum required by law. Under the present policy of the War Department, this regiment is not entitled to a Colonel. Encouraging, is it not? The more desperate the risks of the Lieutenant Colonel who commands in battle, and the greater the loss of his regiment, the less his chance for promotion. The Governor would commission a Colonel in case of a vacancy, but the United States mustering officer can not now muster in a Colonel for our regiment."

This cutting off of the Lieutenant Colonels and Majors of the old battle regiments from promotion, was a gross blunder in our war policy. It was done on the theory of economy. Colonels came too high. It would have been better to cut off the appointment of a Major, leaving always before the field officer, the avenue to promotion. An honorable promotion as a reward and recognition of perilous service, is an inestimable prize to a true soldier. The right policy was pursued with line officers in the companies. When a company became reduced below the minimum, the second lieutenant was cut off and not the captain. This "blunder" was far-reaching in its damaging effect upon the spirits and efficiency of our volunteer army.

(Letter to M. B. G.)   BIVOUAC NEAR WATERFORD, ⎱
   LOUDON COUNTY, VA., JULY 18th, 1863. ⎰

"We crossed the Potomac river at Berlin this morning and came here. We may have some hard marching to end up with another battle, but let us hope that the glorious result to which events are now pointing so plainly, may be attained without the battle. Colonel Bragg has gone home sick. It looks as though the subscriber would command the Sixth regiment for some time. I fear we shall suffer again from heat and dust, but we are moving leisurely now."

MIDDLEBURG, VIRGINIA, JULY 21st, 1863.

"Almost for the first time since coming into the army, I have my headquarters in a house. I am King of this pretty little village while we stay. My regiment is doing provost duty. Are not you glad I have the boys living on the aristocratic rebels of Middleburg? The people board the men wherever they are sent to guard their property. The boys are living high and they are kindly treated. I had a talk with a lady this morning, and she was a refined and gentle woman. She had lost a son, and her nephew had been killed in the war. She had lost 'all she had to live for.' You can not imagine how bitterly she expressed herself against the North and our army. She made no complaint of our men who, she said, did their duty faithfully and kindly. 'I believe,' she said, 'God's blessing will rest upon our soldiers if they take ruin and desolation to every hearthstone of the North, for their wickedness has merited such punishment.' She confessed freely their own waning fortunes, but had 'faith that a just and terrible vengeance would yet come on the North.' Poor old Virginia, she is bitterly reaping her reward. Nothing more plainly foreshadows the bursting of the rebel bubble, than this despair of the first families of Virginia."

I regret that the name of this lady is not preserved. I had received a communication from corps headquarters that Mosby's men had been in Middleburg, and I was directed to put a stop to their being harbored and concealed by the people. There were none but women in the town. I was told to see this lady, as she was the most influential person in the town, and to notify her that if there were further causes for complaint, the guards would be removed from their property. She promised me she would try to control the young women in the matter, and put a stop to it.

"General Cutler now commands our division and General John Newton commands our first corps.

I have been sitting this morning as a member of a special court martial, and all the forenoon we wise doctors have been wrangling over the law and the testimony. I have to go back in a few minutes. We are selected for a dignified and able court. We have one Brigadier General, four Colonels, and two Lieutenant Colonels. We are trying Colonel ——.

Later—I will try to finish my letter though it is quite late and we are to march at daylight. My head is full of hearsay evidence, competency, relevancy and so forth, for we have a fearfully technical court. General H. S. Briggs of Massachusetts, is our President. Colonel Bates of the twelfth Massachusetts is the brightest man on the court. He occasionally makes sad work with technical points. The prosecution of —— is a silly farce."

The Colonel, who was on trial, was a gallant, faithful, and capable officer. His regiment was first in the order of march one morning, but the Colonel overslept, and his regiment was not ready to move at the designated hour. In consequence of this the troops were delayed for a short time. For this somewhat trivial offense, charges were preferred against him. He was punished by a nominal censure.

At this time, whisky was too freely issued to the troops under the term "rations." The effect was very bad, and I published an order forbidding the issue of liquor to the regiment, except with quinine. Hence arose a song composed in imitation of the Surgeon's sick call on the drum, the burden of which was: "Come, Come, Come, Come and get your quinine!" When some of our "soakers" were seen going to sick call, this chorus would break out. General John Newton, our corps commander, said, as I was alone of regimental commanders in making such an order, I could not sustain it. He was mistaken. It enforced itself. ——'s trial grew out of an excessive ration of whisky. The Colonel was drunk on Government whisky, as were most of his men and officers. Whisky as a stimulant to wet, weary and tired soldiers did not compare with hot coffee. After whisky, the men being overstimulated, were wakeful and noisy, and lost their rest. After coffee they went at once to sleep. Sleep, tired nature's sweet restorer, was the thing needful.

GEN R E LEE

MAJ GEN JOHN NEWTON

(Letter to M. B. G.) WARRENTON, VA., JULY 23rd, 1863.

"We marched yesterday from Middleburg to White Plains, and to-day we came here, where I think we will remain a day or two for supplies."

(Letter.) WARRENTON JUNCTION, JULY 25th, 1863.

"Yesterday I was ordered down the Culpepper turnpike to support a battery, and to construct defenses with *abattis*, and to-day was spent marching to this point. We are in a terrible place here. The water is undrinkable, and wood is very scarce. I hope our sojourn will be short. What a calamity to a country to even have an army camp in it! The beautiful country about the village of Warrenton, without fences, without crops, without even garden enclosures, is little better than a desert. There are few more pleasantly situated villages in the land. It is the home of Virginia aristocracy, but you see literally nothing but black veils and mourning dresses. We heard last night the familiar boom of cannon, the first since crossing the river. I do not know what it was.

We have just got to-day's newspaper, which is the first one we have had for a week. So you have had John Morgan near you, if not in Marietta. (Morgan's raid in Ohio.) I shall feel anxious for particulars. Did you run? Did you see any of the rebels? It is coming home to have rebels all around Marietta. But if they were, as reported, at Chester, they must have gone very near Marietta. How did your brave men bear themselves? Better, I hope, than the Pennsylvania militia. I would like the 'Iron Brigade,' for a short time in front of Morgan's ragamuffins."

Of the Morgan Raid in Ohio, my correspondent, M. B. G., wrote me that ten thousand of the Ohio emergency Militia were encamped at a ford on the Ohio river, eight miles below Marietta. They were on the great farm of William P. Cutler. This force was mainly without guns. She named two very prominent citizens who had patriotically joined the militia to repel Morgan. These gentlemen had guns, and they marched arm in arm under the same umbrella, paying a darky to carry their muskets. After accomplishing the eight miles, they were so hot and tired that they declared they would not run if the whole Southern Confederacy came against them. They would contract with the darky to save their muskets, and themselves surrender. She described how Mr. Cutler found sleeping in his hay mow, the man who had beaten him for Congress.

(Letter to M. B. G.) WARRENTON JUNCTION, JULY 27th, 1863.

"The army is now lying in this vicinity getting supplies and clothing, and recruiting its energies, preparatory for future campaigning. We are in a bad place for water and wood. I do not want to fight, but I hope to get out of this desolate land.

General Meade did wisely in not attacking General Lee in his entrenched position at Williamsport, and I am impudent enough to say my opinion is worth more on this point than any man's who is as far away as Marietta.* I examined the rebel fortifications at Williamsport, which were strong and well-constructed, and I think General Meade would have certainly failed to carry them by direct assault. Both flanks of the works were on the Potomac river. We had no other alternative than direct assault. I take no stock in the stuff printed in the newspapers about the demoralization of the rebel army after Gettysburg. They were worn out and tired as we were, but their cartridge boxes had plenty of ammunition, and they would have quietly lain in their rifle pits and shot us down with the same coolness and desperation they showed at Gettysburg.

So you have really had a speck of war at Marietta. I hope Charley† will not bivouac many nights, and that he will keep out of the skirmishing with the rebels.

I think the New York riot is in some respects a fortunate thing. It settles Vallandigham in Ohio, and teaches more clearly than words the propriety of muzzling the Woods and Seymours. The suspension of the draft, though a cowardly policy, was consistent as a military necessity. The country would have been in a fix if General Lee had defeated our army at Gettysburg. That is clear now is it not?"

(Letter to M. B. G.) WARRENTON JUNCTION, JULY 29th, 1863.

"Morgan came nearer than you expected. I am glad he is

---

*On Page 935, Volume XXVII, Part II, War Records, may be found some of this talk by a smart aleck, who writes to Wm. H. Seward.

†Charles B. Gates, her brother, then a young student in Marietta College. He went out to resist Morgan.

captured. Ohio is not a shell, as General Grierson found Mississippi, and 'carrying desolation to northern hearthstones,' is serious business.

We are now clothing our men and recruiting generally, from the effects of our hard campaign. What absurd talk there is in the papers about General Lee's 'escape' from Williamsport."

(Letter to M. B. G.) WARRENTON JUNCTION, JULY 30th, 1863.

"I do not believe there is in Virginia, any such place as 'Endorville.' If there is, General Lee has certainly 'escaped' from it. General H. S. Briggs, of Massachusetts, is to command our division. He was President of our court martial at Middleburg, and I feel well acquainted with him.

I am President of the General Court Martial, which holds its sessions at division headquarters. Colonel Bragg is at home sick. He could not endure the hot sun. No leaves of absence are now granted, except for sickness. —— —— made a piteous appeal. His hard earned property was going to ruin. His wife was sick. His children had the measles, and the dog was not well, but notwithstanding all these troubles, his application was 'unfavorably considered' at army headquarters.

Our division is now doing the picket duty for the corps. The two other divisions are guarding the Orange and Alexandria R. R. There is no appearance of any purpose on the part of Meade to attack the enemy. Four old regiments just passed here on their way to New York to enforce the draft. Many officers and men are being sent from the army to take charge of conscripts. So far as I know, no considerable re-inforcements have been sent to this army since crossing into Virginia, and we are still losing nine-months volunteers by reason of expiration of their service."

One day about this time, I was away attending court martial when our division marched, and, as I galloped after them, I was doubtful whether I was on the right road. I asked a woman if any troops had passed. Raising both hands she replied: "Yes sir, millions and millions of them!"

BEVERLY FORD, RAPPAHANNOCK RIVER,
AUGUST 1st, 1863.

"We are near the railroad crossing. We marched to-day from Warrenton Junction, twelve miles. It was very hot and men were sun-struck in the column. *There is artillery firing and musketry this evening near Brandy Station, I think. The one hundred and sixty-seventh Pennsylvania, a regiment of men who were drafted for nine months service, and who claimed their time had expired, refused to march this morning. They are attached to our brigade and there are about eight hundred men in their ranks. The second, sixth, and seventh Wisconsin were drawn up in front of them with loaded muskets and the commands "Ready! aim!" were given by General Cutler before they would 'fall in.' Upon that incentive however, they fell in with great alacrity. General Cutler himself gave these commands, and I should have felt badly all my life to have had him order 'Fire.' But by showing the men he would order it, the necessity was obviated. I was directed to march my regiment behind the one hundred and sixty-seventh Pennsylvania, and had orders to shoot any man who fell out of the ranks, which I did not do, but I kept a company deployed behind them, who drove them up when they lagged."†

"The State of Wisconsin has sent us a fine stand of colors which will, I understand, be here to-morrow. I wish I could keep our old color lance, which has three bullet holes through it, and two other marks. Think of that slender stick struck five times. It is dark, but still the sullen boom of rebel cannon goes on beyond the river."

This color staff is preserved in the flag room at the Capitol of Wisconsin. Five distinct bullet marks can be seen. There is probably not another color lance in the United States that equals it in the number of its battle scars. It is a National color.

---

*On August first, Brigadier General John Buford, with a division of cavalry, advanced from Rappahannock Station, and drove the enemy's cavalry to the vicinity of Culpepper C. H., where he encountered infantry and was obliged to retire. This was the cause of the firing we heard.

†The question with the men of this regiment was whether they were legally held for nine months from the time that each individual was taken into the service or nine months from the date on which the regiment was mustered into the service as an organization. It made a difference of about two weeks time, upon the average. It was said that the officers of the regiment were themselves conscripts, who had been elected to their positions by the men of the regiment, and it was suspected that they encouraged the men in refusing to march.

Bivouac south of the Rappahannock,
AUGUST 3rd, 1863.

"Yesterday morning we moved in great haste from Beverly Ford, and crossed the river on pontoons at the railroad station. We went into line of battle stretching along in front of the railroad crossing. I do not know but that yesterday was the hottest day I ever experienced. The troops suffered very much, although the march was not long. Thinking that we would remain at Beverly Ford, I took great pains in arranging the regimental camp, and the men were nicely fixed. Dr. Hall is still at Gettysburg attending the wounded of the battle."

Line of Battle south of the Rappahannock,
AUGUST 5th, 1863.

"*We got ready for battle yesterday. Pack mules were hustled back over the river to the rear, stretchers were brought up, and field hospitals established. The enemy attacked our cavalry in front, but were driven back. It was only a reconnoissance in force. Meanwhile a heavy rain came on, drenching us suffering heroes to the skin. I got my wedge tent up to the front before night, and, appropriating a stretcher for a bed, I made myself quite comfortable. We sent away our old flag yesterday, and were sorry to see it go. The new one is a very handsome silk color, (National color) and it has all of our engagements inscribed upon it, except Fitz Hugh's Crossing. I enclose a copy of my letter which accompanied the flag."

Headquarters Sixth Regiment Wisconsin Volunteers,
AUGUST 4TH, 1863.

W. Y. Selleck, Military Agent for the State of Wisconsin :

SIR—I have the honor to acknowledge at the hands of Mr. Taylor, the receipt of the National color, with the names of our battles inscribed upon it, provided by the State of Wisconsin for this regiment. I send to you herewith for transmission to the Governor our old color. It can no longer be unfurled and five bullets have pierced the staff. Its tattered folds and splintered staff bear witness more eloquently than words to the conduct of the men who have rallied around it from Gainesville to Gettys-

---

*See Page 22, Volume XXIX, Part II, War Records, for reports of this affair.

burg. We send it to the people of Wisconsin, knowing what they expect of us, and we promise that the past shall be an earnest of the future, under the beautiful standard they have sent us.

Very respectfully,   R. R. DAWES,

Lieutenant Colonel commanding sixth Wisconsin volunteers.

(Letter to M. B. G.)   AUGUST 5th, 1863.

"We are still south of the river. Our cavalry pickets in front were attacked by the enemy yesterday. There was not much of a skirmish and the rebels soon retired. We (the infantry) were not engaged but I formed my command for action.

Dr. Hall came back yesterday. He has been at Gettysburg ever since the battle attending the wounded, of whom there were thousands. Dr. Preston still remains at Gettysburg in this employment. General Meade is not worshiped but he is highly respected. His judicious and vigorous handling of the troops at Gettysburg and his pursuit after the battle have inspired confidence, which is not lessened by his proper caution at Williamsport. The army is not so fierce to attack the enemy in entrenchments as newspapers represent it to be.

I am glad Dr. Hall is back, as it has been dull with so many of our officers away and he is excellent company."

In this camp I received a letter from my brother, who was in General William T. Sherman's corps during the Vicksburg campaign. He was now in pursuit of General Joseph E. Johnston. It will be seen that we did not have an entire monopoly of hard campaigning :

MESSENGER'S FORD (BLACK RIVER) MISS., ⎱
JULY 27th, 1863.   ⎰

"A little more than a month since we marched from Snyder's Bluff, with three days' rations. We staid at Oak Ridge a week. On the afternoon of the fourth of July (the day Vicksburg surrendered) we started after Johnston's army. My baggage for the campaign was one shirt and two pocket handkerchiefs carried in the valise on my saddle. * * * * The only rations issued were crackers, coffee and salt. Our mess for three weeks have lived on green corn, chickens and sweet potatoes. To-day, for the first time since leaving Snyder's Bluff, I have a tent over my head."

SOUTH OF THE RAPPAHANNOCK, AUGUST 6th, 1863.

"We are disagreeably situated on this (south) side of the river. They will not allow our wagon to come within five miles of us. I was obliged to ride ten miles last night to change my clothing. Whenever the rebel cavalry comes in sight, our pack mules are ordered back over the bridge and we are left destitute. A small portion of our corps is now the only body of troops south of the river.

This army is not 'anxious to get at Lee' until it feels victory reasonably certain, and such a victory as may close the war and crush the rebellion. Then, as always before, we will go in not eagerly, as ferocious stayers-at-home say, but willingly and to win. The 'Iron Brigade' has a record beyond reproach, and a record it will always maintain, but the 'Iron Brigade' does not crave a battle. A battle to veterans is an awful experience. There is not with our men the headlong recklessness of new men, who start in, acting as though they would rather be shot than not, and then lose their organization and scatter like sheep, but there is a conviction from much experience in fighting, that safety is best had by steadiness, persistence in firing, and most of all by holding together. So, with the inducement of pride, duty, patriotism and personal preservation, they will stand together till the last."

SOUTH OF THE RAPPAHANNOCK, AUGUST 8th, 1863.

"Most of the troops of our division have gone back into camp north of the river, but I was placed in command of three regiments, (second Wisconsin, twenty-fourth Michigan and sixth Wisconsin) and Huntington's battery, ('H'—first Ohio) and sent forward to hold a position covering the approaches to the railroad bridge. I hope we will soon be relieved from duty on this side of the river, so that I can get the regiment into camp and have the men clean up. It is hardly fair to require us to do all the outpost duty."

AUGUST 10th, 1863.

"There does not seem to be any prospect of getting relieved from duty on the south side of the river. I am detailed to command this outpost. I have three regiments, twenty-fourth Michigan, sixth Wisconsin, *fifty-sixth Pennsylvania, and Hunt-

---

*This regiment had relieved the second Wisconsin.

ington's battery. I report to General Cutler. The principal hardship is having our wagon two miles away at the brigade camp over the river. We have good water and a good shade, and that is more than can be found north of the river. The situation is assuming the same phase as last spring,—that of chronic apprehension of an advance by the enemy. Their cavalry videttes are in sight. Since the body of our troops have crossed back north of the river, a dash upon us by the enemy has been feared. I have dug riflepits and selected a good position, and I think we can hold out until reinforced from the other side of the river. I believe I will bring my headquarters wagon up in the night and hide it in the bushes."

On August twelfth, the regiment was relieved and sent back into camp.

My service in command of the important outpost, south of the Rappahannock seems to have commended itself to General Briggs, our division commander, for on August fifteenth, he sent me back again.* The regiment however, remained in camp under command of Major Hauser. An advance by the army of General Lee seems to have been feared, and my instructions were to exercise the greatest care and vigilance, and to stubbornly resist an attack until supported from the north side of the river.

(Letter M. B. G.) HEADQUARTERS DEFENSES SOUTH OF RIVER, } AUGUST 16th. }

"I have settled upon my dispositions in case of an attack and feel easy. I have six hundred infantry in the entrenchments and a battery of artillery. The troops are now all under marching orders and something is in the wind. I shall not be surprised if General Lee assumes the offensive. I hardly dare write here why I think so, our communications are so much interfered with. I have my headquarters in a house. There are three

---

*HEADQUARTERS FIRST BRIGADE, FIRST DIVISION, FIRST ARMY CORPS, } SPECIAL ORDER No. 126.   AUGUST 15th, 1863. }
"In compliance with instructions from headquarters first division, just received, Lieutenant Colonel R. R. Dawes, sixth Wisconsin Volunteers, is hereby detailed to take charge of the troops on the south side of the Rappahannock and he will report at these headquarters without delay.
By command, W.W. ROBINSON, Col. seventh Wis. Vols. Com'd'g Brigade.
J. D. WOOD, Captain and A. A. G."

little astonished looking girls with their fingers in their mouths, hanging around the table watching me as I write."

(Letter to M. B. G.) AUGUST 18th, 1863.

"Just now I am living in a house and have good water to drink. My tent back at the regimental camp is in the 'broiling sun,' but I am too old a soldier not to have put up a shade long ago. I have had the men dig a well at the camp, about twenty feet deep, and they now get good water. This army will not 'advance soon.' Our Generals expect to be attacked. There now—that is more than I have any business to write, to trust the mail which Mosby may capture.

There was an exodus from this neighborhood of children of Ham (and they took all the hams with them) last night, to the number of about forty. 'Dey's g'wine ter git out dis yer place, 'fore de southern gemman come.' This morning, for the first time in her life, I presume, the old rebel lady of this house cooked a very poor breakfast for herself and the Yankee Colonel, who boards with her. I have quite an independent command over the river here. There is one Maryland regiment who spend most of their time singing hymns. I found yesterday that some of these men had not a single cartridge in their boxes. The negligence and carelessness of some officers is marvelous.

Did you get the 'Iron Brigade Quickstep' which I sent you?"

The "Iron Brigade Quickstep" was a sheet of music. It was not worthy of its name as it has long since been forgotten.

(Letter to M. B. G.) AUGUST 22nd, 1863.

"I am still in command south of the river. We had a false alarm night before last. Since then my garrison has been reinforced by three hundred men. I want to get back to the regiment, but I cannot get relieved. I command the only force of the army south of the river. I cannot appreciate the policy of holding the Rappahannock line, if our army does not assume the offensive. The country between us and Washington is barren, desolate, and worthless. The communications are constantly exposed, and the line of defense imperfect and easily flanked. We should hardly lose prestige by contracting our lines to Centreville, as no attempt is made in our present position to occupy the attention of the enemy. But I suppose—'*nulla vestigia retrorsum*,' is the motto of our commander. General Briggs left us yesterday. I think likely that General Cutler will have command of the division. I hope so.

Later—I finished my letter at home in camp, having been relieved from duty over the river. The old lady and little girls cried when I came away. They said they knew 'they would lose their chickens, and the soldiers would milk their cow, too.' The poor people were grateful for the protection I afforded them. They have been plundered and robbed by both armies, until starvation stares them in the face. The weather continues very hot, and, with the bad water in this neighborhood, it is beginning to cause much sickness among the troops. The old lady over the river fed me on bread and milk."

(Letter to M. B. G.)   NEAR RAPPAHANNOCK STATION, }
                                   AUGUST 23rd, 1863.   }

"Every idea is roasted out of my head by the heat. The Doctor (J. C. Hall) and I had a discussion to-night on the question,—whether the negro has any love of liberty; whether he desires freedom, or merely imagines more personal comfort in being free. We submitted the following test question to William, to Moses, to Reuben, to Mink, to Mat, and to Sam, all the Africans accessible: 'Which would you prefer—to be a slave with a good master, not much to do, plenty of hog and hominy, and a coon dog, or be a free man and have to scratch for your living?' William, of course, took my side of the question, and preferred freedom, but Mink, a child of influence among our contrabands, followed the coon dog, and the rest of them followed Mink."

Mink argued that if he could pick his master, he had rather be a slave than a Brigadier General. There was no better position. It involved "no 'sponsibility." It was almost the same as to "jine the family." But said I, "Mink, what if your master died?" That would be bad he said, because he might set his slaves free in the will. He had heard of them made "miserable" that way. "They'd rather died themselves." He said a free nigger was "'spized" everywhere he had ever been. But said I, Mink suppose you got a bad master? "Dat's next to bein' a free nigger, sah," was his quick response.

General J. C. Rice of Massachusetts has been assigned to the command of our division in place of General Briggs, who has gone to Alexandria."

(Letter to M. B. G.) AUGUST 24th, 1863.

"William says 'he done never seed it hotter afore.' We have just had a thunder gust. It swept away my letter and came near taking our tent along also. Our only course in such an emergency is to go to bed until the wind will let the candle burn."

RAPPAHANNOCK STATION, AUGUST 27th, 1863.

"I expect Colonel Bragg back to-night. If he comes, I shall honor the day to-morrow, by an application for a leave of absence to come home. Colonel Bragg will likely get his star as a Brigadier General. Colonel Lucius Fairchild was nominated by the Republicans for Secretary of State of Wisconsin. This is accepted as a special compliment to the 'Iron Brigade.'

I am having a busy day, shifting my whole camp, shading it with evergreen bowers, and having the men raise their tents and bunks. I am having a thorough, general police. I propose to have the best camp in this division, and therefore supervise the work myself, not trusting wholly to the officer of the day.

Our new division commander, General J. C. Rice, is especially anxious to have a neat camp. Our men can make a nice enough camp to suit him. We once had from the medical inspector of the army credit for having the best arranged and best policed regimental camp in the Army of the Potomac."

(Letter to M. B. G.) NEAR RAPPAHANNOCK STATION, AUGUST 29th, 1863.

"Colonel Bragg arrived in camp yesterday. I made application for ten days leave of absence. It will be pretty mean if they do not give it to me. There is no field officer in the Army of the Potomac who has kept more closely at his post, or participated in more battles."

(Letter to M. B. G.) SEPTEMBER 3rd, 1863.

"My application for leave of absence was disapproved by our brand-new Brigadier General Rice, at division headquarters, which made me pretty mad, and I went up to see him. The result of our interview was, that he said if I would make another application, he would approve it, and so I started another paper grinding through the mill."

SEPTEMBER 6th, 1863.

"This time General Rice 'earnestly recommended that the application be granted'—a change over the spirit of his dream. General Rice was anxious that I should know his action, and he called me in to see him endorse my application. You had better keep on writing letters just the same. Great preparations are being made for an appropriate celebration upon the reception of the new colors of the 'Iron Brigade.' Ex-Governor Alexander W. Randall will probably make the presentation address.

Conscripts are beginning to come to this army, and a sorry looking set they are. Many are substitutes, who have received large sums of money, and who are old soldiers discharged or deserted, who have come with the deliberate intention of deserting, and again speculating in the substitute money. They are closely guarded. What a contrast between such hounds and the enthusiastic and eager volunteers of 1861. Our men thoroughly despise these cattle and certainly the honor of the old army will not be safe in such hands. I took dinner with Captain Huntington, (commander of the Ohio battery.) He lives well, and so do we now."

SEPTEMBER 8th, 1863.

"I have been for three days on picket. They have just brought in one of our Lieutenants badly hurt by the fall of a horse." (I do not remember who it was.)

SEPTEMBER 12th, 1863.

"General Meade refused to grant my leave of absence. Colonel Bragg endorsed it: 'Lieutenant Colonel Dawes has neither asked nor received indulgences to relieve him from duty. I earnestly recommend the granting of the application.' General Rice, the division commander, endorsed: 'This appears to be such a case, that if the exigencies of the service will permit, I earnestly recommend that the application be granted.' The corps commander, General John Newton, approved the application, but General Meade refused to grant the leave of absence, and returned the paper endorsed: 'The Commanding General declines to grant leaves of absence at the present time, for private considerations.'

I received notice, yesterday, that Colonel Cutler's ordnance returns for 1861 had not been accepted, and I am obliged to go to making up returns for my old company "K," which is a hard job. Is not this system delightful as applied to officers in the field? Here is Colonel Cutler's account of fifty thousand dollars worth of property, once settled with the Government, but it is later discovered that it is not precisely in accord with some technical rule of the Ordnance Office, and now while we are in the field, without our books or papers, we must make up again two-year old accounts, and have them inspected and accepted, before we can receive any more pay, if they choose to enforce the order to stop it.

The paymaster is here now and we will get our pay this time anyhow. I was just now hailed by the Adjutant General of the second army corps,* who is an acquaintance. He said: 'We are going over the river.' I asked him, 'where?' He said: 'To Culpepper, I think.' "

NEAR RAPPAHANNOCK, SEPTEMBER 13th, 1863.

"The sound of cannon comes to us, this morning, from the front. The cavalry corps and the second (infantry) corps are over the river on a reconnoissance. We have orders to support the second corps if they are pushed. Dr. Preston (who had now returned from Gettysburg) says three army corps moved forward this morning. It is surprising that we should be left behind. This looks like a general advance of our lines, and may possibly account for the disapproval of my application for a leave of absence.

Drinking, gambling, and horse racing, are the principal pursuits of many officers of the army, during such lulls in the active service as we are having now.

Next Thursday, General Meade and the 'Johnnies' permitting, we shall celebrate, in an appropriate manner, the presentation of the 'Iron Brigade' flag. There is considerable fighting over the river as I write. Judging from the sound, our men are advancing, and the enemy retiring. A beautifully decorated bower is being constructed, and preparations are being made for a grand affair when the brigade flag comes."

*Francis A. Walker.

(Letter to M. B. G.) SEPTEMBER 15th.

"I have lazy times since Colonel Bragg has returned. There is nothing to read in the army but trash and newspapers. The worst thing of the service is the coarse, boorish manners, which grow upon one, and against which there is little restraint. It is easy not to drink whisky, and not to gamble, and not to swear, but it is hard not to become rough, coarse and uncouth. It is easier to be a gentleman here in moral conduct than it is in personal manners."

BIVOUAC NEAR CULPEPPER COURT HOUSE, ⎱
(Letter to M. B. G.) SEPTEMBER 16th, 1863. ⎰

"We broke camp at daylight this morning and marched ten miles toward the enemy, and are perhaps on the eve of more of the bloody fighting that usually falls to our lot. We are now in bivouac awaiting orders. The sun is very hot and the dust intolerable. We are in a beautiful rolling country, covered with rich farms and fine houses, but no crops are cultivated. As far as I can see to the east and west stretches a broad line of glistening white tents, the line of the army of the Potomac. To the east, we trace it for six miles, and to the west, for four miles. This great white belt is the strength of the North in the cause of justice, freedom and humanity. It does seem that, with the prestige and glory of our victory at Gettysburg, and with the unity and determination this army has shown, its onward sweep should be irresistible.

The sound of cannon has come to our ears all day from the front, and it comes as I write from the direction of the old Cedar Mountain battle field. To us who have so often felt the terrible meaning of this sound, it is not pleasant. The wail of a musket ball that has spent its flight is mournful; the hiss of one at full speed is spiteful. I lay on my back looking into the sky hour after hour on Culp's Hill at Gettysburg, listening to the varied sounds of battle firing. Some of our men imitate the whistle of a shell to perfection.

Our brigade band is now playing 'When this cruel war is over.' Dr. Hall, carried away by the music and by the sentiment, is bothering me with conundrums, 'When will it be over? What will be the result? Will the end of this cruel war establish

National Supremacy or destroy it?' If you think of any good answers you might put them in your next."

BIVOUAC NEAR CULPEPPER, SEPTEMBER 17th, 1863.

"I lay last night on gravel stones about as big as a walnut. To-day I sent Billy out to provide for the case. He got a bushy cedar tree, from which we made a splendid bed. All the roads in this country are lined with cedar, and frequently with osage orange hedges. They are very pretty and pleasant, but we 'heathenish vandals' must have something upon which to rest our weary limbs, and so we appropriate the trees and hedges. There is much grief among the old families here at seeing the landmarks of their childhood and days of their prosperity swept away, and their manifestation of sorrow is sometimes quite affecting. But sorry as it makes us feel, we have to stand it, and take the trees. At Culpepper live the families of Slaughter and Bradford. At Madison University, Wisconsin, I met Clayton and Johnny Slaughter and Hill Bradford. They were young Southern gentlemen. They say Clayton served as an aid-de-camp to General Roger A. Pryor, and Bradford went with the rebel artillery (Kemper's.)

Nothing daunted by our unfortunate march, which prevented our celebration, the "Iron brigade" proposes this afternoon to receive its new flag with appropriate honors. This is the anniversary of our battle at Antietam. The victuals are here and the liquors, but no splendid bower nor distinguished guests."

(Letter to M. B. G.)   SEPTEMBER 18th.

"What a time we had this morning. There came a pouring rain storm in the night, and in the midst of it a gust of wind swept away our tents and left Dr. Hall and me in a sorry plight. In pouring rain and sloppy mud, with no superfluous clothing to speak of to protect us from the elements, we recaptured and raised our fallen domicile and waited in a state of perfect saturation and misery for daylight. This kind of soldiering presents few attractions.

The brigade flag celebration came off according to program, but it was an affair that conferred little honor on the brigade as gentlemen. I feel glad to say there were a few exceptions, but the fact is, the officers of this brigade and the Generals and staff officers within any convenient distance of us were almost unanimously drunk last night. You will see an account of the presentation in the New York Times, as I saw the 'graphic and reliable' correspondent of that paper guzzling champagne and wine with the rest of them.*

(Letter to M. B. G.)

NEAR CULPEPPER, SUNDAY, SEPTEMBER 20th, 1863.

"I rode over to Culpepper Court House this morning. While in the village the house of Dr. Slaughter was pointed out to me. The house in its surroundings and appearance is very respectable and substantial, and I called to inquire after my old college friends. I was gracefully received by a young lady, who to my inquiry touching the health and location of John and Clayton Slaughter, in whom I felt the 'interest of an old college associate,' replied that her brothers were at present absent in the army, but if I would come in she would be glad to tell me of them.

Her mother, a very pleasant and intelligent lady, came in to see me and my visit seemed quite acceptable and pleasant. Why not? I was from Wisconsin, and there, Mrs. Slaughter told me, many of her relatives lived, and with Madison, Wisconsin, were connected many of the most pleasant associations of the family. 'Can you tell me, Colonel Dawes, where Lawson Merrill is? He is my nephew.' He was my classmate in the University and he is now in the United States Navy. 'Can you tell me where †Emory, his brother, is?' I knew that he was an officer in

---

*FLAG FOR THE IRON BRIGADE.—There is on exhibition at the store of Messrs. Tiffany & Co., a beautiful flag, which has been procured for the celebrated "Iron Brigade," of the First army corps, Army of the Potomac. The flag is of regulation size, and made of heavy dark blue silk. It is embellished by a handsome vignette of an eagle, shield and scroll motto, "*E Pluribus Unum*"—the same as on the ten dollar Treasury note. The names of the principal battles in which the brigade has been engaged are handsomely worked, each on a separate scroll. The vignette, the scroll work, and the name of each regiment composing the brigade—the Second, Sixth and Seventh Wisconsin, Nineteenth Indiana and Twenty-fourth Michigan—are all worked in the flag with silk chenille, and the shading is most exquisitely done. A rich and heavy border adds to and completes the effect. The staff is mounted with a massive silver spear head. The flag is the gift of a number of gentlemen from the States of Wisconsin, Indiana and Michigan. It is a fit and elegant tribute to the heroism of one of the most glorious organizations in the entire army.—New York Times.

†Col. Wm. E. Merrill, U. S. Engineers.

our army, but I did not tell her he had been on General Pope's staff. 'Where is William Vilas? John thought everything of him.' My answer was 'He is Lieutenant Colonel of the twenty-third Wisconsin.' Dick Hubbell, another classmate of John's, is a Lieutenant in our army. Her nephew, Burgess Slaughter, is a Captain, and William Slaughter, her husband's brother, is an officer in the Union army. On their mantel was a photograph of Chancellor Lathrop and Clayt's class at the University, all of whom, except Clayt and Bradford, are officers in the Union army.

General Roger A. Pryor has resigned on account of some difficulty with Jeff. Davis, and now Pryor and his aid-de-camp, Slaughter, are privates in the third Virginia cavalry."

This statement is from information received in Culpepper village, and it may be erroneous.

"The war has carried the northern soldiers of the family up, and the southern, down.

I enclose a graphic, though unpretending story, of our drum major's escape from the rebels, (R. N. Smith.) The boy had little idea he was writing for the eyes of the world. Ed Brooks happening to see his letter, secured its publication in a Wisconsin newspaper. It is such spirit as this boy shows, that has made the glory of the old Sixth regiment."

Smith was captured at Gettysburg, and escaping from the rebel guard, he floated down the Shenandoah river on a saw-log, hiding in the daytime and floating only at night.

(Letter to M. B. G.)   CAMP NEAR CULPEPPER, }
                         SEPTEMBER 21st. }

"I have been all day at work making up ordnance returns, some of them for two years ago. All this work must be done over, or we poor ex-captains lose more than we are worth. I do not believe there are any errors in my original returns, but Colonel Cutler's return for the regiment has been rejected. Red tape is well enough for a peace establishment, but, as applied to the extraordinary exigencies of service in the field, it is severe. Officers in the field, who are suffering and risking everything, and scarcely allowed transportation for enough to eat, are required to make returns for the critical scrutiny of officials at

Washington, who seem to reject them on the flimsiest informality. This subjects an officer to stoppage of his pay and allowances, no matter how impossible a loss of papers even in battle, or want of vouchers *pro forma* makes it to correct returns. The clerks at Washington exact the same technical accuracy of the officer in the field, required of the officer in the garrison."

(Letter to M. B. G.) NEAR CULPEPPER, SEPTEMBER, 22nd, 1863.

"I have at last got that ordnance return made up and sent off. It has taken three days hard work, and it is all correct. General Cutler has come back and is in command now of the division. We are all stirred up by the terrible battle at Chattanooga." (Chickamauga.)

(Letter to M. B. G.) SEPTEMBER 23rd.

"We are greatly concerned about General Rosecrans' army. As usual, our active and desperate foe has concentrated his strength on a weaker army. Chattanooga is one of the strategic points of the war. Its simple possession by us forces, ultimately, offensive operations by the enemy, and that is a great point gained if we only avail ourselves of the advantage. But to have the golden opportunity turned into a defeat of our army, and a loss of the point, would be a great calamity."

HEADQUARTERS PICKET, FIRST DIVISION, FIRST ARMY CORPS,
(Letter to M. B. G.) SEPTEMBER 26th, 1863.

"Day before yesterday, very unexpectedly and very suddenly, we left our old camp and marched here to the fords of the Rapidan, to relieve the twelfth army corps, on general outpost duty for the army. I was placed in command of the first division picket, and night and day since, have been very busy on that hardest duty of the service. My line is four miles long, running most of the way along the bank of the Rapidan river. The rebel pickets are very amicably disposed. There has been no firing on this line. The smoke of the encampments of the rebel army rises from every piece of timber, and their earthworks appear on every hill beyond the river. My headquarters are at Morton's Ford. This is a rich country. The houses are fine, and there is evidence of wealth and refinement. The house (Mr.

Robinson's*) where I write has been abandoned on account of its proximity to the lines, but it is now filled with elegant furniture and paintings. The weather is cold for the season. I can see a rebel general and escort riding along on the other side of the river as I look out of my window from my writing. My letter was interfered with. One of the captains on the picket line came to me with the word that a rebel was trying to get into our line. I went out to the point at once and saw several bayonets glistening in the sun in a cornfield on this side of the river. (At this point the rebel line was on the river, and our line was back from the river.) I immediately turned out the grand guard, but discovered that one man only was really advancing, swinging something white over his head. When he saw the grand guard falling into line, he turned to run, but I ordered him to halt on penalty of being shot, and, supposing him a deserter, assured him of safety in coming into our lines. So he came in. His only object was to exchange newspapers, and one of our men had swung a paper as a signal to come over. He had really been enticed into our lines. But having arrested him thus publicly, I could not release him without instructions, so I sent a note to General Newton, and explained the case to him, and asked for instructions, He ordered me to hold the man, which seemed a mean advantage to take, but he was right. I now must go with the general officer to visit the line."
(Letter to M. B. G.)

BIVOUAC NEAR MORTON'S FORD, SEPTEMBER 27th, 1863.

"I was relieved from picket duty last night. The regiment now lies one mile from Morton's Ford, but our wagons are all six miles back, and nothing but headquarters' mail comes up. It is getting cold these nights to sleep on the ground. We build up a fire of logs and spreading our blankets on the ground, lie with our feet to it. My health is better when on this kind of campaigning than when in camp. On that severest of all our marches, from Fredericksburgh to Gettysburg, I gained several pounds in weight. You may hear of me on our way to Chattanooga. The first corps used to serve under General Hooker, and he is to command a western expedition."

---

*War Record has it Robertson.

(Letter to M. B. G.)   BIVOUAC IN THE FIELD, }
                                 SEPTEMBER 29th, 1863. }

"This morning we moved camp a mile or two, to get out of range of the enemy's batteries south of the river, and avoid danger of surprise. There was quite an alarm yesterday morning. What seemed to be a brisk musketry skirmish was heard along the pickets. Drums were rolling, bands playing, artillery rumbling on the roads on the other side of the narrow river. All was under the mantle of a heavy morning fog. Line of battle was formed, and every preparation made to repel any attempt at crossing by the enemy. When the fog raised, not a battalion or battery of the enemy was in sight and not a shot had come near our pickets. What do you suppose the rebels were up to, making all this fuss? *The eleventh and twelfth corps have left this army and are now in Washington. While they are gone, the probabilities of an advance by us are small. Nor do I think while Longstreet is west, the rebels will attack us. We are feeling easier about Rosecrans, but fear he is not master of the situation, and that he has been entrapped by Bragg. Hooker is to command the expedition, eleventh and twelfth corps, if it is not recalled, which some look for now. They say this army was to have fallen back to Centreville, and the strongest corps sent west if the reports had continued unfavorable."

(Letter to M. B. G.)   SEPTEMBER 30th, 1863.

"It is dull here now. I take a ride on my horse occasionally to look at the rebel pickets and speculate on the signal flags, and to enjoy the beautiful weather we are now having. I play chess some and am champion of this division."

---

*See pages 146 to 200, Vol. XXIX, Part 1, War Records for account of movements of 11th and 12th corps by rail to Chattanooga.

CHAPTER X.

At Morton's Ford—The Retreat to Centreville—A Skirmish at Haymarket—Bob Tomlinson—To Thoroughfare Gap—Roast Turkey—Judge Advocate of a Court Martial—General Fairchild —Col. Edward Pye—To Catlett's Station—Adjutant Brooks Captured—General Cutler Resorts to Vigorous Measures—A Gentleman of the Old School—To Rappahannock—A Visit to M. B. G. in Ohio—The Mine Run Campaign.

(Letter to M. B. G.)　　Near Morton's Ford, Oct. 4th, 1863.

"About two hours ago there broke out a roar of cannon. The rebels fired six times into our lines at Raccoon Ford, and for what purpose I do not know. The impression here is that the war has for the present been carried to the west. Here the prestige of victory rests with us and the advantage to be gained by moderate success in Virginia is small."

Morton's Ford, October 9th, 1863.

"This morning I took a long ride to enjoy the bright, beautiful day, and I reconnoitered the enemy's position from Clark's Mountain to Stringfellow's Ford, the extreme left of our army. They are entrenched on a range of hills, completely commanding our approaches throughout the line, and their forts are arranged so as to pour a converging fire upon the principal fords.

The Retreat of the Army to Centreville.

(Letter to M. B. G.)　　Kelly's Ford, October 12th, 1863.

"I know you will excuse my pencil. I forgot to put ink in my haversack in our hurry when we started. At daylight, Saturday, our first corps was massed in front of Morton's Ford on the Rapidan. Orders were given to cross the river and attack the enemy in his entrenchments and our regiment was placed upon the skirmish line to lead the attack as at Fitz Hugh's crossing. The day was consumed in making showy demonstrations in sight of the enemy. *No advance at all was intended, (I was mistaken,) but at night we made a hurried retreat toward Culpep-

---

*See Pages 272—279, and 291—293, Volume XXIX, Part II, War Records.

per Court House. We waited until yesterday at Culpepper for the wagon train of the army to clear the way, and then continued our retreat toward the Rappahannock. Our column was scarcely in motion when the enemy with cavalry, infantry and artillery attacked General Buford, (cavalry,) our rear guard. Our regiment was rear guard for the infantry, so we had a good view of the cavalry fight at a distance of not over a mile. We continued our retreat in plain sight of fighting all the way, until last night we reached Kelly's Ford. So for thirty-six hours we have been on duty. The reason we escaped fighting yesterday was that the enemy did not pursue our column toward Kelly's Ford, but went in the direction of Brandy Station, where the fighting was severe. We fear that Buford's cavalry was badly used. From the high ground near Stevensburgh, we had a fine view of the cavalry resisting the advance of the enemy on the plains toward the Rapidan. The cavalry would form their lines and receive the attack with hot firing, and then wheel by sections and gallop to the rear, reform their lines again, and await another advance of the enemy. The cavalry was finely handled, and behaved admirably."

(Letter to M. B. G.)   KELLY'S FORD, OCTOBER 12th, EVENING.

"I wrote this morning, and in default of a better opportunity, sent the letter by a teamster. All is quiet to-day, although a battle may be impending. I do not think General Meade will force the fighting, but he may not be able to avoid battle. I never saw a cavalry fight upon an open plain before yesterday. General Buford handled his division with great skill and courage, and he performed excellent service in holding back the enemy. He resisted their infantry for twelve miles."

(Letter to M. B. G.)   HEIGHTS OF CENTREVILLE, VA., OCT. 14th.

"After continuous marching night and day, we have outrun the enemy and this afternoon our army is going into position along these heights. We have escaped fighting ourselves, but every day we have heard the thunder of the enemy's guns, pursuing the rear. As I write this letter, the air is full of the noise of battle. We think it is the second corps, and that the battle is near Manassas Junction."

Lucius Fairchild

ROLLIN P. CONVERSE,

CAPTAIN CO B. SIXTH WIS. VOLS.

Battle near Bristoe Station,—between second corps, commanded by General G. K. Warren, and the corps of General Ewell of the Confederate army.

"The rebels are after our wagon train, and we are in fear for it. We hope our first corps train is safe. Will we have a battle here to-morrow? That is the question we are all discussing. The battle roars and lulls as I write. From the sound I do not think our men are losing ground. God help them! You should see our wagon train rushing along the turnpike to the rear. A panic among the thousand or two wagons of this army is a scene."

Six P. M.—"The fight is over down at Manassas, (Bristoe.) Our wagon train appears to be safe."

(Letter to M. B. G.) Centreville,Va., Oct. 15th, 1863, 8 P. M.

"My candle flickers in the wind so that I can hardly write. Think of me rejoicing to-night, in the possession of an ancient pig-pen, as a protection from the drizzling storm. We are in line of battle in rifle pits at Centreville, awaiting the enemy. They have been cannonading our left two miles from here all the afternoon."

(Letter to M. B. G.) Centreville,Va., Oct. 16th, 1863, 8 P. M.

"Not much firing to-day and no battle. I have emerged from my pig-pen to-night, and availed myself of the hospitality of a poor white for shelter to write this letter. His unpretending domicile has its history in being the birth place of the rebel General Benjamin S. Ewell, who is in our front in command of some twenty thousand men. I do not think the enemy will pursue his aggressive movement. It is too late in the season for a campaign north of the Potomac, and I do not think General Lee is strong enough to venture it. General Lee by his forward, and our retrograde movement, has placed our capital before the world as menaced, instead of his own. General Meade, sufficiently strengthened, as I think he has been, should turn upon Lee, and if possible, defeat him on the old battle field of Bull Run. There would be poetic justice in such a history. We have not seen our wagons or valises since we left the Rapidan."

(Letter to M. B. G.)

Centreville, Va., (October 17th or 18th.)

"This morning we 'fell in' double quick at daylight to march to the assistance of 'General Sedgwick at Chantilly,' but the rebels did not attack General Sedgwick. Every day we hear distant cannonading. The weather is delightful and from these heights we have an extended and varied landscape. You can, on clear days, trace the blue summits of the mountains from Harper's Ferry to Culpepper county, and to the south and east you over-look the fighting ground from Bull Run to Fredericksburgh."

*"LINE OF BATTLE, NEAR HAYMARKET, VA., ⎱
(Letter to M. B. G.)   OCTOBER 26th, 1863. ⎰

We left Centreville yesterday morning in a cold, beating rain storm. We marched toward Warrenton by way of the Bull Run and Gainesville battle-fields. The cavalry in our front skirmished with the enemy all day. Toward evening we bivouacked near Haymarket. Cannonading was still going on in front. We had just begun to cook supper when an officer came rushing in with word that our cavalry were attacked at Broad Run by overwhelming numbers. General Newton ordered the brigade out at once to their relief. We double quicked a mile when sharp firing and cheering broke out near the camp we had left. There was firing in front of us and to our left. The enemy's cavalry seemed to be all around us. We formed a line of battle, skirting an edge of timber. The rebel cavalry in our front advanced, but when they saw our line they immediately retreated. We remained until late in the night and then marched back about a mile where we found the whole first corps in line of battle. The seventh Wisconsin lost about forty men who were on picket. We lost one man taken prisoner."

A recent letter from General Bragg gives the history of the 'one man' lost:

"Do you remember Tomlinson of company B? I think they called him 'Bob.' In the early camp-life days, he used to swell and boast of his prowess until he was marked down as a sort of '*Bombastes furioso;*' but he proved as good as he talked.

At Antietam, (you told me this) when you fell back from beyond the corn field the first time, Bob cried out, 'not yet, I have a few more cartridges left,' and he was firing away with his

---

*For reports of action at Buckland Mills, October 19th, 1863, see Volume XXIX, Parts I and II, War Records.

musket in the open field, a target for hundreds to turn their guns on. Bob got a terrible wound in the shoulder at Gettysburg and was sent to hospital, but he ran away and joined us, with his wound all open and unhealed, when we were marching under General Newton as corps commander, toward Thoroughfare. You remember when Fitz Hugh Lee surprised Kilpatrick, near Buckland's, and in hot pursuit, his men came clear on to our camp line, where we were killing beef, and the Sixth was ordered out at double quick in light marching order to repel cavalry, which by that time was more scared than we were, and was getting back on the gallop! Now to come to Bob again, he was left at the commissary, to guard our meat; he had no gun, and being wounded could carry none, but the devil was waked up in him, he got a pistol and took a short cut across a neck of woods to join us, and he was picked up by straggling rebel cavalry. He gave his life to his country in a rebel prison!"

"We have two pack mules for regimental field and staff transportation, upon which we carry plenty of blankets, but no shelter. Our provisions we carry in panniers on the mules. It is two weeks since we have seen our regimental headquarters wagon, and as no sutlers are allowed with the army, we are becoming quite poverty-stricken."

(Letter to M. B. G.)　　　　　Thoroughfare Gap, Virginia, ⎱
　　　　　　　　　　　　　　October 31st, 1863. ⎰

"You can hardly know how comfortable and homelike it seems to-night to get up my wall tent. Since the eighth of this month, I have had nothing over me except the slab cover of the pig-pen at Centreville. To-night the regiment is in camp. It is said that a council of war was held at Gainesville yesterday, and as a result we came here. Just at supper time last night we got our marching orders, and it was midnight before we had accomplished our journey of five miles. It was a night of Egyptian darkness. The column of troops would hitch up two rods and stop fifteen minutes, and then hitch up a rod and a half and stop half an hour. It is always so, marching after artillery over a stony road and rough hills. I often fall asleep on my horse, but whenever the troops ahead start, she starts, and she is in no more danger of losing our regiment than a hound is of losing a fox.

We have a magnificent place here. We are encamped among the Bull Run Mountains, west of Thoroughfare Gap. I climbed this morning to the top of the highest peak and enjoyed the scenery. You will be astonished at our dinner to-day. Roast turkey! Honey! Graham biscuit! It is an epoch, such a dinner in this day of hard tack plain, hard tack fried, hard tack soaked, hard tack crumbled and stewed, or hard tack otherwise compounded with salt pork as the sole staff of life. Colonel Bragg devoted his entire attention to an oven of flat stones and a turnspit for the turkey. This turkey, by the way, paid to us good and true Union soldiers, the penalty of his life for gobbling at one of our men with all the venom and derision of the miserable rebel that he was. Colonel Bragg, to his infinite satisfaction and pride, in two hours and a half, brought on a roast turkey that would have done honor to the table of a lord. He gave me lessons in the art of carving. The Doctor, (J. C. Hall,) who had conscientious scruples that the honey was realized in an improper manner by the man who presented it to the Colonel, visited the premises to investigate, and, being furiously attacked by the bees on account of his Union sentiments, he concluded that the confiscation was just and proper. We do not steal turkeys and honey as a rule, but when a wealthy rebel runs away, leaving everything because our army is coming, we sometimes confiscate rebellious turkey gobblers, and the honey of traitorous bees.

Ohio has done a grand thing in the sweeping defeat of Vallandigham, and I feel proud of my native state."

"NEAR THOROUGHFARE GAP, OCTOBER 23d, 1863.

I have a disagreeable task. Lieutenant Colonel Robert B. Jordon, of the fourteenth Brooklyn, was in command of the picket of our division last Monday at Haymarket when the skirmish took place. Charges have been preferred against him for misconduct in the presence of the enemy. A special court martial has been called by General Newton, commanding the first army corps, with General J. C. Rice as President and your unfortunate correspondent as Judge Advocate. I tried my best to get excused from this duty, but 'Old Prince,' as the boys irreverently call General Cutler,* would not allow me to be excused at all.

---

*General Cutler commanded the division.

Colonel Jordon has employed the best legal advisers he could find to defend him. I spent yesterday and until late at night looking up the case. Never a student of law, I feel not a little nervous in going before so intelligent and dignified a court on behalf of the prosecution in one of the most important cases ever tried in our division."

NEAR BRISTOE STATION, VA., ORANGE & ALEXANDRIA R. R. }
(Letter to M. G. B.)   OCTOBER 25th, 1863, —8. a. m.   }
"We left Thoroughfare Gap yesterday in a cold rain storm. We marched all day, the men wading three creeks waist deep. We went to Brentsville and then after night, countermarched to this point, fording another deep creek by the way. Yesterday was one of the hardest days of all our service, and its effect upon the question of veteran enlistment was decidedly unhealthy."
(Letter to M. B. G.)

CAMP NEAR BRISTOE, OCTOBER 27th, 1863.

"I have been as busy as a man could be for two days with the Colonel Jordon case. To-night my work was closed, the final defense of the accused and the finding and sentence of the Court only to be had. Things are unsettled here. It is impossible to tell whether we will remain in peace this fall or go into battle to-morrow. We hear cannonading every day but never know where it is or what is the cause of it. We are under orders to be ready to move at a moment's notice. Still we always regard the chances as about even of going or staying under such orders.

Since our brilliant retrograde movement to Centreville everything seems in the fog. I think the enemy intend to check and embarrass General Meade on every foot of his advance, to consume his time until General Mud puts an embargo upon army movements. My head is full of my court record, which I have to overlook as my clerk makes it out. Sixty pages of foolscap in testimony ought to cashier a man. Another case is coming before our court. It is of an officer charged with shooting his toes off to keep out of the battle of Gettysburg. What do you think of that kind of a hero? I think him a notorious coward.

Brigadier General Lucius Fairchild was here with his empty

coat sleeve. He is pale and thin. He will be elected. He is to be married soon. The first words he said to me were ' When are you going to be shot? You are the luckiest man in the army.' "

(Letter to M. B. G.)

NEAR BRISTOE STATION,
OCTOBER 29th, 1863.

"The trial of Colonel Jordon is over. I feel as though I had succeeded as well as I had a right to expect. Major Pye, the counsel for Colonel Jordon, issued this little ration of soft soap in his closing address: 'To the Judge Advocate, whose qualities as a gentleman and an officer are apparent upon all occasions, and who has conducted this case with a fairness and ability alike commendable to his head and heart, I return my thanks.' "

Major Edward Pye had been a Judge of the Courts in New York, and it would be quite ungracious to say less than that he was an able lawyer. But to the memory of my esteemed and congenial friend, and my heroic comrade at Gettysburg, who charged with us upon the railroad cut, and who was later killed in battle while leading the ninety-fifth New York in the same gallant manner, I here offer the sincere tribute of respect and admiration. He was a pure, high minded gentleman, a patriot who cordially sustained all the measures of his government to crush the enemy, and a hero who gave his life freely for his country.

Colonel Jordon was convicted by the Court on a part of the charges and sentenced to be dismissed from the service. He was afterwards re-instated to his rank by the President of the United States. The Judge Advocate and all members of the Court Martial joined in recommending this action in consideration of his good character and gallant service before this time.*

(Letter to M. B. G.)

NEAR CATLETT'S STATION,
NOVEMBER 1st, 1863.

This is a beautiful Sabbath day. I have been riding on my horse. Twenty months ago we came here, the advance of the

---

*Members of the Court: Brigadier General J. C. Rice, second brigade, first division; Colonel J. W. Hoffman, fifty-sixth Pennsylvania; Colonel S. H. Leonard, thirteenth Massachusetts; Colonel P. S. Davis, thirty-ninth Massachusetts; Colonel L. Wister, one hundred and fiftieth Pennsylvania; Lieutenant Colonel Walton Dwight, one hundred and forty-ninth Pennsylvania; Lieutenant Colonel R. R. Dawes, sixth Wisconsin, Judge Advocate.

army, and more pleasant homes are seldom found, than we carefully guarded and protected then, under General McDowell. Now nothing but charred ruins and ghostly looking chimneys mark the places of those pretty cottages. Not a fence, barn, nor scarce a vestige of timber remains to identify the spot. In place, the country is covered with the bones of dead horses and mules, and the debris of abandoned camps. Unsightly stumps mark the places of the pleasant groves. It is hard for one who has not seen, to imagine the horrid desolation wrought by war.

The rebel army made a complete destruction of our railroad, (Orange & Alexandria.) In the cuts they put first a layer of pine brush, and then a layer of dirt and stone and brush again. You can imagine the bother and trouble of picking out such a tangle. The cross ties and railroad iron, they built up in kind of cob houses and then set the ties on fire. When the iron was sufficiently heated they bent it around logs in fantastic knots. I saw one or two logs standing up, adorned with neckties of railroad iron, upon which the knots were quite *au fait*.

I saw a pontoon train, those dismal prophets of fighting on the Rappahannock, moving down toward the river this morning. The men say we are soon to be on the march when the boats come. The second and third corps are in front of us. Since General Reynolds was killed, our corps does not seem to be selected for work in the advance. The second corps now does most of the heavy work of making the reconnoissances and covering the retreats. General G. K. Warren of the second corps is the rising young general of this army. I think General Meade intends to push Lee back to the Rapidan again if possible, and Lee, I think, will go, hoping to draw Meade into a general attack upon his works. We are now a kind of side play. The great and decisive campaign will be in the west. There, operations can be carried on through the winter. I enclose a little bit of Virginia cotton that I picked just as it grew."*

---

*This letter from General Cutler deals as gently as possible with the sad truth it discloses:

"HEADQUARTERS FIRST DIVISION, FIRST ARMY CORPS,
BRISTOE, VA , NOVEMBER 1st, 1863.

Editor State Journal: Rumors have reached me, from time to time, that the remains of those men of the 'Iron Brigade,' and of the fifty-sixth Penn-

(Letter to M. B. G.)   NEAR CATLETT'S, NOVEMBER 2nd, 1863.

"The court martial, of which I am Judge Advocate, has been re-convened and I have been relieved from the one of which I was President. Day after to-morrow we are to try the officer who had charge of our corps ambulance train, for leaving wounded rebels on the battle field at Gettysburg over night in a rain storm.

The cavalry went to the front to-day. Rumor says they are going to Hartwood Church, near Fredericksburgh. General Kilpatrick rode by to-day with his usual swagger. I hope he will handle his cavalry better than he did at Haymarket on the nineteenth of last month. He was awfully thrashed there. The sick were all ordered away from the army to-day, which looks like a general advance. Our corps is now quite in the rear of the army, guarding the line of the railroad from raids."

(Letter to M. B. G.)   NOVEMBER 5th, 1863.

"Our Adjutant (E. P. Brooks,) was captured by the rebels to-day. A few days ago, a rather handsome young lady came to our camp and politely solicited a guard for her home, two miles away. The Adjutant was quite attentive, and the lady seemed very gracious. Brooks took out a guard for the premises. To-day she came over to the regiment with some butter to repay the kindness, and Brooks was happy to see her safely home. They were both on horse back. Not more than a mile from camp, Mosby with a few other particular friends of the lady, stepped out of the bushes and captured our badly sold companion in arms. He is to-night walking along obscure bridle paths on a circuitous route to Libby Prison, while a rebel cavalryman has

---

sylvania and seventy-sixth New York volunteers, who fell at Gainesville in the bloody fight of August 28th, 1862, were carelessly buried. Upon examination, a few days since, while passing the battle field on our way to Thoroughfare Gap, it was found to be true. I have to-day had details from all the regiments who fought there sent to the ground, under the charge of Captain Richardson, of the seventh Wisconsin. They have carefully interred the remains. Many of them could be recognized by the positions where they lay, or by articles found about them. As the friends of those who fell will doubtless hear of the loose manner of the first burial, I write to assure them that all has been done that could be to give them decent burial.   Very Respectfully,
                                         L. CUTLER, Brig. Gen."

his horse. William gave me the news thus: 'The Adjutant dun got captivated.'*

The regiment is just now under a cloud. That rainy night at Brentsville, some men of our brigade were guilty of robbing and marauding. General Cutler thinks he has traced some of the property to the Sixth regiment. He has sent an order requiring this regiment to pay one hundred and fifty dollars at his head-quarters within twelve hours. Colonel Bragg has replied to this strange demand that he will cheerfully use every exertion to bring the guilty to punishment. General Cutler seems to think Colonel Bragg is conniving to conceal the men from punishment, and says if such and such things are not done, he will apply to the Secretary of War to have all pay stopped from the regiment. Colonel Bragg says he will do anything to punish the guilty, if there are such in our regiment, but no such absurd order or wild threat shall intimidate him."†

(Letter to M. B. G.)

NEAR CATLETT'S STATION,
NOVEMBER 6th, 1863.

"We had an interesting visitor in camp to-day. He was an old school Virginia gentleman, of one of their patrician families. The old gentleman was a pattern of method and precision in his manners, and there was the urbanity and consideration for others of the true gentlemen of the real old stock. He said that he had been an officer in the 'War of 1812'—that he had General Washington's own pistols. He was well acquainted with President Madison and President Monroe, and edified us with anecdotes and illustrations of the men of his day and generation. His visit was much enjoyed by us all. The old gentleman was carried away by talking, and he said: 'I am eighty years of age. My grandfather was a Virginia gentleman; my great grandfather was a Frenchman, and, begging your indulgence to an old man, I thank God that to-day I stand as they would in this struggle.' Said I: 'My dear Sir, your enthusiasm is worthy of imitation by

---

*It will be seen by this letter that we suspected treachery. The guard was withdrawn by Colonel Bragg. Brooks is not to be blamed for going out, as he had been there to place the guard. He did not himself believe it was treachery, which would have been base to the last degree.

†To be taken "*cum grano salis.*' It is evident I was a little out of humor at the writing.

us who are younger, but your cause is no older in your family than ours is in mine. My ancestors came to New England when yours came to Virginia, and they flourished in Massachusetts, and I thank God I live in the day to fight for their principles.' Said the old gentleman: 'I always did admire a full blown Yankee.' "

(Letter to M. B. G.) NEAR BRANDY STATION,
NOVEMBER 9th, 1863.

*"Saturday morning we marched from Catletts to Morrisonville, and Sunday found us in line of battle with the rest of the army at Brandy Station. Our corps has this time brought up the rear. We have heard continually the cannon of the sixth and the third corps about four or five miles in front. This morning the whole army seems to be at a stand still. We, as usual, do not know what is the reason.

I just heard that General Kilpatrick is at Stevensburgh. If that is so, the enemy have retreated beyond the Rapidan. They would not give us possession of the Stevensburgh heights, which command the ground to the river, without a contest. The day is lowering and the smoke of the camp fires fills our eyes. Sitting on the ground, with my eyes full of smoke, letter writing is hard work."

CAMP NEAR BEVERLY FORD, RAPPAHANNOCK RIVER,
(Letter to M. B. G.) NOVEMBER 11th, 1863.

"Night before last we came back from Brandy Station to the north side of the Rappahannock and encamped. Our first corps is now stretched from Manassas Junction to this point, along the line of the Orange & Alexandria railroad. We sent men out this morning with six days' rations to work on the railroad, which is still uncompleted from Warrenton Junction to the river. We are busily engaged in clearing out the woods and making a good camp, as we think it likely that we shall remain here for a while. I told you about a difficulty between General Cutler and Colonel Bragg. It has all blown over. Not a man was punished, and not a cent was paid."

Not able to call to memory the facts in this affair, I asked General Bragg for his recollections, and he has written me as

---

*Page 614, Volume 29, War Records.

follows: "General Cutler sent his little Orderly, from the third Indiana cavalry up to me with an order, fining the regiment two hundred and fifty dollars,* and ordering it to be paid in twelve hours or our pay would be suspended. The upshot of the whole thing was,—that I laughed him out of it with virtuous indignation, that the Sixth should be charged with the thefts of the fourteenth Brooklyn, and advised him to find out the true culprit, before he took such action. It occurred to the General that he could find out himself, and he summoned Edwin C. Jones of company 'E.' Jones confessed to some knowledge of the affair, and upon being re-assured as to secresy and condign punishment, if he didn't tell what become of the meat, Jones with many protestations that he didn't want to, and it wouldn't be right, yielded and told him 'he saw it going to his own headquarters.' This was the last that I heard of the attempt to prove that the Sixth ate it."

(Letter to M. B. G.)   CAMP NEAR BEVERLY FORD, VA., }
                                   NOVEMBER 12th, 1863.   }

"Our camp is pleasantly located in a fine grove of timber. The nights are frosty, but when we are in camp we can provide against that. The Doctor (Hall) and I have built a log crib, eight feet long, four feet wide, and two feet deep, and packed it full of dry leaves, which makes us a warm and comfortable bed."

(Letter to M. B. G.)   BEVERLY FORD, NOVEMBER 15th, 1863.

"There is as I write, heavy firing in front, and we are under orders to be ready to move. The enemy seems to be reconnoitering or advancing, for the firing is nearer than Cedar Mountain.

We have not marched to-day, and I think now that we will not, but I am obliged to go on picket duty to-night, '*miserabile dictu.*' Captain Philip W. Plummer and two enlisted men from each company, are starting home on recruiting service and to take charge of conscripts for this regiment, as there is a draft going on. You may be sure these men are highly delighted."

(Letter to M. B. G.)   NOVEMBER 16th, ON PICKET.

"I have had a grand gallop over the country this beautiful morning, reorganizing and re-adjusting the picket line of the first army corps. The first night we came here some one established

---

*My contemporary statement, one hundred and fifty dollars, is probably correct.

the line only a few rods from the camps, and it became my duty to correct it. Our first corps' camps are now safely guarded. Everything looks as if our army was soon to make another campaign."

I here received a leave of absence for ten days and hastened to Marietta, Ohio. In making a third effort to secure a leave of absence, I went in person to corps headquarters. My application had the usual "urgent" endorsements which plaintively appealed that I should be granted the favor. General John Newton, now best known as the man who blew up Hell Gate, looked my paper over and I saw no hope in his eye. "Colonel," said he, "you give no reason for this application!" "What's the use of giving a reason!" said I, "sickness or death in the family, or business complications are rejected as reasons in the orders." "Yes," said the General. "Have you any other reason?" "I have," said I, "I want very much to see my girl." "All right, Colonel, you have stated a reason not forbidden in the orders, and I will endorse that you have 'a good and sufficient reason.'" I got all I asked, ten days leave of absence to visit Ohio. General Newton made two friends by this level-headed, official action.

This short visit is remembered as an oasis in the desert of my military life. The weather was delightful, and that dreamy haze, called Indian summer, was upon the hills and valleys of Southern Ohio. For four days, a young couple, oblivious to all others, wandered over the hills or drove on the beautiful roads. Owing to the exigencies of the military service, this four days was all the opportunity we had for meeting until our wedding.

During my absence, the army marched from its camps to engage in the Mine Run campaign.

MINE RUN.

(Letter to M. B. G.) LINE OF BATTLE BEFORE THE ENEMY, }
SOUTH OF THE RAPIDAN, NOVEMBER 28th, 1863. }

"We are lying in mud and water in hourly expectation of moving forward to attack the rebel army in front, in plain view. I caught the regiment yesterday after a hard chase and in a half an hour we were in a skirmish with *Rosser's rebel cavalry. I

---

*Volume XXIX, Page 689, War Records, Report of General L. Cutler.
     "   "   " 687,   "   "   Report of General John Newton.
     "   "   " 904,   "   "   Confederate Colonel T. L. Rosser.

got to the Rappahannock Thursday evening and traveled all night in an ambulance. I am just in time to be in the great battle. I am sitting on a knapsack in the pine woods, my eyes filled with smoke and the clouds full of rain. *We had one man shot yesterday in the skirmish with Rosser's cavalry, lost an arm. The rebels are digging entrenchments as fast as they can and the skirmishers keep up a continual and murderous duel."

(Letter to M. B. G.)   SUNDAY EVENING, NOVEMBER 29th.

"We are still lying in smoke and chilly air waiting our summons for battle and catching with eagerness every rumor. Once to-day we formed a column of assault to charge upon the enemy's entrenchments; but the fearful task was not attempted. The enemy are here in great force and they have worked like beavers at their fortifications. Day before yesterday a bullet cut a hole in my hat and fairly brushed my face and I was covered with dirt by a shell yesterday. I wished myself again on the hill tops of Ohio. It is now so near night that I look for no battle to-day."

(Letter to M. B. G.)   MITCHELL'S FORD, RAPIDAN RIVER, DECEMBER 2nd, 1863.

"The battle did not occur, but great suffering and toil was undergone by our army. We marched all night last night on our retreat and suffered intensely from cold. To-night we are north of the Rapidan. Every preparation was made by General Meade to charge upon the rebel entrenchments. The slaughter would have been great and we feel thankful to have been spared. I can hardly tell you how tired, sleepy and worn out we all are to-night. Our brigade is alone here at Mitchell's Ford. Our corps is at Stevensburgh."

(Letter to M. B. G.)   CAMP NEAR KELLY'S FORD, DECEMBER 4th, 1863.

"To-night, for the first time since leaving Marietta, I have an evening that I can feel is my own. Our communications have been interfered with or suspended, so that I fear you have not received my letters. I got safely to Washington Wednesday

---

*Isaiah F. Kelly, company "B."

night and secured my pass* to the front. I left for the army on the last train that went down Thursday morning and that train they had once decided not to send, as the whole army was moving to parts unknown. We reached Rappahannock station at four o'clock P. M., and the army was gone, nobody could tell certainly where. By hard work and good luck I found a mail ambulance belonging to the fifth army corps headquarters, and by dint of persuasion and a can of preserved peaches, I prevailed upon the men in charge to let me ride with them in their pursuit of the army. We had a freezing night's ride. While we were blundering along in the dark, asking every straggler we could find which road the troops had taken, we were at one time completely at a loss when a drunken straggler was overtaken who swore in round oaths that the fifth corps had gone to 'Jemima Ford's.' He could not be shaken in this statement. After puzzling over it, I suggested that we try the road to Germania Ford. At midnight we found our own wagon train at Germania Ford. Here I donned my fighting armor, borrowed a horse, and at daylight started in pursuit of the army. About ten o'clock A. M., I overtook the column of the first corps near Chancellorsville and resumed my post, my leave of absence not having expired by six hours when I reached the regiment. In a very few moments, musketry was heard in front and our regiment was ordered forward double quick. We deployed the men as skirmishers in the woods. We had been marching on a narrow road through thick woods, our regiment the advance of the first corps. Ahead of us was a wagon train of the fifth corps. Most of the wagons were loaded with ammunition. The rebel cavalry under Colonel Rosser came in by a cross road through the woods and attacked this wagon train, driving away the guards. It was a bold dash to come in between two army corps. We hurried forward through

---

*No. 294.   HEADQUARTERS MILITARY DISTRICT OF WASHINGTON, }
WASHINGTON, D. C., NOVEMBER 25th, 1863. }

Pass Lieutenant Colonel Rufus Dawes to Army Potomac, for the purpose of joining command, via government boat and rail.
This Pass will expire November 26th, 1863.
By order JOHN H. MARTINDALE,
Brig. Gen. and Military Governor.
Issued by E. BENTLY,   H. C. LOCKWOOD,
Captain and A. A. A. G.   Captain and Aide-de-Camp.

the thick woods and opened fire on the rebels as they were trying to hurry off the wagons. They promptly returned our fire and, for a few moments, the shots cracked and whizzed around our heads. We quickly drove them away, killing and wounding several of their men. Before they retreated they set fire to a number of ammunition wagons which blew up with loud and continued explosions, scattering shot, shell and wagon wheels all over the country. One of our men was shot. A rebel cavalry man took fair aim at me and his bullet cut a hole in my hat. He had on a blue United States overcoat and so our men had not fired at him. But when he shot at me, John Kilmartin of company 'G' drew a bead on him and shot him dead. Under his blue overcoat we found the rebel gray. Friday night we reached Locust Grove in our advance against the enemy. Saturday morning, together with the second corps, we moved in line of battle driving the enemy before us through the woods for three miles when we met General Ewell's corps in line of battle at Mine Run. The skirmishing was very hot, but we (ourselves) were subjected mainly to artillery fire. On Saturday, Sunday, Monday and Tuesday, we grimly faced the enemy, hourly expecting to be ordered to attack his works. During all this time, there was a soaking rain until the weather turned so bitterly cold that several men on the skirmish line are said to have frozen to death. As we were without shelter, we suffered much. Tuesday night we retreated back across the Rapidan river. Wednesday morning our brigade marched to Mitchell's ford to meet and resist any attempt at crossing by the enemy. Thursday we marched to Mountain Run and to-day we came here (Kelly's Ford) and went into camp."

I give extracts from General Bragg's letter. written in response to my request for some incidents or personal recollections of Mine Run.

"Do you remember a Council of War, to determine whether we could carry the line in front of us, that cold December day at Mine Run? *Your commanding officer voted No! I had Major Hauser, who was something of an engineer, make a reconnois-

---

*Colonel Bragg.

sance and report. He said the run was breast deep with water, covered with a thin ice, and the opposite bank was protected by a heavy abattis, made by trees with tops felled from the opposite bank into the stream, and also that beyond the abattis covering the slope were batteries in position. All this I explained to the doughty warriors who voted that the position could be carried, but it was no good! They voted the way they thought would please the powers that were. The order in the morning was to charge down the slope, cross the stream,—and carry the line beyond,—the movement to commence at a signal gun on the right, at or about eight o'clock A. M. Our line was formed and arms stacked, with big fires on the front to keep from freezing, while we waited for the order to move on to almost certain death.

On looking along the line, I saw some yellow-headed ganders, in Hauser's 'herd of goose,' (company 'H,') playing poker, for postal currency as stakes. I said: 'Can't you find anything to do but that?' They looked up and said in pigeon English: 'Dis will be no good to us, after de charge, we want all the fun we can get.'

You remember 'Big' Harry Dunn, of company 'E,' Scotch-Irish. His father was a man of position in Edinburgh. Harry, you know, deserted at Belle Plaine, because, being so large, he could not get any clothes that he could get into, but he was brought back, sentenced to some dire punishment, and pardoned for being so good a soldier. He had committed a crime in a foolish pet. Harry that morning, when we were waiting orders to charge, called me to one side and said: 'Write a good report to the old Governor about me, and tell him I was a brave soldier, and please don't say anything about that Belle Plaine affair.' Said I: 'Why, what's the matter Harry? I am as likely to be killed as you,—why give me the message?' 'Oh no,' said he, 'you ain't half as big as I am. My chances are two to one against yours,' and,—the orders were countermanded and no charge was made at all."

CHAPTER XI.

(Letter to M. B. G.)   CAMP NEAR KELLY'S FORD,
                                    DECEMBER 7th, 1863.

"Doctor Hall and I are fixing up our quarters for cold weather. We do not feel sure that we will stay here for the winter, but we hope to. Our men have built fine log cabins and the encampment of the brigade is very respectable. It is curious to see the ingenuity displayed by the men in making themselves comfortable in their log houses. With no tool but the little hatchet, they house themselves snugly and comfortably, and provide all the necessary furniture. To-morrow we will be fixed up in our cabin."

(Letter to M. B. G.)   KELLY'S FORD, DECEMBER 10th, 1863.

"To-night we are in our cabin, and our quarters are cheerful and bright, and for the first time since I left home I can sit down comfortably to write a letter. Our fireplace is a complete success and our chimney is all of brick. Look at the plan of our winter house: W. B. is wood box. F. P., fire place.

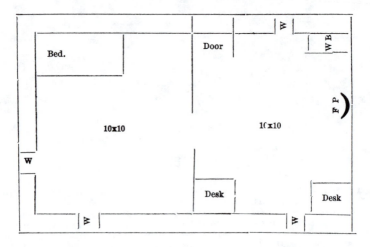

We have a tight board floor and are very comfortably established for a soldier's winter. We are tormented by rumors of a move to a different location.

I have no doubt that our army would have been slaughtered and defeated in any assault upon the enemy's entrenched line, (at Mine Run) after Sunday evening. The morning our corps and the second corps pursued the enemy from Robertson's Tavern, we found them in line of battle beyond Mine Run, without entrenchments. Upon that day and the next, the enemy might have been attacked, perhaps, with advantage. All honor to General Meade, who at risk of personal discomfiture, and at sacrifice of personal pride, had the moral courage to order a retreat without a day of blood and National humiliation to demonstrate its necessity to every dissatisfied carper among the people."

(Letter to M. B. G.)   KELLY'S FORD, DECEMBER 12th, 1863.

"What a noble message from President Lincoln. I do not hesitate to say that I think him a great statesman, and what is better, an unselfish patriot. The high tone of this message, and the unflinching adherence to his great measure of Emancipation, must command the respect of the world and inspire confidence in the ultimate success of a cause so firmly planted on the right. If the full success we hope shall crown our struggle, and slavery with rebellion be swept from the land, the name of Lincoln will mark on history a grand epoch in the progress of civilization.

The author of the Proclamation that gave freedom to four millions of people, and brought the true object and end of our battling before the world, that placed us upon ground consistent with the fearful sacrifices we have made, will have a high place in the respect of this age and the veneration of all succeeding ages. All hail to old Abe! for in the sure omens of final triumph all around, is the dawning glory of his name, as the world's greatest champion of freedom, and Republican institutions. This is not extravagant, for we are in the midst of grand events, and the men who carve their names as representatives of the triumph of right in a struggle of such magnitude, will have a proud distinction in history.

We are watching anxiously the action of Congress on the 'Conscript Law.' The three hundred dollars exemption clause will probably be repealed. The Government should rely entirely upon filling up its old organizations in the recruitment of its army. This regiment, as at present affected, will not re-enlist. The men want to go in cavalry, in artillery, in the navy, or in anything but the business of transporting Government supplies in a knapsack on their shoulders. We have heard from our recruiting party. They are getting no recruits, and the draft in Wisconsin brings money, as I supposed, but very few soldiers, so we are not likely to be filled up with conscripts."

BARABOO, WISCONSIN, DECEMBER 8th, 1863.
COLONEL R. R. DAWES,

DEAR SIR:—"Our elections all went off right this fall. *Bully for the boys in blue.* They did their duty, excepting the —— —— I suppose that regiment would vote for Jeff. Davis, if they were told that he was a Democrat. Every Badger feels proud of our own 'Iron Brigade,' and well they may, for no other has such a reputation or such a record.

My wounded limb is getting quite comfortable. I am however, badly crippled. I get around with two canes pretty well. I can never march on foot again. The draft is over here, and about

---

*The vote of the soldiers is here referred to.

one in twenty of those drafted, will go to the war. They nearly all pay their regular three hundred dollars, (exemption fee.) I have recruited seventeen men recently, and all but one go in cavalry. They are bound to ride. I have tried them all for the Sixth, but it is no use, they must ride. If the Sixth was mounted, it could be filled up. *I could go then.** Sergeants Klein and Fletcher are here. I shall do all I can to assist them, but it is an up-hill business to recruit for infantry.

The merchants are all getting rich. Remember me to Colonel Bragg and Major Hauser.

I shall be happy to hear from you. Please accept my best wishes for your future success, prosperity and happiness. A glorious past is sure. Very truly your friend,

D. K. Noyes."

(Letter to M. B. G.) Near Kelly's Ford, December 14th, 1863.

"The rain is pouring down in floods, and mud unfathomable is the order of things. Colonel Bragg is now in Washington on a seven days leave of absence. †I think his star will soon rise above the horizon. I am fixing up the camp for winter quarters, corduroying the streets, building stables and mess houses."

(Letter to M. B. G.) Kelly's Ford, December 16th, 1863.

"These are rumors of our going back to Centreville. The depletion of the army by sending home veterans, and from various other causes, may cause such a movement. We are getting settled down into camp life with the usual routine of court martial, inspections, picket, and fatigue duty."

(Letter to M. B. G.) Kelly's Ford, December 20th, 1863.

"General Meade has sent orders to this brigade to report at once how many men will re-enlist as veterans. If three fourths of the members of a regiment who are within his department, agree to re-enlist, the regiment, he says, will be ordered home for furlough and to recruit. Commanding officers were directed to submit the question to their regiments. I called the regiment together, and spoke to them for half an hour, explaining fully

---

*Captain Noyes' foot was torn off by the shell at Antietam.

†His promotion as a Brigadier General, which had long been promised.

and as fairly as I could, the inducements offered by the Government to re-enlist as veterans, the prospect of the continuation of war, and the especial advantages of re-organizing as the Sixth regiment. I submitted an agreement for as many as chose to sign, pledging themselves to re-enlist in the sixth Wisconsin, as a veteran volunteer organization, under the various orders on the subject, provided the regiment should immediately upon the re-enlistment of three fourths of its members now within the department, be sent to Wisconsin for a furlough of at least thirty days. Something over eighty men have signed the agreement, but my impression is, that the requisite three fourths will not sign.'

In this camp I received a letter from my brother, Major E. C. Dawes, in General Sherman's corps :

BRIDGEPORT, ALABAMA, DECEMBER 19th, 1863.

"Safe home at last; home to tents, blankets, teams, clothes, hard tack, coffee and pork. It was a hard campaign, that in East Tennessee, but I would not have missed it for anything. * * *

I cannot now give details of our march. We drew no rations from November twenty-ninth, until to-day, (December nineteenth.) Every night we slept in the open air. Every day we marched from seventeen to twenty-five miles. All supplies were foraged from the country or brought to us by the Union people, some of whom walked miles to carry food to the Union soldiers. We cooked our meat on sticks before the fire and made corn cakes on flat boards. We did not have a single thing on wheels with our regiment, except one old ambulance that had no top. Many of our men were without shoes, and often marched over frozen ground with bleeding feet. Very few made any complaint, and none straggled. We have marched continuously since leaving Memphis, October eleventh, without halting at any one place over two days."

(Letter to M. B. G.)   CAMP NEAR KELLY'S FORD,
                               DECEMBER 22nd, 1863.

"Is the regiment going to re-enlist? Very doubtful. One hundred and forty-eight men have signed, up to to-night. I go on picket for two days in the morning."

(Letter to M. B. G.) NEAR CULPEPPER COURT HOUSE,
DECEMBER 27th, 1863.

"Excuse my pencil. Our wagons are loaded. We have had a hard time the past two days. I went on picket on Wednesday morning. Thursday at daylight, the coldest day this winter, our corps left its winter quarters. I had a very severe time gathering up the picket line about four miles long. About the middle of the afternoon we reached Culpepper, and I had to work hard until night to establish a new picket line. I remained on the line all night. This morning our regiment was ordered temporarily into empty houses in the village of Culpepper, until the severe storm now raging is over."

I received an especial kindness on the cold afternoon of our arrival at Culpepper from a rebel citizen. There were about twelve hundred men in the picket details, and I had to establish them on a line of four or five miles according to points designated and given me. But pitying the cold and forlorn condition of the men, this gentleman helped me by his familiar knowledge of localities and roads. His only concern was lest his rebel neighbors might know of his kindness and misinterpret it. His name was Jack Pendleton, and he had served as a member of the Congress of the United States before the war. This assistance enabled my picket reserves to make their tin cups full of hot and refreshing coffee, before the darkness of a cold and stormy night prevented them from gathering fuel for their fires.

(Letter to M. B. G.) CULPEPPER COURT HOUSE,
DECEMBER 28th, 1863.

"We are still in the houses in the village, but are expecting an order that will send us out into the winter storm and mud General Cutler has just called in. He says he thinks it is all right, and that we can stay in the houses. We have a pleasant room, with a fire place, on the second floor of a respectable house. The officers of the corps and division staff are scattered around in comfortable houses in the village. Such quarters for the winter would be grand. Three fourths of the men of our regiment are disposed to re-enlist, but objections are raised to sending them home as a regiment. The men will not go in any other way and if this point is insisted upon, the chance of their re-enlistment is gone."

(Letter to M. B. G.) CULPEPPER COURT HOUSE,
DECEMBER 30th, 1863.

"We are still in Culpepper, and our men are very comfortable in houses. As I write now, the room is full of officers, talking and brawling over the veteran question, and I cannot think of anything else in this awful clatter. We have fine quarters, a large house, one room for an office, one for reception room and one for a kitchen."

(Letter to M. B. G.) DECEMBER 31st, 1863.

"The veteran excitement is unabated. We have present in this army two hundred and ninety enlisted men, who can re-enlist as veterans. Of this number, three fourths must re-enlist to have the regiment ordered to Wisconsin. To-night, one hundred and ninety-five men have been sworn in. It needs twenty-three more men. Our detached men who have been cooks for officers, hostlers, clerks, and teamsters, of whom there are sixty-eight, nearly all decline to re-enlist, but the men who have stood by the old flag through fair and foul weather, and through many bloody battles, almost to a man dedicate their lives and service anew to their country. These men who have stood day after day in the presence of death, who have endured every sort of privation and and suffering, present an example that should bring a blush of shame to the brows of the young men who have failed their country at this crisis."

(Letter to M. B. G.) CULPEPPER COURT HOUSE,
JANUARY 2nd, 1864.

"To-night the quota, two hundred and seventeen men and five recruits, have been sworn in. We are busily engaged in mustering the regiment as veterans. If no unforseen accident intervenes, the regiment will be on its way west next Thursday or Friday."

HEADQUARTERS SIXTH WISCONSIN VETERAN VOLUNTEERS,
(Letter to M. B G.) CULPEPPER COURT HOUSE,
JANUARY 4th, 1864.

"Yesterday we unfurled our flag from the windows of headquarters in token of success. 'We have hung our banner on the outer wall, and the cry is still they come.' There are two hundred and thirty-three men sworn in, and five companies mustered."

(Letter to M. B. G.)   CULPEPPER COURT HOUSE, }
               JANUARY 6th, 1864. }

"The regiment is paid in full, and camp and garrison equipage has been turned over to the Quartermaster's department, and everything is in readiness. I rode yesterday through snow and mud to army headquarters, fifteen miles there and back, to get the order to go to Wisconsin. General Williams (Seth Williams, A. A. G. Army of the Potomac,) said the order would be made, but he would not give it to me, and he has since telegraphed that six hundred men only can be sent away from the first army corps. This may cut us out altogether. I represented the interest of the regiment at army headquarters the best I was able, and felt troubled not to have succeeded in getting the order, for the men are impatient and suspicious, after being trifled with so much. The seventh Wisconsin has gone, and is now far on its way to Wisconsin."

The order came on a bitterly cold afternoon. The re-enlisted regiment took freight cars for Alexandria, on their way to Wisconsin. The men who did not re-enlist and the recruits, remained in the camp of the second Wisconsin, which did not re-enlist as an organization. We were all night on the Orange and Alexandria railroad without fires, and there was great suffering. One man was so severely frozen that he was left in the hospital at Alexandria. We proceeded west via Baltimore, Harrisburgh, and Pittsburg. At Pittsburg I left the regiment and went to Marietta, Ohio, where I arrived January 14th, 1864.

The regiment met with a splendid reception upon its arrival at Milwaukee. The Board of Trade of the city provided a dinner at the Newhall House, and public exercises were conducted in the hall of the Chamber of Commerce. In an account of the affair, the Milwaukee Sentinel says: "The Sixth regiment proceeded from their quarters at Broadhead's Block, to the Chamber of Commerce, escorted by six companies of the thirtieth Wisconsin under Colonel Daniel J. Dill,—formerly a Captain in the Sixth,—and the Milwaukee Light Infantry under Captain Nazro.

At a few minutes past one o'clock the cortege made its appearance, headed by Christian Bach's excellent band, playing : 'The Year of Jubilee.' The veterans marched into the hall and the escort was dismissed. As the regiment entered, they were greeted with salvos of cheers. They formed in the center of the room in close column by company, and at the command of Colonel Bragg, brought their pieces to an order with a thug that elicited rounds of applause."

The address of welcome was made by Ex-Governor Salomon. General Fairchild, Secretary of State of Wisconsin, and Mayor O'Neill of Milwaukee, made speeches of welcome, and other prominent citizens of Milwaukee took part in the speech making.

My purpose in leaving the regiment at Pittsburg was to fulfill my engagement of marriage with my correspondent, M. B. G. The wedding took place Monday morning, January 18th, 1864, at half past five o'clock, at the residence of Beman Gates, in Marietta, Ohio. The ceremony was performed by Rev. Thomas Wickes, D. D. There were few guests present beside the family connections residing in Marietta. My wife and I immediately took the train for the west to join the regiment at Milwaukee. A heavy snow storm set in which delayed our progress. We were all day getting from Cincinnati to Hamilton, Ohio, twenty-four miles. A day was consumed going from Hamilton to Valparaiso, Indiana. At this point we found a strike of locomotive engineers on the Pittsburg, Ft. Wayne & Chicago R. R., and we took a sleigh and drove across the country twelve miles, to the Michigan Central Railroad, where we boarded a freight train and arrived in Chicago on Thursday evening, in triumph in the caboose. Of course under such circumstances, the trip was in every respect delightful. We reached Milwaukee Friday evening, where the headquarters of the regiment during the veteran furlough was established. During our stay of about four weeks, we were at the Newhall House a part of the time, and a part of the time with the family of a Mr. Roddis. Here we met congenial and sympathizing fellow boarders, in Mr. J. Middleton Arnold and wife, who, like ourselves were an extremely newly married couple. Mr. Arnold was a soldier in the twenty fourth Wisconsin, and his wife was from Ipswich, Massachusetts.

My wife, who had followed every movement of our regiment through my correspondence, saw in a hall in Broadhead's Block, the stacks of muskets with belts and cartridge boxes hanging upon them, as left by the column when broken for the men to visit their homes. She never saw more than this of the sixth Wisconsin regiment. As I was riding on the icy streets in the city of Milwaukee on my crippled horse, which had been shot at Gettysburg, the animal fell in turning a corner. My left ankle was dislocated and badly sprained. I was unable to walk without crutches for several weeks, and obtained a leave of absence upon a surgeon's certificate of disability, and I accompanied my wife to Marietta, Ohio. This accident was regarded as a great piece of good fortune. Upon the expiration of the veteran furlough, the regiment returned to its camp near Culpepper, Virginia. I was unable to return to the field until the twenty-first of March, 1864.

HEADQUARTERS SIXTH WISCONSIN VETERAN VOLUNTEERS, ⎱
(To my wife.)   NEAR CULPEPPER, MARCH, 22nd, 1864. ⎰

"I arrived safely last night. I came down with General Cutler, who provided me with a good dinner and gave me an ambulance in which to ride over to camp. (I was still lame from the effects of my sprain.) I found the regiment encamped two miles from Culpepper and quite comfortably quartered. There are one hundred and eleven recruits, and more are coming. William Jackson was delighted with the pipe you sent him. He is now chief steward of our mess.

Major Hauser's resignation has been accepted, and he has gone. General Grant is fixing up headquarters in Culpepper village. He will be a near neighbor to us. He shows good judgment in establishing himself with the first army corps. The impression here is that our army, properly re-inforced and strengthened, will make a vigorous advance on Richmond."

(To my wife.)   HEADQUARTERS SIXTH WISCONSIN VOLS., ⎱
                 MARCH 22nd, 1864. ⎰

"I am on my old duty again. I received yesterday a detail as President of the general court martial of our division. Our court will sit near General Grant's headquarters and I shall see the hero of the day often. He is to arrive in Culpepper to-morrow. My ankle gets stronger every day but I am still quite lame. General James S. Wadsworth is to command our division."

(To my wife.) MARCH 24th, 1864.

I was greatly surprised yesterday to see Captain William J. Dawes (eighth Wisconsin) come riding into camp. On account of a very severe wound in his foot, received at Corinth, he is going into the veteran reserve corps. This morning we are to ride over to Pony mountain to see the rebels beyond the Rapidan. The weather has been very cold and there is not less than six inches of snow on the ground, but it is a fine morning and a pleasant day to ride.

Seven o'clock P. M.—We have returned from our ride to the signal station on Pony mountain. We came through Culpepper just in time to see General Grant. He looks like a plain common sense man, one not to be puffed up by position nor abashed by obstacles."

HEADQUARTERS SIXTH WISCONSIN VETERAN VOLUNTEERS,
FIRST DIVISION, FIRST ARMY CORPS, MARCH 26th, 1864.

(To my wife.)

"The room in which our court martial sits is opposite General Grant's headquarters. We see him every day. He looks differently from what I had expected and my impressions are favorable. He holds the life of the Nation almost in his own hands. God help him and our country! There is a desperate struggle before us. Both sections seem to have chosen this as the ground for the last grand conflict. If we gain it, in my opinion, the rebellion will be crushed. General Wadsworth will command our new division which will be in the fifth army corps, and General G. K. Warren will command that Corps. Direct your letters as usual until I advise you what the arrangement is. It will be a swallowing up of the old first army corps with the fifth corps, which hurts our feelings very much. We think the first army corps has deserved something better than obliteration."

HEADQUARTERS SIXTH WISCONSIN VETERAN VOLUNTEERS,
FOURTH DIVISION, FIFTH ARMY CORPS, MARCH 27th, 1864.

"*Dear Father*:—The army receives with great satisfaction the compliment of the personal leadership of the Lieutenant General, but the army can fight no more heroically under General

Grant than it did under General McClellan at Antietam, or General Meade at Gettysburg. There is a measure to human achievement. Give General Grant men enough of the tried valor and experience of this fighting army of the Nation and I think he can go to Richmond and, with the occupation and isolation of Virginia, crush the rebellion. We believe he will not undertake the great work in the light of such abundant experience without strength adequate to the enterprise, and we feel confident that, as you say, 'Grant will take Richmond this campaign.'"

NEAR CULPEPPER COURT HOUSE, MARCH 27th, 1864.

"*My dear wife:*—We have had a complete re-organization of our army. Our old first corps is merged into the fifth corps under the command of General G. K. Warren. I like General Warren for a corps commander. We are, in the re-organization, the first brigade, fourth division, fifth army corps. General Cutler commands our brigade and General Wadsworth our division.

We have had a pleasant Sabbath. A gentleman from Massachusetts, the Rev. Lewis F. Clark, pastor of the Congregational church at Whittiersville, Massachusetts, (born in Southhampton, Massachusetts,) who is connected with the Christian Commission, came to our camp and desired to hold religious service. It was a beautiful morning, and after inspection, the regiment was turned out to attend divine service. Mr. Clark preached a short and excellent sermon to the regiment, which was formed in a hollow square. The service was impressive, and it is an honor to our regiment that every man behaved with a reverence becoming the occasion. We all took dinner with Mr. Clark at Colonel Bragg's tent. He corresponds with Dr. Justin Perkins, of the Nestorian mission in Persia. He knows all about Mr. Shedd (my brother-in-law, a missionary in Persia) and has read his published letters with much interest, and he quoted from them. He knew more about the mission than I did. He regards Dr. Perkins as one of the benefactors of the age. He told several anecdotes of his life. He knew of my great grandfather, Rev. Dr. Manasseh Cutler, and about my great grandfather, Colonel William Dawes, who rode from Boston with Paul Revere to arouse the people the night before Lexington. He was quite witty over my Yankee pedigree. He made me feel quite blue. You will perceive that we had a pleasant visitor. He is a graduate of Andover and an exceedingly bright and intelligent gentleman. He left his church for six weeks to come to the army in the service of the Christian Commission."

Dr. Clark was pleased with the decorous behaviour of our men, and he was inclined to attribute it to the moral influence of our "Christian commandant," as he styled Colonel Bragg, to the great delight of Dr. Hall and myself. Dr. Clark privately asked Dr. Hall to what denomination Colonel Bragg belonged. Dr. Hall replied that the Colonel was "so modest and reticent about his religious affiliations" that he had never told us.

"Our recruits are a fine set of fellows and they take up their new business readily. I do not fear that the honor of the regiment will ever suffer in their keeping. I inspected the regiment this morning and looked them all over carefully."

(To my wife.) NEAR CULPEPPER, MARCH 29th, 1864.

"I am going over some day soon to Culpepper to play chess with a rebel gentleman, named Mr. Mosee, who says 'he has beaten the Confederate army and is anxious to beat the Union army.' This morning we stood shivering two hours in line of battle to be reviewed by General Grant. An incident occurred upon this review, which was characteristic of General Grant. The troops were drawn up in line of battalions en masse doubled on the centre. There was a cold drizzle of rain, and as General Grant, at the head of his staff and escort, rode slowly along in front of the line, regiment after regiment gave loud cheers in his honor as he approached. This had become customary in our army when the troops were reviewed by the commanding General. General Grant made no recognition of the intended compliment. I was in command of the regiment and observing this felt provoked. I turned to the regiment and said: 'As General Grant does not seem to think our cheering worth notice, I will not call for cheers. Maintain your position as soldiers.' When General Grant came to the sixth Wisconsin, the military salutes required were performed with exact precision and the men stood motionless as statues. He evidently expected us to cheer him as the others had; but when he saw us performing only our exact and formal duties as soldiers, he took off his hat and made a low bow

to us, and to our colors dipped in salute to him as commander of
the army. It was to say, 'I did not come here for a personal
ovation.' It was a genuine Grantism and our men were highly
pleased at it. They said, 'Grant wants soldiers, not yaupers.'"

(To my wife.)   NEAR CULPEPPER, MARCH 31st, 1864.

"Major Hauser has been appointed a Consul to Switzerland
and he will soon start with his wife for Europe. Captain Philip
W. Plummer will be Major in place of Hauser. He is a pleasant
gentleman and will be an agreeable member of our mess. Adjutant Brooks is out of Libby Prison at last and will soon return to
to the regiment."

(To my wife.)   CAMP NEAR CULPEPPER, APRIL 4th, 1864.

"General James S. Wadsworth, is now in command of
our division, and we begin at once to feel the old fellow
trying in his own level headed way to ferret out abuses. For instance: 'All officers applying for leave of absence must state the
date and length of their last leave.' He is a thorough and able
commander.

The men are drawing commutation money for the rations to
which they were entitled while on the veteran furlough and I
have to sign all these papers in duplicate. About all the time
that I am not on court martial, I am writing my name. William
Jackson, now our chief steward, provides well and serves up
dinners that are the envy of all around us. It is impossible to
get good cooks and competent servants now, and we should be
badly off if it were not for William. He is anxious that
General Grant shall succeed this spring, for an advance of our
lines of twenty miles would enable him to find his mother, which
he can never hope to do if the rebellion prevails."

(To my wife.)   NEAR CULPEPPER, APRIL 8th, 1864.

"This morning the regiment is to be inspected by Colonel
Osborne, Inspector, at General Wadsworth's headquarters, and
every man is busy polishing his gun and brasses and blacking his
shoes. Our men will not allow themselves to be surpassed in
neatness of appearance.

There was a great horse race yesterday near Stevensburgh.
Our horse lost more than $1000 for our friends who bet their

money on horse races. I am glad the horse got beaten. They have been gambling on it for a year and this I hope will put a stop to it. This dose was badly needed."

(To my wife.)   NEAR CULPEPPER, APRIL 9th, 1864.

"There are increasing indications of active work. Sutlers are being sent to the rear, baggage reduced, and leaves of absence forbidden. General Warren says in his order, that sickness or death of near relatives will not be considered as a reason for granting leaves of absence. His idea of an extreme case is likely the same as General Newton's. We expected the ninth corps, General Burnside's here, but I do not know that it has come. I have not been very well for the last two days."

(To my wife.)   NEAR CULPEPPER, APRIL 12th, 1864.

"There is a lively hum of preparation throughout the army for active operations. On the 15th of April, all sutlers or camp followers of every description must be out of the army under severe penalty, and all available men are being gathered up, armed and equipped for service in the ranks. Soon the dreaded rattle of musketry will be around us. The incessant rain storms have so raised the streams as to carry away nearly every railroad bridge between here and Washington.

Our camp was enlivened last night by a decided genius. He spoke and sang patriotic songs to our boys for two hours. He kept his audience in an uproar. He was amusing, pathetic, patriotic, almost thrilling in his climaxes after the most approved style of oratory. He is doing a good work in his way. His utterances were encouraging to the soldiers and his entertainment highly acceptable to them, wearied by the monotony of camp life.

A report was called for from army headquarters of how many officers of veteran regiments had 'signified their intention to serve a new term of three years.' Colonel Bragg reported 'none in this regiment.' The course of our State Governors is not calculated to encourage the army. The most severe criticism is made of Governor Brough of Ohio. He has inaugurated a system of throwing obstacles in the way of the promotion of veteran officers and soldiers. The Governor of a State, free from danger and with little knowledge of the military service of the general Government, in point of propriety and good sense ought not to have control of the appointment or promotion of officers who are in the field, in the Army of the United States. One of our companies is now without officers and we are not able to get the Governor of Wisconsin to appoint them, and this while we are preparing for an active campaign against the enemy. Week after week he has delayed sending the commissions asked for by Colonel Bragg, making frivolous, and to us, contemptible objections. For example, 'you have not stated whether this man is first sergeant,' when there is no first sergeant in the company. Again: 'This officer cannot be promoted until the Governor is notified by the War Department of the resigned officer's discharge,' when the officer was not discharged by order of the War Department. The War Department can not know of his discharge for a month to come, and then would not notify the Governor of Wisconsin, because that is not required. Besides, the Governor has been notified long before by our Colonel, who is the proper authority. Or: 'The Governor has determined not to appoint out of the line of promotion in the individual's own regiment.' The important places in the new regiments, where the experience and example of the veterans are of vital importance, are given too often to politically influential civilians, who hang around and tease for them. Shame on such a policy. No such folly is practiced by the rebels. Instead of rushing in new and green organizations, they are constantly filling up, by conscription or otherwise, their old regiments. That is one reason why we can't whip Lee's army."

The following extracts from an article by Colonel E. C. Dawes, in the National Tribune of August 14th, 1890, state succinctly these radical differences in the military policy of the contending powers:

"In the Confederacy after 1861, all soldiers were enlisted 'for the war.' There was scarcely a new regiment organized after 1862. Recruits and conscripts were assigned to old regiments, whose ranks were thus kept full. Promotions were promptly made to fill all vacancies. Each infantry and cavalry company had three Lieutenants. Brigades, divisions, and army corps, were commanded by officers of appropriate rank. Brigades as a rule retained the same organization from the beginning of the war to the end.

In the Union army there was perpetual change. Men were enlisted for all periods, from three months to three years. Under each call for troops, new regiments were organized. Each infantry and cavalry company had two Lieutenants. Promotions were not permitted in old regiments if the number of officers on the rolls was proportionately greater than the number of enlisted men. The chances for promotion were therefore in inverse ratio to the service performed. Brigades and divisions were changed with each campaign, and were seldom commanded by officers of proper rank.

Some examples from the records will illustrate these differences: General Joseph E. Johnston's army by its return of June 10th, 1864, numbered for duty, 6,538 officers and 64,340 enlisted men. General Sherman's army by its return June 30th, 1864, with 100,851 enlisted men for duty, had but 5,219 officers."

(To my wife.)   NEAR CULPEPPER, APRIL 15th, 1864.

"I had the honor of an introduction to General G. K. Warren yesterday. He is a keen-looking fellow of small stature, about my own complexion, black eyes and hair, and quite young looking. His address is gentlemanly and pleasing."

(To my wife.)   NEAR CULPEPPER, APRIL 17th, 1864.

"The enemy are evidently preparing themselves to meet the advance of this army, and if possible, repel it. Our army is being considerably augmented, not so much however, I think, as the country generally supposes.

The Rev. Warren Cochran has been appointed chaplain of our regiment. He is a Congregationalist and said to be an able man. He has a son, who is a recruit to the regiment, and he wishes to be with him in the service. Our regiment has been announced in general orders as first in excellence in the division in cleanliness of clothing and persons of the men, and in good condition of arms and accoutrements."

General Wadsworth had announced that he would publish in general orders, the regiment in his division that stood first in soldierly qualities, discipline, cleanliness, and condition of arms, but the time for the inspection was not given. The order for inspection came to brigade headquarters and was there discovered by Colonel Bragg at midnight, and the inspection was to be at eight o'clock A. M. Bragg has written of this circumstance: "It was a stunner, and I thought aimed to bring down our high pretensions." The Colonel called out all the Captains after midnight, and we had a preliminary inspection at daylight in the morning, after which the men went to bed and apparently fell fast asleep. At eight o'clock Colonel Osborne, the inspector, came. Colonel Bragg writes: "He stopped at my tent and waked me up, and I pretended that it was the first I had heard of an inspection, and grumbled about their playing such tricks on us. As I ranked Osborne, you turned the regiment out, and such a regiment those fellows never saw, as Osborne himself told me in 1865 at a Camp-fire one night. He admitted that he expected to take us unawares, and wanted to know how we got ready. I told him they always kept themselves that way in camp, to which he answered 'Bosh.'"

"The manner in which the whole opposition party in Congress has shown sympathy for the traitorous sentiments of Representative Long, of Ohio, has created a profound impression in the army. It is asked how many reverses to our plans and our arms will bring the great political party these people represent to Mr. Long's conviction of the necessity of recognition. They have shown favor to Mr. Long's avowal upon the floor of Congress of his conviction of our defeat, and of the triumph of our enemy.

I attend court martial every day. We have an important case pending. Judge McCunn of New York City, under provisions of a law of New York, enacted in pursuance of a provision of the Constitution of the United States, that the militia cannot be called into the service of the United States for a longer period than two years, discharged from the service, by the decree of a municipal court of New York city, a member of the fourteenth Brooklyn, which was a regiment of New York state militia, mustered into the United States service for three years unless sooner discharged. The Provost Marshal arrested the man as a deserter, disregarding the decree of the court, and our court is trying him on a charge of desertion. Important questions are involved in this case."

The provision in the Constitution is that "No appropriation of money," to raise and support armies, "shall be for a longer term than for two years."

(To my wife.)   NEAR CULPEPPER, APRIL 22nd, 1864.

"Captain Philip W. Plummer has been appointed Major, vice Hauser. Adjutant Brooks came unexpectedly into camp last night. I must say he never looked better in his life, and imprisonment in Libby seems to have agreed with the young man. He tells amusing stories of life in Libby. General Neal Dow, who was a prisoner, had coffee sent to him by his friends. Brooks says he wanted some of that coffee, and he sent a young Lieutenant, who did not know Dow, to commiserate with him upon the burning of his fine distillery. The ludicrous explosion that followed, enabled Brooks to steal a tin cup of coffee from the hot coals. Brooks says he got ninety dollars in rebel money, for three dollars in gold, and that Mosby sold his (Brooks') horse for two thousand dollars in rebel currency. We had a fine little brigade review in honor of the Governor of Wisconsin, who is here, (Governor Lewis.)

(To my wife.)   NEAR CULPEPPER, APRIL 26th, 1864.

"I occupied the time yesterday playing chess with old Mr. Mossee, the rebel gentleman in Culpepper, of whom I have written you. We played ten games and won five each. The old fellow is a strong player. He spends his time studying calculus and chess for want of something else to do. He has a daughter living with him, whom he calls 'Puss,' which rather disturbs my equanimity, as I dislike silly nicknames. But the daughter's tenderness for her father is beautiful. I am afraid I shall be short of socks before the campaign is over. The sutlers have all left the army and nothing of the kind can be procured here. Our people are building forts around Culpepper, either as a blind or to fortify this point as a base of supplies."

(To my wife.)   NEAR CULPEPPER, APRIL 27th, 1864.

"Burnside's corps are arriving at Alexandria, which of course, is a preliminary to an immediate movement by this army."

(To my wife.)   NEAR CULPEPPER, APRIL 28th, 1864.

"The seventh Indiana regiment, under Colonel Ira B. Grover, has been added to our brigade. This is a large and remarkably fortunate regiment. They claim to have been in seventeen battles with less loss than we sustained at Gettysburg. General Wadsworth's division must be seven thousand strong. The seventh Wisconsin received fourteen Indians, apparently wild from the woods, as recruits yesterday. Some of them cannot speak our language. I have Reuben greatly exercised, for I tell him that no delicacy is so choice to an Indian as roast nigger, unless it be a coon. As Reuben considers himself both he sees no chance to escape. Mr. Mossee and I, yesterday, played seven games. I won four; he won two and one was drawn. It was hard work to beat the old man, but I did it this time, and the Union army is ahead. The drawn game was a joke. This is the position:

Black.

White.

I have the white men and the move and draw the game. To be caught thus asleep annoyed the old gentleman greatly. He had a sure thing."

(To my wife.) NEAR CULPEPPER, APRIL 29th, 1864.

"We are to try a Major to-morrow on the charge of drunkenness, and other charges too disgraceful to write on paper. It is discouraging to find such men in respectable and responsible positions in the army. I saw a regular war dance in the camp of the seventh Wisconsin last night. The Indians are Chippewas. General Rice saw our returned enlisted men who had been prisoners at Belle Isle, in Richmond. 'No one,' he says, 'who has not seen them, can imagine the dreadful condition of these men.'"

(To my wife.) CAMP NEAR CULPEPPER, MAY 1st, 1864.

"Our new Major, Philip W. Plummer, came into camp yesterday from Wisconsin, where he has been on recruiting service. He has enjoyed his stay in Wisconsin and is in high spirits at his promotion. He looks finely. May 2nd.—You must tell me where Charley's regiment is to be stationed. He will not have an unpleasant duty in his one hundred days of soldiering."

Charles Beman Gates, only brother of my wife, was a member of the Junior class in Marietta College. He was nineteen years of age. He had joined the one hundred and forty-eighth Ohio regiment under the call for men to serve one hundred days, and he was First Lieutenant in company "A."

(To my wife.) CAMP NEAR CULPEPPER, MAY 3rd, 1864.

" 'We move at midnight.'"

When the orders to march to the Wilderness came, two culprits who belonged to our regiment were in confinement at Gen. Wadsworth's headquarters to be taken to the penitentiary at Sing Sing, New York. One had been sentenced to a term of five years and the other to a term of three years. They begged piteously to be allowed to join the regiment and fight in the coming battles. They said they had rather be killed than go to the penitentiary. Upon Colonel Bragg's voucher that they would fight if released General Wadsworth granted their request. They never left the skirmish line until both were shot and severely wounded. At Petersburg, after the campaign, I applied to the President of the United States for their pardon, pleading their bravery and their suffering in battle. Under the rule in such cases, all the evidence before the court was submitted together with the application. The pardon was granted by President Abraham Lincoln.

CHAPTER XII.

The Wilderness—Laurel Hill—The Bloody Angle and Spottsylvania.

On the early morning of May 4th, 1864, the grand column of the Army of the Potomac was on the march to cross the Rapidan, the fifth army corps in advance. At the head of our division rode General James S. Wadsworth, gray-haired and noble in his appearance and bearing, and grand in every element of character and manhood. We crossed on the pontoon at Germania Ford, and marched into the Wilderness. Word passed over the land that General Grant was moving, and with almost breathless anxiety our people awaited the result. For days no word came from beneath the dark shadow, to relieve the almost agonized anxiety of my young wife. It was known that there was desperate and incessant fighting, but it was wholly impossible to get particulars from the front. Her kind father, (Beman Gates) left his business, and putting aside all else came to Washington to get the first word possible from me, and to be at hand to aid me in case of need. My uncle, Wm. P. Cutler, almost equally concerned, sent the first word of encouragement that reached my wife. The battles in the Wilderness and near Spottsylvania, will first be given in the correspondence which is arranged in the same order that it came to my wife, as the most graphic as well as the most accurate manner of restoring the experiences of that time.

(Telegram.)   CHILLICOTHE, OHIO, MAY 10th, 1864.

"Morning papers contain lists of casualties among officers. Rufus' name not among them. General Wadsworth killed. Lee retreating.   W. P. CUTLER."

This was the first list published. The telegram gained six hours time before delivery of the morning papers at Marietta.

Letter from Beman Gates to my wife,—his daughter:

"*My dear Mary*:—"I am convinced that during the first six days of battle, Rufus escaped injury. I have sought information from every possible source, and have obtained as full lists as practicable of all casualties. There are several wounded men from the sixth Wisconsin who came up on the boat last night, and whom I will see before closing this letter. This morning I went to the Georgetown hospital where the officers are mostly sent, to see Dr. Preston, reported as Surgeon of the sixth Wisconsin. He could give me no information, having started here before the army moved. Over seven thousand men have already reached here, but a majority of them are slightly wounded. The more severely wounded are kept at Fredericksburgh. I get more information through the Sanitary Commission than from all other sources, but in the present hurry and confusion, it is very difficult to get any information that is reliable. The loss of men has been terrible, and I fear the slaughter will continue for some days yet. Everything is being done by the Government and by the Sanitary Commission to relieve the wounded, but great suffering must result from the inability to give prompt aid. I am now waiting to see the Wisconsin State Agent, (W. Y. Selleck) and if I can get any information, I will add it to this letter. If I get any reliable information from Rufus I will telegraph at once."

"2½ o'clock P. M.—I have just come from one of the hospitals where I found three men wounded from the sixth Wisconsin. They all belong to company 'C.'* One of them was wounded in the first day's battle, and two in the second. They say that Bragg is in command of a Pennsylvania brigade, and Dawes, of the regiment. They speak in the very highest terms of him and say that in the second day's fight, when the division was driven,† the colors fell back, when Colonel Dawes seized them in person, marched forward and planted them under a heavy fire, and brought the men up to line. Major Plummer was killed in the first day's fight, and Captain Converse, company 'B,' was killed.

---

*Norman S. Bull, Albert P. Sprague, C. H. Clary.

†Longstreet's attack when General Wadsworth was killed and our lines broken.

These were all the officers killed or wounded badly up to Sunday night.* The Wisconsin State Agent says that officers from the seventh Wisconsin, who came up last night, report that when they left Sunday night, Rufus was all right. The Agent expects later news to-night, and if I hear anything unfavorable I will telegraph you, and go down to the front on the first boat. I have a pass and shall take charge of the sanitary and medical stores for the Ohio Relief Association. I do not know how to leave my business, but if I can be of service, I feel that I ought to go. Your husband is proving himself a brave and true man and an excellent officer; indeed, he has done this long ago. But he is now winning fresh laurels, which for your sake, for his mother's and sister's sake, and for the country's good, I pray that he may live to wear for many years.

Your affectionate father,
BEMAN GATES."

WASHINGTON, MAY 13th, 1864.

Extracts from a letter to Mrs. Gates.—"I expect to start to Fredericksburgh in the morning. I shall get to Belle Plaine, eighty miles down the Potomac, before night, and shall then have to walk or ride ten miles or so to Fredericksburgh. Whether I go farther or not will depend upon circumstances when I get there. My pass will allow me to go to the front if I can get there, and I cannot tell now where that will be. At latest dates, Rufus was safe, but there has been severe and almost constant fighting and very heavy losses. The reports this evening continue encouraging as to our general success, but the thousands of wounded who are arriving here from the last week's battle make a man weep, and their sufferings prompt me to do what I can for their relief. If I only had good health, I could do much, and when I am not sick I can do a little and can not hesitate to offer my service. I wrote Mary this afternoon and have not heard anything since. Her anxiety is of course painful, and I trust the dreadful suspense may soon be happily relieved. Whatever may be the result, she may well be thankful that she has had a husband who was willing to put his life at hazard in the defense of his country.

---

‡An error on the part of his informants.

Nobly has he sustained the service, and long may he live to enjoy the blessings of the government he has served so well. I feel anxious about Charley (his son), but I cannot say he ought not to go. I do not know but I ought to go too."

Saturday A. M., 14th.—"I am off for the army. I leave my valise here, taking nothing but a shirt and my shawl. Rufus' name does not appear in any list; the latest I could get he was well. Captain W. N. Remington, of his regiment, was admitted to a hospital last night, wounded. When he left, Rufus was all right. The fighting is not over yet."

P. S.—"I have seen the Wisconsin State Agent. He has reports from the sixth regiment as late as Wednesday, at which time Dawes was well. He has the report that Colonel Bragg, commanding a Pennsylvania brigade, was killed on Tuesday or Wednesday, but does not credit it." B. G.

LINE OF BATTLE, MAY 11th, 1864.*

(To my wife.)

"Through God's blessing I am yet alive, and beside the fearful tax upon my energies, mental and physical, have nothing to complain of and everything to be thankful for. For six long days we have been under the deadly musketry. On the morning of May 5th our brigade lost near eight hundred men; the same night a hundred more; the next morning two hundred more. We marched all night to come here (7th), and next day (8th), we charged the enemy and were repulsed, and the †next day (10th), we twice attacked and were driven back, and every moment the balls, shot and shell have whistled around us. Major Plummer, Captain Kellogg, Captain Converse, Lieutenant Pruyn and Lieutenant Graetz are in their graves. Captain Remington, Lieut. Timmons and Lieut. J. L. Converse are wounded. The perils of the last week have been fearful. I cannot hope to pass thus safely through another such. Colonel Bragg commands a brigade of Pennsylvania troops and I have commanded the regiment since the second day. Our loss in killed and wounded is about one hundred and forty men. The battle must soon be

---

*We were confronting the enemy in a log breast work at Laurel Hill, near Spottsylvania Court House.

†Error, 10th is the day of the attacks referred to.

renewed. I cannot write now. The frightful scenes of the last week make my heart almost like a stone."

OHIO STATE MILITARY AGENCY, WASHINGTON, D. C.
(To Mrs. Beman Gates.)   MAY 14th, P. M., 1864.

"I have been hard at work for eight hours, buying stores and gathering sanitary supplies, and expect to leave at five o'clock. We hope to reach Belle Plaine (six miles below Acquia Creek), about midnight, and to get to Fredericksburgh early in the morning. If I can get to the front, I shall, and I hope that will be Richmond.

The losses have been immense, but not so heavy as reported. The highest authorities here say that twenty thousand will cover all up to Thursday's battle. We are taking medicines, vegetables, lemons, tobacco, lint, bandages, &c., and hope to do many a poor fellow some service.

The city is literally full of people seeking out their wounded friends, in the hospitals, and as they arrive. The hospitals are in nice order, and amply provided. Twenty thousand beds have been provided for the wounded.   BEMAN GATES."

(To Mrs. Beman Gates.)   BELLE PLAINE, SUNDAY, A. M.,
               MAY 15th, 1864.

"We were delayed in getting off last night, and did not get here until near morning. There will be great difficulty in getting forward,—except by walking. I shall try to get to Fredericksburgh to-day, though I have a bad headache. The roads, since the last rain, are horrible. There are eight thousand rebel prisoners here. No more wounded will be brought here at present, as it would kill the poor fellows to ride here. They will be kept at Fredericksburgh. I send this to Washington by a mail messenger from the front, who left Grant's head-quarters yesterday morning. There was no fighting on Friday, but heavy firing was heard yesterday P. M., from which it is inferred that the contest was renewed. There is great want of nurses at Fredericksburgh.   BEMAN GATES."

LINE OF BATTLE NEAR SPOTTSYLVANIA COURT HOUSE,
(To my wife.)   MAY 14th, 1864, 11 A. M.

"By the blessing of God I am still alive. We have had continued fighting and hardship since I wrote two days ago, beyond what I can now describe. We charged upon the enemy's rifle pits again on Thursday, and were as usual driven back. *Thursday night, May 12th, we stood in mud over my boot tops, firing all night. Yesterday,—13th,—we were under fire all day, and last night we marched all night. I am troubled very much lest I have been reported killed in the New York papers. The report was extensively circulated by one of my men. I can never tell, if I live through it, the sufferings of this campaign. The army has earned the lasting gratitude of the people. Do not give me up if you see me reported killed. Such things are often mistakes. The end is not yet, though, and I cannot avoid, my dear wife, saying that the probabilities of coming out safely are strongly against me. If we may only finish this horrible business here, our lives are of poor moment in comparison. The loss of my regiment now amounts to over one hundred and fifty men killed and wounded, many of our best and truest."

LINE OF BATTLE NEAR SPOTTSYLVANIA, MAY 15th, 9 A. M. (To my wife.) "I find this morning that I am reported killed in the New York papers.† The report may be verified before this awful struggle is over, but I may still escape, and to have this unnecessary burden of trouble thrown upon you, is very trying. I am almost prostrated with over exertion and with fighting, but alive and well, and feeling more hopeful. Colonel Bragg is alive and well. He has been published as killed, and is troubled lest the same shock has come to his wife. I received your letter of the second, (May) last night. I have had two letters since the first day of the battles. Our army is fearfully exhausted and worn out."

FREDERICKSBURGH, Va., MONDAY A. M.,
(To Mrs. Beman Gates.)   MAY 16th, 1864.
"I walked from the Potomac here yesterday, the last four miles

---

*Thursday night, May 12th, we were at the point now famed in history as the "Bloody Angle" or "Angle of Death," where General Hancock had captured General Edward Johnson's division.

†The New York Tribune reported me in a list of killed, which the paper said had been carefully verified, and paragraphed the item thus: "Colonel Dana of the sixth Wisconsin was killed yesterday, while gallantly leading his men to a charge. This regiment has suffered terribly." It escaped the notice of my wife, because it was not published in the Cincinnati papers.

in a very severe rain and hail storm. I am sick but hard at work. * * * The latest news from the front is that Rufus was well and safe Saturday P. M. There was a report two days ago, that he was killed on Wednesday, but I have talked with M. Dempsey, First Lieutenant of company 'A,' twenty-fourth Michigan, who left the front yesterday, and he says that on Saturday afternoon between two and three o'clock he saw Colonel Dawes and talked with him. The Chaplain of the Twenty-fourth says that Dempsey is a reliable man.

You cannot conceive of the suffering here. Every house, barn, and shed is a hospital, and although everything possible is done, the accommodations are imperfect. The roads by the late rains are so cut up, that the transportation of the wounded men to the river is in many cases fatal. The delay in receiving sanitary and hospital stores is very great. It is impossible to get reliable information from the front. Last night it was currently reported that Grant was falling back, and that General Warren's corps would be in Fredericksburgh. This morning men from the front report, that our general hospital was yesterday advanced to Spottsylvania, and that General Grant had issued a congratulatory order. One hour we hear that Butler is in Richmond, and the next that he has been whipped. We know almost nothing, except that on every hand are thousands of brave men suffering and dying. The Sanitary and Christian commissions are doing a great deal, but their supplies cannot be got forward. The stores that I started with are yet at Belle Plaine, but I hope will be got through to-day. I send this to Washington by an Ohio man, who is going there with a wounded son, and he will mail it from there upon his arrival. BEMAN GATES."

LINE OF BATTLE NEAR SPOTTSYLVANIA, MAY 16th, 9 A. M.

(To my wife.)—"Last night we were ordered to charge the enemy's entrenchments, provided he attacked Burnside's corps on our right, but no attack was made and for the time being we were spared another scene of horrid butchery. We know absolutely nothing of what is going on outside of our army or even within it. We have had no newspapers since May 3rd, and get only a pitiful handful of mail for cooks, orderlies and lieutenants of staff at the various headquarters. Put 'Headquarters First

Brigade, Fourth Division, Fifth Corps,' on your letters and perhaps some may get through."

LINE OF BATTLE, MAY 17th, 1864, 6 A. M.

(To my wife.)—"I have to be thankful for another day of life and safety. There was no considerable fighting anywhere along the line yesterday. There was an order this morning that the artillery throughout the whole line should open on the enemy and I heard the bugles sounding at daybreak, but the fog is so thick now they can not do anything. The loss of the regiment as near as I can now arrive at it is, sixteen killed, one hundred and nineteen wounded, and fourteen missing. Most of our missing men are now known to be wounded and some are killed. I have commanded the regiment since leaving the Wilderness on the seventh of May. The enemy in our front are in plain view. Spottsylvania Court House is directly in our front. Day after day we stupidly and drearily wait the order that summons us to the fearful work."

LINE OF BATTLE NEAR SPOTTSYLVANIA COURT HOUSE, MAY 18th, 8 A. M. 1864.

(To my wife.)—"Alive and well this morning. There has been sharp fighting to our right, indeed there is heavy skirmishing along the whole line as I write. I have heard that your father is at Fredericksburg. It is impossible to communicate with him."

LINE OF BATTLE NEAR SPOTTSYLVANIA COURT HOUSE, MAY 19th, 7 A. M., 1864.

(To my wife.)—"We are occupying the extreme right of our army and we are strongly entrenched. (This seems to be an error; there were other troops on our right.) The battle will be to our left unless the enemy attack us. (They did so the same evening). It is impossible to conjecture when this campaign will end or what will be the result. The country, as usual, has been unduly exultant. This campaign has been by far the most trying I have known. We have had eight days and nights of constant toil and battle. Colonel Bragg does well with his Pennsylvania Brigade. General Cutler commands our division since General Wadsworth was killed. (Fourth division, fifth corps). We hope to get our first regular mail to-day since May 2nd. I look for it very anxiously.   One man says I have been reported killed in all the papers and another man says I have not been, and that he has seen all the lists."

LINE OF BATTLE NEAR SPOTTSYLVANIA, MAY 20th, 1864.

(To my wife.)—"Who should come riding to the battle front but your good father. I saw him for only a few moments, but I was greatly rejoiced and encouraged. His visit did me more good than I can tell you, and for him to come to the front was an undertaking of no little peril, as it proved. He barely escaped getting into a battle, but he is all right at Fredericksburgh. I sent Philip Gaubatz with him and he is back.

Our hearts were rejoiced also this morning at receiving our mail. I got five letters from you. I will not try to write how burdens are lightened and how life comes back. I find (by the mail,) that the Wisconsin State Agent telegraphed to Wisconsin that I was killed and my body burned. I saw many bodies burning (at Laurel Hill,) in the brush between the lines, set on fire by burning wads from the muskets.

I was very much alarmed about your father. The battle was on the road to Fredericksburgh, directly in our rear. The rebels attacked us. This does not look like Lee was entirely defeated, does it?* (General B. S. Ewell commanded the troops of the enemy in this action and portions of the second and fifth corps and General Tyler's foot artillerists were engaged on our side). The enemy are probably re-inforced, and I do not believe General Grant will again attack them in their entrenched position. Your letters came to me truly when I was 'sick with the horrors of war.'"

---

*Mr. Gates had ridden out from Fredericksburgh to Spottsylvania Court House on a very poor animal, and upon his return I gave him my own horse and put our little drummer boy, Philip Gaubatz, of company "F," on his horse to bring back my own horse. Mr. Gates first saw the rebel line of battle approaching and he asked Philip what troops those were. He ejaculated "The Shonnies!" and burying his spurs in the flanks of the old plug, started for Fredericksburgh on a gallop. My horse caught the spirit of the occasion and they barely passed the flank of the rebel army corps before the firing began.

Mr. Gates was much indebted to the fact that he was an old newspaper man, as he fraternized with the correspondents. What that body of men did not know about getting around in the army was past finding out. He was provided with a horse by a correspondent who promptly stole another for his own use, and he came to the front on the pass of C. C. Coffin, (Carleton.)

THE BATTLE OF THE WILDERNESS.

No official report of the action of the regiment in this battle has been made. In 1874 I wrote some personal recollections of our experiences in that strange and terrible struggle called the Wilderness.

On the night of May 4th, 1864, the regiment was in bivouac near the "Old Wilderness Tavern." On the morning of May 5th, when Wadsworth's division of the fifth army corps was ordered to advance upon the enemy, our brigade was formed in two lines of battle, the sixth Wisconsin on the left of the second line.

Seventh Indiana.

Sixth Wisconsin.

After the troops had been formed, we all lay down in the woods to await the order to advance. There were in the ranks of the regiment three hundred and forty-seven men who carried muskets, and twenty-three commissioned officers—a total of three hundred and seventy combatants. It was a bright and pleasant morning, and the woods were filled with the twitter of birds. Colonel Bragg and all of our officers gathered under a great oak tree, and were chattering and chaffering in the highest spirits. The first call to advance was an order for a company to go forward as skirmishers. Colonel Bragg designated Captain John A. Kellogg with his company "I," for this duty. We were told that our movement was to be a reconnoissance. As Kellogg got up to go, Major Philip Plummer said: "What word shall I send to your wife?" "Never mind my wife," replied Kellogg "Look after Converse' girl!" Captain Converse said: "Plummer will be shot before either of us, leave your messages with Dawes, he is the only man they can't kill!"

Colonel Ira B. Grover's seventh Indiana regiment was directly in front of us, in the first line of battle, and it was our duty to follow them at a distance of one hundred paces. It was with the greatest difficulty that we could keep in sight of them in the brush. We soon lost connection on our right, but we followed the colors of the seventh Indiana. When tangled in a thicket we heard Colonel Grover order his regiment to advance at a double quick. Colonel Bragg directed me to hasten forward with our regiment as fast as practicable through the brush, while he ran ahead to keep in sight of the colors of the seventh Indiana. It is now known that Wadsworth's division had partially lost its direction in this march which may explain the trouble we fell into. Instead of facing the enemy as we should have been, we were more in this position:

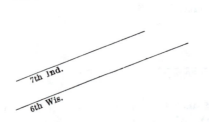

As we hurried along there was a great outburst of musketry. Major Plummer shouted to me: "Look to the right!" Probably his last words. There came the enemy stretching as far as I could see through the woods, and rapidly advancing and firing upon us. I ordered a change of front on the color company, to bring the regiment to face them. Directing Major Plummer to attend to the left wing, I gave orders to the right wing, but the Major was shot and killed, and the regiment stood with reference to the enemy, something like this:

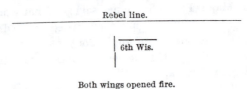

We here lost forty or fifty men in a very few moments, including Major Philip W. Plummer, Captain Rollin P. Converse, and

Lieutenant James L. Converse of company "G." The brush now served us well. Our smaller body of men could move faster than the heavy lines of the enemy could follow. The rebels came on yelling and firing. The little band, as always under fire, clung around its colors. We rallied and formed twice or three times and gave the enemy a hot reception as they came on. When the rebels ceased pursuing us, we found ourselves alone as a regiment and lost in the woods, and we lay flat on the ground, not knowing certainly which way to go to join our troops. Colonel Bragg did not find the seventh Indiana, but he almost ran into the midst of the rebel army. He joined us as we fell back. Here came to us a man who had been on the line of skirmishers with company "I," and he said: "Captain Kellogg is killed, I am certain of it." We were in the woods between the hostile lines and we felt our way cautiously back to the open ground around the Lacy House, where our corps was being formed after this repulse. We here constructed a log breast-work and remained in it until near evening of May fifth. At this time, General Wadsworth's division was detached from the fifth corps and ordered to the support of General Hancock's second corps on our left. Our brigade had hot musketry fighting from the start, but the enemy was driven back a long distance through the woods. We were fighting troops of the corps of General A. P. Hill. At dark the firing died down to the skirmish line. We lay upon the ground surrounded by dead and dying rebel soldiers. The sufferings of these poor men, and their moans and cries were harrowing. We gave them water from our canteens and all aid that was within our power. One dying confederate soldier cried out again and again: "My God, why hast thou forsaken me!" On this night Colonel Bragg sent out Sergeant Lewis A. Kent, who crept around the skirmish line along the whole front of Wadsworth's division and located the enemy. For the important information thus obtained, Colonel Bragg says he received no thanks from his superior officers.

On the early morning of the sixth of May, the fighting was renewed. Again we drove the enemy through the woods. The four lines of battle of Wadsworth's division were formed thus, with reference to the second corps, which was also advancing in several lines.

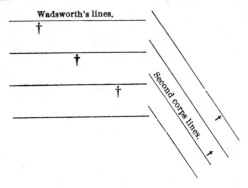

When the two came together, the men became jammed and crowded, and there was much confusion. *When Longstreet's attack upon us began, it first struck the right flank of General Wadsworth's division. General Wadsworth seeing his lines broken and scattered by the rebel onset on his flank, rode at once forward through his lines and I saw him pass through the ranks of the one hundred and forty-ninth Pennsylvania in the front line on our left, and ride in front of that regiment. He was instantly killed. Later on that day, I asked Lieutenant Earl M. Rogers who was serving on his staff, why he did so, as he rode to certain death. I remember the reply that "Bony" made: "My God, Colonel, nobody could stop him!" Our regiment fell back in good order in the same direction we had advanced, and we were not pursued by the enemy, who moved on against the lines of the second corps.

In the Wilderness our loss was three officers and five men killed,—one officer and thirty-nine men wounded,—one officer and fourteen men missing, a total of sixty-three.

---

*"At 4:30 A. M. on the 6th, we moved forward, attacked the enemy and drove him across the Plank Road, where a junction was made with the second corps. The division was then formed in four lines, the left resting on the Plank Road. These lines were by order of General Wadsworth closed in mass to avoid the artillery fire of the enemy. *While in this position* it (the division) was furiously attacked by infantry and artillery, driven back and badly scattered." Report Brigadier General L. Cutler, commanding Wadsworth's division.

On the morning of May 7th,*Colonel Bragg was placed in command of the third brigade, fourth division, fifth corps, the brigade referred to in my account of the battle of Gettysburg as Roy Stone's Pennsylvania Bucktails. The men of this brigade had squirrels' tails in their caps. The original regiment of Pennsylvania Bucktails had deers' tails to adorn their caps, but the demand for soldiers was beyond the supply of deers' tails in Pennsylvania. The Junior Bucktails, as they were called, had all of the soldierly qualities ever possessed by their predecessors in the title. Colonel Bragg was selected for this command of Pennsylvania troops because he was a brave, efficient and experienced commander of men in actual battle. Brigadier Generals were plenty, but not of this quality. His pending appointment as a Brigadier General still hung fire. That was more under the control of the members of Congress from Wisconsin than of his superior officers. I quote from Colonel E. C. Dawes:

'The Army of the Potomac, including the ninth corps at the opening of the Wilderness campaign, contained forty-one infantry brigades, twenty-six of which were commanded by Colonels. The Army of Northern Virginia, including Longstreet's corps, contained thirty-five infantry brigades, thirty-one of which were commanded by Brigadier Generals. Of the brigades in the Army of the Potomac which took part in the battle of Gettysburg but six in May, 1864, were composed of the same regiments as in July, 1863. All of the advantages of organization were clearly with the Comfederate Army.' "

On the seventh of May while in the presence of the enemy in the Wilderness I succeded to command of the regiment, in which duty I continued until the expiration of my term of service in the army. On the afternoon of May 7th, the soldiers in the lines of the rebel army in our front began a loud cheering, which continued to run along their lines for nearly half an hour. Its significance I have never learned. At 8 P. M., of this day the movement of the fifth army corps toward Spottsylvania Court House commenced by the Brock road. We were on the march

"*I placed it (Stone's brigade) under command of Colonel E. S. Bragg, 6th Wisconsin Volunteers, who retained command until the brigade was detached from the division, June 5th, doing good service." Report General L. Cutler.

during the entire night, and on the eighth of May we were in line of battle in the vicinity of Todd's Tavern, where the cavalry were engaged with the enemy. We continued our march toward Spottsylvania and before our arrival the second division of our corps under General John C. Robinson had attacked and been repulsed. About 10 A. M. our brigade was formed to assault the enemy at a point called Laurel Hill, near Spottsylvania Court House. *"This was perhaps the most formidable point along the enemy's whole front. It's densely wooded crest was crowned by earthworks, while the approach, which was swept by artillery and musketry fire, was rendered more difficult and hazardous by a heavy growth of low cedars, the long, bayonet-like branches of which interlaced."

In the formation for attack, Colonel W. W. Robinson, commanding the brigade, placed my regiment upon the right of the front line. I at once threw forward skirmishers and discovered that the enemy were themselves advancing upon us. I ordered the men to kneel upon the ground and fire upon them as soon as they appeared through the brush. There were no troops upon our right and our skirmishers came running in from that direction and reported the enemy moving forward without opposition. We had here a sharp musketry engagement, but our brigade was outflanked in both directions and we were obliged to retreat as best we could through the woods and undergrowth.† We crossed an open field and on the opposite side we reformed our line and repulsed several attempts of the enemy to advance over the field. Upon this retreat Lieutenant Howard F. Pruyn, commanding company "A" was killed. He disdained to run, and while striving to rally his men he fell. He had been promoted from the ranks for bravery, and he had taken part in every battle and had uniformly distinguished himself for efficiency and courage. Captain William N. Remington, of company "K," won especial and honorable mention for his conduct upon this occasion, as did also Corporal John E. Hart, of company "E," who was killed.

---

*Swinton's History of the Army of the Potomac.

†"My right being uncovered and unsupported, was attacked in flank from the woods and we were obliged to retire a short distance." Report General L. Cutler.

Along the edge of timber skirting the open field we constructed a strong log breastwork, which may be called our base of operations during the five days of fighting at Laurel Hill. This breastwork was in the valley. The rebel line of entrenchments was upon the hill-top. The skirmishers of each army occupied the tangled brush and woods between the lines, and they kept up, day and night, a ceaseless and deadly fire. Our men in the entrenchments were constantly harassed by the fire of the enemy's sharpshooters, who were posted in trees or upon higher ground. On the morning of May ninth a determined effort was made to drive back the enemy's skirmishers, and thirty men were ordered from the Sixth for this service. I called for volunteers, and that nervy little German, Lieutenant William Golterman, immediately stepped forward. Sergeant George Fairfield, of company "C," was his gallant and efficient assistant in command. The conduct of our skirmishers, who throughout the fighting at Spottsylvania were volunteers in every effort made to drive back the enemy, is worthy of the highest praise. The Indians of the seventh Wisconsin regiment took an active part in this skirmishing. They covered their bodies very ingeniously with pine boughs to conceal themselves in the woods. When skirmishers advanced from our lines, they would run across the open field at the top of their speed, and numbers of them were shot while doing so. Upon this run the Indians would give a shout or war whoop.

At 12.30 P. M., on the tenth of May we advanced to an assault upon the enemy in their entrenched position at Laurel Hill. We came suddenly upon their works without being aware of their proximity, on account of the thick brush, and we received a very destructive enfilading fire. Lieutenant Oscar Graetz, commanding company "F," was killed, and Captain William N. Remington and Lieutenant John Timmons were severely wounded and the loss of the regiment was severe. The conduct of officers and men under these trying circumstances was excellent. I moved by the right flank to get under the brow of a hill. We were not two hundred feet from the enemy. Here we were mixed together with the twelfth Massachusetts regiment, (Colonel James L. Bates). The enemy poured over us a continual storm of bullets.

We now saw the bodies of our soldiers burning in grass and leaves which had been ignited by the musketry. Major General Warren soon came running up the hill to have a look at the rebel works, when I seized his yellow sash and pulled him violently back. Colonel S. S. Carroll was with him. To have exposed himself above the hill was certain death. I accompanied General Warren to another point where we secured a good view of the rebel works. As I passed along with the General I noticed Private Aaron Yates, of company "K," creeping up the hill to get a shot at the enemy, and I sharply ordered him back to his company. When I returned he lay on the ground dead. Captain Robert Hughes, of the second Wisconsin, lay dead above the brow of the hill, and the flames in the burning grass were coming toward the body. Lieutenant William H. Harries made a line of suspenders taken from his men, and crawling flat upon the ground, he endeavored to cast a lasso over the upturned foot, but failed in the attempt. After remaining for a time which I cannot estimate under the brow of this hill, clinging to the ground to escape the bullets, we again retreated to our breastworks. On the evening of this day (tenth), a grand column of assault was formed, but no attack was made. Until the morning of the twelfth of May we remained in our breastworks, subjected to the ceaseless fire of the enemy's sharpshooters. There was a space of perhaps ten feet in our works which it was almost certain death to go upon. Men were sent to me from Berdan's Sharpshooters, who had globe sights on their rifles, to dislodge the rebel marksman who had the range on this spot, but two of them were here severely wounded.

The morning of the twelfth of May, the most terrible twenty-four hours of our service in the war, dawned upon us worn and exhausted by five days and nights of continuous service under fire of the enemy. In the early morning we again charged upon the enemy at Laurel Hill. Our brigade was in the front line and Colonel Bragg's brigade was in the second line. We came upon one of General Crawford's brigades (Pennsylvania Reserves), who lay in a breastwork near the rebel line. Here a halt was made. Colonel Bragg, for some reason, now assumed command of our two brigades and ordered me to lead my regiment forward to encourage the rest to follow. I quote from my own official report: "Lieutenant Chas. P. Hyatt, Acting Aide on the staff of Colonel W. W. Robinson, communicated the following order: 'Colonel Bragg directs that the sixth Wisconsin move forward.' I immediately ordered the regiment forward. The men sprang over the breastwork with great alacrity, closely followed by Colonel Bragg's brigade (the Junior Bucktails), and a few of General Crawford's men, and they (our regiment), continued advancing under a heavy and destructive fire for several rods, when, finding no line on my right or left, so far as I could see through the timber, such men as were in front of the breastwork having thrown themselves upon the ground and commenced firing, I ordered my line to halt and fire until the troops on the right and left should move to our support. After a few minutes of rapid firing, suffering meanwhile severe loss, convinced of the futility of striving without support to advance through the abattis in our front, while to remain longer was wanton sacrifice of life, I ordered my men back behind the breastwork. * * * The fire of the enemy at such short range was unusually fatal, a large proportion of the wounds proving mortal. I can not speak too highly of officers and men. They advanced to this desperate assault readily and earnestly and stood up (upright) with heroic tenacity when it became evident that their effort could not achieve success."

There was no disorganization or demoralization in falling back under fire to the breastwork. Several of my best and truest men were killed. This assault was manifestly hopeless at the outset. Company "H" suffered terribly, owing to the fact that they stood where a road passed through the woods. Their First Sergeant, a fine soldier, Nicholas Snyder, was killed and half of the men present were killed or wounded.

On the afternoon of May twelfth the brigade marched four miles to the left,* with orders to assist the sixth army corps, who were fighting over the breastworks at the "Bloody Angle." As we lay in reserve several of our men were wounded by scattering

---

"*On the 12th we were under arms at daylight and again assaulted the enemy's works without success. * * * I was ordered to report with my command to Major General Wright."(sixth corps.) Report General L. Cutler.

shots from the enemy. We were in plain view of this dreadful struggle, one of the fiercest and most deadly of the war. The lines of colors of both armies stood waving within twenty feet of each other and there was a continual roar and crash of musketry. About dusk, in the midst of a driving rain storm, we marched, two miles perhaps, to our right, and began in the night the construction of a breastwork ; then my regiment was selected for picket duty. Another order came, and it required that we should march back at once to the "Bloody Angle." The unbroken roar of musketry continued in the darkness of the night. We formed our line in rear of the troops engaged and our orders were to move forward to their relief. The mud was half boot top deep and filled with the dead of the battle, over whom we stumbled in the darkness. Upon reaching my position I ordered the regiment to open fire.

We stood perhaps one hundred feet from the enemy's line, and so long as we maintained a continual fire they remained hidden in their entrenchments. But if an attempt to advance was made, an order would be given and they would all rise up together and fire a volley upon us. They had constructed their works by digging an entrenchment about four feet deep, in which at intervals there were traverses to protect the flanks. This had the effect of making a row of cellars without drainage, and in them was several inches of mud and water. To protect their heads, they had placed in front logs which were laid upon blocks, and it was intended to put their muskets through the chinks under the head logs, but in the darkness this became impracticable and the head log proved a serious obstruction to their firing. For eighteen hours without cessation our troops aimed their muskets at these head logs, some of which were destroyed, and the bullets passing beyond in this plane cut off the tree, the stump of which may now be seen in the Ordnance Museum of the War Department at Washington. This tree stood behind the enemy's works. This is the true explanation of that phenomenon.

But to return to our own experience. I soon found that the supply of cartridges in the boxes of the men would not hold out. I systematized the firing from right to left of companies and sent half a dozen men after cartridges. One man only returned and he brought a wooden box of packed cartridges weighing, I believe, eighty pounds. To wade through the mud on that awful night, stumbling over the dead, and carrying that heavy box, was a labor of heroic faithfulness which merits the highest praise. During the early hours of the night the rain poured down in torrents. Sometime in the night I suspected that the enemy were retreating, and I crawled up with one man and satisfied myself that they had gone. I then ceased firing and my exhausted men lay down as best they could and some laid their heads upon the dead and fell asleep. In the morning the rebel works presented an awful spectacle. The cellars were crowded with dead and wounded, lying in some cases upon each other and in several inches of mud and water. I saw the body of a rebel soldier sitting in the corner of one of these cellars in a position of apparent ease, with the head entirely gone, and the flesh burned from the bones of the neck and shoulders. This was doubtless caused by the explosion of a shell from some small Cohorn mortars within our lines. The mortar shell is thrown high in the air, and comes down directly from above.

On the morning of May 13th, the men were in a deplorable condition of exhaustion, and I marched the regiment away from the horrible scenes at the "Bloody Angle," and allowed the men to lie down and rest in the woods near at hand. The other regiments of the brigade had marched back to their old position at Laurel Hill. During the afternoon we marched to that point and rejoined the brigade. All night of May 13th, we were on the march. For an account of this night's march I will quote from Swinton's History of the Army of the Potomac: "The fifth corps, during the night of May 13th, marched from its position on the extreme right, to take position on the extreme left. * * The march began at 10 P. M. The wet weather, however, had badly broken up the roads, and the night being one of Egyptian darkness, the move was made with immense difficulty. The route of march was past the Landrum House to the Ny river, which had to be waded. Across the Ny the route followed no road, but traversed the fields and a piece of woods, where a track had been cut. Here, midway of the journey, a dense fog arose and covered the ground so that not even the numerous fires that had been built to guide the column could be seen. The men, exhausted with wading through mud knee deep, and in the darkness, fell asleep all along the way."

On May 14th we constructed an entrenchment directly in front of Spottsylvania Court House, where we remained until the movement of the army in the direction of the North Anna river. The casualties in the regiment from May 8th to 21st, near Spottsylvania numbered eighty-three. Two officers were killed and three wounded. Eight men were killed, sixty-five wounded, and five missing.

ECHOES OF SPOTTSYLVANIA.

The following is a letter from my father to the Honorable Salmon P. Chase. At the top of the sheet is a slip cut from a daily newspaper.

"Colonel Dawes of the sixth Wisconsin was killed yesterday while gallantly leading his men to a charge. This regiment has suffered terribly."

MAUSTON, JUNEAU COUNTY, WISCONSIN, MAY 18th, 1864.

HON. S. P. CHASE,

"*My dear Sir:*—The Colonel Dawes referred to, I greatly fear, is my son, Lieutenant Colonel Rufus R. Dawes, who was in command of the sixth Wisconsin Veteran Volunteers, fourth division, fifth army corps. He was in command on Tuesday, the 10th inst., when he is reported as having been killed. He commanded the regiment also at Antietam and Gettysburg. He had escaped unharmed through fifteen hard fought battles. He was shot down, as I am informed, while waving his battle flag and exerting himself to the uttermost to steady his ranks when wavering. I write to ask whether the Government cannot rescue his remains from the rebel woods near Spottsylvania. My esteemed friend, is it too much for me to ask of you, to place this letter in the hands of the proper authorities, coupled with such an endorsement as will secure a compliance with my request? * * * *

Very truly yours,

HENRY DAWES.

P. S. There is a bare possibility that my son is living either as a prisoner or in hospital. Any definite and reliable information will be most gratefully received."

The letter is endorsed as follows: "D 205—S. A. O. 64. H. Dawes, Mauston, Wisconsin, wants information of Colonel Dawes of the sixth Wisconsin regiment, killed at Spottsylvania. C 1103, May 30th, 1864. Surg. General Report."

This next is in the handwriting of Salmon P. Chase: "Respectfully commended to the Secretary of War. If it be at all possible, I earnestly desire that Judge Dawes' wishes concerning his brave son may be gratified. S. P. CHASE.
MAY 28th, 1864."

"Respectfully referred to the Surgeon General, for any information he has or can obtain, relating to Colonel Dawes. By order of the Secretary of War. LOUIS H. PELOUZ, Ass't Adj't Gen'l.
W. D. May 30th, 1864."

"Respectfully referred to Medical Director McParlin, Army of the Potomac, for report. These papers to be returned with report. By order of the Acting Surgeon General.
C. H. CRANE, Surgeon U. S. A.
S. G. Office, May 31st, 1864."

"HEADQUARTERS ARMY OF POTOMAC, M. D. O., }
NEAR COLD HARBOR, JUNE 5th, 1864. }
Respectfully referred to the Medical Director fifth corps for report. These papers to be returned.
THOMAS A. MCPARLIN,
Surgeon U. S. A., Medical Director."

"HEADQUARTERS FIFTH ARMY CORPS, M. D. O., }
JUNE 6th, 1864. }
Respectfully referred to Surgeon Chamberlain, Surgeon in Chief fourth division, for report. These papers to be returned promptly. JOHN J. MILHAU, Surgeon U. S. A.,
Medical Director Fifth A. C."

"HEADQUARTERS FOURTH DIVISION, FIFTH ARMY CORPS, }
JUNE 7th, 1864. }
Respectfully referred to Surgeon J. H. Beech, twenty-fourth Michigan. Surgeon in charge of first brigade.
C. N. CHAMBERLAIN,
U. S.V. Surgeon in Chief, fourth division, fifth army corps."

Respectfully referred to Lieutenant Colonel R. R. Dawes Please to return report through Medical Department.

J. H. BEECH, Surgeon 24th Michigan, Surgeon in Chief 1st brigade, 4th division, 5th corps A of P.

The following is from the Mauston Star, of Juneau County, Wisconsin:

"Lieutenant Colonel Dawes probably killed.—The Chicago Tribune has a dispatch from its correspondent in the Army of the Potomac, in which we find this sentence: 'Colonel Dana of the sixth Wisconsin was killed yesterday, (Tuesday 10th inst.) while gallantly leading a charge of his regiment. This regiment has suffered terribly." We think the name given is a misprint, and that the name meant is that of our neighbor Lieutenant Colonel Dawes of that regiment. Fearing this, we have no heart for comment.

It may be a glorious fact that the old Sixth has again well sustained its fame as one of the best regiments in the gallant and ever true 'Iron Brigade.' Yet, for all that, who can read the last sentence of the dispatch 'this regiment has suffered terribly,' without a shudder. All here, wives, children, parents and friends, dread yet long for the receipt of the official returns of the killed and wounded, and waiting, suffer agonies unspeakable.

Later from the sixth regiment.—Just as our paper is ready for the press we have letters from Washington informing us that Colonel Bragg, Lieutenant Colonel Dawes, and Captain Kellogg of the sixth regiment are killed, and that Captain Remington is wounded. No other names are given, but we are told that the regiment is nearly destroyed, having been, as usual, in the hottest part of the fight. This sad news with the almost certainty that others of our neighbors have fallen, casts a gloom over our village.

Colonel Dawes left here as Captain of the company raised in this county, company 'K,' sixth regiment. Captain Kellogg was his First Lieutenant. Both have written for themselves a glorious history, as brave, patriotic and good soldiers. A bright future was before them. Their memory will yet live. They sealed their devotion to the cause of freedom and good government with their lives, and their mourners are our whole community."

From the Mauston Star of May 25th, 1864.

"Lieutenant Colonel Dawes died as he had lived, doing his duty. He was gallantly leading his regiment, charging the rebel line, when, the fire being very severe, his men began to waver. To encourage and stimulate them he seized the colors and called them forward. This rendered him a conspicuous mark and a bullet from a rebel sharpshooter pierced his brain. He died covered with glory. His last word was a cheer for victory."

In my youth I was inclined to be angry at these publications; but in my age I am growing quite proud of them.

CHAPTER XIII.

General Cutler was now in permanent command of our division. In this great and trying campaign he proved himself to be one of the bravest and most faithful commanders in the Army of the Potomac. I quote from his official report, an account of our movement from Spottsylvania toward the North Anna river:

"At 10:50 A. M., on the twenty-first of May, I was ordered to retire my line and move to the left. I withdrew successfully, and moved off toward Guinea's Station. My pickets, however, were attacked while retiring, and about forty men were captured. I marched to Guinea's Station and from there crossed the Matapony and encamped, sending the first brigade forward about three miles on the road toward the North Anna." My own report says that our brigade (first brigade,) entrenched a line in front of the Po river near Thornburg. We were in plain view of the Telegraph road, and along that road passed the rebel army corps of General Longstreet. I had a line of skirmishers out and I lay on the ground a long time on the skirmish line and watched this moving column of the enemy. We marched on after the enemy had passed and followed them on the Telegraph road. They fired upon us with artillery, which retreated as we advanced. That night we camped near Harris' store, and at five o'clock, A. M. on May twenty-third, we marched again toward the South. At 5 P. M. we crossed the North Anna river at Jericho Ford, and the division was massed on the southern bank. We were now directed to cook our supper, and the worn, tired, hungry soldiers

LYSANDER CUTLER,

BREVET MAJOR GENERAL U. S. VOLS.

RUFUS R. DAWES,

BREVET BRIGADIER GENERAL U. S. VOLS.

obeyed the order with alacrity. As was my custom at every halt, I took out my pencil and paper and began a letter to my wife.

(To my wife.)   MAY 23rd, 1864, 6 P. M.

"Alive, well, south of the North Anna river in the advance of the fifth corps. Battle to-morrow—."

Here the crack of the rifles of the inevitable rebel skirmishers put an end to writing letters and making coffee. We were attacked in great force by the enemy.

BATTLE OF JERICHO FORD.

(To my wife.)   BATTLE FIELD, MAY 24th, 8 A. M.

"I had barely scratched off a word to you when General A. P. Hill's corps of the rebel army attacked the portion of our corps south of the North Anna river, hoping to make a Ball's Bluff rout of our troops. For an hour the fight raged with great fury. My regiment stood and fought like men, and by God's blessing our loss was small, only one man killed, twelve wounded. (Two killed and eleven wounded). We are now in line of battle awaiting the enemy. God only knows what the day may bring forth. We came near being driven into the river, but the enemy has lost vigor in attack. Their men are getting so they will not fight except in rifle pits. My conclusion is that General Hill's corps could be defeated on an open field by half their number of resolute men. The very positive evidence of progress has greatly encouraged this army. I wonder if a man can go forever without being hurt in battle. It does seem as though your prayers were shielding me."

I quote from my own official report the account of the commencement of the action of the sixth Wisconsin in the battle of Jericho Ford: "About six in the evening the enemy's skirmishers appeared on our right, when the brigade moved rapidly forward (my regiment on the left), to form on the right of the first division of this corps, already in position in the woods in our front. In compliance with directions of Colonel Robinson commanding the brigade, I placed my regiment in position on the right of a breastwork occupied by troops of the first division (Griffin's), and on a prolongation of their line. I experienced much difficulty, owing to the thick and tangled brush. I immediately threw forward skirmishers to cover my front."

On came the enemy and back came my skirmishers. I could hear heavy musketry and the charging yell of the rebels, but in the thick pine brush I could see nothing. The troops of the first division in the rifle pits on my left opened a fire of musketry. I ordered my men to kneel and fire toward the enemy on our right who were attacking our own brigade. I sent Adjutant Brooks to look out of the edge of the woods and report to me the progress of the battle. He came running back and reported the enemy driving our brigade in confusion over the open field. This outflanked us on the right. I had the regiment change front to throw my line facing the enemy on our flank, and while doing so a regiment of the first division broke and ran. They ran through our ranks and broke the regiment. I called a rally on the colors just outside the woods, and every man of our regiment fell into his proper place. Here in the open field was Captain Mink's battery firing away, and no infantry supporting it. Captain Orr with a portion of the nineteenth Indiana, and Captain Shippen with the battalion of Berdan's Sharpshooters, reported to me as the senior officer on the field. I put them in line on my right and moved my force in line of battle to the relief of that glorious soldier, Captain Mink, and it was not a moment too soon. We met the enemy at the battery, and here came gallantly to our support, the eighty-third Pennsylvania of the first division. We drove the enemy back. Colonel Robinson had fallen back to the North Anna river and General Cutler ordered me to join the second brigade of the division with my command, which I did. We now advanced in a new line of battle and we swept the enemy before us from the field. I quote from my own official report: "Being separated from the brigade I was directed by General Cutler to report to Colonel J. W. Hoffman, commanding the second brigade, with my command. After dark the line was advanced several hundred yards and entrenched. My men were working during almost the entire night upon the breastworks. Through this affair the conduct of officers and men, with small exceptions, was admirable. Lieutenant John Beely was twice wounded. The gallantry of Lieutenant Beely throughout the campaign was conspicuous, but upon this occasion I esteem his conduct in remaining upon the field after being seriously wounded until struck down by a second bullet, which penetrated his lungs, worthy of special commendation, Corporal William Hickok, of company 'C,' was killed. No braver soldier, or more worthy young man has given life in this struggle."

Excepting the sixth Wisconsin and nineteenth Indiana, the regiments of our brigade were moved at dark across the North Anna, and bivouacked in the woods. Our colored servants asked at brigade headquarters where our regiment could be found, and they were told that it was with the others. But they searched in vain and late at night they held a council. Young William Jackson alone said: "Youse can say what youse a mind to, I'se done gwine over the river!" He waded the stream waist deep and some hours later, one of our men heard in the darkness, the words: "Whar's the sixth Wisconsin?" The poor boy was almost exhausted, but he found us. For miles in that dark night he had stumbled along the lines, carrying a heavy coffee pot and a full supper for our mess. To him the officers of the sixth Wisconsin owed this comforting relief from hunger and exhaustion, for I shared it with them all.

BATTLE OF THE NORTH ANNA.

(To my wife.) LINE OF BATTLE, MAY 25th, 1864.

"We are again closing our lines for a desperate battle. The bullets clip through the green leaves over my head as I lie behind the breastwork writing. I have had no full night's sleep since May 7th, when I took command of the regiment. Day after day, and night after night we have marched, fought and dug entrenchments; I have not changed my clothing since May third. We have not seen, and seldom communicated with our wagon train. I have not composure to write, as the bullets are coming so thickly through the limbs, and some poor wounded soldiers are near me."

(To my wife.) LINE OF BATTLE, MAY 26th, 7 A. M.

"The hot firing of yesterday has died down this morning to only about ten or twelve shots a minute. We are confronting the enemy precisely as at Spottsylvania, when your father visited me, except that our lines of battle approach each other more nearly. It is raining steadily. I have a little shelter tent with logs piled up at the end toward the enemy to stop bullets, and I lie on the ground as I write. I presume General Grant will not make an assault upon the enemy in their entrenchments. They get stronger in men as we get nearer Richmond, and their works are probably as elaborately prepared as those at Spottsylvania. Our battle on Monday evening, (Jericho Ford) is probably as severe and general as any that will be fought on this line. The repulse of Butler has a material bearing upon the situation here.

The rain storm became violent. A little run near my tent assumed the proportions of a torrent, and drove me out into the storm. I hope you will get the poor pencil scrawls I have sent you during the campaign. For the first four days I had absolutely no opportunity to write, and not until after our occupation of Fredericksburgh was there any mail sent away from the army. You are mistaken about that first week, being the most encouraging in my war experience. We were* repulsed and slaughtered in every attack we made. By continued, persistent, and generally unsuccessful assaults and charges, and by skillful maneuvering, General Grant worried out the enemy and forced him to fall back by flanking him, when too much exhausted and demoralized to fight us in the open field. He has forced him back of the North Anna. Now I conjecture the next effort will be to form a junction with Butler in the direction of West Point, by again moving around the enemy's right flank, constantly as before threatening him with battle, should he leave his entrenchments."

It will be seen by this letter that the general plan for the movement of the Army of the Potomac was quite well understood in the army.

"You have me too badly wounded in your picture. I should stand a poor chance of getting alive to Fredericksburgh and Washington. But the picture is very attractive, and I shall endeavor to get the wound in the next battle."

(To my wife.)   SUNDAY MORNING, MAY 29th, 1864. ⎫
        NEAR HANOVER TOWN. ⎭

"Two days and nights of incessant marching has placed us within seventeen miles of Richmond, the heart of the rebellion. A glorious achievement! The thousands of this army are full of

---

*This refers to our own corps.

admiration and gratitude for the man who has pushed back the rebel army thirty miles without a general battle. (North Anna to Cold Harbor.) The nearer we get to an investment of Richmond, the less we regard our danger of bloody fighting, and our men are intensely anxious to get forward as far as their legs without help of their muskets will carry them. Our advance is now within fourteen miles of Richmond. We are now waiting in line to move forward."

This letter breathes of the inspiration of victory, and shows what a tonic there is to a weary soldier in success. We crossed the Pamunky at 11:30 A. M., on the 28th, and on the 29th moved forward to Hawes' store. On the 30th, we again moved forward and became engaged in battle.

BATTLE OF BETHESDA CHURCH.

LINE OF BATTLE TWELVE MILES FROM RICHMOND,
(To my wife.)   MAY 31st, 1864.

"We were again in battle yesterday, but nobody was hurt. There was a great deal of double quicking in the dust and building breastworks. My force was a reserve. I am now in command of three regiments, the sixth Wisconsin, seventh Wisconsin, and nineteenth Indiana. I commanded this force in the battle. I report to Colonel Bragg. I am feeling in much better spirits. We cannot help hoping the worst is over, now that our great leader has pushed the enemy almost to the wall, without a general battle since Spottsylvania. The enemy was repulsed last night with great loss, in their attack upon us. If we can force the enemy to attack us in entrenchments, we shall feel quite happy over the prospect.

We have reason to hope Major Plummer may be alive, badly wounded, in the hands of the enemy. Captain Thomas W. Plummer, his brother, commands the regiment, while I command the three regiments."

Captain Thomas W. Plummer was a quiet and faithful officer. He was one of those men of whom little is said but much expected, and in his case there was never any disappointment.

I was ordered to move my command in the battle of Bethesda Church, with the utmost haste in the direction of the Pennsylvania Reserves, who were being attacked by the enemy, and whose term of service had expired. It was a supreme test of the fidelity of these men to their country, but the old Reserve never in its long and arduous service in the war, fought a better battle than they did upon this day. I ran the men through the dust and heat and formed them on the right of the Reserves in line of battle. In this movement I came upon a brass band belonging to one of our *Pennsylvania regiments. They were playing the air to which these words were sung during the war:

"McClellan is our leader, he is gallant and strong,
For God and for freedom, we are marching along."

Before we had reached them, the Pennsylvania Reserves had repulsed the enemy. I formed my line in the woods on the right of the Reserves and was ordered to construct a breastwork. The men had been for days in the sun and dust, and they now came into a shady woods. I established the regiment upon the left and rode toward the right, completing the establishment of the line. I then rode back to the left to see how the men were progressing in the construction of their breastwork. I found them stripped of coats and shirts, and engaged in killing "gray backs," *pediculus vestimenti.* They said it was the first shade they had been in for a week, and they must improve their opportunity. This pest was a grievous trial, and it was assuming serious proportions in the army. The only effective remedy was to boil the shirts. These garments being woolen shrunk under this process, so that the men could with difficulty get into them.

There was a law authorizing a field officer to frank letters for enlisted men thus: "Soldier's letter.—R. R. Dawes, Lieutenant Colonel sixth Wisconsin Veteran Volunteers." Once a man brought to me one of his shrunk up shirts in a package, to be franked by mail. He said he thought it would about fit the baby.

COLD HARBOR CAMPAIGN.

(To my wife.)   LINE OF BATTLE, MAY 31st, 6 P. M.

"Alive and well. There has been heavy fighting along most of the line. Of the results we know nothing. There is a hot fire going on on our left as I write."

---

*It was the band of the eighth Pennsylvania Reserves and I suppose they played to encourage the men who were fighting.

(To my wife.)   LINE OF BATTLE, JUNE 1st, 6 P. M.

"I am alive, well, and just as dirty as I can be. Can not get time even to get into a creek, and there is no creek to get into. No fighting for us since I last wrote, of any serious account, but constant marching, countermarching and building breastworks."

Extracts from letters from my brother with Sherman's army, received in the works at Cold Harbor:

RESACA, GA., MAY 16th, 1864.

"On May 12th, our regiment was transferred from the fourth division, fifteenth corps, to Morgan L. Smith's second division, fifteenth corps and we were assigned to Lightburn's second brigade. We were in the battles of the 13th and 14th, and were close to the rebel works all day of the 15th. We lost fifty men killed and wounded. The charge of our division on the 14th, capturing the rebel rifle pits east of Camp creek, was the prettiest thing I ever saw. We uniformly whipped the rebels in our front. Our men were absolutely wild with enthusiasm. The regiment was highly complimented by Generals Logan, Smith, and Lightburn, and Colonel Jones has been especially recommended for promotion by them."

KINGSTON, GEORGIA, MAY 21st, 1864.

"On this campaign we have no tents. Field officers are permitted to take only what they can carry on their horses. Our marching order has just come in. We start Monday, the 23rd. The order says, 'take twenty days' rations of hard bread, coffee, and salt, and expect to be independent of the railroad' for that time. We will meet and defeat the rebel army somewhere between here and Atlanta.

We have a large and well appointed army, well officered and in better spirits than I ever saw an army in my life. The railroad trains from Chattanooga, ran to Kingston as soon as the army reached there. Next Friday is my twenty-fourth birthday; perhaps we will have another fight by that time.* Colonel Jones has just sent up the official report of the regiment at Resaca. In it he was kind enough to say: 'Major Dawes, whose coolness and

---

*As will be later seen Major Dawes came within one day of it in his guess. Friday was the 27th; Saturday, May 28th, was fought the battle of Dallas.

courage did much to inspire the men, is worthy of particular mention.'"

(To my wife.)   LINE OF BATTLE, JUNE 3rd, 1864, 6 P. M.

"Yesterday afternoon and all day to-day, battle has been raging around us, but by a kind Providence our part has been light. One man killed and seven wounded are our total casualties for the two days. We are strongly entrenched and only artillery can harm us. We can not show our heads above the works without being immediately shot at. The men try putting hats on ramrods and sticking them up and sometimes get a bullet through the hat.

Thirty-one days to-day this terrible campaign has dragged along. God grant it soon over. We know absolutely nothing of how the battle is going. We can only do our duty and hope all is well."

To protect my own headquarters I piled up logs in an angle and threw a pile of earth in front of them.

LINE OF BATTLE, JUNE 4th, 3 P. M.

"We are still hiding away from bullets of rebel sharpshooters. The line of works where we are is very crooked and we get bullets and artillery shots from nearly all points of the compass. But so long as our orders only require us 'to hold our line at all hazards,' we are well satisfied with our part in the battle. I can not tell you how tedious and trying this campaign has become. Thirty days of toil, danger and bloodshed, and we can see yet small prospect of an end to it. We are nine miles from Richmond, and our left, by desperate fighting, is said to have been pushed nearer. Our casualties in the regiment now amount to one hundred and seventy men killed and wounded. By general orders we make a daily report of killed and wounded, and we always have some. How long will it take to whittle us away? Our new chaplain reported for duty to-day. He came directly to the front where the bullets were whistling. I like his looks. He is a graduate of Oberlin College. He brings us little news. If we could know something it would be a little easier to be all day in our holes, waiting and dreading the future. It seems as though my sensibilities were deadened by this constant, wearing pressure. I do think this army has shown itself the longest suffering and hardest fighting army of the war. A shell exploded to-day in the log breastwork I had put up for my headquarters, and it showered us with dirt, and one fragment came through but did no injury."

The arrival of our Chaplain, as it was attended with no casualty, was rather an amusing affair. Ignorant of the danger attending such an exposure of himself, he came directly to the front. In approaching our line from the rear, it looked like a bee hive, but nothing could be seen of the enemy, except the puffs of powder smoke of the sharpshooters. In daylight it was almost certain death to come under their aim. We saw a lone man walking deliberately ·toward our headquarters. In vain the soldiers shouted "Lie down!" "Tree!" "Gopher!" "Grab a root, you —— old fool!" Blissfully unconscious that he was a target and a walking miracle to have escaped injury from the enemy's fire, Mr. Cochran had no thought that these remarks were addressed to himself.

By some foolish order, the drummer boys of the regiment had been sent out to the breastworks that day, and I took them in my fort. They were young and full of life, and Larry O'Neal, of company "D," while dancing, at which he was an expert, got outside the works and received a bullet in his knee. He never danced again. The Chaplain was indeed a God-send to this poor suffering boy. He dressed his wound with almost the skill of an experienced surgeon.

Lawson Fenton, of company "A," incautiously raised his head above the breastwork. A bullet passed through his brain, a great portion of which protruded from the wound. He was a brave soldier and a favorite with his comrades and with his officers. Lieutenant Howard J. Huntington prepared with great care a head board for his grave, which was dug in the darkness of the night succeeding and the head board was inscribed; but on the next morning Fenton was still alive, and it was three days before life became extinct. Poor fellow! he was wounded severely at Antietam; and when I visited our boys in Smoketown hospital, near that field, I found him bravely enduring his suffering and cheering all by his hopeful spirit.

On the evening of June fifth we moved to near Cold Harbor. Colonel E. S. Bragg was assigned to command of our brigade, relieving Colonel Robinson.

(To my wife.)   Gaines' Farm, June 6th, 1864.

"I have received your father's note announcing Charley's death. How strange that so suddenly, while you have suffered so long in dread of harm to me, I am safe, and Charley is called to his grave. Truly, we can not tell what is in store for us. I am well. We marched all night. We had a sharp skirmish yesterday."

Charles Beman Gates had been tenderly cherished by a devoted father and loving mother, and as he was only two years younger than my wife, they had been in life inseparable companions.

He was not prepared for the stern hardships of war, but when I was at Marietta I saw that he was full of zealous ardor to act a part in the great historic drama. He said to me, "You belong to the 'Iron Brigade'; how do you think I will feel to take no part in the war, and be in the same family?" Of tall and manly figure, he was a splendid youth, and he was of warm and noble impulses, and of pure and lofty character. As I lay in the works at Cold Harbor, I saw William Jackson come running toward us. He dodged from tree to tree, and crawled upon the ground to escape the fire of the rebel sharpshooters. A letter had come from Washington directed to be delivered "quickly." It said: "Charley died at Harper's Ferry on Tuesday."

(To my wife.)   Banks of the Chickahominy, }
                      June 8th, 1864, 4 P. M. }

"We came down here to-day, and are located on the left flank of our army, and we are at last out from under the fire of the enemy. I have enjoyed the luxury of a good wash, a change of clothing, and a *mess of wild strawberries*. It does seem pleasant to get even for a few hours out of the presence of death, suffering and danger. Our spirits rise wonderfully. It is impossible for one who has not undergone it, to fully understand the depression of spirits caused by such long, continued, and bloody fighting and work. Colonel Bragg said yesterday: 'Of all I have gone through, I can not now write an intelligent account. I can only tell my wife I am alive and well. I am too stupid for any use.' We are having the first quiet day for more than a month. General Cutler said that this is the first day, for that length of time, that no man in the division has been reported killed or

CHARLES B. GATES,

FIRST LIEUT. CO. A. 148TH OHIO.

NATIONAL GUARD.

EPHRAIM C. DAWES,

MAJOR 53RD OHIO VOLS.

BREVET LIEUT. COLONEL U. S. VOLS.

wounded. The weather is bright and sunny, and our location is delightful.''

BIVOUAC NEAR RAILROAD CROSSING OF CHICKAHOMINY, }
(To my wife.)   JUNE 9th, 1864. }

"All is quiet here with us. We can plainly see the enemy south of the Chickahominy. Our pickets are friendly, and we get the morning papers from Richmond by 10 o'clock in the forenoon. We have heard from Captain Kellogg as alive and a prisoner. I at once wrote to his wife informing her of the fact. He has come back to her out of the grave, for we all believed him dead. Colonel Bragg has been assigned to command of our brigade. I have great trouble in getting the company business attended to, so many of our officers are gone.''

In this bivouac the new chaplain addressed the men in strong, earnest, and well adapted sermons. His talk was patriotic as well as religious, and highly acceptable to our men. Mr. Cochran was too old a man for the hard service he had undertaken, and he soon became very sick.

BIVOUAC ON CHICKAHOMINY, JUNE 11th, 1864.

"*My dear sister*:—From what Mary says, I have great hope that my poor brother is not so desperately hurt as your note would indicate. But, at best, I fear he is terribly wounded. I have strong faith that he will not die, but I know he must suffer long and acutely, and perhaps be sadly disfigured. The surgeons tell me that bullet wounds in the jaw seldom prove fatal, though always intensely painful and distressing, on account of neuralgia, and are liable to interfere with the voice. His sufferings he will bear patiently, like a true man, as he has always proved himself. To be severely wounded is something he has prepared himself to meet, and he will accept his fate, I know, bravely and cheerfully. It will be gratifying to hear that he is at home, where he will get every care and comfort, and where his chances for recovery are many times increased. If he gets safely home, I shall feel very sure he will get well. Poor Charley! How strange, all should be struck down and I safe through days and weeks of this perilous storm of battle. We have to add to the list on our flag, Wilderness, Laurel Hill, Spottsylvania, Jericho Ford, Shady Grove Church, and Cold Harbor, where fifty thousand men have fallen, and no harm has come to me. Surely a kind Providence has watched over and preserved me through the 'Valley of the Shadow of Death.'"

Extract from a letter from Major E. C. Dawes of June 11th, 1864, received in this camp.

"I was shot at Dallas, Georgia, two weeks ago to-day. We were in rifle pits. The rebels charged us. We gave them an awful licking. The bullet struck the left side of my lower jaw and, the surgeons say, 'carried away the body of the inferior maxilla to near the angle." It took off my lower lip, tore the chin so that it hangs down, took out all the lower teeth but two, and cut my tongue. It is a horrible looking wound and will disfigure me, but the doctors say they can fix up a face for me. It will be slow healing. A few minutes before I received this wound I was hit in the back of the head. It did not hurt much and is not at all serious, although it is not yet healed.

Our regiment has done splendid fighting this campaign, and has made a reputation second to no regiment in the 15th army corps."

A wounded soldier's journey home. Written by my brother in 1864.

"I was shot late in the afternoon of May twenty-eighth, and remained in the field hospitals, at and near Dallas, Georgia, until the night of May thirtieth.* About ten o'clock at night of the thirtieth a wagon train was sent under strong escort to the railroad at Kingston, about thirty miles distant. All of the wounded who were able to travel in the wagons were permitted to go. The surgeons advised me to go in this train. They said that if I remained around the hospital the chances were that I would contract gangrene or erysipelas and die, and that I should get home as quickly as possible. My old friend Haydn K. Smith, correspondent of the Chicago Journal, volunteered to go to Nashville with me. I could hardly have got along without him. He

---

*Every attention possible was paid me by the surgeons, Dr. H. W. Nichols, who had especial charge of me, and Dr. C. P. Brent, Surgeon in Chief of the division, as well as our own surgeons, Dr. W. M. Cake (then medical director of the fourth division), and Dr. John A. Lair (who had charge of the regiment), who came to see me whenever they could. Colonel Jones sent me twice each day a bulletin from the regiment, which was still in the trenches from which we had repulsed the assault on the 28th.

had been with the army enough to know what to do and to whom to apply in an emergency. My colored servant, Wesley Benson, accompanied me. He was a faithful and competent young man but he could not read writing and I could not talk.*

The wagon train unwound itself at midnight. I got into one of the wagons and sat on a bag of corn. The different surgeons bid me good bye. I sat on that bag of corn all night. The road was very rough, much of the way through dark woods. My wound was much inflamed and my tongue so swollen that it was almost impossible to swallow. The misery of that night's ride was indescribable. Early next morning Major Patrick Flynn, of the ninetieth Illinois, who was commanding the train guard, saw me and brought up the only ambulance in the train. It was loaded with mail bags, but Major Flynn threw some of them in the wagon and put me in the ambulance and helped fix the mail bags so that I could rest on them. Mr. Smith got a canteen of cold water. I managed to swallow a little of it, but the effort was so painful that I almost concluded not to try again. The day was very hot and the road was very dusty. About noon we crossed the Etowah river on a bridge. Near the end of the bridge was a house where there were some Union soldiers and some women.

One of the women brought out a great yellow bowl filled with buttermilk and handed it to me. I was weak with hunger, faint from loss of blood and burning with thirst. I crammed the bowl into my mouth with both hands, despite the awful pain, and drank nearly the whole of the buttermilk. It revived me at once. It satisfied both hunger and thirst, and settled the question of supplies. I could walk and I could eat, and felt that my worst troubles were over.

The train reached Kingston between five and six o'clock in the evening. There seemed to be no adequate preparation for the wounded. But the agents of the Sanitary Commission were there. They took possession of a large house with a shaded yard and went to work to prepare food. Mrs. Bickerdyke and Mrs. Johnson were in charge. I camped in a corner of the porch,

---

*For a long time Major Dawes could not speak a word. His full powers of speech were ultimately restored by one of the most extensive and skillful surgical operations of this kind performed during the war.

surrounding the house, where there was a projecting room. I could not lie down, for breathing was then impossible. I could not rest the back of my head against anything, for the wound there was very painful, and I was obliged to sit up in some place where I could rest the side of my head. This corner filled every requirement. One of the women brought me a bowl of soup. I took off my bandage to drink it. She looked at me, burst into tears, and ran away. An old gray haired surgeon came in to dress the wound. At sight of it he turned very white and went away. Mr. Smith had gone to ascertain about the railroad trains, and Wesley was hunting a newspaper, so I went out myself to find a surgeon. Fortunately my good friend, Dr. Edwards of the fortieth Illinois, who had been attached to our regiment in the East Tennessee campaign and messed with me, met me in the yard. He spent an hour dressing my wound and gave Wesley full and careful instruction how to care for it; that night I slept well. Next day, June 1st, about noon, a train of empty freight cars backed down in front of the house. Mr. Smith came in with the news, that all the wounded who were able to walk, were to go to Chattanooga on that train. I got into a car with a large number of others; so many that all had to sit up. Many of them were badly wounded, but all were in high spirits. At Resaca, as the train stopped, I was startled at the sight of Wm. D. Gaby, a soldier of company "K," of our regiment. At the battle, on May 13th, he was shot dead as we all supposed. The ball struck him in the forehead, but glanced and came out the top of his head. The train reached Dalton at dusk. I was very tired, and getting out of the car walked along the platform to a car where there was more room. It was occupied by a dying officer, with a surgeon and a detail of men sent to care for him, and endeavor to get him far enough North to meet his father and mother who were hurrying down in answer to a telegraphic summons. The officer was Lieutenant George B. Covington, Adjutant of the seventeenth Indiana regiment. He died before the train left Dalton. The surgeon seeing that I was badly wounded and very weak, gave me some stimulant and put me on Covington's cot, raising the head so I could rest. I went to sleep, but at Ringgold, woke with a start to find my bandages drenched with blood from some small arteries under the tongue, which had sloughed away. I stopped it by cramming a towel under my tongue. This weakened me very much and made me afraid to sleep again. About midnight the train reached Chattanooga. There was no one at the depot to tell us where to go. I saw the row of hospitals on the hill near by and started toward them. A guard cried: "Halt!" "Halt!" but I did not care whether he shot me or not, and pushing past him, opened the door of the nearest building, which was the officers' ward. The nurse on duty was a wounded soldier. He knew exactly what to do, dressed my wound carefully, fixed a cot so that I could rest comfortably, and I slept until the surgeon came around in the morning. Mr. Smith after some trouble, secured a pass for me to Nashville. The nurse fixed up a large roll of bandages and a bottle of beef tea and gave them to Wesley for me. The train left at three P. M., June 2nd. It consisted of a number of empty freight cars with a single second class passenger car attached. The car was pretty well filled. I sat on the rear seat, (the seats were plain boards) with my back to the other passengers, as I was obliged to change my bandages frequently. The train went via Stevenson, Huntsville and Decatur, and did not reach Nashville until late in the afternoon of June 3rd. This railroad ride was the most trying experience of all. My wound was sloughing freely, my tongue was very much swollen and it was almost black. I suffered a great deal of pain, and to swallow was exquisite torture. At Nashville I was taken to the officers' hospital. Under the efficient care of Dr. J. H. Green,* the surgeon in charge, I improved rapidly, and having obtained a leave of absence, was able to leave for home June 6th."

---

*"OFFICERS' HOSPITAL, NASHVILLE, TENNESSEE. JUNE 6th, 1864.

Major Dawes, fifty-third regiment, O. V. I., was admitted to this hospital June 3rd, on account of gunshot wound received at Dallas, Georgia, May 28th. The body of inferior maxilla is entirely carried away to near the angle. He informs me that some loose fragments of bone were taken away since he received the wound, and that he has had secondary hemorrhages several times since sloughing commenced.

The wound was sloughing freely when admitted and very offensive, but by the use of solution of chloriated soda two days, the slough has all disappeared, and the wound is now granulating. Have dressed it four times a day, syringing it out freely with cold water. Swelling and discoloration of tongue is abating slowly. Have not attempted to remove any of the spicula, on account of tendency to hemorrhages while sloughing.

J. H. GREEN."

CHAPTER XIV.

A Change of Base—To the James River—Petersburg—Repulsed—Worn, Weary and Discouraged—The Trenches—Disorganization from Losses—Colonel Bragg Promoted—Out of the Trenches—Rising Spirits—Adjutant Brooks' Expedition and its Fate—Captain Kellogg in Rebel Prison—His Escape—Captain Lewis A. Kent—Lieutenant Earl M. Rogers Wounded—Mortar Shell—Ice—Our Chaplain Finds a Cow—Appointed to a Responsible Duty—Cowards and Inefficients—Cuyler Babcock—Commissioned Colonel—The Muster Out—Questions as to Term of Service—Dr. Hall Promoted—Mine Explosion—In Camp—Mustered Out and Honorably Discharged—The Ordnance Sergeant.

(To my wife.) WILCOX'S LANDING, JAMES RIVER, }
JUNE 15th, 1864. }

"Another change of base to the James river. It is very refreshing to get to the beautiful slopes on this broad river. We left our camp on the Chickahominy Sunday evening. We were in line of battle all day. Monday night we marched to St. Mary's church, and yesterday we came here. Our army is crossing the river on steamers and on a pontoon at Fort Powhatan. General Grant does not hesitate to uncover Washington. We hear distant cannonading in the direction of Richmond. I think it probable the enemy are pushing down this way to see what we are doing."

(To my wife.) SOUTH BANK, JAMES RIVER, }
JULY 16th, 12 M. }

"We have a rumor that General Hancock has taken Petersburg. If he has not it will cost us a bloody battle. Dust, dust, dust is our special inconvenience just now. Here comes our corps general and staff, and we must 'fall in' to march."

PETERSBURG.

(To my wife.) LINE OF BATTLE BEFORE PETERSBURG, }
JUNE 19th, 1864, 7 A. M. }

"Yesterday afternoon in another hopeless assault there was enacted a horrid massacre of our corps. Our brigade charged half a mile over an open field, under the musketry fire of the enemy. We had five men killed and thirty-five wounded. (The actual loss was greater than here reported.) We are now lying in rifle pits from which it is almost certain death to raise our heads. Our corps must have lost very heavily yesterday. It is awfully disheartening to be ordered upon such hopeless assaults. My regiment was selected with others to make a night attack on the enemy's entrenchments, and we formed in line to do so, but the order was countermanded."

General Cutler says in his official report: "In this affair I lost in killed and wounded about one third of the men I had with me, and among them many valuable officers." He says also that none of his troops got nearer than "seventy-five yards of the enemy's works."

(To my wife.) LINE OF BATTLE BEFORE PETERSBURG,
JUNE 21st, 1864.

"I am sitting in a hole four feet deep, eight feet long and three feet wide, shaded by green boughs and quite cool and pleasant for a hot day. This is my regimental headquarters. Sergeant Major Cuyler Babcock, who is Acting Adjutant, sits at the other end of the hole, and we are company for each other. To raise a head in daylight above the surface of the ground is almost certain death, for it will draw the fire of a dozen sharpshooters. Babcock knows nothing about Latin, but I taught him to-day about twenty lines of Cicero's first oration against Catiline, and so we pass our time. Few of our men are hurt and none need be. Sometimes a foolish fellow will imagine he wants a drink of water badly enough to risk his life to get it, and he generally loses his life trying to run for it. We have lost forty-five men before Petersburg, six killed. The suicidal manner in which we are sent against the enemy's entrenchments is discouraging. Our brigade was simply food for powder in the assault day before yesterday."

(To my wife.) LINE OF BATTLE BEFORE PETERSBURG.
JUNE 21st, 1864.

"We are completely holed, and ground-hogging for a steady living becomes very tedious. Colonel Bragg has notice of his nomination as a Brigadier General."

On this day (June twenty-first), was shot and mortally wounded Levi Pearson, of Company "A." He was the last one of three brothers who had served in that company. William Pearson was killed in the charge upon the railroad cut at Gettysburg and Jesse Pearson lost his life in the bloody and fruitless charge upon the entrenchments of the enemy at Petersburg on June 18th, three days before his brother Levi fell.

(To my wife.)   LINE OF BATTLE BEFORE PETERSBURG, JUNE 22nd, 8 A. M.

"Still skulking in our holes, and dirty, dusty places they are, but the Johnnies leave us no alternative. William brings my breakfast and enough for a cold dinner up to the works before daylight, and supper after dark. We can see the spires of Petersburg about two miles away to the northwest. There seems to be a severe musketry fight going on this evening to our left and troops have been moving that way all day and yesterday."

(To my wife,)   BEFORE PETERSBURG, JUNE 23rd, 7 P. M.

"I have lain all day in this dirty hole and am too stupid for any use. The Calcutta black hole was not more disagreeable and the constant shower of rebel bullets are the chains that keep us imprisoned. Things look rather blue, I must confess, about Petersburg."

(To my wife.)   LINE OF BATTLE BEFORE PETERSBURG, JUNE 25th, 1864.

"Imagine a hole three feet wide and four feet deep in the middle of the street, and a sun perfectly sweltering in its rays and you have our quarters, from which we can not raise our heads."

The seven days in the Petersburg hole closed on this evening. We had a passage way out to the line of the regiment. Cuyler Babcock, my companion, was a most worthy young man. He had performed the duties of Adjutant since the battles on the North Anna and he continued to do so until killed in the battle of the Weldon Road, August 18th, 1864. The work of preparing descriptive lists for our great number of wounded men in hospitals and of getting straightened out in our various returns and accounts was very difficult. The loss of company officers and of papers added to the general confusion. Babcock was an expert and he helped everybody with an impartial generosity and with untiring industry.

(To my wife.) BEFORE PETERSBURG, JUNE 26th, 1864.

"We have been drawn back from the rifle-pits, comparatively out of range of the enemy's bullets, and we are in the woods. The weather is intensely hot, and very trying upon our poor men in the entrenchments. It is now Brigadier General Bragg.

The long continued fighting has put us very much behind in our business. Many of our poor wounded men are waiting and

---

This poetical and striking description of the works at Petersburg was published August 14th, 1864, by a member of the 188th Pennsylvania regiment, then in the trenches:

"OUR HOUSE IN THE FRONT."

You have never seen our house in the "front,"
Our house that is built for the battle's brunt;
I tell you, then, 'tis a wonderful home,
With its earthen floor and its starry dome.
No mortal structure can reach so high,
For the dome itself is the vaulted sky.
The walls of the loamy earth are made,
With trunks of the forest oaks inlaid.
It boasts of a narrow and lengthy hall,
Where our belted knights are seated all,
Keeping their vigils by night and day,
Ready to join in the deadly fray.
Our carpet and couch are the earthy ground,
Our chairs are woodblocks scat'ered around.
"Hard tack" boxes our tables make,
Where daily our scanty meals we take.
Our pantry is carried slung over the back—
A medley of coffee, pork, and "tack,"
All jumbled up in a haversack.
We ask no fire or lamp-light here
Whilst the moon and stars in the heavens appear.
No urchin's prattle or infant's squall
Is ever heard in our martial hall;
But morning, noon, and night as well
Resounds the scream of the villainous shell,
And the fatal "zip" of the minie ball.
Death in the trenches, Death in the air,
And grim Death rioting everywhere;
Thus we bear the battle's brunt
In this, the hall of "Our House in the Front!"

watching in hospitals for their descriptive lists, so that they can draw their pay. I am doing all in my power to get them made and sent off. Our wagon is kept miles away from us." (Our papers were in this wagon.)

General Cutler says in his official report: "The changes in the command have been so frequent and the losing of nearly every original brigade, regimental, and company commander renders it impossible to make anything like an accurate account as to details. * * * I can not close this report without saying how deeply I felt the loss of the many brave officers and men who have fallen in this campaign."

(To my wife.) JUNE 26, 1864.

"I have been washed, shaved and shampooed, and feel wonderfully revived. I have got some hams, soft bread, flour and biscuit; the latter luxury comes from the Christian Commission. You may be sure I am feeling much better and more cheerful. Brooks (Adjutant E. P. Brooks,) has been sent out by General Grant on an expedition to cut rebel railroads. He has thirty picked men of his own selection from our brigade, and they are armed with Spencer rifles and mounted. (There were seven men from the sixth Wisconsin.) He aims to cut the Danville road at

LOSSES IN THE SIXTH WISCONSIN.

	Killed		Wounded		Missing		Aggregate
	Officers	Men	Officers	Men	Officers	Men	
Wilderness, May 5th—7th,	3	5	1	39	1	14	63
Spottsylvania, May 8th—21st,	2	8	3	65		5	83
North Anna, Tolopotomy, Bethesda Church, } May 22nd—June 1st,		2	1	9			12
Cold Harbor, June 2nd—15th,		1		6		1	8
Petersburg, June 16th—30th,		7	2	38		10	57
Petersburg, July 1st—31st.		1		3			4
Total	5	24	7	160	1	30	227

Killed, 29; Wounded, 167; Missing, 31; Total: 227. The regiment entered the campaign with an aggregate of 370 men and received in recruits and returned men, 10. The loss of 227 was from an aggregate of 380.

Roanoke station.* I have received through Mrs. Kellogg a letter which she received from her husband, Captain Kellogg, who is in the confederate prison at Macon, Georgia. Major Plummer is dead and I shall recommend Captain Kellogg for appointment as Major."

CONFEDERATE MILITARY PRISON, MACON GA., }
JUNE 6th, 1864. }

"My dear wife : – I have again an opportunity of writing, which I gladly improve. My health is as good as it ever was, the climate seems to agree with me. My treatment is, and has been, probably as good as the Confederate Government can afford. The rations are corn meal, bacon, beans and rice, just the same as they issue to their own troops. The weather is delightful, not too hot in the day time, while the nights are cool. The circumstances of my capture are as follows : On the morning of the fifth (May,) I was ordered to take my company and support a line of skirmishers who were ordered to advance and attack the enemy. Soon after the line was engaged it became necessary to bring up the reserve, which I did and deployed them as skirmishers and was hotly engaged. My loss was severe, how many I can not tell. Soon after the brigade charged the enemy. I ordered my line to advance as they were deployed with the brigade, which they did. We drove the enemy's line of battle and were driven in turn. I was captured in the endeavor to rally our troops. Am very anxious to hear from the regiment. Please write to Dawes and enclose this. Love to all friends, and I remain, dear wife,   J. A. KELLOGG."

This is a shrewd and remarkable letter. Captain Kellogg intentionally mis-states the real condition of things in that horrible pest hole, Macon Military Prison. His object was to make sure that his letter, which was to be read by the officers of the prison, would be sent to his wife. As a matter of fact, his published story of his prison experience narrates that he ate a rat while in

---

*Lieutenant Brooks had carefully prepared a plan for this undertaking, which met the approval of General Grant, to whom he was commended by the letters he had received from General Pope for his especially efficient service for that General in his campaign. This entire party was captured by the enemy. If we may credit the Confederate reports they were, owing to the negligence of their commander to put out the proper guards, surprised and captured by a much smaller force.

this horrible place. He shows the solicitude of the brave soldier for his own military honor, and fully explains the circumstances of his capture and says: "Please send this letter to Dawes," his nearest friend in the regiment. This brave man and heroic leader needed no vindication with any of his comrades or his commanders. Captain Kellogg was afterward sent to Charleston, S. C., and placed with other officers, under the fire of our own batteries, which bombarded that city. When on the way back from Charleston to that delightful summer resort, the Macon prison, he jumped at midnight from a rapidly running train of cars. He was chased by blood hounds, and stood for hours chin deep in the water to avoid them. In South Carolina, while gaunt with hunger and reduced almost to despair, he appealed to an aged negro. The old man had never before seen a Yankee soldier, and stood appalled at the apparition. "Will you betray us?" said Kellogg. "No sah," said the old man, "There's not a slave in South Carolina would betray you." The negroes fed Kellogg's party, ferried them across rivers, and aided and piloted them on their way to the best of their ability. After enduring incredible privations, he safely passed through all perils and came into the Union lines in Tennessee.

(To my wife.)   BEFORE PETERSBURG, JUNE 28th, 1864.

"We are to go out to the entrenchments to-night to relieve the second brigade, but as there is no firing on the line in our front, the service is not hard. I am trying to get my company business straightened out, but the loss of so many officers, and the confusion resulting from so long an inattention to returns, makes a great deal of trouble. I fear our pay rolls will be defective."

HEADQUARTERS SIXTH WISCONSIN VETERAN VOLUNTEERS, ⎫
(To my wife.)   JUNE 30th, 1864. ⎭

"We are getting fixed up for a muster for pay, and are pretty well straightened out, but accounts and returns have become inextricably confused in this campaign."

The constant repetition of this complaint indicates how serious the disorganization had become, through the grievous losses in the campaign. The case of Captain Lewis A. Kent, serves well to illustrate these conditions. When Lieutenant James L. Converse of company "G," was killed in the battle of the Wilderness, that company was left under command of Second Lieutenant John Timmons, who was also wounded and disabled in the battle of Spottsylvania. Lieutenant Timmons had notified me that he would not accept promotion because it involved a re-muster for three more years of service, and he wished to hold his legal claim to a discharge on July 15th, the expiration of the term of service of the regiment. I accordingly assigned Sergeant Kent to duty as Captain of company "G," on the 10th of May, 1864. I have made an error in earlier statements of this case, in fixing the date of this order as May 7th, which is not material. No braver, more efficient or more dashing company commander fought in our line. He carried a musket and the flash of his bayonet was always seen leading the line in desperate places. On the 18th of June at Petersburg a minie ball passed through his left shoulder, shattering the arm, piercing the body, breaking two of his ribs, lacerating the left lung, and lodging next to the spine.

Until we settled down at Petersburg, there was literally no opportunity to apply to the Governor of Wisconsin for a Captain's commission for Kent. When the commission came it was dated subsequent to June 18th, the day he received his wound. Although he received this terrible wound while performing most gallant service* as a Captain, for fourteen years he received only the pension of a Sergeant. In 1878 his old commander, General Bragg, was in Congress and through his efforts a law was enacted, granting Captain Kent the pension due his rank and service. There is a tinge of romance about the service of this young officer. When the war broke out he was a student in Beloit College, but his home was at Blacksburg, Virginia, and most of the male members of his family were in the service of the Confederacy.

---

*The 18th of June was indeed a dark day for the faithful little regiment. Lieutenant Earl M. Rogers, in command of company "I," was shot through the body and wounded almost in the same terrible manner as Acting Captain Kent. Lieutenant Rogers was again on duty the next October, and he was in the battles of Hatcher's Run. He was brevetted as a Major. His wound did not close however, until 1866. He served afterward as a Lieutenant in the Regular Army, and was engaged in an Indian campaign. Lieutenant Howard J. Huntington was also badly wounded here.

(To my wife.) BEFORE PETERSBURG, VA.,
JULY 2nd, 1864.

"We are again out of those hot trenches and back in the woods. If the army remains here, in six days we will go out again for a tour of duty in the trenches. There is not so much shooting now, although every few moments a huge mortar shell fired by the rebels, comes straight down from the clouds and bursts with a terrific explosion in our lines. The weather is very hot, but I get ice every day and plenty of it. There is an ice house on our skirmish line. I have some boys who have the nerve to go out and get the ice at night, in spite of the fact that rebel sharpshooters keep a constant fire on the ice house. There is one good thing, corps headquarters can't put a guard over it, and gobble it away from us, and appropriate it to their own use. William wants very much to come home with me."

(To my wife.) BEFORE PETERSBURG, JULY 4th, 1864.

"General Cutler is anxious to make up a Colonel's command of eight hundred and forty men for me, and have me muster in for three years, on my commission as Colonel, which will be issued by the Governor.

Our chaplain was sick, and some where in the rear of the army he found a cow. Now that he has gone to the general hospital, the cow has reverted to me. I draw rations for the cow as a mule. Dr. Hall and I have plenty of fresh milk and we unite in gratitude to the Chaplain.

We are to go up to-night for two days' duty in the trenches.

The boys who go out of the service on the fifteenth of this month are becoming anxious. The Pennsylvania Reserves were in battle the day after their time had expired. Twelve days is a short time, but much history can be made here within that period."

(To my wife.) IN THE TRENCHES BEFORE PETERSBURG,
JULY 5th, 1864.

"We have entered into a treaty of peace with the 'Johnnies' and men on both sides stand up in fearless confidence in each other's good faith. To the right of us Burnside's negroes occupy the trenches. Master and slave meet on equal terms and the hostility is implacable. They fire night and day on both sides. A lady came up to our front line this morning. About a thousand rebels got up on their works to stare at her, and at least two thousand of our men. The quiet is very pleasant, and I hope that the continual whizzing of bullets will not again be heard." (To my wife.) BEFORE PETERSBURG, JULY 7th, 1864, 8 P. M.

"We are back again in the woods, where we are exposed only to rebel shell, which occasionally come howling over. There is a battery of thirty-two pounders, which fires directly over us, and that draws the enemy's fire. I was detailed to-day by order of General Meade as President of the commission to investigate the 'capacity, qualification, propriety of conduct and efficiency of such officers of the fifth army corps as may be brought before it.' This is the highest honor of my military service."

HEADQUARTERS, ARMY OF THE POTOMAC, }
JULY 6th, 1864. }

Special Order, No. 179, Extract.

Under the authority of the 10th Section of the Act of July 22nd, 1861, a Board to consist of

Lieut. Col. R. R. Dawes, 6th Wisconsin Vols.

Major M. C. Welsh, 7th Indiana "

Captain A. B. Pattison, " " "

will meet at such time and place as the Com'dg General, fifth corps may designate, to examine into the capacity, qualifications, propriety of conduct and efficiency of such officers of Volunteers, serving in the fifth army corps, as may be ordered before it.

By command of Major General Meade.

(Signed) S. WILLIAMS, Ass't Adj't General.

To have been appointed by General Meade as President of the Examining Board of the fifth army corps was indeed an especial "honor of my military service." This was a position of the highest trust and responsibility. The object of the commission was to summarily weed out incompetent and cowardly officers. If the commission so recommended, an officer would be promptly dismissed from the service by order of the Secretary of War. Curious cases were brought before the Board. I remember a case of a Captain who had drank a decoction of powdered slate pencils in vinegar to render himself unfit for service. During this unexampled campaign of sixty continuous days, the excitement, exhaustion, hard work and loss of sleep broke down great numbers of men who had received no wounds in battle. Some who began the campaign with zealous and eager bravery, ended it with nervous and feverish apprehension of danger in the ascendancy. Brave men were shielded if their records on other occasions justified another trial, which ordinarily resulted well, but cowards met no mercy. They were dismissed and their names published throughout the land, a fate more terrible than death to a proud spirited soldier.

There were among officers and men some who would even shoot off a finger or attempt to inflict a wound upon themselves in other non vital parts. Ordinarily the "damned spot" caused by the powder burn, remained to tell its story.

(To my wife.)   BEFORE PETERSBURG, JULY 8th, 1864.

"General Cutler's plan is to consolidate the second, fifth and sixth regiments, which he wishes me to command as Colonel.

I have recommended Sergeant Major Cuyler Babcock for appointment as Adjutant, in place of Brooks, whom I shall assign to a company."

(To my wife.)   BEFORE PETERSBURG, JULY 10th, 1864.

"We are in the trenches again, but the rebel infantry is very friendly. A villainous shell occasionally shrieks over our heads, but does no further harm than to create a kind of shivering sensation that 'the Angel of Death has spread his wings on the blast.'"

STATE OF WISCONSIN, SECRETARY'S OFFICE, }
MADISON, JULY 5th, 1864. }

COLONEL RUFUS R. DAWES:

"Dear Colonel:—Yours of the 26th of June received, and I take great pleasure in informing you that I have this moment put the seal on your commission as Colonel, vice Bragg, promoted. If you have time, I would like a letter from you, giving your idea of the situation.   Yours truly,

LUCIUS FAIRCHILD."

(To my wife.)   BEFORE PETERSBURG, JULY 13th, 1864.

"We are busy making the papers for the muster out of our men, whose terms of service expire, and they are nearly wild at the prospect of seeing once more their long separated families and their homes. The men who go now were not on the veteran furlough, and few of them have seen their homes for more than three years. Some have passed through twenty battles and nearly all have marks of wounds received in battle. I am myself the only man who has passed unharmed through every battle and skirmish of the regiment. I have been sitting on our commission for examination of officers. We have to haul over the coals the Captain commanding the ——."

The term of service of nine commissioned officers expired on the 15th of July. But owing to ambiguous and conflicting orders on the subject of mustering commissioned officers, issued by the War Department, the authorities in the Army of the Potomac refused to discharge officers without an order from the Department. This involved delay and action at Washington upon each case. All were finally mustered out excepting one Lieutenant. It had been the practice to receive officers into the service for the emaining or unexpired term of their regiments. The result of an order forbidding such musters was, that if an officer did not wish to pledge himself for a new term of three years, he refused to accept promotion. Second Lieutenant John Timmons had been offered a commission as Captain of his company "G," but he declined to accept it for this reason, and the appointment was given to Sergeant Lewis A. Kent. Pending the granting of his discharge by the War Department, Lieutenant Timmons was "mustered out forever by a minie bullet" in the battle of the Weldon Road.

(To my wife.)　　　　BEFORE PETERSBURG, JULY 17th, 1864.

"There is a prevailing impression that siege operations have so far progressed as to bring another attempt upon the enemy's works when the mine is exploded. (It appears from this letter that we knew about the work upon the mine, which was not exploded until the 30th of July.) There is now no mortar or artillery firing along the line. Before to-day the enemy would throw a mortar shell into our lines at intervals of about fifteen minutes."

(To my wife.)　　BEFORE PETERSBURG, VA., JULY 22nd, 1864.

"We are in the trenches to-day, and about once an hour a

mortar shell is thrown by the enemy. When we hear the chug of the mortar firing, we all run into the bomb proofs and we have time to do so, but we have to be quick about it. Dr. A. W. Preston has been discharged for disability and I have taken great pleasure in recommending Dr. Hall for promotion.

I strolled along our line of entrenchments to-day. It would seem that our army is impregnably entrenched. I have been appointed President of our division court martial, and as I am President of the fifth corps examining commission, my hands are full. There is an immense amount of digging in this siege of Petersburg."

MINE EXPLOSION.

(To my wife.)   BEFORE PETERSBURG, JULY 30th, 1864.

"Shortly after daylight the mine was exploded and at that signal every cannon and mortar on the line opened on the enemy. There was for some reason a long delay in setting off the mine. I was lying in a bomb proof taking a nap, when I felt a jar like an earthquake. I jumped out in time to see probably the most terrific explosion ever known in this country. A fort and several hundred feet of earthworks were literally hurled into the air. It is hardly possible that any man lived who was in the line.

Our men gained the enemy's works and took their line, and the position held would have broken the rebel army. But victory stands with the enemy, who drove our men out and regained all they had lost. I stood on the top of our log house and saw the rebels charge upon our men. (General Mahone commanded this force.) We had three men wounded on the skirmish line. The pile of dead around the ruins of the fort is very large."

(To my wife)   NEAR PETERSBURG, AUGUST 1st, 1864.

"We are to-day about four miles from the enemy and upon the extreme left of the army. It seems comfortable to get almost out of hearing of the shooting. I have put the regiment into camp and I have fixed up a fine and shady bower for my headquarters. Day before yesterday's failure will likely make summer bowers fashionable for this army. We hear that the paymaster is coming with four months pay. Lieutenant John Timmons of company 'G' expected to be mustered out on July 15th, and supposing of course that he would be, as was his legal right, I recommended the Governor to appoint Sergeant Lewis A. Kent Captain over Timmons, and now poor 'Tim,' in addition to being conscripted, is jumped.''

(To my wife.)   NEAR PETERSBURG, AUGUST 5th, 1864.

"The weather is very hot and things go on with the usual stale monotony of a summer life in camp. Occasionally we hear a burst of cannon and mortars in the distance, but we are out of the way of them. We have orders to get under arms at daylight every morning.

We live very well. I still have the cow; she gives all the milk Dr. Hall and I can drink or use, and we are very popular with our friends. We have plenty of vegetables. Dr. Hall has received his commission as Surgeon. The other officers now with the regiment whose terms of service have expired are Lieutenants John Timmons, H. B. Merchant, and William Golterman. The five officers absent from the regiment, whose terms have expired, have been mustered out and honorably discharged.''

HEADQUARTERS FOURTH DIVISION, FIFTH ARMY CORPS, }
AUGUST 9th, 1864. }

Lieutenant Colonel Rufus R. Dawes, Commanding Sixth Wisconsin Veteran Volunteers:

*"COLONEL:—I have just received a communication from the War Department authorizing me to muster out yourself and Second Lieutenant William Golterman of your regiment.

Very respectfully

R. MONTEITH,

Capt. and A. C. M., 4th Div., 5th A. C.''

"Lieutenant Colonel R. R. Dawes, of the sixth Wisconsin

---

*From the Official Army Register of the Volunteer Force of the United States Army, 1861—1865, I take the following:

"Mustered out on expiration of term of service: Lieutenant Colonel Rufus R. Dawes, August 10th, 1864, (Brevet Brigadier General, March 13th, 1865.) Captain Thomas W. Plummer, July 25th, 1864. Captain Charles H. Ford, July 29th, 1864. Captain William N. Remington, October 11th, 1864. First Lieutenant Lloyd G. Harris, July 23rd, 1864. First Lieutenant John Beely, July 25th, 1864. First Lieutenant William S. Campbell, October 11th, 1864. First Lieutenant Earl M. Rogers, March 10th, 1865, (Brevet Major, March 13th, 1865.) Second Lieutenant Howard J. Huntington, July 23rd, 1864. Second Lieutenant William Golterman, August 10th, 1864. Second Lieutenant Hiram B. Merchant, September 6th, 1864.

veteran volunteers, whose term of service has expired, left for the north two days since. The Colonel enlisted as a private, and was at once promoted Captain of the company. In 1862 he was made Major of the regiment, and in 1863 Lieutenant Colonel. When Colonel Bragg was promoted to brigadier general, Colonel Dawes received a colonel's commission, but in consequence of the regiment being badly cut up, he could not be mustered. Having been in all the fights of this army since it left the Peninsula in 1862, his record is one of which any officer might well feel proud.

During the late engagement I saw one of our men being brought from the field with a fractured thigh. By his side on the stretcher was his musket and equipments. When asked why he attempted to save his gun, and he so badly wounded, his answer was: 'Captain is a bully little fellow, and the Ordnance Department isn't going to stop his pay on account of carelessness on my part.'"

The above is from the "Sunday Morning Chronicle," of Washington. "Cron-i-kill!" the news boys shouted as they sold the papers in the army. The writer, as might be suspected from the story about the wounded soldier, was our Ordnance Sergeant, Jerome A. Watrous. His was the intricate and difficult task of keeping track of our muskets, bayonets, shoulder belts, waist belts and their plates, cap boxes, primers and cartridges. He wore red chevrons and in that day they well accorded with the ruddy glow of his fresh and boyish cheeks. But he had enlisted in 1861, served through all and re-enlisted as a veteran. There was yet time to show his qualities in a wider field of action. He became Adjutant of the regiment and served as Adjutant General of Colonel John A. Kellogg's brigade of three thousand five hundred men in the great campaign that ended with Appomattox. He was brevetted Captain for his efficient and gallant service.

CHAPTER XV.

I had returned to Washington to make my final settlement and close my business account as a regimental commander when I wrote this letter:

(To my wife.) WASHINGTON, D. C., THURSDAY EVENING, }
                              SEPTEMBER 1st, 1864. }

"I am safely here to-night, somewhat tired from the journey. I am fairly heart-sick at the stories of blood I hear from the old regiment. Captain Hutchins was killed. Full of the satisfaction of his new commission, he met death in his first battle. But the saddest of all, Timmons was killed. Poor, murdered Timmons! His legal right to be discharged was as clear as mine and just the same. It seems almost certain to me that I could never have lived through another such carnival of blood. Only eighty men are left in the ranks for service."

THIRD DIVISION HOSPITAL, SEPTEMBER 4th, 1864.

"DEAR COLONEL: I received your kind letter some time since, and I should have answered it before only that I have been very sick since you left us. I know that you will be surprised to think of my being in a hospital, but it is so, and just at a time of all others that I wanted to be with the Sixth. Captain (Thomas) Kerr (the senior captain,) was sick at the time of the battle, (battle of the Weldon Road, August 18th, 19th and 21st,) and if I could have been there I would have been in command of the regiment in one of its hardest battles. The regiment never did better than under Captain (Charles P.) Hyatt. I came on to the field just as Hyatt lost his leg, and commanded the regiment in the rest of the fight and until I came back to hospital again. (It will be noted that Captain Remington got up off of a sick bed in the hospital to go to the regiment when he learned that it was in battle.) Poor Timmons is dead and out of the service. His application for discharge came back the other day asking if he had taken the 'veteran furlough?' General Bragg returned it with the endorsement: 'This officer has taken his long furlough. He was killed in the battle.'

The old division is broken up, and our brigade is in Crawford's division, the third brigade. The second brigade was sent to the first division. An effort is being made to have all of the troops of the old first army corps put into one division. From what I hear I think it will be done, but I do not know who will command it. I have a prospect of going home Monday morning on sick leave. I remain, as ever, your friend and well wisher,

WILLIAM N. REMINGTON,
Captain Company 'K', Sixth Wisconsin."

It will be remembered that this brave man and splendid soldier was shot in one shoulder at Gettysburg, while rushing for the rebel flag and he was shot in the other shoulder on the 10th of May at Laurel Hill. So late as 1882 he had not received a pension, nor asked for one until 1879. He then apologized for asking a pension on the ground that his "boys were all girls." I was a member of the 47th Congress from Ohio. The one-legged veteran, Captain E. M. Truell, of Wisconsin, asked me one day, as I had been a Wisconsin soldier, if I knew Captain Bill Remington of the Sixth. Of course I did, and he then told me that Remington needed only the affidavit of his regimental commander to complete his claim. Captain Remington was in Northern Dakota, and he had lost track of his regimental commander in Ohio. Truell and I made quick time for the

---

LOSSES AT WELDON ROAD, AUGUST 18th to 21st.

		killed		wounded		missing		aggregate
Officers:		2;		3;		0;		5
Men	"	7;	"	23;	"	10;	"	40

Total, 45

DR. JOHN C. HALL,

SURGEON SIXTH WIS. VOLS.

JOHN A. KELLOGG,

COLONEL SIXTH WIS. VOLS.
BREVET BRIGADIER GENERAL.

pension office, and it did not take me long to "call up that case" and swear it through. I soon received a letter from "Captain Bill" and he said: "If an Angel from Heaven had appeared to help me, I could not have been more surprised." Poor fellow! He did not live long to enjoy the benefits.

General Bragg has written: "You name Charley Hyatt. Captain Charles P. Hyatt was a gentleman and a soldier, with a manner as gentle as a woman. He was an excellent officer, and I was especially fond of him in command of a skirmish line. The hotter the fire, the cooler he grew, until, if I were telling a camp fire story, I would say that he 'froze the water in his canteen.' I made a special Aide-de-camp of him on my staff, and in the battle on the Weldon Railroad, I placed him in command of the Sixth in my front line. He fought the regiment splendidly. The next day we were attacked in strong force in our works and the assaulting party came so close that they could not get back, and they threw up their hands. The firing ceased and I detailed Captain Hyatt to take the sword of the commanding officer. He did so, and while returning, a stray shot came flying across, and it tore off Hyatt's leg. He suffered an amputation and was sent to Alexandria, from where he wrote me a cheerful letter. He was moved again to Philadelphia,—gangrene set in, and glorious man that he was, he died a soldier's death."

HEADQUARTERS SIXTH WISCONSIN VETERAN VOLUNTEERS, }
ON WELDON R. R. NEAR PETERSBURG, SEP'T. 10th, 1864. }

"Dear Colonel:—Your favor reached me in due time, and would have been answered before this had it not been for my ill-health. I got quite sick soon after you left, and was obliged to go to division hospital and stay there some three weeks. I returned to the regiment two days ago, and think I shall be able to remain with it. * * * Of course you have heard all, and more than all about the fights here, on the 18th, 19th and 21st of August by our corps, resulting in our getting and holding a piece of the Weldon R. R. The 18th and 21st, we gave the 'Johnnies' all they wanted, did a good thing. On the 19th, we got the worst of it rather. For our regiment particularly, it was a bad day. Captain Hutchins and Adjutant Cuyler Babcock were killed, and Lieutenant John Timmons, whose application to the Secretary of

War to be mustered out was still pending, was mustered out of the service forever by a minie bullet. This seems hard, for he would have succeeded with his application. Lieutenant Merchant was mustered out by order of Secretary Stanton three days ago, after risking his own life in four battles, after his term of service had expired. But the most unjust and meanest thing the Government could do, it did. It was ordered that his muster out should date from *July 15th*, thus robbing him of six weeks pay for perilous service, he was compelled to perform. This may be just and right, and it may be the proper way to increase the patriotism of officers, but the obliquity of my moral perceptions is such that I cannot see it.

I congratulate you on getting out when you did, and your wife and friends also. I often think it was almost Providential. These last battles might have proved that you too are mortal. And then,—but why speak of distress so fortunately perhaps avoided? I trust you will have all manner of happiness and success in business at home, and long outlive the present disastrous years of the Republic.

You desire to have yours and General Bragg's reports of the last engagements you were in. I will try to get copies and forward them to you.

You remind me of my promise to write the history of the regiment from last October, and request me not to neglect it. I have been in no condition to write it yet, and until a few days ago, it has been difficult to get access to the books and papers from which to obtain the proper data. But our teams are with the regiment now, and I have no excuse to neglect the matter longer. I advise you not to put too much trust in my executing this labor of love even.

Grant seems to be giving a look of permanency to our occupation of this line. He has nearly completed a railroad from City Point to the Yellow Tavern, Warren's headquarters, and the extreme left of our line on the Weldon Road. It was close by this tavern that we lost in the three battles I have mentioned, three officers and thirty-seven men, most of the casualties occuring on the 19th, and reducing our regiment to less than one hundred men all told, for duty. But this is aside from my present subject. Our line of works makes a loop around the tavern, and back upon itself for six or eight miles. This, of course, is to protect our rear and the new railroad. A depot for storing supplies is to be built near the camp of our brigade, and we shall soon present a business and town-like appearance. We have our baggage, and wall tents. The new Doctor and myself are getting domiciled in one of the latter. We have a tolerably dry camping ground, but we are surrounded by marshes of indefinite extent, and the malarial poison begins to tell on our men. But the Sixth is as good at fighting fevers as fighting 'Rebs,' so we are hopeful.

Well, Colonel, how does the war look to you from the standpoint of civil and domestic life? Have you joined the grumblers who severely ask, 'Why does not the Army of the Potomac move?' I think not. Have the recent successes south and west increased your confidence in our final triumph? Perhaps it was owing to my illness, but to tell you the truth, I have been for the last two months, a good deal discouraged; have almost despaired of the Republic. But I feel a little better about matters now.

What about the political aspect? The presidential question seems to be reduced to a choice between 'Old Abe' and 'Little Mac.' On one side is war, and stubborn, patient effort to restore the Union, and National honor; on the other side is inglorious peace and shame, the old truckling subserviency to Southern domination, and a base alacrity in embracing some vague, deceptive political subterfuge, instead of honorable and clearly defined principles.
                                        Truly yours,
                                            JOHN C. HALL."

It will be noticed that all were sick. The exhaustion, mental, as well as physical, of the long and terrible campaign which had lasted from May 5th until August 22nd, without cessation, did much to aid the marshes in producing this result.

General Bragg has written: "John Timmons, of company 'G', Second Lieutenant, was another noble fellow. He was an Irishman, quiet, but full of humor and brim full of pluck. When J. L. Converse was killed in the Wilderness, he refused promotion and announced his purpose to muster out at the end of his enlistment. When we received orders to move to fight the battle of the Weldon Railroad, John's time was out and he was waiting the arrival of a muster out officer. I urged him to remain in camp, knowing all the circumstances of his intended marriage. But when the regiment moved he went with us, and in the battle of the second day he was shot and instantly killed.

Little Hutchins, (Captain William Hutchins,) originally fourth Corporal of company 'B,' reached the Captaincy of his company and wore his rank for the first time in that battle and was shot at the time Timmons fell.

Babcock, of company 'C,' (Sergeant Major,) was shot, while lying in the trenches at the Weldon Railroad, by a ball that struck the limb of a tree overhead and deflected, striking him on the top of the head, producing instant death. He had his commission as Lieutenant and Adjutant in his pocket, but went to the grand encampment beyond the river, for muster.

You must not think I am proposing to write your book, but I send you these incidents and sketches for you to reject or mould, as you choose, into your narrative.

Upon the principle that I remember to have seen on a pamphlet of Indian stories in old Brandt's time in the Susquehanna valley

'Gather up the fragments—let nothing be lost,
To show the next ages what liberty cost.'

Sincerely your friend,

EDWARD S. BRAGG."

Upon his return from rebel prison, Captain Kellogg found his promotion awaiting him, and he has written: "I proceeded at once to my home in Wisconsin and made a short visit there. I went from thence to Madison and obtained an order assigning enough drafted men to fill the regiment to the maximum and proceeded with them to the regiment in the field. It was then lying on the Jerusalem plank road, near City Point. Here I found many changes. The regiment was commanded by Major Thomas Kerr, who was a Lieutenant when I left.* Nearly every officer on duty when I left the regiment the previous May was

---

*An error; he was appointed Captain in 1863.

either promoted, killed or mustered out.

The following February, 1865, General Bragg having been ordered to Washington, with a portion of his command, the balance was re-organized by adding to the sixth and seventh Wisconsin and the independent battalion of the 2nd Wisconsin, the ninety-first New York heavy artillery, commanded by Colonel Tarbell, the brigade numbering about three thousand five hundred men. I was assigned to its command and had the satisfaction of participating in the last campaign, and of witnessing the final ending of the war of rebellion at Appomattox on the ninth of April, 1865. Among the troops who laid down their arms at this surrender was the 13th Georgia, the same regiment that had captured me on the eighth day of May 1864."

On the nineteenth of October, 1864, Major Kellogg was promoted to Lieutenant Colonel, and on December tenth to Colonel and Major Kerr was on the same date appointed Lieutenant Colonel. The veterans and recruits of the second Wisconsin were consolidated with the Sixth on November twenty-second, 1864, and Captain Dennis B. Daily, of the old second, was appointed Major of the Sixth, as re-organized. Colonel Kellogg brought about four hundred and fifty drafted men to fill the ranks of the regiment, as he states, "to the maximum." For the history of the service of the regiment under Colonel Kellogg I have no data beyond the official records, and these have not yet been fully published.

One more duty yet remained before I was done with my service in the war. It was to be with my brother while he passed through the ordeal of the surgical operation. This was performed in a building at Fairmount, near Cincinnati, Ohio, which was then used as an officers' hospital. Dr. George C. Blackman, one of the most skillful surgeons in the country at that time, performed the operation. My aunt, Miss Julia P. Cutler, wrote to our sister in Persia, giving my own contemporary description of the operation.

MARIETTA, OHIO, SEPTEMBER 24th, 1864.
"MY DEAR JANE:—Just before bed time Rufus and Mary came in, he having come up from Cincinnati to-day. Dr. Blackman performed the operation at the officers' hospital. Rufus

remained with him through the whole, and helped hold his hands while it was done. He was an hour and a half under the surgeon's knife and not under the influence of chloroform. During the four months which intervened since the wound was received, the jagged flesh had been put together and a sort of chin formed, so we hoped that the operation would not be an extensive one, but in this we were disappointed. The flesh was all cut loose, then a gash cut through the cheeks on both sides to the angle of the jaw; slits were then cut parallel with them, in the same direction, so as to get a loose strip of flesh an inch wide, which was only attached to the face at the angle of the jaw. These strips were pulled and stretched so as to meet over an artificial under jaw and teeth, to form an under lip. The tightening and stretching of these strips caused the upper lip to be pushed out of place and protrude, so a gore had to be cut out on each side and sewed up. Then the flesh which had been loosened from the chin was put back and trimmed so as to fit in with the new under lip. He lay upon the table unbound, Rufus holding his left hand. His self possession was remarkable, obeying every direction of the operator, turning his head as directed, until the agony and the loss of blood exhausted him, and only a shiver ran through his frame. After it was over and stimulants administered he rose and walked upstairs to his room. Dr. Blackman considers the operation a great success. He invited a number of physicians to be present. One of them told Rufus that a man who could, endure what Major Dawes had that day would bear burning at the stake."

It is a pathetic memory to me that when my brother had been told that the operation was over, Dr. Blackman, looking at his work, said: "Major, I must finish up with two more stitches." The Major, to whom there was left no voice, raised up one finger to plead for only one. I cried: "Dr. Blackman, don't touch him," and he then raised up both fingers and the two stitches were taken. During the operation he came near strangling with the blood in his mouth, and in a spasmodic effort to get his breath, threw out the false teeth and jaw, which were not replaced. It is perhaps well that they were not, but this made necessary a month later a second operation of comparatively limited extent. To the casual observer no trace appears under the full beard now worn by Colonel Dawes, but a glance will show the marks of the "gores" cut in his upper lip. Captain Wm. Wilson, now of Cleveland, Ohio, and Captain W. R. Thomas alternated with me in holding my brother's hand.

Here are a few exceptional records to which "without invidious discrimination," as the official reports say, I may call attention.

Edward A. Whaley, of company "C," enlisted April 30th, 1861, and he re-enlisted as a veteran volunteer. He was promoted to Corporal, First Sergeant, Captain and Major by brevet. He was wounded at South Mountain, at Petersburg and at Five Forks. His right leg was amputated. It may be said that there is a good deal left of Major Whaley, who still lives, a much respected and honored citizen, and as modest as he was unapproachably faithful, brave and true.

James Whitty, of company "A," was wounded at Gainesville, at South Mountain, at Fitz Hugh's Crossing and at the Wilderness. His left leg has been amputated.

Sergeant Allison Fowler, of company "A," a re-enlisted veteran, was wounded at South Mountain, at Gettysburg, at the Weldon Road and killed at Hatcher's Run, February 6th, 1865.

Frank Hare, of company "B," a re-enlisted veteran, was severely wounded at Antietam, was wounded and a prisoner at the battle of the Wilderness. His leg was amputated by a Confederate surgeon.

Peter Adrian, of company "C," was a recruit, who came to us February 18th, 1864. He developed a remarkable capacity for stopping bullets. He was wounded at Spottsylvania, at the Weldon Road, and at Five Forks, He was mustered out with the regiment.

First Sergeant Jacob Lemans, of company "C," was wounded at Gettysburg, at Petersburg and at Five Forks.

Lieutenant George D. Eggleston, of company "E," was wounded at Antietam, at Gettysburg and at Spottsylvania.

Sergeant Leo Gotsch, of company "F," was wounded at Antietam, at Petersburg and at Hatcher's Run,

Henry Steinmetz, of company "F," was wounded at Antietam, at Gettysburg and at the Wilderness.

Nathan Burchell, of company "I," was wounded at Antietam, at Laurel Hill and at Five Forks.

William J. Revels, of company "K," was wounded at South Mountain, at Gettysburg and killed at the Weldon Road.

Sergeant James P. Sullivan, of company "K," was wounded at South Mountain and discharged as disabled. He re-enlisted in the regiment and was again badly wounded at Gettysburg. Nothing discouraged, he re-enlisted again as a veteran at the end of his second term.

Corporal Dugald Spear, of company "D," was wounded at Antietam, at Gettysburg and killed at the Weldon Road.

On page 263, in the account of the battle of the Wilderness I say: "On the afternoon of May seventh the soldiers in the line of the rebel army in our front began a loud cheering, which continued to run along their lines for nearly half an hour. Its significance I have never learned." Since this was printed I have found in the 'History of Gregg's Brigade of South Carolinians,' published by J. F. J. Caldwell, an officer of the first regiment of South Carolina Volunteers, a full history of the affair. I quote from this author: "While we were closing up here a pace at a time, the grandest vocal exhibition took place that I have heard. Far up on the right of the Confederate line, a shout was raised. Gradually it was taken up and passed down until it reached us. We lifted it as our turn came and handed it to the left, where it went echoing to the remotest corner of Ewell's corps. This was done once with powerful effect. * * * Again the shout arose on the right, again it rushed down upon us for a distance of perhaps two miles. Again we caught and flung it joyfully to the left, where it only ceased when the last post had huzzahed. And yet a third time this mighty wave of sound ran along the Confederate lines. The effect was beyond expression."

William Jackson came home with me as he desired. First I found employment for him as a waiter in a hotel and next in the service of a railroad company. He needed no more help. His sterling qualities won success. For twelve years he served as a station baggage master in our city. He then started in business for himself, and April 7th, 1886, he died of consumption. He had accumulated a handsome property and with his brother owned a fine home, a store building and other property. Few young men do better, who enjoy the best advantages. Every dollar of his first two year's earnings he saved to get his mother. His brother was then a boot-black in the St. Charles hotel in Washington. The proprietor of that hotel took a kindly interest with me, and William's brother, Moses Jackson, a brave and true man, was sent to Spottsylvania County, Virginia, to find their mother. He was successful in the search. He found her in 1866 still held as a slave by a brute named Richardson. Moses brought his revolver to bear on Richardson, and he was obliged to push and drive before him his mother and a sister, while he held at bay this Richardson. Night and day Moses pushed them through on the march to Washington, and the proprietor of the St. Charles hotel sent me a telegram announcing the safe arrival of the party. I sent a card to be pinned on the woman's dress, giving her destination and the route. The neat, gentlemanly station baggage agent, who then always wore the army blue, awaited with a swelling heart the arrival of the train. Only by this card could he recognize his mother. She had been whipped and choked, so that her power of speech was almost gone, owing to injury of the throat and palate. The daughter was an idiot, rendered so by blows upon her head. Poor William! he could not bear to take this bitterness to my wife, with whom he had so often talked and planned in joyous anticipation of this event, but he went to my mother, and saying: "Mrs. Dawes, see what slavery has done!" he broke down in an agony of grief and disappointment. Bravely he took up the burden. The sister soon died. Mrs. Jackson was an unusually bright woman and before the war, as her associations had been with a good family, she was all her son imagined her. She outlived both of her faithful sons, and she lived in the enjoyment of comfort and even luxury. The gratitude of Mrs. Jackson was amusing as well as touching. She put Abraham Lincoln as the first man and myself as the second. She could not speak to me on the subject, because her partly paralyzed tongue would not act, owing to her excitement, so she put on her best one day and came to tell my wife her tale of overflowing thankfulness, but she could not speak a word only "William will done write it."

An examination of the Adjutant General's Report of Wisconsin, a most complete and admirable work, shows that I have done injustice to the marksmanship of the rebels in the railroad cut at Gettysburg. They did hit Captain Marston. He was not knocked out, but kept the field as I remember.

After Seventeen Years.

House of Representatives, Washington, D. C.,
December 18th, 1881.

"*My dear wife:*—I have to-day worshipped at the shrine of the dead. I went over to the Arlington Cemetery. It was a beautiful morning and the familiar scenes so strongly impresssed upon me during my young manhood, were pleasant. Many times I went over that road, admiring the beautiful city and great white capitol, with its then unfinished dome, going to hear the great men of that day in Congress. An ambitious imagination then builded castles of the time when I might take my place there. Now at middle age, with enthusiasm sobered by hard fights and hard facts, I ride, not run with elastic step over the same road, with this ambition at least realized, and warmth enough left in my heart to enjoy it. My friends and comrades, poor fellows, who followed my enthusiastic leadership in those days, and followed it to the death which I by a merciful Providence escaped, lie here, twenty-four of them, on the very spot where our winter camp of 1861—1862, was located. I found every grave and stood beside it with uncovered head. I looked over nearly the full 16,000 head-boards to find the twenty-four, but they all died alike and I was determined to find all. Poor little Fenton who put his head above the works at Cold Harbor and got a bullet through his temples, and lived three days with his brains out, came to me in memory as fresh as one of my own boys of to-day, and Levi Pearson, one of the three brothers of company 'A,' who died for their country in the sixth regiment, and Richard Gray, Paul Mulleter, Dennis Kelly, Christ Bundy, all young men, who fell at my side and under my command. For what they died, I fight a little longer. Over their graves I get inspiration to stand for all they won in establishing our government upon freedom, equality, justice, liberty and protection to the humblest."

To my living comrades this book will be my greeting and farewell, for we can never again rally on our color. If I have brought back to you, by the printing of my contemporary papers, something of your own feelings and experiences in those days of glory, which you had lost, and if I have said aught to fan to life the yet smouldering spark of fiery zeal for the honor and glory of the "Old Sixth" regiment, I am content. It is a matter of sincere regret that many noble deeds and some brave men are overlooked. But remember I was not then a historian. I was then only writing to my family, friends and M. B. G., (my best girl), who were personally strangers to you all. I wonder that so much was saved. Enough is recorded, here and elsewhere, to show the generations yet to come that our band was of the finest quality of heroic mettle, and "equal," as General McClellan wrote, "to the best troops in any army of the world."

The shadows of age are rapidly stealing upon us. Our burdens are like the loaded knapsack on the evening of a long and weary march, growing heavier at every pace. The severing of the links to a heroic and noble young manhood, when generous courage was spurred by ambitious hope, goes on, but you have lived to see spring up as the result of your suffering, toil and victory the most powerful nation of history and the most beneficent government ever established. While you are in the sear and yellow leaf your country is in the spring-time of the new life your victory gave it. This is your abundant and sufficient reward. It now only remains for me to lay aside my pen, as I did my sword, and again take up my business.

The following statements are taken from the valuable publication of Colonel W. F. Fox, entitled "Regimental Losses in the Civil War."

"The regiment left Wisconsin July 28, 1861, proceeding to Washington, where it was assigned to the brigade which was destined to fill such a glorious place in the annals of the war. The Sixth had the advantage of a year's drill and discipline before it was called upon to face the enemy in a general engagement, its first battle occurring at Manassas—August 28th and 30th

—where it lost 17 killed, 91 wounded, and 11 missing. The regiment lost at South Mountain, 11 killed, 79 wounded and 2 missing; and at Antietam, three days after, 26 killed, and 126 wounded. Under command of Colonel Dawes, it won merited distinction at Gettysburg in the battle of the first day; all histories of that field mention the manœuver—and the part taken in it by the Sixth—by which a part of a Confederate brigade was captured in the railroad cut. The casualties at Gettysburg were 30 killed, 116 wounded, and 22 missing. Upon the re-organization of the army in March, 1864, Wadsworth's division was transferred to the fifth corps, and with it the Iron Brigade, under General Cutler. The regiment lost at the battle of the Wilderness 8 killed, 40 wounded, and 15 missing; at Spottsylvania, 10 killed, 69 wounded and 5 missing; at Hatcher's Run (Dabney's Mills), 13 killed, 81 wounded, and 7 missing; at Gravelly Run, 5 killed, 34 wounded, and 32 missing. Major Philip W. Plummer was killed at the Wilderness."

In his investigation of comparative losses in battles, Colonel Fox has included about two thousand regiments which were more or less engaged with the enemy. In the number of men killed in battle, the sixth Wisconsin regiment is tenth upon the list. Only nine regiments engaged in the war suffered a greater loss in killed. The second Wisconsin, according to Colonel Fox, suffered the greatest loss in killed in proportion to the whole number upon its rolls of any regiment in the Union army during the war. Col. Fox says: "The 'Iron Brigade' suffered a greater proportionate loss in battle than any other brigade in the Army of the Union."

SIXTH WISCONSIN INFANTRY.

IRON BRIGADE—WADSWORTH'S DIVISION—FIRST CORPS.

(1) COLONEL LYSANDER CUTLER, BREVET MAJOR GENERAL.
(2) COLONEL EDWARD S. BRAGG, BRIGADIER GENERAL.
(3) COLONEL RUFUS R. DAWES, BREVET BRIGADIER GENERAL.
(4) COLONEL JOHN A. KELLOGG,   "   "   "

COMPANIES.	KILLED AND DIED OF WOUNDS.		
	Officers	Men.	Total.
Field and Staff..	2		2
Company 'A'	1	28	29
" 'B'	2	25	27
" 'C	1	14	15
" 'D'	1	28	29
" 'E'	2	15	17
" 'F'	3	17	20
" 'G'	2	23	25
" 'H'	0	19	19
" 'I'	0	37	37
" 'K'	2	22	24
Totals..	16	228	244

224 killed—12.5 per cent. of total enrollment.

Of the 1,058 men originally enrolled, 170 were killed—16 9 per cent.

Total of killed and wounded, 867; missing and captured, 112; died in Confederate prisons, 20.

BATTLES.	K. & M. W.	BATTLES.	K. & M. W.
Gainesville, Va.,Aug. 28, '62...... 14		North Anna, Va........ 3	
Manassas, Va., Aug. 30, '62 11		Bethesda Church, Va............... 2	
South Mountain, Md.................16		Petersburg, Va. June 18th.........10	
Antietam, Md...........................40		Petersburg Trenches, Va............ 5	
Fitz Hugh's Crossing, Va.......... 5		Weldon Railroad, Va..... 12	
Gettysburg, Pa........................41		Dabney's Mills, Va , Feb. 6, '65...24	
Wilderness, Va, May 4-6, '64.....15		Gravelly Run, Va..................... 9	
Spottsylvania, Va., May 8th 3		Five Forks, Va........................ 7	
Spottsylvania, Va., May 10th.....12		Picket Line, Va, Aug. 31, '62..... 1	
Spottsylvania, Va., May 12th..... 3		Prison guard, Salisbury, N. C... 1	
Spottsylvania, Va., May 13th..... 6		Detail, Artillery Service........... 4	

List of battles according to the United States Army Register: Cedar Mountain, Rappahannock, Gainesville, Groveton and Bull Run, South Mountain, Antietam, Fredericksburg, Fitz Hugh's Crossing, Chancellorsville, Gettysburg, Haymarket, Mine Run, Wilderness, Spottsylvania, North Anna, Tolopotomy, Bethesda Church, Cold Harbor, Petersburg, Weldon Railroad, Hatcher' Run, Oct. 27, 1864, Hatcher's Run, Feb. 6-7, 1865, Gravely Run, Five Forks.

RELATED MATERIALS

A Selected Critical Bibliography

This selected bibliography is presented for those who wish to pursue the career of Rufus Dawes' Sixth Wisconsin Volunteers and the Iron Brigade. In addition to contemporaneous newspaper materials and the reports of the Adjutant Generals of Wisconsin, Indiana, and Michigan, the following may be consulted.

BOOKS

Three published accounts by Iron Brigade contemporaries of Rufus Dawes are available:

History of the Sauk County Riflemen, Philip Cheek and Mair Pointon, privately published, 1909.

"Sauk County Riflemen" was the popular name of Company A of the Sixth Wisconsin Volunteers. Cheek and Pointon were members of the company and this book is their joint account of its history. Much of the material in the book is based on contemporaneous letters and journals and the Dawes' book is also used as an authority. The book also includes a quantity of "recollected" facts and anecdotes which enlarge its charm but are of limited historical value.

History of the Twenty-fourth Michigan, O. B. Curtis, Detroit, 1891.

O. B. Curtis was an enlisted man in the Twenty-fourth Michigan Volunteers, that state's representative in the Iron Brigade. After a brief introduction based on secondary sources, his history begins with the raising of the regiment in Detroit in the summer of 1862 and continues until the regiment was withdrawn from combat in Virginia in February, 1865, and sent to a draft rendezvous at Springfield, Illinois. The book is not as well-written as Dawes' book and includes the reminiscences of a number of Curtis' comrades. Despite this, it is valuable historically as a source of facts. Of unusual interest are the statistical data concerning the ages, backgrounds and occupations of the Michigan men. These materials were painstakingly assembled and are doubtless reliable.

Personal Recollections of the Civil War, John Gibbon, New York, 1928.

Based in part on his letters written at the time, and also reflecting a study of the *Official Records*, this is General Gibbon's posthumously published story. Only a part of the book is concerned with the Iron Brigade, because Gibbon's command of that organization covered only the period from May 7, 1862 until November 4, 1862. Prior to this time, he commanded Battery B of the Fourth U. S. Artillery. After leaving the Iron Brigade, he progressed from division commander to a major generalship of volunteers and command of the Twenty-fourth Corps in the Army of the James. He was involved in intense combat at Fredericksville, Chancellorsville, and Gettysburg, and in Grant's final Virginia campaign. At Appomattox he was one of the Federal commissioners in charge of the surrender. All of these events are recounted in his book.

In addition to these books, a recent history exists:

The Iron Brigade, Alan T. Nolan, New York, 1961.

This book is a formal military history of the Iron Brigade. It is based on extensive study of published unit histories and personal accounts, the *Official Records*, contemporaneous newspapers, and manuscript materials. The story of the brigade is told in the context of the war as a whole.

THE OFFICIAL RECORDS

Known formally as *War of Rebellion, Official Records of the Union and Confederate Armies*, these 128 volumes were published by the Government Printing Office during the period from 1882 to 1900. They are the basic source material for any military study of the Civil War. Because of the casualties of officers and other such exigencies, there are gaps in the reports for the Sixth Wisconsin Volunteers, the Iron Brigade, and the other regiments of the brigade. The reports became especially rare in 1864 and 1865 because of the almost constant combat. Available reports for the Iron Brigade and its regiments are as follows:

Brawner Farm–August 28, 1862

Report for the Iron Brigade (by General John Gibbon) *O.R.*, Series I, Volume XII, Part 2, page 377. (See also Gibbon's later letter, Series I, Volume XII, Part 2, page 380.)

Report for the Sixth Wisconsin Volunteers (by Lt. Col. Edward S. Bragg) *O.R.*, Series I, Volume XII, Part 2, page 382.

Second Bull Run–August 29–30, 1862

Report for the Iron Brigade (by Gen. John Gibbon) *O.R.*, Series I, Volume XII, Part 2, page 379.

South Mountain–September 14, 1862

Report for the Iron Brigade (by Gen. John Gibbon) *O.R.*, Series I, Volume XIX, Part 1, page 247.

Report for the Second Wisconsin Volunteers (by Col. Lucius Fairchild) *O.R.*, Series I, Volume XIX, Part 1, page 252.

Report for the Sixth Wisconsin Volunteers (by Lt. Col. Edward S. Bragg) *O.R.*, Series I, Volume XIX, Part 1, page 253.

Report for the Seventh Wisconsin Volunteers (by Capt. John B. Callis) *O.R.*, Series I, Volume XIX, Part 1, page 256.

Report for the Nineteenth Indiana Volunteers (by Col. Solomon Meredith) *O.R.*, Series I, Volume XIX, Part 1, page 249.

Antietam–September 17, 1862

Report for the Iron Brigade (by Gen. John Gibbon) *O.R.*, Series I, Volume XIX, Part 1, page 248.

Report for the Sixth Wisconsin Volunteers (by Lt. Col.

Edward S. Bragg) *O.R.*, Series I, Volume XIX, Part 1, page 254.

Report for the Seventh Wisconsin Volunteers (by Capt. John B. Callis) *O.R.*, Series I, Volume XIX, Part 1, page 257.

Report for the Nineteenth Indiana Volunteers (by Capt. William W. Dudley) *O.R.*, Series I, Volume XIX, Part 1, page 251.

Fredericksburg–December 12–15, 1862

Report for the Iron Brigade (by Gen. Solomon Meredith) *O.R.*, Series I, Volume XXI, page 475.

Report for the Iron Brigade (by Col. Lysander Cutler) *O.R.*, Series I, Volume XXI, page 478.

Chancellorsville–April 29–May 6, 1863

Report for the Iron Brigade (by Gen. Solomon Meredith) *O.R.*, Series I, Volume XXV, Part 1, page 266.

Report for the Second Wisconsin Volunteers (by Col. Lucius Fairchild) *O.R.*, Series I, Volume XXV, Part 1, page 270.

Report for the Second Wisconsin Volunteers (by Lt. Col. George H. Stevens) *O.R.*, Series I, Volume XXV, Part 1, page 271.

Report for the Sixth Wisconsin Volunteers (by Col. Edward S. Bragg) *O.R.*, Series I, Volume XXV, Part 1, page 271.

Report for the Seventh Wisconsin Volunteers (by Col. William W. Robinson) *O.R.*, Series I, Volume XXV, Part 1, page 273.

Report for the Nineteenth Indiana Volunteers (by Col. Samuel J. Williams) *O.R.*, Series I, Volume XXV, Part 1, page 269.

Expedition Down the Northern Neck–May 20–May 26, 1863

(Commanded by Colonel Henry A. Morrow; included Second and Sixth Wisconsin, Nineteenth Indiana, and Twenty-fourth Michigan)

Report of Colonel Henry A. Morrow, *O.R.*, Series I, Volume XXV, Part 1, page 1112.

Gettysburg–July 1–3, 1863

Report for the Second Wisconsin Volunteers (by Major

John Mansfield) *O.R.*, Series I, Volume XXVII, Part 1, page 273.

Report for the Sixth Wisconsin Volunteers (by Lt. Col. Rufus R. Dawes) *O.R.*, Series I, Volume XXVII, Part 1, page 275.

Report for the Seventh Wisconsin Volunteers (by Col. William W. Robinson) *O.R.*, Series I, Volume XXVII, Part 1, page 278.

Report for the Twenty-fourth Michigan Volunteers (by Col. Henry A. Morrow) *O.R.*, Series I, Volume XXVII, Part 1, page 267.

Spottsylvania–May 7–13, 1864

Report for the Sixth Wisconsin Volunteers (by Lt. Col. Rufus R. Dawes) *O.R.*, Series I, Volume XXXVI, Part 1, page 618.

The Virginia Campaign–May 21–25, 1864

Report for the Sixth Wisconsin Volunteers (by Lt. Col. Rufus R. Dawes) *O.R.*, Series I, Volume XXXVI, Part 1, page 621.

Weldon Railroad–August 18–21, 1864

Report for the brigade which included the Sixth and Seventh Wisconsin, the Nineteenth Indiana and the Twenty-fourth Michigan Volunteers (by Brig. Gen. Edward S. Bragg) *O.R.*, Series I, Volume XLII, Part 1, page 534.

Hatcher's Run–October 27–28, 1864

Report for the brigade which included the Sixth and Seventh Wisconsin and the Twenty-fourth Michigan Volunteers (by Brig. Gen. Edward S. Bragg) *O.R.*, Series I, Volume XLII, Part 1, page 507.

Weldon Railroad–December 7–11, 1864

Report for the brigade which included the Sixth and Seventh Wisconsin and the Twenty-fourth Michigan Volunteers (by Brig. Gen. Edward S. Bragg) *O.R.*, Series I, Volume XLII, Part 1, page 507.

Boydton Plank Road–March 31, 1865

Report for the brigade which included the Sixth and Seventh Wisconsin Volunteers (by Col. John A. Kellogg) *O.R.*, Series I, Volume XLVI, Part 1, page 883.

The Appomattox Campaign–March 29– April 25, 1865
Report for the brigade which included the Sixth and Seventh Wisconsin Volunteers (by Col. John A. Kellogg) *O.R.*, Series I, Volume XLVI, Part 1, pages 882, 885.

MANUSCRIPTS

In the archives of the State Historical Society of Wisconsin at Madison may be found a number of manuscript materials of Wisconsin Iron Brigade personnel. These materials represent all three of the Wisconsin Iron Brigade regiments. Those of the Sixth Wisconsin are as follows:

The Bragg Papers.

The war letters of Edward S. Bragg, a distinguished commander of the regiment, to his wife. Also included are letters to Bragg from General Gibbon and other officers.

The Chapman Papers.

Chandler B. Chapman was a Surgeon with the Sixth Wisconsin Volunteers. These are his war papers and letters and include a number of contemporaneous medical forms pertaining to the regiment.

The Cook Papers.

The war letters of John H. Cook, an enlisted man of the regiment.

The Fairfield Papers.

George Fairfield was another enlisted man of the regiment. His papers include his diary, kept during the war, and a number of letters to him from his comrades.

The Gallup Papers.

Andrew Gallup was an officer of the regiment. His papers include a number of memoranda and letters and clothing and equipment returns for the regiment.

The Haskell Papers.

These are the war letters of the celebrated Frank A. Haskell, covering his career which began when he was a captain and adjutant of the Sixth Wisconsin in 1861 and ended with his death as Colonel of the Thirty-sixth Wisconsin at Cold Harbor in 1864.

A. T. N.

INDEX

Of persons, places and organizations mentioned. (Con.) indicates Confederate, (n) reference to notes. Numbers indicate pages.

A.

B.

C.

O.

P.

Q.

R.

S.

T.